# The Regulation of Franchising in the New Global Economy

# The Regulation of Franchising in the New Global Economy

Elizabeth Crawford Spencer

*Bond University, Australia*

**Edward Elgar**

Cheltenham, UK • Northampton, MA, USA

Published by
Edward Elgar Publishing Limited
The Lypiatts
15 Lansdown Road
Cheltenham
Glos GL50 2JA
UK

Edward Elgar Publishing, Inc.
William Pratt House
9 Dewey Court
Northampton
Massachusetts 01060
USA

A catalogue record for this book
is available from the British Library

Library of Congress Control Number: 2010925996

ISBN 978 1 84844 866 7

Typeset by Servis Filmsetting Ltd, Stockport, Cheshire
Printed and bound by MPG Books Group, UK

# Contents


*List of figures, tables and boxes* vi
*Foreword* Andrew Terry viii
*Acknowledgements* xi

Introduction: The regulation of franchising in the new global economy 1
1. Reconceiving regulation 14
2. The market interaction as private regulation 46
3. The contract as private regulation 76
4. Purpose and scope of franchise-specific regulation and the UNIDROIT Model Law 116
5. Worldwide survey of franchise-specific regulation 133
6. Summary of trends in franchise-specific legislation 212
7. Legislation impacting upon negotiation and formation of franchise contracts 226
8. Legislation impacting upon the performance of and exit from the agreement 263
9. Future directions for the regulation of franchising 313

*Appendix 1 Franchise legislation worldwide* 322
*Appendix 2 Content of disclosure* 327
*Index* 351

# Figures, tables and boxes

## FIGURES


6.1 The presence of franchise-specific legislation and/or a trade association 213
6.2 Civil law and common law jurisdictions of the world 217
7.1 Number of items of disclosure required 237


## TABLES


1.1 Selected principles of regulatory process 40
2.1 Franchise trade association promotions claims 60
4.1 Purposes of regulating franchising 118
4.2 Definitions used in franchise regulation worldwide 122
5.1 US state franchise, business opportunity, and relationship statutes 151
6.1 Tools used in franchise regulation worldwide 219
7.1 Summary of disclosure requirements 230
7.2 Disclosure content requirements 232
7.3 Registration requirements 250
8.1 Conduct legislation worldwide 264
8.2 Australia's proposed unfair terms legislation 269
8.3 Examples of mandatory contract terms in franchise-specific legislation 272
8.4 Legislation prescribing aspects of performance 276
8.5 Dispute resolution requirements 282
8.6 Legislation with respect to termination and right of renewal 290
8.7 Common requirements of trade association codes of conduct or ethics 308

## BOXES

2.1 Mendelsohn's features of business format franchises 48
2.2 The importance of uniform system standards 68
8.1 Mediation in Australia 284

# Foreword

Franchising is, in the words of Australia's 1997 *Fair Trading Report*, 'an increasingly popular form of economic organisation providing an alternative means of expanding an existing business or an alternative means of entering an industry'. It is a method of business operation which has revolutionised the distribution of goods and services in most industry sectors and has transformed the business landscape of most countries. As franchising increases its influence internationally the issue of its regulation assumes increasing significance. The regulation of entrepreneurial activity – of which franchising is one of the purest expressions – is never straightforward. The regulatory debate – initially in relation to the need for a dedicated regulatory regime and then as to its shape and content – is sustained and often passionate. Dr Spencer's pioneering book makes a valuable contribution to this debate.

The OECD has pointed out that 'entrepreneurship and business activities are shaped not only by markets, but also by regulatory and administrative environments established by governments'. This is particularly true of franchising. In some cases, such as those of China and Vietnam, the introduction of a regulatory regime recognising franchising as a legitimate and viable method of business operation has been a necessary prerequisite to the development of a viable domestic franchise sector. In most cases however the reason for embracing dedicated franchise regulation is to address what the recent Australian *Opportunity not Opportunism* report described as 'differing expectations about the obligations of each party to the agreement' and an 'asymmetric power dynamic within franchise agreements, with potential to lead to abuse of power'. Dr Spencer is not ambivalent in her belief that monitoring and regulation are necessary to address potential areas of abuse to ensure that the economic and welfare objectives promoted by franchising are not frustrated by inappropriate conduct that can result not only in financial and social cost to franchisees, but also lead to costly market inefficiencies. In this she is not alone.

For many years the US was in splendid isolation in imposing a franchise specific regime on its franchise sector to supplement the underlying commercial laws of general application. California – the cradle of business format franchising – was the first jurisdiction to adopt franchise specific regulation. Its 1971 Franchise Investment Law, based on the securities law model, imposed franchisor disclosure and registration requirements and was followed at the end of that decade by a federal disclosure law. The international community, although quick to embrace the US franchise model, was not enthusiastic about embracing the US manner of its regulation. By the year 2000 only 17 countries had introduced franchise-specific legislation. There has nevertheless been a significant trend to legislation since then and today over 30 countries have dedicated franchise regulation.

The catalyst for legislative intervention has been the increasing recognition that franchise contracts are, in the language of the Privy Council *in Dymocks Franchise Systems (NSW) Pty Ltd v Todd* [1] 'not ordinary commercial contracts' and that, in the words of Australia's 2008 *Opportunity not Opportunism* report, abuse of the 'inherent and necessary imbalance of power in franchise agreements . . . can lead to opportunistic practices'. While there is increasing recognition of the 'relational' character of franchising, the extra-legal norms which explain relational contracting in the context of contracting equals are less compelling in the context of the typical business format franchise which is characterised by both an information imbalance and a power imbalance. Judicial developments have not progressed to the stage where the general underlying law provides adequate protection for franchisees. Legislative solutions have been increasingly sought. Yet, while the case for remedying the information imbalance by mandatory prior disclosure is widely accepted today – and is indeed the rationale for UNIDROIT's *Model Franchise Disclosure Law* – the power imbalance raises more sensitive issues and remains a difficult, and a controversial, issue.

Dr Spencer argues that franchising must be understood in terms of its risks and that the question is not whether to regulate but how to regulate. This sentiment has increasing support internationally. It may have been regarded as radical at an earlier stage in the development of franchising but today has wide and increasing support as domestic sectors struggle with the challenge of regulating this dynamic and unique business relationship. Commercial risk is an inevitable incident of entrepreneurship and business creation in a free enterprise society. The challenge for franchise regulators is to minimise those risks arising from the unique dynamics of the franchising relationship while leaving the commercial risks to the parties themselves. Although there is increasing international recognition of the need to regulate beyond the scope of the underlying business laws of general application, there is no unanimity among the 30 regulated sectors as to the appropriate regulatory tools let alone the extent of their application. Prior disclosure, registration, controls on conduct or dispute resolution are utilised either individually or in a range of combinations and permutations by

---

1 [2002] 2 All ER (Comm) 849 at 871.

the regulated regimes and there is little consistency in scope or extent even among those jurisdictions adopting the same regulatory strategy.

Dr. Spencer urges governments to embrace regulatory process that is consultative, identifies the harms and potential solutions, implements appropriate tools, monitors outcomes, and adjusts accordingly. Such process, she suggests, will result in 'increased permeability among layers of governance, and so enhance their effectiveness'. Her belief that, through proper process, all layers of governance can interact more effectively together hinges on collaborative process, a process in which the regulator's new role is not to impose rules, but to promote best regulatory process. This, she notes, is not an easy transition, but it is a significant one.

Dr Spencer has performed a valuable service to the international franchising community in writing this book. Its strength is not simply in making the case for franchise regulation which those who practise franchising in a regulated environment such as Australia readily acknowledge has had a strong and positive influence on sector development for the benefit of all stakeholders. Dr Spencer's comprehensive survey of franchise regulation globally and her conceptual analysis of the regulatory tools applied makes a very important contribution to the regulatory debate. Of particular interest is her argument that alternative regulatory approaches, including self-regulatory mechanisms, should be explored and that legislative intervention where necessary and appropriate should draw on the full range of regulatory tools.

I, like the author, believe that the question for domestic franchise sectors is not whether to regulate but how to regulate and her comprehensive survey and analysis of regulatory strategies and tools will be a valuable resource not only for unregulated sectors which are considering regulation but also for regulated sectors as they refine and reshape their regulatory scheme.

Dr Spencer's hope for her book is that it will lead to a better understanding and harmonisation of franchising regulation. Given the massive political, social, economic and commercial diversity of the international franchising community her hope for harmonisation may be too optimistic: even UNIDROIT's *Model Franchise Disclosure La*w has been influential as a beacon rather than as a template. But, Dr Spencer's hope for a better understanding of franchising regulation will undoubtedly be met. This is the strength of her contribution.

Andrew Terry
Professor of Business Regulation
The University of Sydney

19 August 2010

# Acknowledgements

I would like to acknowledge the hard work of my good friend Maria Nicolai, and that of many other research assistants who have been involved in the course of preparing this manuscript. I am grateful for the cooperation of the Franchise Council of Australia in the early days of my research. I would like to thank Bond University Faculty of Law for its support, and the many senior members of the faculty for their continuing patience, guidance, good advice, and for keeping their doors open. I would like to thank Jenny Buchan for her unflagging friendship and support. Andrew Terry, Rupert Barkoff, Andy Selden, and Lorelle Frazer, thank you for your encouragement, your help, and your friendship. I am truly grateful for the loving support of so many wonderful colleagues and friends over these years as I have laboured over this project. I am grateful to my parents and my family for their love and support. Most importantly, I am grateful to my children, Nina and Sam, to whom I dedicate this book.

The law is as stated at 1 January 2010.

# Introduction: The regulation of franchising in the new global economy

> 'In the time of the legendary King Arthur, the quest for the Holy Grail was the highest spiritual pursuit for a knight. Today, franchise reformers search for their own Holy Grail – a convenient formula to deliver balance and equity to the franchise relationship which is commonly characterised by both a power and an information imbalance.' [1]

The concept of business-format franchising originated in the United States of America in the late 1950s and saw rapid expansion there in the 1960s and 1970s. As the phenomenon of business-format franchising has taken hold in many countries around the globe regulation of the sector internationally has increased with a trend toward regulation that has been particularly notable in the years since 1990. The franchise sector was first regulated in the 1970s in the US and Canada. In 1980 only the US and Canada had franchise-specific legislation. By 1990 France and Mexico had joined them. By the year 2000 about thirteen jurisdictions had implemented franchise-specific legislation including Australia, Brazil, the People's Republic of China, Taiwan, Indonesia, Malaysia, Romania, and Spain.

Since the year 2000 another 16 countries have followed suit. Today about 30 countries, or about one-third of the countries where franchised business operates, have enacted regulation directed specifically towards franchising or with the specific intention to capture franchising. These countries include Canada (four of ten provinces: Alberta; Ontario; New Brunswick; Prince Edward Island), the US, Barbados, Brazil, Mexico, Albania, Belarus, Belgium, Estonia, France, Italy, Lithuania, Moldova, Romania, Russia, Spain, Sweden, Ukraine, People's Republic of China, Indonesia, Japan, Kazakhstan, South Korea, Kyrgyzstan, Macau, Malaysia, Vietnam, Taiwan, and Australia. The countries included in this list where regulation is not strictly or solely franchise-specific, but where the intention has been to capture franchising include Albania, Belgium,

1 Andrew Terry, 'Franchising and the Quest for the Holy Grail: Good Faith or Good Intentions?', 23rd Annual International Society of Franchising Conference, San Diego, CA, February 2009.

Belarus, Estonia, France, Georgia, Kyrgyzstan, Lithuania, the People's Republic of China, Taiwan, Russia and Ukraine.[2]

The reasons for the increase in regulation of the sector include an increase in international franchise activity and the recognition of franchising as a unique business model that demands a particularized regulatory scheme. Currently the forms the laws take are not uniform, despite the promulgation in 2002 of the UNIDROIT Model Franchise Disclosure Law. Many countries have responded to problems in the sector with regulatory measures, but some countries, such as England, Germany and the Netherlands, seem to do well with no sector-specific legislation at all. Other countries, such as Sweden, have enacted only minimal regulation. Variation in legislation is to be expected because regulation in each jurisdiction must respond to its own particular circumstances and requirements and because regulation as governance reflects the global diversity of conceptions about the kind of people and societies we are and aspire to be.

At the same time there is also a compelling argument for harmony in regulation internationally to the extent that it is feasible and practicable. Consistency in private law provides a legal framework of private rights as the foundation for social interaction. An international legal regime facilitates transactions, enhances credit facilities and reduces borrowing costs.[3] In order to maximize the benefit of such harmonization, regulation should be understood and applied as consistently as is practicable.

This book is an undertaking that has been motivated principally by two factors. The first is a discernible trend globally to regulate the franchise sector. The second is the lack of consensus on what that regulation should look like. 'The increasing influence of franchising has . . . been accompanied by an increasingly vigorous debate as to the regulatory environment for franchising.'[4] It is hoped that the global survey and analysis of this aspect of the regulation of the franchise sector provided here will lead to better understanding and harmonization of that regulation.

The book is organized in three parts. The first provides introductory material, an overview of the nature of regulatory theory as well as an overview of the nature of the franchise sector. The second part comprises a survey of the regulation of the sector. The survey of regulatory measures

---

[2] Venezuela is not included as the legislation directed toward franchising in that country is only for the purposes of exempting franchising from certain competition law requirements.

[3] See http://www.uniformlaw.org/important.php at 14 December 2009.

[4] Andrew Terry, 'A Census of International Franchise Regulation', 21st Annual International Society of Franchising Conference, Las Vegas, Nevada, 24–25 February 2007, 3.

provides an indication of where we are in the progress toward the optimum regulatory program for the sector globally, and an orientation for future plans for regulation. The third part of the book offers a comparative analysis of the current approaches to regulating in light of the concepts for optimum regulation suggested by current regulatory theory.

This book challenges some of the commonly-held myths about both regulation and franchising; first, with the proposition that franchising in fact does have risks and dangers for its participants, and second, with the proposition that appropriate regulation can help to minimize the damaging effects of these risks and so benefit the health and competitiveness of the sector overall. Rather than reinforcing the belief that franchising is low risk, this book argues that franchising must be understood in terms of its risks. This is the logical starting point for regulatory intervention. Rather than reinforcing the belief that regulation is something to be avoided, this book argues that there are multiple levels at which regulation operates, and that it can and should be properly calibrated in order to provide sophisticated, appropriate regulation at each 'layer' of governance.

## RECONCEIVING REGULATION

There is a commonly-held belief that regulation is bad for business, and that the heavy hand of government intervention in peoples' private affairs should be avoided at all costs. Such a belief may often be justified; but as often it is not. It is said that judgments are alienated expressions of needs, and certainly there are needs that are not being met by regulation.[5] The widespread mistrust of regulation is the result of years of high costs and intangible benefits of regulation that have eroded public confidence in the efficacy of regulation. In 2001 the US Office of Management and Budget estimated the cost of federal regulations at $380 billion per annum, or about ten percent of the US gross domestic product (GDP) (more than half the output of the US manufacturing sector).[6] Despite the high cost that it is asked to pay for regulation, however, the public does not see its worth. A 2004 report showed that 53 percent of Americans agreed that 'Government regulation of business usually does more harm than good.'[7] Clearly, needs are not being met.

It is true that inefficient regulation can erode confidence, impede growth,

---

[5] M. Rosenberg, *Nonviolent Communication: A Language of Life* (2003) 52.

[6] James L. Gattuso, 'Reforming Regulation to Keep America's Small Businesses Competitive' (2004) The Heritage Foundation <http://www.heritage.org/Research/Regulation/tst052104a.cfm#_ftn2#_ftn2> at 14 December 2009.

[7] <http://people-press.org/report/?pageid=756> at 23 December 2009.

and retard needed change. It may limit the expansion of consumer choice, reduce entrepreneurial initiative, and often advantages some unfairly at the expense of others, small business for example.[8] Because many regulatory costs fall disproportionately on small business; if regulation is ineffective, small business feels it first. [9] There are, however, significant benefits to efficient and effective regulation, though they are often harder to quantify than the costs. Appropriate regulation can enhance economic growth and competitiveness, as regulatory regimes support the growth of local economies and global economic development.[10]

As the current global financial crisis continues to unfold, there can be no doubt that there are consequences to regulatory inaction. In place of neo-conservative principles of de-regulation and unbounded faith in markets, there is a renewed appreciation of the potential benefit of effective regulation to enhance competitiveness by ensuring effective and fair commerce. There is in the public discourse an 'increasing sense of anxiety surrounding deregulation' because market processes cannot be relied upon to adequately serve the public interest.[11]

Properly targeted and implemented regulatory measures can reduce costs of unfair practices and failed business, reinvigorate consumer confidence and stimulate investment. An effective regulatory scheme can attract foreign investment and facilitate local expansion overseas. Some experts advise businesses to seek out areas with progressive regulation in terms of concern with social problems, and to set internal goals that meet or exceed regulatory standards because this ultimately leads to advantage as

---

[8] Sveinbjörn Blöndal and Dirk Pilät, 'The Economic Benefits of Regulatory Reform' (1997) 1 OECD Economic Studies No. 28 [29] <http://www.oecd.org/dataoecd/22/21/2733617.pdf> at 14 December 2009.

[9] A Crain and Hopkins study found that firms employing fewer than 20 people faced regulatory costs of almost $7,000 per employee, compared to an average of $4,700 for all firms, not including indirect burdens and secondary costs. See W. Mark Crain and Thomas D. Hopkins, 'The Impact of Regulatory Costs on Small Firms: A Report for the Office of Advocacy, US Small Business Administration,' RFP No. SBAHW-00-R-0027.

[10] Sveinbjörn Blöndal and Dirk Pilät, 'The Economic Benefits of Regulatory Reform' (1997) 1 OECD Economic Studies No. 28 [30] <http://www.oecd.org/dataoecd/22/21/2733617.pdf> at 14 December 2009. On the distinction between the regulation of standards and the regulation of competition, see Michael E. Porter, *The Competitive Advantage of Nations* (1990). The topic is also discussed in John Braithwaite, 'Responsive Regulation for Australia' in Peter Grabosky and John Braithwaite (eds), *Business Regulation and Australia's Future* (1993).

[11] Karen Gustafson, 'The New Economy and Internet Regulation: Discourses of Inevitability' (Paper presented at the 57th Annual International Communication Association Conference, San Francisco, CA, 24 May 2007).

other jurisdictions modify their regulations to follow suit.[12] A well-defined legal structure is indispensable for the effective functioning of any business operation and the lack of comprehensive legislation can lead to greater complexity, ambiguities and uncertainty. Commercial interests in any jurisdiction therefore should seek to promote a measured approach toward achieving effective and efficient regulation in order to enhance competitiveness and the effective function of markets and, ultimately, to enhance the quality of life in both economic and social spheres.

Regulation is inevitable. All commerce is underpinned by a legal framework and infrastructure. Not only that, all commerce is regulated privately; specifically at the 'layers' of market and contract the parties use various means to control the nature of their interactions. The question then is not whether to regulate, but how to regulate.

The global financial crisis provided a stark reminder that the economic climate and the regulation of business in economies around the globe can and do impact each other significantly. Regulating business in a post-global-financial-crisis world is likely to involve greater emphasis on the prophylactic benefits of regulation, as a result of a widespread disillusionment with laissez-faire approaches that allow unscrupulous people to profit to the detriment of all. There is less tolerance for 'sharp' business practice and a greater recognition that we all pay for financial opportunism, often on a grand scale, and that we need regulation for the benefits and competitive advantage that good governance can offer.

However, increasing complexity in markets and higher levels of specialization mean it is harder than ever for regulators to comprehend and respond to risks in the marketplace. During the financial instability in the US prior to World War II Franklin D. Roosevelt was able to shut the banks, to take time to analyse and address the particular problems that had caused the most damage to the economy.

Today, it appears to be impossible to unravel the interconnected web of global trade and finance, and the luxury of sufficient time to fully analyse problems and formulate plans seems to be a relic of a bygone era. Further, there seems less consensus than ever on what the role of government can and should be in market intervention:

> Welfare economics supports the concept that failure to satisfy the conditions for perfect competition can justify government intervention in markets . . . but this market failure approach is open to question . . . The difficulty facing regulatory

---

[12] Peter Grabosky and John Braithwaite (eds), *Business Regulation and Australia's Future* (1993) 88, citing Michael E. Porter, *The Competitive Advantage of Nations* (1990).

> authorities is how to differentiate between situations requiring intervention and those that do not . . . in general, government intervention is not necessarily the only or even the best solution to instances of market failure . . . also, spillover effects of regulatory actions in one jurisdiction can impact on other jurisdictions and necessitate coordination in a globalised economy.[13]

The answers therefore have to be quicker, with greater reliance on insider/expert knowledge and with awareness of synergies of the ecologies of markets and industries. They must be more self-regulatory, responsive and reflexive, with greater reliance on the expertise and on-the-spot assessments of the participants themselves.

The answers also must be global and broad-based in perspective as the new global economy is more interconnected than ever before. The concept of globalization can mean many things; in this book it is used to refer to, 'a process in which the structures of economic markets, technologies, and communication patterns become progressively more international over time'.[14] The growth of international trade, the expansion of transnational enterprise, and increased interactions of financial markets are components of this process which has significant implications for national economies and global change.[15]

The Malaysian franchise sector's targeted expansion into Middle Eastern markets illustrates the connections among countries and regions such as Southeast Asia and the Middle East and among industry sectors such as tourism and fast food:

> The Malaysians have been particularly successful in the area of introducing new food and fashion brands to the Gulf. Malaysia's current drive, promoting itself as a preferred holiday destination for people from the Gulf, is assisting the drive to export Malaysian brands. Tourists experience the local brands abroad and readily accept them in Saudi when they are introduced. The tourist drive further enhances the concept of brand Malaysia?[16]

---

[13] Boon-Cheye Lee, 'Regulation and the New Economy' (Working Paper 02-18, University of Wollongong, NSW, Australia, 2002) 15–16. Available at <http://ro.uow.edu.au/cgi/viewcontent.cgi?article=1063&context=commwkpapers> at19 December 2009.

[14] OECD, 'Environment and Globalisation: Background Report for Ministers' (Report for meeting of the Environment Policy Committee at Ministerial Level, Environment and Global Competitiveness, 28–29 April 2008) < http://www.oecd.org/dataoecd/3/59/40511624.pdf> at 19 December 2009.

[15] Rhys Jenkins, Jonathan Barton, Anthony Bartzokas, Jan Hesselberg and Hege Merete Knutsen, *Environmental Regulation in the New Global Economy: The Impact on Industry and Competitiveness* (2002).

[16] Franchiseek Limited, 'Saudi Arabia Franchise Statistics' (2009) <http://www.franchiseek.com/Saudi_Arabia/Franchise_Saudi_Arabia_Statistics.htm> at 14 December 2009.

No single company is driving the expansion of Malaysian franchising in the Gulf region; instead the entire Malaysian franchise sector is the brand in this process of market development and international expansion, facilitated by effective regulation. 'The need for countries to cooperate and coordinate their policies is perhaps the key conclusion. . ..'[17]

Finally, the answers must also be based on durable human values. Current academic literature reflects this; it is about 'humanizing the firm', recognizing the economic value of trust and integrity in commercial environments. What is needed is regulation of commerce both on a human and a municipal scale that comprehends and responds to global conditions. Just as franchising itself combines local 'touch' with worldwide proportions, regulation must comprehend the multiple layers of commercial interaction and respond to them with careful, balanced measures in order to maximize the productivity of commercial enterprise while minimizing its inefficiencies and negative externalities.

## THE IMPORTANCE OF FRANCHISING

In the post-World War II period franchising has proved to be a remarkably successful business model, adaptable to many different industries and commercial applications as well as to the sharing of intellectual property for social welfare initiatives. Though franchising is often identified with the 'small end of town', franchising in fact represents big business and small business alike. Today, franchised businesses operate in about two-thirds of the approximately 192 countries in the world and make a major economic contribution. McDonald's Corporation has over 31,000 stores in approximately 120 countries,[18] and in 2008 reported sales revenue of US$23.5 billion.[19] Yum! Brands (owner of the Kentucky Fried Chicken, Pizza Hut, Taco Bell and Long John Silver brands) has 35,345 stores in over 100 countries and in 2008 reported revenue of US$11.3 billion.[20]

---

17 Boon-Cheye Lee, 'Regulation and the New Economy' (Working Paper 02-18, University of Wollongong, NSW, Australia, 2002) 16. Available at <http://ro.uow.edu.au/cgi/viewcontent.cgi?article=1063&context=commwkpapers> at 19 December 2009

18 McDonald's Corporation, 'Frequently Asked Questions' (2009) McDonald's <http://www.aboutmcdonalds.com/mcd/students/faq_for_students.html#10> at 19 December 2009.

19 <http://finance.econsultant.com/mcdonalds-2008-revenue-profit-2009-fortune-500-rank/> at 23 December 2009.

20 <http://www.yum.com> at 23 December 2009.

Franchising is also a major sector of many national economies, where its efficient operation impacts economic, social and political conditions. While reliable measurements of activity in the franchise sector are notoriously difficult to obtain, reports from many jurisdictions do suggest its importance. In Canada franchising revenues are estimated at $30 billion, accounting for approximately 10 percent of GDP. In the US about 40 percent of all US retail sales may be attributed to franchise units, franchising is also estimated to account for approximately 10 percent of GDP. In Peru approximately 70 Peruvian and foreign franchise businesses now operate, generating an estimated 3,250 direct jobs and sales reaching US$375 million. In Belgium the annual sales turnover through these outlets is about €2.4 billion, or about 6 percent of retail trade. The total market for franchising in Finland was estimated at $5.4 billion. German franchising, with sales at about US$2 million, accounts for about 1.6 percent of total national GDP. Annual sales through franchise outlets in the Netherlands accounted for approximately $23 billion worth of sales in 2004. In India franchising accounts for 3 percent of India's total retail; the market is estimated to be €2 billion. In Malaysia, by some estimates franchising contributes over 12 percent of the country's GDP. In Japan more than 1,000 franchisors operate over 198,000 outlets and generate an annual turnover of more than US$142 billion. In Singapore franchising accounts for an estimated A$80 billion (12 percent of the GDP). And the list goes on.

Franchising is not only an important part of the global economy currently, but also it is on the increase worldwide.[21] In Norway there are approximately 250 different franchising systems in operation, an increase of 32 percent since 1998.[22] Sixty of the 107 franchises currently operating in Romania have been established during the last two years.[23] In Egypt continued growth is expected at an annual rate of 10 to 20 percent,[24] while an average annual growth rate of 25 percent is estimated for the region of the Middle East.[25] In New Zealand the sector is expected to continue to

---

[21] Diez-DeCastro, Navarro-Garcia, Rodriguez-Raz, Rondan-Cataluna, 'Membership in the Franchising System: A Worldwide Analysis' (Speech delivered at the 22nd Annual International Society of Franchising Conference, Saint-Malo, Brittany, France, 20–21 June 2008).

[22] Britt Hestenes, 'Franchising in Norway' (2006) United States of America Department of Commerce <http://www.buyusainfo.net/docs/x_3120014.pdf> at 28 December 2008.

[23] Roxana Negutu, 'Romania – A New Player On The Market' (30 May 2008) http://www.franchise-update.com/article/573 at 19 December 2009.

[24] <http://www.nixonpeabody.com/publications_detail3.asp?ID=2795> at 25 December 2009.

[25] <http://www.ameinfo.com/156782.html> at 25 December 2009.

grow at up to 20 percent per annum, while in Australia the sector continues to grow domestically, and about 20 percent of its franchisors are looking at expanding overseas.[26]

The franchise business model is expanding because of its potential as a versatile and dynamic organizational form. It is a model that has been described by law and economics theorists as 'federated', combining large-scale economies of big business with the local 'touch' of local enterprise.[27] The many benefits of franchising include its ability to facilitate the efficient expansion and adoption of good business practices; to rapidly develop intellectual property both domestically and internationally; to promote the growth of small business; and to provide a vehicle for investment as well as for training of fledgling entrepreneurs in both mature and developing economies. Franchising combines the advantages of small- and large-scale enterprise; it is personal and accessible, while at the same time it achieves important economies of scale and international brand recognition.

This book is focused on the regulation of the franchising sector, especially on franchise-specific legislation. Because legislation by governments only comes into play when there are problems that need to be addressed, by its very nature this book is about problems in the franchising sector. This is not meant in any way to detract from the successful organizational form that franchising represents. Franchising continues to grow, continues as a successful business form, and that is exactly why the regulation of this sector is important and should comply with best practice, representing the highest examples of integrity and expertise in regulating.

## THE REGULATION OF FRANCHISING IN THE NEW GLOBAL ECONOMY

The book is arranged in two parts. The first part deals with both regulation and franchising in conceptual and practical terms. Chapter 1 establishes the regulatory context for the survey of the regulation of franchising, which is based on a 'new learning' on regulation, with a focus on three concepts. The first is the importance of self-regulatory tools and strategies. The

---

26 'An Overview of the Status of Franchising Internationally', http://www.afdb.org/fileadmin/uploads/jai/Course-Materials/04-FRANCHISING-WITHIN-SME-DEV-STRATEGY/day1/1.3-louw-an-overview-of-the-status-of-franchising-internationally.doc. at 25 December 2009.

27 See, eg, Oliver Williamson, *Markets and Hierarchies: Analyses and Antitrust Implications* (1975); Oliver Williamson, *The Economic Institutions of Capitalism* (1985).

second is that regulation as governance happens at multiple 'layers', all of which must be considered in any regulatory program. The third concept is that regulation should follow a process that encompasses reliable information and the input of all stakeholders through democratic, participative process. These concepts serve as the underlying framework for theoretical approach to regulation in the book.

The first part of the book continues with the thread of the 'new learning' as it outlines in Chapters 2 and 3 the governance of franchising at private 'layers' of market and contract, and its implications with respect to the franchise relationship. The phrase 'the franchise relationship' refers to the relationship between franchisor and a franchisee. Legislation directed towards that interaction is described as 'franchise-specific legislation'. As the Explanatory Report for the UNIDROIT Model Law points out, one of the characteristics of franchising is that a number of areas of law are involved, many of which are already regulated. It is therefore, 'difficult to justify adopting a discipline specifically for franchising in relation to, for example, contract law, choice of law and jurisdiction, or intellectual and industrial property law'.[28] A comparison of the legislation regarding all these aspects of franchising, though significant, lies outside the scope of this study.

Chapter 2 describes the fundamentals of the interaction between franchisor and franchisee at the level of the market. Some of the problems that arise frequently in the course of the franchise relationship are outlined, with the caveat that this material is presented only to provide an understanding of the issues for the purposes of this book. It is in no way intended as a substitute for participation in regulatory process in any given jurisdiction. The main issues that are raised for this purpose are the importance of uniformity, the corollary of which is franchisor control, and lack of reliable information about the sector and about franchise systems, which leads to asymmetries of information and acts as a substrate for the promulgation of myths.

Chapter 3 proceeds from the premise that best practice in regulatory process requires a comprehensive understanding of the context of regulation. Because the context of regulating franchise relationships is contract,[29] an accurate understanding of the nature of the contractual agreement is

---

[28] UNIDROIT, 'Model Franchise Disclosure Law: Explanatory Report' (2002) p. 13. <www.unidroit.org/english/modellaws/2002franchise/2002modellaw-e.pdf> at 19 December 2009.

[29] Gillian Hadfield, 'Problematic Relations: Franchising and the Law of Incomplete Contracts' (1990) 42 *Stanford Law Review* 927, 939: '[T]he heart of franchising's legal structure is still contract'.

critical to understanding the relationship. Chapter 3 explains the full implications of the fact that franchise agreements 'are long-term, standard-form contracts',[30]first in theory and second through an examination of contract terms in franchise agreements as they represent the competing interests of franchisors and franchisees.

Though its benefits are well-documented, franchising does have risks for both parties, but the risks are easier for franchisors to address through careful drafting of contract terms than they are for franchisees. In fact, franchisors often shift their business and financial risks to franchisees. The contextual framework for understanding the regulation of franchising provided in the first part of the book suggests that franchising carries risks that are reinforced by the parties' private self-regulation through their market and contractual interactions. Therefore, the market inefficiencies and social welfare problems that may result do warrant public intervention.

The second part of the book provides a global survey and analysis of how the sector is currently regulated through statutory regulation, franchise-specific legislation. Chapter 4 outlines the articulated purposes of sector-specific legislation where it is available. It also surveys the scope of the legislation according to the various definitions used for franchising in the legislation.

Chapter 5 provides a general country-by-country overview of legislation globally. For each jurisdiction that regulates the sector some general statistical information about population and economic productivity are included to provide a context for the survey information about the regulatory climate. The survey gives information about disclosure; registration; other pre-sales measures; measures targeted towards performance of the agreement; dispute resolution; good faith where applicable; and in some cases administration and enforcement.

The survey in Chapter 5 of this legislation provides the material for an analysis of trends in the statutory regulation of franchising. Chapter 6 begins the book's analysis and discussion of franchise-specific regulation, identifying the common themes and trends. Chapter 7 summarizes the tools and approaches used in franchise-specific regulation with respect to regulation through disclosure, registration, and other pre-sales measures such as cooling-off and standards and qualifications. Chapter 8 deals with legislation directed toward the conduct of and exit from the franchise

---

[30] Gillian Hadfield, 'Problematic Relations: Franchising and the Law of Incomplete Contracts' (1990) 42 *Stanford Law Review* 927, 946. Having made this observation, Hadfield focused the balance of her analysis primarily on the incompleteness of the contract rather than the standard form or the combination of the two.

relationship, in other words performance-oriented legislation, including mandatory content; prescribed procedures for dispute resolution, transfer and termination; and also a requirement of good faith. Chapter 9 concludes with some discussion of directions for the reconception of regulation at all 'layers' of governance.

This book surveys franchise-specific regulation globally; it is not a comprehensive manual or analysis of regulation of the franchising sector in any given jurisdiction. Rather, it surveys legislation from a broad perspective in order to identify patterns and trends and so to serve as a starting point for understanding the regulation of franchising as well as other commercial regulation, taking into account the context of the relationship, the nature of the contract, and the nature of the commercial interaction. Rather than a practice-oriented resource, this book identifies patterns in statutory intervention in the sector and provides a conceptual analysis of the regulation of the franchise sector globally. Such information can lead to better analysis of how such tools work, to what extent they are effective and in what combinations they may best be applied to achieve agreed regulatory objectives.

While it has not been within the scope of this book to survey case law in each jurisdiction, this is an important area for further study as each jurisdiction, region and/or legal tradition will have a history of case law and landmark cases, such as *Scheck* in the US or the *Pronuptia* case in Europe, that have implications for the legal landscape and the regulation of the sector in these jurisdictions.[31] It is also beyond the scope of this volume to survey business practices at the level of the market or contractual interaction. Obviously these aspects are also crucially important in assessing the regulatory regime in any given jurisdiction. The material presented here is, therefore, only one piece of a much larger picture.

Ideally, perhaps in the ten-volume revised version of this book, this assessment will encompass, *inter alia*, analysis of market usage and practice and contractual conventions in drafting and interpretation in each jurisdiction, with special attention to implied terms such as good faith. Such research would also examine various other factors influencing the regulatory environment such as the level of economic development; capitalist versus communist traditions; political and social factors; and cultural attitudes to business, themselves a product of religion, politics and economics.

It is also beyond the scope of this book to assess the effectiveness of regulation in achieving its ends in any given sector, or to determine whether regulation of the franchising sector in any given jurisdiction comports with

---

31 *Scheck v. Burger King Corp.* (756 F. Supp. 543 (S.D. Fla. 1991)) and *Pronuptia* Case, European Court of Justice, Case 161/84, 1986 CMLR 414.

what is suggested as best regulatory practice, in terms of getting the best information, identifying the harms and selecting the best tools and strategies to address them; whether the process fully engages all the stakeholders; whether there is transparency and legitimacy. In practice every jurisdiction must engage in a process of gathering information about the conditions specific to it, to consult with stakeholders, to identify the specific risks and to address them.

What this book does aim to provide is a contextualized comparison of current practice in addressing the problems in franchising against the range of possible tools that are in theory available. The impetus for this survey of current regulatory regimes for the franchising sector globally grew out of research into the operation of the Australian franchise sector, where, after 30 years of experimentation with the regulation of the franchise sector, there is still no consensus about the effectiveness of the regulatory program for franchising. Four government inquiries into the regulation of the franchise sector in the past three years suggests that Australia has not yet achieved the best regulatory regime for its own particular requirements. There is even less reason to believe that it should be exported to other jurisdictions with their own particular circumstances, political, economic and social conditions and varying objectives. The question that this research sets out to answer is whether there is an ideal formulation for the regulation of the franchising sector, and if so, to identify the essential characteristics of that formulation.

For those who seek to understand them, the worlds of regulation and franchising may be both the stuff of myths. Perhaps the possibility of achieving a successful regulatory program tailored to the franchising sector is a myth in itself. But even if delivering balance and equity to franchising is a fairy tale, there are nevertheless lessons to be learned from fairy tales; and the quest for a grail, however futile, often brings out what is beautiful and worthwhile in the human spirit.

# 1. Reconceiving regulation

'Man's capacity for justice makes democracy possible, but man's inclination to injustice makes democracy necessary.'[1]

Public mistrust of regulation has become a norm, embodied in the idea that if government refrains from regulatory activity, people will have increased freedom, money, time and resources to live as we choose. Former US President Ronald Reagan labelled the phrase 'I'm from the government and I'm here to help' the nine most terrifying words in the English language. But such thinking, however appealing, reflects a narrow view of regulation. This chapter explores what regulation has become, how it has evolved to the current 'new learning', which reconceptualizes regulation as governance. This chapter outlines the 'new learning' on regulation according to three key principles:

- the importance of self-regulation in expanding the potential for creative solutions to effectively serve regulatory purposes;
- a widened perspective of regulation, as it functions at every 'layer' of a contractual interaction, in which self-regulation plays an integral role in a broadened perspective on governance and tools of regulation; and
- an acknowledgement of the importance of process because its broadened scope renders regulatory process more complicated, proper process at all stages of regulation becomes more critical, from information collection to problem identification through selection of tools, implementation, and monitoring and management.

These new approaches to regulation provide the framework for the subsequent treatment of franchising and its regulation in this book.

[1] Ursula M. Niebuhr (ed), *Remembering Reinhold Niebuhr: Letters of Reinhold and Ursula M. Niebuhr* (1991).

## THE EVOLUTION OF REGULATORY THEORY

Commentators and academics employ a range of different meanings for the term regulation, 'with varying amounts of lack of discipline'.[2] Among this diversity of meanings are the following:

- the promulgation of rules by government, usually a specialized agency, including enforcement and monitoring;
- any direct state intervention in the economy; and
- all mechanisms of social control or influence, affecting all aspects of behaviour, intentional or not. [3]

'Traditional regulation' is a term sometimes used to describe a democratically elected legislature making laws which are then enforced through the civil or criminal procedure of the courts. It may also be referred to as 'hard law'. By contrast, 'soft law' is a term used to refer to any regulatory process other than the traditional process.[4]

The term 'regulation' and related terms such as 'regulatory practice', 'regulatory process' are commonly used to refer to regulation by direct intervention, that is by an outside regulator. This form of regulation is also referred to as 'statutory' or 'legislated' regulation or intervention, or simply as 'legislation' or 'statute'.

The term 'regulation' is increasingly used in academic literature in the broadest sense of governance, 'the intentional activity of attempting to control, order, or influence the behaviour of others'.[5] In advocating this approach the editors of the journal *Regulation and Governance* describe their mission as one of opening regulatory studies to move 'the boundaries of regulation toward the boundaries of governance'.[6]

---

[2] Julia Black, 'Critical Reflections on Regulation' (2002) 27 *Australian Journal of Legal Philosophy*, 11–13.

[3] Julia Black, 'Critical Reflections on Regulation' (2002) 27 *Australian Journal of Legal Philosophy*, 11–13. Black observes that they are 'sometimes using all three meanings within the same document' and concludes that 'conceptual confusion is indicated by definitional chaos'.

[4] European Consumer Law Group, 'Soft Law and the Consumer Interest' (March 2001) <http://ec.europa.eu/consumers/policy/eclg/rep03_en.pdf> at 14 December 2009.

[5] Julia Black, 'Critical Reflections on Regulation' (2002) 27 *Australian Journal of Legal Philosophy 1*.

[6] John Braithwaite, Cary Coglianese and David Levi-Faur, 'Can regulation and governance make a difference?' (2007) 1(1) *Regulation & Governance*, 1–7.

With the expanding range of meanings for regulation,[7] it is important to describe precisely what form and what meaning of regulation is intended. Qualifiers of the term help to distinguish the intended meaning, as well as to represent different attitudes to regulatory activity.

In this book, regulation is intended to be construed in the broad sense, being that regulation is about the control and governance of the business relationship between franchisor and franchisee.

According to this broader conception of regulation, there is no longer a question of whether or not to regulate; instead, there is a question of governance. If we choose not to regulate in the traditional sense of government intervention, there will still be governance in the relevant market, through contract and by dispute resolution. It is therefore necessary to understand the nature of governance at the market, contract and dispute resolution 'layers' in order to fully inform a determination of whether traditional legislative intervention is warranted, and, if warranted, what form it should take.

Regulatory theory evolved towards the current, broader view of regulation as governance with insights borrowed from the biological and social sciences. Early theories of regulation focus on the nature of the interests involved and on the question of whose interests prevail in the regulatory process.[8] The 'public interest' theory[9] considers regulation as a state response to abuses in a regulated sector.[10] Stemming from the public choice theory of law and economics, it focuses on the implementation of law as the result of political process.[11] Public interest regulation requires a disinterested, efficient, expert and competent regulator. Problems with this approach stem from the clash of values in determining what is in the 'public interest', as well as problems due to lack of funding and training of regulatory administrators.[12] 'Private interest' theory[13] de-emphasizes

---

[7] Hugh Collins, for example, uses the term, 'meta-regulation' to refer to the collection of forces and actors that contribute to regulatory process. Hugh Collins, 'Regulating Contract' in C. Parker et al. (eds), *Regulating Law* (2004) 13.

[8] 'Regulatory process' is used here to designate the process of determining what regulatory action is needed, selecting the appropriate mix of tools, and implementing and monitoring that regulatory action.

[9] Also known as public choice or normative-positivist theory.

[10] Johan Den Hertog, 'General Theories of Regulation' in Bouckaert et al., *Encyclopaedia of Law and Economics, vol II: The Regulation of Contracts* (2000).

[11] Nicholas Mercuro and Steven G. Medema, *Economics and the Law* (1997) 84.

[12] Baldwin and Cave suggest that the public interest vision may really only be viable in the early stages of the regulatory 'life-cycle'. Life cycle theory is introduced below. See Robert Baldwin and Martin Cave, *Understanding Regulation: Theory, Strategy and Practice* (1999) 20.

[13] Also known as Chicago or economic-libertarian theory.

ideology and policy goals. Instead, it regards regulation as a reflection of the private interests that influence regulatory process. The purpose of regulation, according to this theory, is to serve the special interests of the individuals who shape it.[14]

'Interest group' theory views regulation as the result of the inputs of interested parties. Regulatory process is a negotiation of interests, and the resulting regulation represents a compromise of both public goals and private interests. Competing groups engage in a struggle for power in which the prevailing groups formulate regulations that may exclude other legitimate interests.[15]

'Capture' theory places greater emphasis on the process of regulating. Capture theory concerns itself with economic and political influence over the regulator, where industry may take advantage of being 'regulated', for example, by using regulation to protect itself from competition or to insulate itself from further government scrutiny. While cooperation between the regulated industry and the regulator may result in legislation that carries greater force of buy-in, capture theory highlights the risk of the regulator becoming subject to the influence of the regulated interest.

The 'life-cycle' theory of regulation, as conceived by Bernstein, identifies four stages in the life cycle of a regulator; these stages are gestation, youth, maturity, and old age.[16] Each stage is characterized by the role of the regulator, but also by the changing nature of legislation and enforcement, and third party influence. This theory views the confluence of regulated and regulator interests as a natural step in the institutional development of the regulator. At some stage the regulator may even take a protective and proprietary stance vis-à-vis the regulated industry. Therefore, in the interests of legitimacy and transparency, regulation can be successfully implemented by an outside agency only if it is subject to regular, independent monitoring and review.[17]

'Institutional' theories emphasize the roles of organizational structures

---

[14] Roman Tomasic (ed), *Business Regulation in Australia* (1984) 16–17; See also Johan Den Hertog, 'General Theories of Regulation' in Bouckaert et al., *Encyclopaedia of Law and Economics, vol II: The Regulation of Contracts* (2000) 9–14. Den Hertog refers to this theory as public choice theory.

[15] Robert Baldwin and Martin Cave, *Understanding Regulation: Theory, Strategy and Practice* (1999) 21.

[16] David Levi-Faur, 'Theories of Regulation' (1999) School of Political Science, University of Haifa, Israel <http://poli.haifa.ac.il/~levi/regutheories.htm> at 14 December 2009.

[17] H.K. Colebatch, 'Regulation and Paradigms of Organization: Six Theses' in Roman Tomasic and Ric Lucas (eds), *Power, Regulation and Resistance: Studies in the Sociology of Law* (1986) 20.

and rules in shaping regulation as the entire process of designing regulation is informed by institutional context.[18] Before looking at the rule-making process, therefore, it is necessary to consider the institutions of both the regulator(s) and regulated interest(s), including their history and development, their evolution from other institutional relationships, and the perceptions of effectiveness that different types of regulation have had in that context.

The 'force-of-ideas' theory suggests that regulation is influenced by economic, technical, social, and institutional pressures.[19] Force-of-ideas explains why some goals and values are favoured in determining objectives of regulation at any given time.[20]

Whereas traditional theories of regulation centre on whose interests prevail in the regulatory process, later theories, such as the 'institutional' and 'force-of-ideas' theories reflect a further expansion of the conception of regulation, and the growing interest in systems-based approaches, self-regulation and reflexive regulation.[21]

More recently, 'systems' theory has shifted the focus to communications and organizational principles, feedback and responsiveness.[22] Adapted from biology and based on communications and organizational principles, systems theory signals a further shift in emphasis from direct intervention to process. It conceives of the organization as a system of complex sets of interdependent parts that interact as they adapt to constantly changing

---

18 Robert Baldwin and Martin Cave, *Understanding Regulation: Theory, Strategy and Practice* (1999) 27.

19 Robert Baldwin and Martin Cave, *Understanding Regulation: Theory, Strategy and Practice* (1999) 27.

20 An example of this might be the debate between Butler, Eliot and Manning on the legitimacy of corporations law. Butler and Eliot judge corporations law a success because they focus on utility (i.e. a useful tool to enable economic and productive expansion), while Manning sees it as flawed because his focus is on responsibility (insufficient controls over those in power within corporate organizations). See James W. Hurst, *The Legitimacy of the Business Corporation in the Law of the United States, 1780–1970* (1970) 156.

21 Teubner's conception of reflexive law is that it involves a new kind of legal self-restraint. Rather than taking over regulatory responsibility for the outcome of social processes, reflexive law restricts itself to the installation, correction, and redefinition of democratic self-regulatory mechanisms. See Günter Teubner, 'Substantive and Reflexive Elements in Modern Law' (1983) 17(2) *Law & Society Review* 239–86.

22 Many of the concepts are related to autopoietic theory as applied to law and other social sciences. See Günter Teubner, 'Law as An Autopoietic System' (Paper presented at the LSE Complexity Study Group Meeting No 3, London, 18 June 1997).

environments. Feedback within the system is critical to enable regulation to be responsive and adaptable.[23]Consultation with and responsiveness to a wide range of interests in regulation are important in the interests of transparency and building trust. Participation also reduces regulatory risks and curbs 'information monopolies'.[24]

Reconceptualizing regulation as governance is part of the 'new learning' on regulation and focuses on three key concepts: the importance of self-regulation; the widened scope of regulation, as it functions at every 'layer' of a contractual interaction; and the importance of process.

The concept of self-regulation is also derived from the biological sciences.[25] 'Self-regulation' is now used generically to refer to any mechanism whereby a subject exercises control over itself to maintain the stability of its function.[26] Rather than a precise concept, 'it may be defined as a process whereby an organized group regulates the behaviour of its members'.[27]

Self-regulation in business can be defined as 'internal regulation of the industry by the industry through its own procedures'.[28] Originally identified with 'the professions' where rules of conduct and rights of practice for professions were set and enforced by professional organizations, today self-regulation has extended to other areas, most notably financial regulation.[29] Disillusionment with the burden and inefficiencies of substantive regulation fuelled the development of these approaches:

---

23 Systems may be open or closed. An open system 'is a set of objects with attributes that interrelate in an environment. The system possesses qualities of wholeness, interdependence, hierarchy, self-regulation, environmental interchange, equilibrium, adaptability, and equifinality'. 'Equifinality' is defined to mean the same results with different inputs or processes. See S.W. Littlejohn, *Theories of Human Communication* (2nd ed, 1983) 32.

24 See Jacobs & Associates, <http://www.regulatoryreform.com> at 14 December 2009.

25 Self-regulation is part of the process of homeostasis by which a system regulates its internal environment to maintain a stable condition by means of multiple equilibrium adjustments carried out by interrelated regulatory mechanisms; see <http://en.allexperts.com/e/h/ho/homeostasis.htm> at 23 December 2009.

26 As the state of the terminology in this developing field of study indicates, there is no single conception of self-regulation; Black identifies four basic forms of self-regulation as 1) mandated self-regulation; 2) sanctioned self-regulation; 3) coerced self-regulation; and 4) voluntary self-regulation. See Julia Black, 'Decentring Regulation: Understanding the Role of Regulation and Self-regulation in a "Post-Regulatory" World' (2001) 54 *Current Legal Problems* 103, 118.

27 Neil Gunningham, Peter Grabosky and Darren Sinclair, *Smart Regulation: Designing Environmental Policy* (1998) 50.

28 Neil Gunningham, Peter Grabosky and Darren Sinclair, *Smart Regulation: Designing Environmental Policy* (1998).

29 Anthony I. Ogus, *Regulation: Legal Form and Economic Theory* (1994) 107.

> Günter Teubner articulated his famous regulatory 'trilemma' of 'circumvention, perversity and negative feedback' that resulted in a pathology of increasingly elaborate and legalised regulation that was ultimately ineffective. Julia Black summarises these critiques of regulation: [t]he instruments used (laws backed by sanctions) are inappropriate and unsophisticated (instrument failure), . . . government has insufficient knowledge to be able to identify the causes of the problems, to design solutions that are appropriate, and to identify non-compliance (information failure), . . . implementation of the regulation is inadequate (implementation failure) and/or . . . those being regulated are insufficiently inclined to comply (motivation failure).[30]

These critiques stimulated a 'new learning' on regulation with self-regulation, and also the concept of 'decentred' regulation, at its core.

> In the area of consumer policy decentred approaches appear in a heightened emphasis on self-regulation, the creation of greater opportunities for consumers and others to participate in policy making and implementation.[31]

As an alternative prescription for failures of state-centred regulation,[32] decentred regulation is characterized by:

> . . . complexity, fragmentation and construction of knowledge, fragmentation of the exercise of power and control, autonomy, interactions and interdependencies, and the collapse of the public/private distinction.[33]

Cooter suggests that centralized law is 'not even plausible for a technologically advanced society'.[34] Decentralization goes hand-in-hand with self-regulation because, 'efficiency requires that as economies develop, the enforcement of custom in business communities becomes more important as part of the regulation of business'.[35]

---

30 Iain Ramsay, 'Regulatory Capitalism and the "New Learning" in Regulation' (2006) 28 *Sydney Law Review* 9.

31 Iain Ramsay, 'Regulatory Capitalism and the "New Learning" in Regulation' (2006) 28 *Sydney Law Review* 9. For a full discussion on the range of meanings of the term 'decentred regulation', see Julia Black, 'Decentring Regulation: Understanding the Role of Regulation and Self-regulation in a "Post-Regulatory" World' (2001) 54 *Current Legal Problems* 103.

32 Julia Black, 'Critical Reflections on Regulation' (2002) 27 *Australian Journal of Legal Philosophy* 1, 4.

33 Julia Black, 'Decentring Regulation: Understanding the Role of Regulation and Self-regulation in a "Post-Regulatory" World' (2001) 54 *Current Legal Problems* 103.

34 Robert D. Cooter and Ulen Thomas, *Law and Economics* (2000) 1647.

35 Robert D. Cooter and Ulen Thomas, *Law and Economics* (2000) 1647.

Often used in connection with self-regulation, responsive and reflexive regulation are emerging concepts that emphasize greater inclusiveness and participation by all stakeholders.[36] Reflexive law and responsive regulation suggest new theoretical perspectives with respect to the function of industries, sectors, and 'systems'.

'Reflexion' is a process through which specialized subsystems of society mediate and integrate their functional role in the larger society as a whole; it establishes processes and procedures for private actors to determine their own substantive outcomes.[37] Reflexive regulation prescribes inclusive procedures for parties to recognize existing and future problems and to develop their own solutions.[38] The imposition by the regulator of rules and standards is replaced by 'process, organisation, and the distribution of rights and competencies'.[39] Reflexive law is self-regulation in that the private actors determine substantive outcomes through the reflexive process.[40]

'Responsive' regulation refers to a collaborative process between a regulator and the regulated interest where the cooperation of the regulated interest offers a better chance of finding a solution. This more inclusive approach to regulation better represents stakeholder interests.[41] However, it requires a commitment to involve stakeholders:

---

36 See Günter Teubner, 'Law as An Autopoietic System' (Paper presented at the LSE Complexity Study Group Meeting No 3, London, 18 June 1997); H. Willke, 'Autopoiesis and Organized Complexity' (Paper presented at the LSE Complexity Study Group Meeting No 3, London, 18 June 1997); E.W. Orts, 'Reflexive Environmental Law' (1995) 89 *Northwestern University Law Review* 1227; David Hess, 'Social Reporting: A Reflexive Law Approach to Corporate Social Responsiveness' (1999) 25(1) *Journal of Corporate Law* 41; W. Eisenberg, 'The Responsive Model of Contract Law' (1984) 36 *Stanford Law Review* 1107. While these terms sometimes appear to be used synonymously, Collins argues that responsiveness and reflexion are distinct concepts. See Hugh Collins, 'Regulating Contracts' in C. Parker, C. Scott, N. Lacey and J. Braithwaite (eds), *Regulating Law* (2004). Teubner also explored the distinctions. See Günter Teubner, 'Substantive and Reflexive Elements in Modern Law' (1983) 17(2) *Law & Society Review* 239–86.

37 For more on autopoietic theory see H. Rottleuthner, 'The Limits of Law: The Myth of a Regulatory Crisis' (1989) 17 *International Journal of the Sociology of Law* 273; Rottleuthner, 'Biological Metaphors in Legal Thought' in Günter Teubner (ed), *Autopoietic Law: A New Approach to Law and Society* (1998).

38 David Hess, 'Social Reporting: A Reflexive Law Approach to Corporate Social Responsiveness' (1999) 25(1) *Journal of Corporate Law* 41, 136–40.

39 Sanford E. Gaines and Cliona Kimber, 'Redirecting Self-Regulation' (2001) 13 *Journal of Environmental Law* 157.

40 David Hess, 'Social Reporting: A Reflexive Law Approach to Corporate Social Responsiveness' (1999) 25(1) *Journal of Corporate Law* 41, 51.

41 Hugh Collins, *Regulating Contracts* (1999) 65.

> [R]esponsive regulation needs to respect the 'paramount values' of democracy, participation, and citizenship . . . [G]overnance arrangements in both economic and social spheres should be decided through careful consideration of the various interests and conditions obtaining in different settings, following full public and local debate about policy goals and the best means to their achievement.[42]

Reflexivity and responsiveness are interdependent. Christine Parker asserts that:

> If law is to be pluralized, it must be both reflexive and responsive – it must be aimed at catalysing processes of social coordination for people to agree on values – but it must also take up these values and apply them to the processes in order to make participation in these processes of deliberation possible in the first place and to critique their outcomes and not just the processes themselves.[43]

Parker explains that, according to these concepts, substantive goals cannot come from inside law itself but only from political discussion outside of law. Nevertheless, law plays a role in ensuring free and fair discussion and in the implementation of the substantive justice goals that result.[44]

There are several advantages attributed to reflexive and responsive self-regulation. Many governments, including the United Kingdom, Canada and Australia, have embraced these concepts, attracted to their potential to

- tap into the expertise and technical knowledge of the regulated activity;
- directly involve the parties who have better knowledge about technical problems in regulating a particular market;
- better integrate institutional knowledge about the need for action, about the relative merits of alternative types of action, and a surer sense of what standards are practical;[45]

---

[42] Peter Vincent-Jones, 'Contractual Governance: Institutional and Organisational Analysis' (2000) 20 *Oxford Journal Legal Studies* 317, 351.

[43] Christine Parker, 'The Pluralization of Regulation' (2008) 9(2) *Theoretical Inquiries in Law*, 369.

[44] Christine Parker, 'The Pluralization of Regulation' (2008) 9(2) *Theoretical Inquiries in Law*, 369.

[45] Governments can hire the technical expertise needed to draft regulations, but this method is slower in perceiving the need for action than where parties are directly involved in the relevant market action. John Wallace, Denise Ironfield and Jennifer Orr, 'Analysis of Market Circumstances where Industry Self-Regulation is Likely to be Most and Least Effective' (2000) Tasman Asia Pacific Pty Ltd. <http://www.treasury.gov.au/contentitem.asp?NavId=&ContentID=1128> at 15 December 2009. See also Peter Vincent-Jones, 'Contractual Governance: Institutional and Organisational Analysis' (2000) 20 *Oxford Journal Legal Studies* 317, 351.

- more accurately target problems of the industry in a way that is neither over- nor under-broad;
- harness market forces to deliver greater benefits where business is prepared to promise more than the law requires;
- can encourage innovation;
- improve consumer choice;
- quickly develop and adapt to changing conditions;
- ensure that various interests and externalities are taken into account;[46]
- allow for gradual adjustments;[47]
- reduce costs of more 'heavy-handed' intervention due to reduction of formalized processes and rules, information search costs, monitoring and enforcement costs, and costs to practitioners in dealing with regulators;[48] and
- protect and give new means of expression to values such as individuality and autonomy.[49]

A number of commentators agree that self-regulation, where the regulator 'agrees to stay out of the detail' and the regulatee 'agrees to go beyond the mere letter of the law', can enhance the effectiveness of statutory regulation.[50] Self-regulation is thought to offer flexibility, expert design and sensitive enforcement, where statutory regulation can be bureaucratic, inexpertly designed, and rigidly enforced.[51] Julia Black credits self-regulation with the potential to take the issue of compliance into the boardroom, helping executives 'see the moral wood from the technical trees'.[52] Parker suggests that self-regulation has the potential to 'heal the rift between individual ethics, social values and the culture of business.'[53]

---

[46] David Hess, 'Social Reporting: A Reflexive Law Approach to Corporate Social Responsiveness' (1999) 25(1) *Journal of Corporate Law* 41, 51.

[47] David Hess, 'Social Reporting: A Reflexive Law Approach to Corporate Social Responsiveness' (1999) 25(1) *Journal of Corporate Law* 41, 136.

[48] Anthony I. Ogus, *Regulation: Legal Form and Economic Theory* (1994) 107.

[49] They may not appear in a familiar form and instead can be expected to take the form dictated by the interests of the stakeholders involved in the process of regulation. See, eg, Sanford E. Gaines and Cliona Kimber, 'Redirecting Self-Regulation' (2001) 13 *Journal of Environmental Law* 157; European Consumer Law Group, 'Soft Law and the Consumer Interest' (March 2001) <http://ec.europa.eu/consumers/policy/eclg/rep03_en.pdf> at 14 December 2009.

[50] Sanford E. Gaines and Cliona Kimber, 'Redirecting Self-Regulation' (2001) 13 *Journal of Environmental Law* 157–84.

[51] Julia Black, *Rules and Regulators* (1997) 79.

[52] Julia Black, *Rules and Regulators* (1997) 79, 219.

[53] Christine Parker, 'The Pluralization of Regulation' (2008) 9(2) *Theoretical Inquiries in Law*, 369.

Ogus argues for a wider perspective on self-regulatory alternatives in order to fully tap their potential.[54]

Self-regulation is an important phenomenon, with the potential to deliver effective measures at reduced costs, but one that also risks becoming ineffective if it is not monitored and managed. Self-regulation is an integral part of an expanded perspective on governance and tools of regulation, which makes the process more complicated, but also increases the potential for creative solutions to effectively serve regulatory purposes. This expanded perspective on tools, layers, strategies is also an expanded perspective on process and participation.

## LAYERS OF GOVERNANCE

Theoretical approaches to regulation have evolved from interest-based to process-based to systems-based approaches. This evolution has encompassed a wide range of organizational structures and inputs. It has expanded the range of potential actors in regulatory processes beyond regulatory activity as the province of watchdog government agencies to today's preference for self-regulatory strategies and tools.[55] It has also expanded conceptions of the range of tools that can be employed at regulatory 'layers', both public and private in a 'multi-layered' system of governance.[56] 'Layers of governance' is a term commonly used in reference to the Internet and information systems technology.[57] Hugh Collins refers to a 'multi-layered system of governance' of contractual relationships that involves less reliance on the judicial system and legislation and greater emphasis on markets and contracts.[58]

More diverse actors are included in the regulatory process, as well as a

---

54 Anthony I. Ogus, *Regulation: Legal Form and Economic Theory* (1994).

55 Stewart Macaulay, 'The Real and the Paper Deal: Empirical Pictures of Relationships, Complexity and the Urge for Transparent Simple Rules' (2003) 66(1) *Modern Law Review* 44–79. The work of S. Macaulay and I. Macneil among others underpins Collins' conception of the contractual framework, the relationship, and the deal.

56 Hugh Collins, *Regulating Contracts* (1999).

57 There are four 'layers' to the internet: the physical network layer; the logical layer; the application layer; and the content layer. See, eg, UNCTAD, '"Layers principle" should be respected in internet governance, report recommends' (Press Release, 16 November 2006) <http://www.unctad.org/Templates/Webflyer.asp?docID=7680&intItemID=1528&lang=1> at 15 December 2009.

58 Hugh Collins, 'Regulating Contract Law' in Christine Parker (ed) et al., *Regulating Law* (2004) 29.

greater range of layers, strategies and mechanisms as part of the regulatory mix. Here too, there is a departure from traditional views of regulation, in particular the distinctions between private and public regulation.[59]

The first layer of governance consists of private, non-legal mechanisms of regulation through market interaction. The second layer consists of private, non-legal and legal mechanisms of regulation through contract. 'Private regulation' refers to parties' regulation of their own activities through interactions in the market and through the use of private contractual agreements. The third layer is a public or quasi-public layer, court interpretation of contract, and the fourth layer is also public, regulation by statute.

Within each regulatory layer, both private and public, there is a range of instruments, processes and strategies. Each of these layers functions interdependently with the others. As the law is said to be a seamless web, regulation is a web of instruments and interactions.

Self-regulatory mechanisms are not only private but also can be used in public forms of regulation. Disclosure and mediation, for example, are self-regulatory tools which the parties themselves are responsible for implementing, but their implementation is within the rubric of public governance. The use of self-regulation in conjunction with public regulation is sometimes referred to as 'co-regulation'.[60]

Private law does not take the place of public regulation, but its role takes on new significance. Because it vests control over a commercial relationship in those best equipped to interpret it, the parties themselves, private regulation is more contextualized, sophisticated and efficient and so should be preferred to public, substantive, command-and-control regulation.[61] Collins' preference for private layers of regulation is supported by the work of Braithwaite and others; self-regulatory mechanisms populate the base of Braithwaite's 'enforcement pyramid'.[62] This preference for private regulation is, however, balanced by acknowledgement that it must work in concert with public regulation.[63] The following sections explain in more detail the contribution each layer makes in the governance of commercial arrangements.

---

59 Hugh Collins, *Regulating Contracts* (1999) 358.

60 Julia Black, *Rules and Regulators* (1997) 50.

61 Hugh Collins, *Regulating Contracts* (1999).

62 John Braithwaite, 'Responsive Regulation for Australia', in Peter Grabosky and John Braithwaite (eds), *Business Regulation and Australia's Future* (1993).

63 Hugh Collins, 'Regulating Contract Law' in Christine Parker (ed) et al., *Regulating Law* (2004).

## The First 'Layer': Market Regulation

'The market' as a layer of regulation includes a variety of mechanisms, sometimes referred to as non-legal sanctions.[64] Non-legal sanctions are often relied upon:

- in the case of flexible or vague commitments, where it makes sense for the participants in a market to self-regulate rather than for courts or regulators that are not experts to intervene;
- where the stakes are low relative to litigation costs;
- where mechanisms for enforcing a bond are already in place to serve some other social or economic function;
- where transactors closely monitor each other, so that information and competition contribute significantly to the effectiveness of self-regulation; or
- in a market that involves highly sophisticated transactors, whose knowledge and information allow them to effectively play a significant role in the regulation of market behaviour.[65]

In all these instances it may be more appropriate for contractual behaviour to depend on reputation, ethnic and family connections, and other elements of non-legal regulation and not on detailed and carefully written contracts enforced by disinterested courts.[66]

Transaction-specific investment is a non-legal means to control a relationship; it binds the party making the investment and gives greater leverage to the contracting party who has not made such investment. Another method is the manipulation of a relationship-specific advantage, such as the posting of a 'hostage', that is an asset a party exposes to the control of the other party.[67] The 'repeat deal' is another market mechanism, but one that is less effective in interactions such as franchise contracts where

---

[64] David Charny, 'Nonlegal Sanctions in Commercial Relationships' (1990) 104 *Harvard Law Review* 375, 392.

[65] For a detailed discussion of non-legal sanctions, see David Charny, 'Nonlegal Sanctions in Commercial Relationships' (1990) 104 *Harvard Law Review* 375, 425.

[66] Eric Posner cited in Paul Steinberg and Gerald Lescatre, 'Beguiling Heresy: Regulating the Franchise Relationship' (2004) 109 *Penn State Law Review* 105, 132–3.

[67] Oliver E. Williamson, 'Credible Commitments: Using Hostages to Support Exchange' (1983) 73(4) *The American Economic Review* 519–40.

parties are in long-term relationships, and so there the need for a repeat deal is less likely.

Market regulation also has collective dimensions. One is competition, which may take the form of competition for favourable contract terms and/or competition for fair complaint mechanisms. Another is reputation. Reputation is particularly effective when information is available in the market and participants have the ability to utilize it. There are often conditions that must be considered in determining which of these can be used to what effect. The 'repeat deal' is another market mechanism of self-regulation. The 'repeat deal' is not as effective where parties are in long-term relationships, as the likelihood of a repeat deal is lower. Reputation is particularly effective when information is available in the market and participants have the ability to utilize it. Interpretive communities are another collective measure; they can provide a shared understanding of rules and context so that less precision and specificity is required in regulatory intervention.[68] Corporate social reporting is '[a] means of assessing the social impact and ethical behaviour of an organization in relation to its aims and those of its stakeholders'[69] and it assists responsiveness to social goals.[70] Finally, codes of ethics and practice may provide a collective means of governance that functions largely at the market layer.

Increased emphasis on market regulation offers several practical advantages. As a form of self-regulation it can reduce the need for direct legislated intervention. Firms seeking competitive advantage through innovation and development of new products and services are considered to have the strongest incentives to give customers what they want in terms of price and quality. Of all the mechanisms of regulating contractual relationships, it is in theory the market that best ensures participation of all stakeholders. Because it represents the highest potential for stakeholders' participation consistent with current conceptions of best practice in regulatory process, market regulation is the starting point in evaluating appropriate regulatory mechanisms. As a starting point, it is hard to overstate its importance, 'Markets, both domestic and international, are greater potential

---

68 Julia Black, Rules and Regulators (1997) 31.

69 David Hess, 'Social Reporting: A Reflexive Law Approach to Corporate Social Responsiveness' (1999) 25 *The Journal of Corporation Law*, University of Iowa, 41–3.

70 David Hess, 'Social Reporting: A Reflexive Law Approach to Corporate Social Responsiveness' (1999) 25 *The Journal of Corporation Law*, University of Iowa, 41–3.

instruments of control than governments and investors, and financiers in particular, and may have a profound influence.'[71]

Nevertheless, despite the advantages and the potency of regulation by means of market mechanisms, market inefficiencies due to information asymmetry, externalities, and imperfect competition occur in the franchise sector as they do in most commercial contexts.[72] Market relationships do not always represent a balance of interests of all stakeholders. Inefficiencies at this layer of governance may necessitate the use of other forms of regulatory intervention.

### Regulating the Franchise Sector at the First 'Layer' of Governance

Market regulation of franchising includes mechanisms such as the use of hostages, sunk investments, control over information, and the 'repeat deal'. The first three are used extensively, mostly by franchisors in controlling the interaction with franchisees. The 'repeat deal' is of limited utility to either party because of the long-term nature of franchise contracting.

Reputation is potentially very effective in contracting that has consumer-like dimensions such as franchising. The effectiveness of reputation depends on availability of information in the market, and participants' ability to utilize it. Private, independent initiatives, such as *bluemaumau.org* in the US, are useful for this purpose.[73] There are also collective initiatives through trade associations' programs. Many franchise trade associations have recognition and awards programs. The International Franchise Association (the IFA) has a recognition/awards program and the Franchise Council of Australia (the FCA) also has an awards program for franchisors, although in the latter case recognition is based primarily on financial success.

Codes of Ethics and Practice are very important in franchising. Many franchise organizations use codes of ethics or practice, including the British Franchise Association, the Italian Franchise Association, the International Franchise Association (US), the Franchise Association of South Africa, as well as organizations in Canada, New Zealand, the Philippines, Singapore

---

[71] Neil Gunningham, Peter Grabosky and Darren Sinclair, *Smart Regulation: Designing Environmental Policy* (1998) 22.

[72] John Wallace, Denise Ironfield and Jennifer Orr, 'Analysis of Market Circumstances where Industry Self-Regulation is Likely to be Most and Least Effective' (2000) Tasman Asia Pacific Pty Ltd. <http://www.treasury.gov.au/contentitem.asp?NavId=&ContentID=1128> at 15 December 2009.

[73] See http://www.bluemaumau.org and http://www.tenthousandfeet.com.au at 16 December 2009.

and Hong Kong. At a regional level, the European Franchise Federation also has a Code of Ethics.

### The Second 'Layer': Contract as Regulation

As part of the multi-layered system of governance, contract is another means of self-regulation. The contract is used by the parties to procedurally regulate drafting and negotiation. Once the contract is signed, the standards set by the parties constitute a form of self-regulation governing performance.[74]

Contract is a layer of self-regulation designed, drafted and agreed to by the parties. 'Many contracts are therefore analogous to regulation themselves, for they purport to establish binding standards for future conduct . . . The private law of contract . . . delegates to the parties a substantial power to fix the rules'.[75] Contract is also integrally related to market and non-legal methods of regulation, so there is some overlap in market and contract as means of self-regulation.

Contract regulates substantively not only by its terms but also through the contract attributes, such as the standard form and relational attributes. The standard form, for example, is cost-effective and efficient for mass transactions, but has potential to impose terms on the non-drafting side that may erode commitment to the deal and the relation. The relational quality of the contract is also used to contain transaction costs, but unspecified terms may require court interpretation, and so invoke another layer of regulation.

Parties govern their relationship through the negotiation of express contract terms, including hostages and restraint of trade clauses, and terms that specify dispute resolution procedures. Here, effectiveness depends on the bargaining power of the parties and their ability to place a value on terms.[76] Contractual terms are typically used by individual parties, but are amenable to collective regulatory initiatives.

Standards can be agreed upon expressly or by terms implied by course of dealing. (This is distinct from contract terms implied, for example, by

---

[74] Hugh Collins, *Regulating Contracts* (1999) 63.

[75] Hugh Collins, 'Regulating Contract Law' in Christine Parker (ed) et al., *Regulating Law* (2004) xxvi.

[76] See, eg, Oliver E. Williamson, 'The Economic Institutions of Capitalism' (1986) 17(2) *RAND Journal of Economics* 279; Oliver E. Williamson, 'Credible Commitments: Using Hostages to Support Exchange' (1983) 73(4) *The American Economic Review* 519–40; Antony W. Dnes, 'Franchise Contracts', The Nottingham Trent University <http://encyclo.findlaw.com/5890book.pdf> at 15 December 2009.

consumer-protection legislation such as sale of goods legislation.) The parties may not specify some terms per se, but in the process of contracting they are taken to be aware of mandatory and default rules imposed on them by courts and legislatures.[77] Default rules analysis is an important area of contract law that examines how courts fill the gaps in contracts when terms are not specified by the parties.[78]

Specificity of contract terms establishes certainty, but sacrifices flexibility. On the other hand, the use of vague terms such as 'reasonableness' may be combined with a permissive character to increase discretion in application and interpretation. Vagueness is consistent with compliance strategies, and relationships where trust is important. The use of discretion in contracts risks opportunism and hold-up, but is often necessary due to future uncertainty. Trade-offs for granting discretion may include lower costs and price breaks, or they may be less tangible.

Not only in entering the contract, then, but also in performing the terms of an agreement the parties 'control' their own interaction. The standards in the contract comprise a form of self-regulation that develops throughout the performance of the contract.

Like every other layer of regulation, contract as governance has drawbacks as well as strengths. In franchising the contract is drafted and controlled by the franchisor. As a regulatory tool it serves the interests of the franchisor, which are often not aligned with the interests of franchisees (or those of other stakeholders). A franchise contract therefore may not represent the interests of all stakeholders.[79] Where private mechanisms lead to inefficiencies or undesirable social consequences, public regulation through court interpretation or legislation may be called for.

## Regulating the Franchise Sector at the second 'Layer'of Governance

While 'the law of contract is a fundamental mechanism of social order', 'the evidence from empirical studies of contractual behaviour indicates

---

[77] Hugh Collins, *Regulating Contracts* (1999) 63.

[78] See, eg, Jay M. Feinman, 'Relational Contract and Default Rules' (1993) 3 *Southern California Interdisciplinary Law Journal* 43; Omri Ben Shahar, 'Agreeing to Disagree: Filling Gaps in Deliberately Incomplete Contracts' (John M. Olin Center for Law and Economics Working Paper No 2, University of Michigan, 2004); George Dent, 'Lawyers and Trust in Business Alliances' (2002) 58 *The Business Lawyer* 45.

[79] Regarding stakeholder analysis see S. Watson and G. Gunasekara, 'Regulating Business Format Franchising: Familiar Solutions for Novel Problems' (2006) 12 *NZBLQ* 174.

the marginal and sometimes socially disintegrative effects of the law of contract'.[80] This debate has been fuelled by research indicating that the paper document is not of primary importance to business people.[81] Macaulay claims that business people fail to plan and draft carefully, to consult legal advisors, to consider their rights, and to utilize the courts with the result that the importance of contract in business relationships is overstated.[82]

In a sense contract is indeed of small significance in franchising. It is only one of many documents that support the relationship. It is not referred to as much as the operations manual, or even the lease or finance agreements. Many franchisors say that the contract only comes out of the drawer in the case of a dispute, a view that supports the idea that more intimately-bound firms behave in a less strictly contractual way.[83] Franchise systems, because of the closeness of the association between franchisor and franchisee, might therefore be expected to put less emphasis on the agreement as the long-term relationship means parties are likely to rely on other means to govern the relationship.

Nevertheless, franchisors continue to draft contracts, franchisees continue to agree to them, legislators continue to address them, and courts continue to interpret them. The role of contract in franchising has been explored in management and economics, for example in how contract is used to govern the relationship as it establishes an organizational structure that reduces transaction costs.[84] Contract provides:

---

80 Hugh Collins, Regulating Contracts (1999).

81 See, eg, Stewart Macaulay, 'The Real and the Paper Deal: Empirical Pictures of Relationships, Complexity and the Urge for Transparent Simple Rules' in David Campbell, Hugh Collins and John Wightman (eds), *Implicit Dimensions of Contract: Discrete, Relational and Network Contracts* (2003); Ian R. Macneil, 'Contracts: Adjustment of Long-Term Economic Relations under the Classical, Neo-classical, and Relational Contract Law' (1978) 72 (6) *Northwestern University Law Review* 854.

82 'Contract law in action is a defective product, promising far more than it can deliver.' Macaulay cited in Christian Joerges (ed) *Franchising and the Law: Theoretical and Comparative Approaches in Europe and the United States* (1991) 189.

83 George Dent, 'Lawyers and Trust in Business Alliances' (2002) 58 *Business Lawyer* 45, n 120.

84 See, generally, Deepak Agrawal and Rajiv Lal, 'Contractual Arrangements in Franchising: An Empirical Investigation' (1995) 32(2) *Journal of Marketing Research* 213; James A. Brickley, 'Incentive Conflicts and Contractual Restraints: Evidence from Franchising' (1999) 42 *Journal of Law and Economics* 745; Francine Lafontaine and Kathryn L. Shaw, 'The Dynamics of Franchise Contracting: Evidence from Panel Data' (1999) 107 *Journal of Political Economy* 1041;

- an early point of contact between the parties;
- the subject of negotiation between the parties about the nature of their ongoing relationship;
- a form of governance of the franchise organization, and the parameters for performance during the relationship as an alternative to planning, promise and competition;[85]
- a matrix of overlapping roles of franchisor and franchisee, serving both as a means for parties to organize themselves and as a guide to public entities (courts and regulators) on how to interpret the relationship;
- mechanisms for the franchisor to:
    - monitor a franchisee,
    - provide performance incentives,
    - allocate risk,
    - manage externalities, information asymmetry, and
    - facilitate information search, entrepreneurship and interdependence;
- a sales tool as it is a piece of the package for which the franchisee is paying and so can signal to the buyer that the seller's entire package is an attractive one;[86]
- methods of conflict management and resolution, with the potential to promote the long-term strength of the relationship (even if the contract only comes out of the drawer in case of a dispute, this role is an important one because disputes are critical to the relationship, and can be handled in a variety of ways; the contract is central to processes of negotiation, mediation, and litigation, and it helps the parties to predict outcomes of dispute settlement processes);

---

Francine Lafontaine and Margaret E. Slade, 'Incentive Contracting and the Franchise Decision' , Ch 5 in Kalyan Chatterjee and William F. Samuelson (eds), *Game Theory and Business Applications* (2001); G. Frank Mathewson and Ralph A.Winter, 'Territorial Restrictions in Franchise Contracts' (1994) 32(2) *Economic Inquiry* 181; Janet E.L. Bercovitz, 'An Analysis of the Contract Provisions in Business Format Franchise Agreements' (2000) International Society for New Institutional Economics <http://www.isnie.org/ISNIE00/Papers/Bercovitz.pdf> at 15 December 2009; S. Watson and G. Gunasekara, 'Regulating Business Format Franchising: Familiar Solutions for Novel Problems' (2006) 12 *NZBLQ* 174.

[85] See Oliver Williamson, 'Transaction-Cost Economics: The Governance of Contractual Relations' (1979) 22(2) *Journal of Law and Economics* 233.

[86] Jim Penman writes that it should be 'an offer too good to refuse'. Jim Penman, *What Will They Franchise Next?: The Story of Jim's Group* (2003).

- an outline of the parties' rights and obligations at the end of the relationship by way of transfer or termination; and
- a guide to third parties such as:
    - suppliers and investors;
    - lawyers, lenders, prospective business partners and other third parties with an interest in the relationship who, though not a party to it, will also look to the contract for clarification of what is expected; and
    - courts and regulators, for whom contract is not only an important layer of private regulation but also an instrument of public regulation in judicial interpretation of the relationship and in direct intervention, especially disclosure.

The contract is important in franchising. The use of contract as a means of private, self-regulation raises a number of issues involving:

- the effects of the standard form of contract;
- the relational nature of the contract;
- the use of particular terms; and
- whether complementary regulatory measures from public 'layers of governance' are needed to ensure that the contract serves stakeholders efficiently and equitably by influencing or addressing issues such as:
    - Drafting of contract terms (currently used on an individual basis, but amenable to collective use);
    - Negotiation of terms, including dispute resolution procedures (here, effectiveness depends on the bargaining positions of the parties, and their ability to place a value on different contract terms. Standard-form contracting as a cost-effective and efficient means of engaging in multiple transactions, but with a potential to impose terms on the non-drafting side that may erode commitment to the deal and the relation);
    - Contract duration, for example a long or short term (shorter contract duration may benefit franchisors and some jurisdictions impose minimum contract durations);
    - Relational contracting, which is a means to reduce transaction costs of engaging in long-term contracts but requires flexibility and trust;
    - Specificity of contract, which is used in contracts to establish certainty but also sacrifices flexibility for the party that commits to specific terms;

- Use of discretion risks opportunism and hold-up, but this is often necessary due to future uncertainty in long-term contracts; and
- The use of vague terms (for example 'reasonableness' may be combined with a permissive character to increase discretion in application and interpretation; trade-offs could include lower costs or price breaks, but in franchising these tend to be less tangible because a franchisee gets the franchisor's commitment to the brand).

Chapter 3 is devoted to an analysis of the nature of franchise contracts, not only the type of contract that it is, but also its terms. That analysis suggests that public interpretation and intervention may be needed to play a role in ensuring that the contract provides two sorts of balance, a balance of values of freedom of contract against public policy values in favour of good faith and fair dealing; and a balance of specificity of terms against flexibility and discretion to accommodate the uncertainty of the long term.

**The Third 'Layer': Court Interpretation**

Thus the judiciary is another layer of regulation; its primary role lies in interpretation and enforcement of contracts and statutes. As the judiciary supports both the private self-regulation of the contract as well as legislated rules, and:

> the court system, generally regarded as having nothing to do with regulatory activity, can be a regulator as well as enforcing laws compelling market activity.[87]

Court interpretation of contract involves express and implied terms, using both literal and contextual interpretation. Courts may employ particular methods for the interpretation of certain species of contract and courts may also regulate through default rules of contract. Implied terms can include good faith, a duty of care and fiduciary duties. Courts may engage in evaluations of fairness procedurally, of the contracting process, formal requirements and criteria for validity; and substantively, of the intentions of the parties, taking into account the explicit terms of the contract as well as the context in which the contract was made and the implicit understandings of the parties. This role of the judiciary, however, is not at all clear. The

---

[87] Warren Pengilley, 'Competition regulation in Australia: A Discussion of a Spider Web and its Weaving' (2001) 8 *Competition and Consumer Law Journal* 51.

extensive debate over default rules analysis underscores the uncertainty over the circumstances under which parties' intentions should be considered insufficiently clear or not to be enforced.[88]

When courts do interpret contracts based upon extrinsic values, there is no definitive and immutable balance of collective interests and no procedure to establish which competing values and interests should guide the courts' interpretations and interventions. The inevitable vagueness of principles of unfairness, unreasonableness, good faith and unconscionable conduct results in uncertainty for contracting parties' planning purposes.[89] They are all subject to wide variation in judicial application and the courts exhibit varying degrees of restraint in interpretation. Günter Teubner observes, 'Law lost its formalism as the politicization of contract law has increased since the 1960s'[90] and that judges rewrite contracts in translating the policy goals of legislation into contracts. Promissory estoppel and restitution further compound problems of interpretation.[91] In interpreting contract law, the courts may be forced to rely upon the same filtering devices as tort law, such as proximity, duty, causation and remoteness, but with these devices come the same problems of subjectivity and indeterminacy.[92]

Collins argues that private regulation by the parties is less effective due to lack of particularity in contracts and courts' inconsistent and unpredictable interpretation of fairness, reasonableness, and good faith.[93] His view underscores why courts need access to reliable data to inform their deliberations. The courts' role in regulatory process is one that relies upon and must be informed by the other tools in the multi-layered system.

The role of the courts is essential in the interpretation of franchise contracts, particularly of the franchise contract as a relational contract requiring contextual analysis. The debate over the extent to which literal or contextual interpretation may be appropriate, as well as the debate over default rules is important in franchising. Also relevant are the principle of

---

88 Juliet Kostritsky, 'When Should Contract Law Supply a Liability Rule or Term: Framing a Principle of Unification for Contracts' (2000) 32 *Arizona State Law Journal* 1283.

89 Hugh Collins, *Regulating Contracts* (1999) 232.

90 Günter Teubner, 'Law as An Autopoietic System' (Paper presented at the LSE Complexity Study Group Meeting No 3, London, 18 June 1997).

91 See, eg, David Charny, 'Nonlegal Sanctions in Commercial Relationships' (1990) 104 *Harvard Law Review* 375.

92 See D. Charny, 'Nonlegal Sanctions in Commercial Relationships' (1990) 104 *Harvard Law Review* 375 for discussion of how extra-contractual duties that arise with promissory estoppel, restitution, and tort further compound problems of contractual interpretation.

93 Hugh Collins, *Regulating Contracts* (1999).

good faith as it varies in application among common and civil law jurisdictions, and related concepts such as reasonableness and unconscionable conduct. There is even potential for application of a principle of fiduciary obligation.

## The Fourth 'Layer': Statutory Intervention

Statutory intervention, also known as state, legislative or direct intervention, is regulation in the commonly-used sense of the term – formal, legislated regulation by a governmental organization or agency. The term 'command-and-control' is sometimes used to refer to this type of regulation, though this is increasingly less accurate with the trend toward co-regulatory strategies.[94] Statutory regulation may impose substantive requirements, such as prescriptive and/or performance standards. It may also involve procedural standards such as information disclosure, cooling-off periods, licensing and registration. Procedures may also be prescribed for dispute resolution processes and public education programs.

There are two fundamental purposes for statutory intervention in commercial enterprise, to promote efficient markets to alleviate market failure; and to protect the public welfare (for example, by protecting franchisees as consumers and as small businesspeople, third parties such as end-user consumers, suppliers and creditors). Regulatory measures often serve both purposes, but in commercial contexts the greater weight is often placed on the former. Even in franchising where protection of a franchisee may be acknowledged, the more compelling arguments are those of efficiency.

While markets, through competition, are generally considered to be the most efficient means of allocating society's resources, competition does not lead to efficient and equitable outcomes when its operation is hindered by information asymmetry, externalities, moral hazard or transaction cost inefficiencies.[95] Statutory intervention in commercial activity 'corrects' these market imperfections in the interests of economic efficiency.[96]

While statutory intervention addresses a variety of forms of market

---

94 Neil Gunningham, Peter Grabosky and Darren Sinclair, *Smart Regulation: Designing Environmental Policy* (1998) 39. Discussion of the pros and cons of direct regulation and innovations at 40–50.

95 John Wallace, Denise Ironfield and Jennifer Orr, 'Analysis of Market Circumstances where Industry Self-Regulation is Likely to be Most and Least Effective' (2000) Tasman Asia Pacific Pty Ltd. <http://www.treasury.gov.au/contentitem.asp?NavId=&ContentID=1128> at 15 December 2009.

96 Robert Baldwin and Martin Cave, *Understanding Regulation: Theory, Strategy and Practice* (1999) 17.

failure in the construction of markets, the same interventions can also influence the outcomes of market interactions. Regulation may, for example,

- ensure provision of socially desirable products and services where free market competition fails to provide continuity and availability of a good or service;
- prevent anti-competitive and predatory pricing practices in order to promote efficient market function;[97]
- allocate scarce goods in the public interest; and
- ensure the availability of a public good.[98]

There are, of course, drawbacks to direct intervention. Statutory regulation can be bureaucratic, inexpertly designed and rigidly enforced.[99] It may fail to elicit socially responsible behaviour from corporations because society has become too complex for effective control by such intervention. This has been labelled the 'juridification' problem, in which direct regulation becomes too complex and distanced from its subjects, overly burdensome, over-broad or under-inclusive.[100]

This, among other concerns, may lead to the criticism that there is 'too much regulatory law'.[101] Related to the juridification problem are issues concerning implementation, such as the concern that the legislature delegates a large degree of discretion to regulatory agencies. This compounds the problem of 'normative legitimacy', that lawmaking procedures have become distanced from the democratic procedures that establish legitimacy.[102] Finally, substantive regulation can encroach on individuality and autonomy, key values formerly protected by formal rules.[103] As discussed earlier, the search for solutions to the problems associated with substantive intervention leads back to self-regulation and private measures.

---

97 Regulated through the Trade Practices Act 1974 (Cth), not the Code.

98 Categories adopted from Robert Baldwin and Martin Cave, *Understanding Regulation: Theory, Strategy and Practice* (1999) 17.

99 Julia Black, *Rules and Regulators* (1997) 79.

100 <www.leblogpolitique.be/wp-content/uploads/wp05_14.pdf> at 23 December 2009.

101 David Hess, 'Social Reporting: A Reflexive Law Approach to Corporate Social Responsiveness' (1999) 25(1) *Journal of Corporate Law* 41, 50 and 139.

102 David Hess, 'Social Reporting: A Reflexive Law Approach to Corporate Social Responsiveness' (1999) 25(1) *Journal of Corporate Law* 41, 50 and 139.

103 Sanford E. Gaines and Cliona Kimber, 'Redirecting Self-Regulation' (2001) 13 *Journal of Environmental Law* 157.

### Regulating the Franchise Sector at the Fourth 'Layer' of Governance

Among the regulatory tools that are used by governments in legislation aimed to influence the franchise relationship, the principal means used is the imposition of standards. In the context of 'command-and-control' regulation, standards can take several forms. Performance standards define responsibility in terms of problem to be solved or goal to be achieved. These standards tend to be outcome-focused; they work well when there is a certain target to be met that is easy to monitor and measure. Because of the need for flexibility and adaptability to such a wide range of commercial undertakings, performance standards are not frequently used in franchise-specific legislation. Where monitoring and measurement are more difficult, as is the case with franchising, then procedural standards, such as requirements of procedures for entry into contracts, resolution of disputes or termination of contracts, are often used toward the same result. Indeed procedural standards are by far the most commonly used measure in the regulation of the franchising sector. Prescriptive standards dictate requirements in form and/or substance. They are considered to be less well adapted to self-regulation as they are imposed, and monitored and measured, externally by the regulator. They include warranties, good faith requirements, prescribed contents of the agreement, prohibition on vertical restraints between franchisor and franchisee, and minimum contract duration.

Chapter 5 provides a full survey of the legislation regulating the franchise sector, while Chapters 6, 7 and 8 consist of analysis of the use of the regulatory tools. Much more will be said about the choice of regulatory tools in these chapters. The remainder of this chapter will focus upon directions toward best practice in regulatory process in order that the best choices can be made from the available range of regulatory tools.

## TOWARDS A MODEL OF BEST-PRACTICE FOR REGULATORY PROCESS

Determining best practice in regulatory process for any particular sector or industry is a complicated task, and there is, as yet, no formulation of best practice for regulation of the franchise sector. General principles of best practice in commercial regulation provide some guidance. Such principles acknowledge that regulation should ideally be tailored to the needs of the activity being regulated. Theories on how to achieve this continue to evolve. With the rapid developments in concepts of best practice in regulation, there is a wide range of approaches to tailoring best practice for regulation of specific types of activities or sectors, such as workplace health and safety, utilities, environmental regulation and regulation of professional services. There is a diversity of formulations of best practice in regulating. Respected authorities offer varying conceptions of how to design regulatory process. Sorting through the many formulations of best practice in regulatory process can be confusing and lends itself to picking and choosing from among them in order to arrive at the comforting conclusion that whatever the nature of a particular regulatory program may be, it complies with some formulation of best practice.

Despite the diversity in regulatory practice, some common themes do recur across many of the various formulations of best practice. A comparison of the principles that should guide regulatory process as put forward by Ogus in 1994, Gunningham, Grabosky and Sinclair in 1998 and the OECD Guiding Principles for Regulatory Quality and Performance in 2005, suggests some of these and is presented below in Table 1.1.

Some shared themes in these formulations are simplicity, identifying the problems, orientation to ends and goals, choosing the right tools, inclusive and self-regulatory process, less intervention, more responsiveness and fuller participation. Interestingly, these themes are echoed in some other current theories of regulatory process.[104]

## Core Elements of Regulatory Process

Julia Black describes the new 'normative propositions' of regulatory strategies as hybrid, combining governmental and non-governmental actors; multi-faceted, using a number of different strategies simultaneously or sequentially; and indirect.[105]

The impetus for these strategies derives from systems theories, involving a process of coordinating and balancing interactions between actors and systems using a variety of techniques.[106] Emerging empirical research on

---

104 See, for example, Malcolm K. Sparrow, 'PLENARY 4: Effective Regulation' (Paper presented at the 25th International Organisation of Securities Commissions (IOSCO) Annual Conference, Sydney, 14–19 May 2000) <http://www.asic.gov.au/asic/pdflib.nsf/LookupByFileName/plen_4_sparrow.pdf/$file/plen_4_sparrow.pdf> at 15 December 2009.

105 Julia Black, 'Decentring Regulation: Understanding the Role of Regulation and Self-regulation in a "Post-Regulatory" World' (2001) 54 *Current Legal Problems* 103, 111.

106 Labelled by some as the strategies of the 'new regulatory state', these include proceduralization, collibration, feedback loops, and 'above all countering variety with variety.' See Julia Black, 'Decentring Regulation: Understanding the Role of Regulation and Self-regulation in a "Post-Regulatory" World' (2001) 54 *Current Legal Problems* 103, 111.

*Table 1.1 Selected principles of regulatory process*

| Professor Ogus' recommendations for regulatory process[a] | OECD principles for best practice in regulation[b] | Gunningham, Grabosky and Sinclair recommendations for regulatory process[c] |
|---|---|---|
| Identify the issue – keep regulation in proportion to the problem | Serve clearly identified policy goals, and be effective in achieving those goals | Use a complementary instrument mix, as varied methods can reinforce and support each other |
| Keep it simple – go for goal-based regulation | Have a sound legal and empirical basis | Prefer less intervention, because direct intervention is not as efficient, effective or as politically acceptable as self-regulation[d] |
| Provide flexibility for the future – set the objective rather than the detailed way of making sure the regulation is kept to | Produce benefits that justify costs, considering the distribution of effects across society and taking economic, environmental and social effects into account | Allow for escalating regulatory response up an instrument pyramid that should include government, business and third parties (and that builds in regulatory responsiveness and triggers) |
| Keep it short | Minimize costs and market distortions | Use third parties as surrogate regulator |
| Try to anticipate the effects of regulation on competition or trade | Promote innovation through market incentives and goal-based approaches | Encourage business to move beyond compliance[e] Often, this is accomplished through increased self-regulatory measures |
| Minimize costs of compliance | Be clear, simple, and practical for users | |
| Integrate with previous regulations | Be consistent with other regulations and policies | |
| Make sure it can be effectively managed and enforced | Be compatible as far as possible with competition, trade investment-facilitating principles at domestic and international levels[f] | |
| Make sure it will work and that you will know if it does not | | |
| Allow enough time[g] | | |

*Table 1.1* (continued)

---

*Notes:*

[a] Anthony I. Ogus, *Regulation: Legal Form and Economic Theory* (1994) 339.

[b] OECD Guiding Principles for Regulatory Quality and Performance (2005) Organisation for Economic Co-Operation and Development <http://www.oecd.org/dataoecd/24/6/34976533.pdf > at 15 December 2009.

[c] Neil Gunningham, Peter Grabosky and Darren Sinclair, *Smart Regulation: Designing Environmental Policy* (1998).

[d] Neil Gunningham, Peter Grabosky and Darren Sinclair, *Smart Regulation: Designing Environmental Policy* (1998) 391.

[e] Neil Gunningham, Peter Grabosky and Darren Sinclair, *Smart Regulation: Designing Environmental Policy* (1998), 387–422.

[f] Guiding Principles for Regulatory Quality and Performance (2005) Organisation for Economic Co-Operation and Development <http://www.oecd.org/dataoecd/24/6/34976533.pdf > at 15 December 2009.

[g] Anthony I. Ogus, *Regulation: Legal Form and Economic Theory* (1994) 339.

regulation offers some fresh perspectives on the variety of means and processes available for any particular regulatory purpose.[107] No one instrument or layer of regulation is always the right one, but greater legitimacy can be achieved if all layers of governance are considered as part of a process of regulation that is participative, democratic and reflexive.

Thus, current theories of regulation have shifted in focus from interests and outcomes to process. Within these democratic, participative processes there are choices to be made among different levels of regulatory action, different instruments, and different strategies within each layer. This implies also a need to consider synergies and contra-indications for the various mechanisms and tools used in regulation.[108] Equipped with a more comprehensive perspective of how each layer of regulation works and how the mechanisms of regulation work within them, it should be easier to identify interactions and synergies. It should also be easier to evaluate the need for adjustment in any particular mechanism in the 'layers of governance'.

While much of what is written about new conceptions of regulation is devoted to the instruments of regulation, these new conceptions of regulatory activity also called for a broader range of actors, a frequent focus on regulatory tools notwithstanding. Braithwaite's 'enforcement pyramid' is populated by tools, but as he himself explains:

---

[107] See, eg, Neil Gunningham, Peter Grabosky and Darren Sinclair, *Smart Regulation: Designing Environmental Policy* (1998); Lisa Bernstein, 'Opting out of the Legal System: Extralegal Contractual Relations in the Diamond Industry' (1992) 21 *Journal of Legal Studies* 115.

[108] Neil Gunningham, Peter Grabosky and Darren Sinclair, *Smart Regulation: Designing Environmental Policy* (1998).

> 'There is no standard or optimal pyramid advanced here as providing a simple model for solving all our regulatory problems. . . . The important conclusion is about the need to move our regulatory institutions away from the simplistic and mechanistic models of economic rationalism, legalism and government command-and-control. This means genuine empowerment of all the stakeholders in a regulatory dialogue where each stakeholder comes to understand the concerns of the other and stands ready to respond positively to them so long as their own concerns are responded to positively by others.'[109]

The regulatory pyramid might better be thought of as a matrix. Regulatory process now encompasses various layers and tools of regulation, but the relationships among them are not linear.[110] Regulation may be voluntary or may involve self-regulation. It may involve direct intervention or co-regulation. The challenge is, through designing and refining a matrix of regulatory tools, to identify the most efficient and effective mix of tools to accommodate the dynamic requirements of any given context, whether that context is environmental regulation, financial services or the franchising sector.[111]

Malcolm Sparrow distils his recommendations for regulatory process into one phrase, 'Pick important problems, and fix them.'[112] Along with this prescription, recurring themes in Sparrow's work are principles of good regulatory process, such as determining the nature and scope of the problem, the consideration of cost-benefit, making the regulation clear in terms of policy and compliance, review, and consultation with parties.

Sparrow claims that regulatory craftsmanship requires the use of many different tools, which should be employed to suit the task, not vice versa:

> [t]he essence of craftsmanship is having them all, knowing how to use them, and being quite judicious when you will use each one.[113]

---

[109] John Braithwaite, 'Responsive Regulation for Australia', in Peter Grabosky and John Braithwaite (eds), *Business Regulation and Australia's Future* (1993).

[110] Neil Gunningham and Darren Sinclair, 'Designing Smart Regulation', Organisation for Economic Co-Operation and Development <http://www.oecd.org/dataoecd/18/39/33947759.pdf> at 15 December 2009.

[111] The work of Hugh Collins; Julia Black; Gunningham and Grabosky; Martin and Cave; and Baldwin, Scott and Hood; among others, call for the expansion, diversification and improved calibration in the use of regulatory tools.

[112] See Malcolm K. Sparrow, 'PLENARY 4: Effective Regulation' (Paper presented at the 25th International Organisation of Securities Commissions (IOSCO) Annual Conference, Sydney, 14–19 May 2000) <http://www.asic.gov.au/asic/pdflib.nsf/LookupByFileName/plen_4_sparrow.pdf/$file/plen_4_sparrow.pdf> at 15 December 2009.

[113] Malcolm K. Sparrow, 'Innovating in a Regulatory Environment' (Speech delivered at the National Environmental Innovations Symposium, Kansas City, 6 December 2000) <http://www.epa.gov/innovation/symposium/docs/sparrow.pdf> at 15 December 2009.

Sparrow also identifies three 'core elements' in reformed regulatory process:

- The first element is a focus on results, which involves rejecting reliance on output measures in favour of 'more meaningful' impact measures.
- The second element is to adopt a problem-solving approach that includes systematic identification of important problems, risk assessment and prioritization. Sparrow also notes that enforcement should not be overlooked or neglected.
- The third element is to invest in collaborative partnerships to form a shared purpose through collaborative agenda setting. Engagement of multiple parties can lead to more effective interventions, and optimal leveraging of scarce public resources.[114]

Sparrow's prescription is supported by the process recommended by Gunningham, Grabosky and Sinclair in *Smart Regulation*, which involves determining objectives, defining the character of the problem and generating the range of available options to address problems and achieve objectives. Like Sparrow, Gunningham, Grabosky and Sinclair call for greater consultation and participation.[115]

This need is especially relevant to the regulation of franchising. Given the lack of reliable information about the sector to inform regulatory policy, legitimacy through expertise by third party regulators is not a solution for the regulation of franchising. There is also a low likelihood of generating the required level of interest and funding and harnessing the required expertise. As it is unrealistic to expect an external regulator to formulate a regulatory program that comprehends the interaction of all layers of regulation, the focus on tools should be balanced by a greater emphasis on stakeholder participation in the legitimate processes of regulating.

Despite its simplicity, Sparrow admits that his prescription is not easy, and has been 'experienced by those who have grappled with it' as different, intellectually and analytically demanding, organizationally awkward and 'unrelentingly difficult'.[116] It usually calls for a change in regulatory style,

---

114 Malcolm K. Sparrow, 'PLENARY 4: Effective Regulation' (Paper presented at the 25th International Organisation of Securities Commissions (IOSCO) Annual Conference, Sydney, 14–19 May 2000) <http://www.asic.gov.au/asic/pdflib.nsf/LookupByFileName/plen_4_sparrow.pdf/$file/plen_4_sparrow.pdf> at 15 December 2009.

115 See Gunningham et al., *Smart Regulation: Designing Environmental Policy* (1998) 380–7.

116 Malcolm K. Sparrow, 'PLENARY 4: Effective Regulation' (Paper presented at the 25th International Organisation of Securities Commissions (IOSCO)

and here, Sparrow's model echoes Julia Black's conclusions. According to Sparrow, the 'old model', characterized by enforcement, was 'reactive, adversarial, incident-driven' and 'hard'. The new, 'soft' model, characterized by a re-orientation toward compliance assistance and customer service, is about prevention, partnerships, and problem-solving.[117]

The substantial challenge for regulatory agencies is 'to construct a framework, so that . . . innovative methods come forward at the right time, in the right place, for the right job'.[118] For the franchising sector the adoption of such a framework is the first step toward creating an effective and robust regulatory process.

## Streamlining Regulation Through Broadened Scope and Improved Effectiveness

Public apathy towards regulation is justified, but an overly cautious approach to regulating may risk exposing economic efficiency and public welfare objectives to greater uncertainty. It may also reduce the potential for regulation to promote competitiveness. Current theories of regulation imply a greater potential for effective regulation according to a broader conception of what regulating is, more diverse actors, and a wider range of regulatory instruments at all the layers upon which they operate.

In the broad sense of the term, it is impossible to eliminate regulation. It is not a question of whether to regulate; the important question is how to regulate. The goal is efficient and effective regulation that is good for business, for the competitiveness of economies and for stakeholders' interests.

The new regulation is systems-based, often self-regulatory and multi-layered. It emphasizes process that collaborates rather than interferes with business, and it encompasses a diverse range of participants and a wide choice of tools to regulate, the capacity of which is greatly increased because regulation can involve virtually any form of governance.

---

Annual Conference, Sydney, 14–19 May 2000) <http://www.asic.gov.au/asic/pdflib.nsf/LookupByFileName/plen_4_sparrow.pdf/$file/plen_4_sparrow.pdf> at 15 December 2009.

117 Malcolm K. Sparrow, 'Innovating in a Regulatory Environment' (Speech delivered at the National Environmental Innovations Symposium, Kansas City, 6 December 2000) <http://www.epa.gov/innovation/symposium/docs/sparrow.pdf> at 15 December 2009.

118 Malcolm K. Sparrow, 'Innovating in a Regulatory Environment' (Speech delivered at the National Environmental Innovations Symposium, Kansas City, 6 December 2000) <http://www.epa.gov/innovation/symposium/docs/sparrow.pdf> at 15 December 2009.

In an era where 'regulatory studies have emerged at the cutting edge of paradigmatic change in the social sciences',[119] there is hope for the reestablishment of public confidence in regulation. The theoretical foundation for evaluating regulation presented in this chapter rejects casting regulatory activity in a limited role as a necessary evil in favour of a more multifaceted and versatile role that expands the meaning of regulation; expands the range of instruments, tools and participants; and is truly worthy of public confidence.

In a 'multi-layered system of governance', the term regulation encompasses not only statute and court interpretation, but also markets and contract. It is regulation in which public and private governance are purposefully employed in concert with the potential for enhanced efficacy:

> The insights of the reflexive capacity of private law combined with the collective policy orientation of public regulation can provide the springboard for more productive regulation.[120]

This book makes no assumptions regarding the suitability of particular regulatory tools because tools should be selected as a result of good regulatory process from the full range of options, methods, strategies, techniques and rules to achieve, for any given sector at any given point in time, the optimal mix.[121] Such an all-encompassing system presents a challenge in implementation. This is why current theories, which continue to be refined with ongoing research, emphasize that in order to improve understanding and enhance legitimacy in regulation, there is no substitute for a process that includes full stakeholder participation in gathering information and measurements; identifying tools; and selecting, implementing, monitoring and revising those tools.

These new theoretical approaches do not suggest a need for more regulatory intervention and greater regulatory burdens. On the contrary, regulatory process that comprehends all these aspects has the potential to respond to the exigencies of the sector more effectively and with greater precision so that less intervention may be required.

---

[119] John Braithwaite, Cary Coglianese and David Levi-Faur, 'Can regulation and governance make a difference?' (2007) 1 (1) *Regulation & Governance* 1–7.

[120] Hugh Collins, *Regulating Contracts* (1999) 361.

[121] For more information on sequencing instrument combinations and multi-instrument mixes see Neil Gunningham, Peter Grabosky and Darren Sinclair, *Smart Regulation: Designing Environmental Policy* (1998) 444–7.

# 2. The market interaction as private regulation

> 'If someone says that he can think or talk about quantum physics without becoming dizzy, that shows only that he has not understood anything whatever about it.'[1]
> 'Behind the appearance of simplicity the franchise arrangement is probably one of the most complex relationships.'[2]

Any discourse on the regulation of the franchise sector requires an understanding of how the parties in the franchisor-franchisee relationship regulate their interaction privately. This chapter discusses market interaction which sets the stage for the contracting process and for subsequent stages of the franchise relationship. It examines the roles and motivations of the franchisor and franchisee in the market interaction by exploring:

- the fundamental nature of the franchise structure and the legal relationship between a franchisor and its franchisees;
- the social and cultural conditions conducive to franchising, as well as the economic reasons that underlie a franchisor's choice of the franchise business model;
- the early stages of a franchise system, system development and recruitment of franchisees;
- the motivations behind, and the issues surrounding, a franchisee's choice to participate in franchising;
- the problems associated with a lack of information about systems and the sector; and
- an explanation of the importance of uniformity as the underlying justification for the imbalance of power and information that characterizes the relationship.

---

[1] Murray Gell-Mann, <http://www.quantumstep.nl/english/quantumstep_eng.html> at 16 December 2009.

[2] Andrew Terry, 'Understanding the franchise relationship' (Press release, Australian School of Business, University of New South Wales, 10 September 2008) <http://www.asb.unsw.edu.au/newsevents/mediaroom/media/2008/september/Pages/franchiserelationship.aspx> at 15 December 2009.

## FRANCHISING STRUCTURE AND LEGAL RELATIONSHIP

### A Taxonomy of Franchising

Despite efforts to define it, a cogent, consistent legal definition of franchising has so far proved elusive. Perhaps because of this, legal approaches to franchising are rarely straightforward. Almost every text on franchising begins with an attempt to answer the question, 'What is franchising?'[3]

*Black's Law Dictionary* defines a franchise as a licence from the owner of a trademark or trade name permitting another to sell a product or service under that name or mark. Among the 30 countries that regulate 'franchising', eight employ a term that fails to translate directly to the term 'franchise'. Where such a term is used, it refers to a right; conferred with respect to intellectual property, a trademark or a brand. Depending on the jurisdiction there may be a discernible system controlled by the franchisor, assistance, information-sharing, and/or support; and/or a payment by a franchisee to the franchisor.

Franchising is a marketing channel, a business structure, a legal relationship, and a form of governance.[4] As a legal relationship a franchise is a contractual arrangement for the transfer of a right. It is a license to operate the franchise unit at a specified location or geographic area and to use the franchise's intellectual property, including its operations manual and images, to the extent permitted by the scope of the licence. Often franchising represents the most effective means for an owner of a trademark and other intellectual property relating to a business system to obtain revenue from that intellectual property, while at the same time maintaining the requisite control to preserve and enhance its value. Finally, franchising is, in itself, a form of governance. It is a structure used to manage and control the interactions of people engaged in a commercial activity. In the sense that regulation is governance, every participant in franchising is in some sense regulating or seeking to regulate. Generally speaking, there are three categories of franchise system. The attributes of each category reflect the chronological development of franchising in the modern era. As with any

---

[3] 'The threshold problem of defining "franchising" plunges us immediately into the complexity of this modern organizational form,' Gillian Hadfield, 'Problematic Relations: Franchising and the Law of Incomplete Contracts' (1990) 42 *Stanford Law Review* 927, 930.

[4] See Barkoff and Selden, *Fundamentals of Franchising* (2007); M. Mendelsohn, *The Guide to Franchising* (6th ed, 1999).

### BOX 2.1 MENDELSOHN'S FEATURES OF BUSINESS FORMAT FRANCHISES

1. A franchise relationship is founded upon a contract which should contain all the terms agreed upon.
2. The franchisor must first develop a successful business format (the system) which is identified with a brand name which may be a trademark, service mark and/or trade name.
3. The franchisor must initiate and train the franchisee in all aspects of the system prior to the opening of the business so that the franchisee is equipped to run the business effectively and successfully and assist in the opening.
4. After the business is opened the franchisor must maintain a continuing business relationship with the franchisee in the course of which it provides the franchisee with support in all aspects of the operation of the business.
5. The franchisee is permitted under the control of the franchisor to operate under the branding (trademark, service mark, trade name) format the business systems developed and owned by the franchisor and to benefit from the goodwill associated therewith.
6. The franchisee must make a substantial capital investment from his own resources.
7. The franchisee must own his business.
8. The franchisee will pay the franchisor in one way or another for the rights which he acquires and for the continuing services with which he will be provided.

process of evolution, the lines are not distinctly drawn and a franchise system may fall into more than one of these categories.

The first and simplest category is the product franchise. Here, a franchisor is a distributor who supplies goods to a retailer with the understanding that the retailer will have the exclusive right to sell goods in a particular area of the market. This market is usually, but not always, defined in geographic terms. Gas stations, car dealerships and some clothing companies are examples of this category. Early examples of franchising were product franchises, such as the beer franchises in England and Germany that began in the 1800s, some of which still persist today.

The second category of a franchise system, sometimes collapsed into the first, is the processing or manufacturing franchise. Here, the franchisor provides the particular specifications or a specific element which the franchisee uses in producing the product. Soft drinks are a good example of the manufacturing franchise.

The third type, the business-format franchise, developed in the post-war period from the mid 1950s. In a business-format franchise arrangement the franchisor provides franchisees with a comprehensive, often extensive, operating system. Each franchisee must comply with the requirements of the system or risk losing the franchise. Many fast food restaurants, hotel chains, video rental and travel agents are examples of this category. In Australia, where franchising is a mature sector, business format franchising is the most common form of franchise. Of a total of about 708 franchise systems reported in Australia in 1999, 677 were business format franchises.[5] Mendelsohn identifies eight common characteristics of business format franchises (see Box 2.1 on p. 48).[6]

Because most modern franchise systems are business-format franchises, in this book the term 'franchising' and related terms such as franchise, franchisor and franchisee are used in reference to the practice of business-format franchising, unless stated otherwise.

## SOCIAL, CULTURAL AND ECONOMIC CONDITIONS CONDUCIVE TO FRANCHISING

Business-format franchising is about the rapid deployment and exploitation of intellectual property. When Ray Kroc began selling the business-format for McDonald's restaurants in the mid 1950s, social and economic conditions in the US were ideal for growth in the sector. Those conditions, in particular, were:

- positive attitudes, both politically and socially, toward small business;
- highly-developed communications systems that facilitate pervasive advertising and enable nationwide (and international) brand-name recognition; and
- high levels of tertiary activities, including service and knowledge-based industries with heavy customer interface as well as retail and services that could be well-served by small, dispersed outlets.[7]

---

[5] Lorelle Frazer and Scott Weaven (Griffith University), *Franchising Australia 2002 Survey*, (2002) at 3.

[6] M. Mendelsohn, *The Guide to Franchising* (6th ed, 1999) 11.

[7] Some of the factors described here are derived from the work of Stanworth and Curran. See John Stanworth and James Curran, 'Colas, Burgers, Shakes and

Increased consumer mobility and an increase in the real income of consumers further contributed to the post-war franchising boom in the US.[8] The increased prevalence on a global scale of these conditions has contributed to the growth in international franchising in recent years.

Extensive research has been devoted to the question of why a business makes the choice to segregate (operate as a franchise system) rather than integrate (expand through company-owned and -operated outlets).[9] Most franchise systems operate company-owned units and license franchised units. A typical mix might be about 25 percent company-owned to 75 percent franchised units, but the ratio varies widely, even within industries. The topic remains a subject of research and debate and the answers are as complex as the social, economic, and political conditions that inform them. In saying that, two frequently cited motivations in the choice to franchise are resource acquisition theory and transaction cost efficiency/agency theory.[10]

### Resource Acquisition Theory

According to 'resource acquisition theory' the phenomenon of franchising can be attributed to its advantages in capital-raising.[11] Franchising helps a franchisor raise capital because franchisees provide a source of both start-up

---

Shirkers: Towards a Sociological Model of Franchising in the Market Economy' (1999) 14(4) *Journal of Business Venturing* 323, 344.

[8] G. Frank Mathewson and Ralph A. Winter, 'Competition Policy and Vertical Exchange' (1985) 7 *Collected Research Studies*.

[9] See Blair and Lafontaine, *The Economics of Franchising* (2005). Williamson describes franchising as a hybrid, federated structure. See also Paul H. Rubin, 'The Theory of the Firm and the Structure of the Franchise Contract' (1978) 21 *Journal of Law and Economics* 223; Brickley, Dark and Weisbach, 'An Agency Perspective on Franchising' (1991) 20 *Financial Management* 27; Mathewson and Winter, 'The Economics of Franchise Contracts' (1985) 28 *Journal of Law and Economics* 503.

[10] There are other theories for the franchise structure. See Antony W. Dnes, 'A Case-Study Analysis of Franchise Contracts' (1993) 22 *Journal of Legal Studies* 367, 391 for information search theory; Alanson P. Minkler, 'An Empirical Analysis of a Firm's Decision to Franchise' (1990) 34(1) *Economics Letters* 77 for entrepreneurial theory.

[11] For an overview of economic theories of franchising see Mehta and Pelton, 'Limitations of Existing Theories: A Need for "A General Theory of Franchise Relationships"' (Paper presented at the 14th Annual International Society of Franchising, San Diego, 19–20 February 2000); Sue Birley, Benoit Leleux and Stephen Spinelli, 'Franchising your Way to Riches? An Analysis of Value Creation in Public Franchisors' (1997) Babson College <http://www.babson.edu/entrep/fer/papers97/birley/birl.htm> at 15 December 2009.

and working capital in exchange for the right to use a successful business concept and to operate the franchise unit. Because a franchisee accepts the financial responsibility and risk for establishing and running the new unit, this business structure offers a uniquely effective method of harnessing the financial equity (as well as the 'sweat equity') of a franchisee to fuel rapid expansion and increase market penetration for the franchise system.

Franchising thus enables rapid, steady growth for a franchisor with reduced exposure to business risk. A viable business concept in a highly dynamic and competitive market must be implemented quickly, due to the danger of losing market share and brand awareness in markets where new ideas are quickly replicated by competitors.[12] The capital investment of franchisees provides a franchisor with a low-risk means to meet the capital costs of rapid expansion. Franchising thus enables a business to efficiently manage exponential growth by providing access to capital that can fuel expansion in collapsed time frames.

### Transaction Cost Theory

The 'transaction cost theory' of economics considers franchising from a principal/agent perspective. While resource acquisition theory has been well-supported in the literature, many studies emphasize transaction cost and agency theory.[13] Transaction costs can be defined as:

> [H]eterogeneous costs that arise in economic activity. In many deals, parties have to find each other, communicate, measure and inspect the goods that are to be purchased, draw up the contract using lawyers, keep records, and so on. In some cases, compliance needs to be enforced through legal action. All these entail costs in terms of real resources and time, termed *transaction costs*. The reality of these costs contrasts with the frequent assumption of a perfectly clearing, frictionless market.[14]

Transaction cost economics uses the transaction as the basic unit of economic analysis and applies this economic analysis to organizational theory, the law of contracts, and the contracting process to explain the economics of organizations.[15] According to this approach, organizational

---

[12] See John J. Gillman, 'Broken Sticks – Why Mergers may fail to Garner Market Share' (1992) 13(5) *Managerial and Decision Economics* 453, 455.

[13] The term 'transaction cost' is sometimes used interchangeably with 'agency cost' because transaction costs are often related to agency relationships.

[14] Craig Calhoun (ed.), *Dictionary of the Social Sciences* (2002).

[15] Nicholas Mercuro and Steven G. Medema, *Economics and the Law* (1997) 147.

structures are interpreted as adaptations to economize on transaction costs. Effectively the transaction type determines the choice of governance structure, as certain business structures minimize the transaction costs of producing and distributing a particular type of good or service.[16] The transaction type is reflected in the contract or set of contracts binding the participants in the business structure, which explains why these structures are categorized not simply by the transaction type but also by the kind of contract involved.

Williamson classed franchising as a hybrid form which he described as 'federated'. In the federated model large and small entities combine to take advantage of the disparate economies of scale of linked production and marketing processes, while also saving on coordination costs.[17] This model seems especially apt for larger, more established franchise systems. McDonald's, for example, can contract for beef on a massive scale in Brazil, while retaining the local 'touch' of individual franchise units. The per-unit cost of developing a franchise system may be less than the amount required to open one additional company store. At the same time, through the development and operation of small units, the franchisor is freed of day-to-day unit operation and local market concerns, while still receiving information about these functions.[18]

Transaction costs can be divided into two broad categories, coordination costs and motivation costs. Coordination costs arise from coordinating agents' activities. The costs of coordinating specialized agents such as costs of obtaining information, coordinating input in production, and costs of monitoring and measurement are mainly caused by bounded rationality (imperfect knowledge).[19] In franchising, this means that information

---

16 Oliver Williamson, 'Transaction-Cost Economics: The Governance of Contractual Relations' (1979) 22(2) *Journal of Law and Economics* 233, 233–261. On the implications of Williamson's work on regulation of contracts see Hugh Collins, *Regulating Contracts* (1999), 259.

17 See Oliver Williamson, *Markets and Hierarchies: Analyses and Antitrust Implications* (1975); Oliver Williamson, *The Economic Institutions of Capitalism* (1985); Oliver Williamson, 'Transaction-Cost Economics: The Governance of Contractual Relations' (1979) 22(2) *Journal of Law and Economics* 233, 233–61. The original concept is based on the work of Ronald Coase, which has been developed by Oliver Williamson.

18 This function has given rise to the 'information search theory' of franchising.

19 See, for example, George J. Stigler, 'The Economics of Information' (1961) 69 *Journal of Political Economy* 213; A. Armen Alchian and Harold Demsetz, 'Production, Information, Costs and Economic Organising' (1972) 62 *American Economic Review* 777; Yorman Barzel, 'Measurement Cost and the Organization of Markets' (1982) 25 *Journal of Law and Economics* 27.

asymmetry and uncertainty over future conditions lead to coordination costs, for example, in recruitment and transfer with respect to the selection and substitutability of franchisee. The franchise form helps contain coordination costs by allowing a franchisor to enter into an employment-like relation with franchisees without the usual costs and risks associated with employment. A franchisee pays to set up the unit, enjoys fewer compensatory benefits, fewer statutory protections and takes on more of the operating risk than would an employee.

Franchisors select this business form in order to shift the responsibility for site selection, training and management, local administration and leasing.[20] As one franchise system website explains, 'Most of the stores will run as franchises to reduce the risk of liabilities, such as leases and employees, to the company.'[21] By committing their capital, resources, as well as contractual and tortious liability vis-à-vis, *inter alia*, lessors, debtors, employees, suppliers and consumers, franchisees share the risk burden in the franchised business and often take it over altogether.

Motivation costs include the costs of motivating agents to align their interests to avoid cheating or other opportunistic behaviour as well as costs of monitoring.[22] Franchising keeps motivation costs down because a franchisee, unlike an employee, has a financial interest in the performance of its unit. A franchisee's equity investment ensures a commitment to the success of the business so that a franchisor can reduce costs of incentives and monitoring. Further, most franchisees directly manage their businesses themselves (as an added assurance they are often required to do so according to terms of the contract).

Transaction costs may also include liability for other obligations that arise in connection with the relationship, such as franchisor liability for the tortious or contractual liability of franchisees, as well as costs of obtaining information. Another transaction cost benefit of franchising is the savings in the cost of obtaining information. As Williamson's 'federated' model highlights, franchising is a way for a franchisor to guarantee free access to market information from many independently-owned local units.

The choice to franchise is thus motivated largely by franchisor considerations of capital efficiency and transaction costs. The infusion of outside

---

20 Andrew J. Sherman, *Franchising and Licensing* (3rd ed, 2004) 12–13.

21 Reed Business Information, 'Strathfield in tune with franchising' (30 March 2009) [4] < http://www.franchise.net.au/Article/Strathfield-in-tune-with-franchising/474958.aspx> at 16 December 2009.

22 Oliver Williamson, *Markets and Hierarchies: Analyses and Antitrust Implications* (1975); Oliver Williamson, *The Economic Institutions of Capitalism* (1985).

capital together with cost savings allow for expansion over geographically dispersed markets.

If there is an adequate supply of well-qualified franchisees, a well-run franchise structure successfully facilitates the rapid recruitment and training of qualified, motivated management. It also contains transaction costs such as coordination, motivation and monitoring costs, drafting and negotiation of contracts, and it facilitates intra-organizational information-sharing and innovation.

There are other theories supporting the choice to select a franchise structure such as information search theory and entrepreneurial theory. Other theories have focused on the franchise contract as a tool in bonding or screening or a combination of both.[23] Still others invoke concepts of relationship and conflict management.[24] Research continues in these areas as resource acquisition and transaction cost theory remain central in explanations of franchising.

**Early Stages of Franchise System Development**

Once the decision has been made to franchise a business concept, a franchisor invests time, money and effort in formulating, developing, testing and marketing the franchise concept and system and assumes the business risk in the development of pilot stores, company-owned stores and the system as a whole. System development is an important part of the calculus of the franchisor/franchisee relationship. If the franchisor invests sufficient resources in the development of the system, the product is more likely to be satisfactory to franchisees and less susceptible to problems as the relationships between the franchisor and its franchisees develop in later stages. The system development stage underscores the fact that the franchisor is the original bearer of the risk of system failure, but also that the franchisor has control over the system and knowledge that is superior to that of a franchisee, and that the franchisor is in a position to shift much of that and other risks to its franchisees.

Potential sources of conflict in the relationship at the system development stage or arising from system development include the profitability of the system, inadequate development by the franchisor of concept and systems, and inadequate investment by the franchisor in the brand. The

---

[23] Antony W. Dnes, 'A Case-Study Analysis of Franchise Contracts' (1993) 22 *Journal of Legal Studies* 367, 391.

[24] Alanson P. Minkler, 'An Empirical Analysis of a Firm's Decision to Franchise' (1990) 34(1) *Economics Letters* 77.

system may not be well-conceived and developed to provide the benefits that a franchisee has been led to expect. This is one reason why franchisee due diligence is important. Disclosure can aid prospective franchisees in that process, and should be structured and monitored to ensure that it is achieving its purpose.

**Recruitment and Screening of Franchisees**

Once the franchisor has the system up and running it will begin to focus its efforts on recruitment and screening of franchisees. Interviews with franchisors indicate that they consider the selection of franchisees a critical factor in the success of the system.[25] Transaction costs in relation to recruitment and a limited pool of available, qualified franchisees can lead to a choice to integrate, and the hiring of managers for company-owned stores rather than selling franchise units to be operated by franchisees. If qualified franchisees are in short supply, however, franchisors may be tempted to accept franchisees lacking the proper qualifications to make a success of the business, and may fail to adequately screen and select franchisees. If resource acquisition, information search or other motivations take precedence, the franchisor may be inclined to accept under-qualified franchisees rather than make the shift to company-owned units.[26] Those franchisors that are motivated predominantly by the income generated by selling franchises may sell to franchisees who are not adequately screened, and who fail to understand the true nature of the enterprise and who may fail to adequately self-screen.

The result of ineffective screening is that opportunistic behaviour may be more prevalent, and the costs of other methods of controlling transaction costs, such as monitoring, may increase. A franchisor's investment in screening is a coordination cost that can reduce motivation and monitoring costs through the selection of franchisees who are highly motivated to achieve greater returns on their own equity investments.[27]

As another way to contain these costs, franchisors write contracts to ensure

---

[25] One of the most important problems franchisors face in Australia is a shortage of qualified franchisees. See, quoted in Derek Parker, 'Franchising', *The Australian* (Sydney) 30 June 2006: 'The main constraint we are facing is a shortage of good franchisees.'

[26] Francine Lafontaine and Margaret E. Slade, 'Incentive Contracting and the Franchise Decision' in Kalyan Chatterjee and William F. Samuelson (eds) *Game Theory and Business Applications* (2001).

[27] B. Elango and Vance H. Fried, 'Franchising Research: A Literature Review and Synthesis' (1997) 35(3) *Journal of Small Business Management* 68, 74.

that they have the requisite discretion to manage problems with underperforming franchisees, but these contractual provisions only come into play long after franchisees have committed their equity to the project with little protection because they failed to fully appreciate the risk at that early stage.

The franchisor is less vulnerable to each single unit failure than is the individual franchisee operating that unit. Apart from the risk to the franchisor's reputation, the franchisor's risk is contained because the franchise fee is designed to cover the franchisor's costs of establishing each new franchise unit.

> In recruiting an investor to open up a new franchise outlet the franchisor is, to a large degree, gambling with someone else's money. [F]ranchisors gain financially when an investor opens a new outlet, perhaps even if that outlet fails. Some franchisors may have invested minimally in the franchise system, but even those who have a large stake in the system may commit little or no resources to a new outlet. Indeed, the franchisor may receive an up-front franchise fee and, thus, may reap immediate financial gain even if the outlet fails quickly. In the event of failure the franchisor may be the only buyer for the franchisee's capital equipment, and may do so at a deeply discounted price, perhaps reselling it to a future franchisee at a substantial markup.[28]

Payments to franchisors by franchisees are the life blood of a franchise system. The fees paid by franchisees to join the system are an important part of the fee structure. Franchise systems are understandably likely to sacrifice screening considerations, where their risk is low anyway, in order to generate higher revenues. Because of the risk-reward equation from a franchisor's perspective, it is marketing to franchisees, and not screening, that often seems to take precedence.

## FRANCHISEE MOTIVATIONS

Franchisor motivations to franchise are well-documented in the economic theory, but economic theories of organizational structure generally give less weight to the extent to which the structure benefits the consumer of the product of the firm, or suppliers or creditors with whom the firm does business. Such theories therefore prove less helpful in understanding franchisee motivations, 'Because of the way industrial economists work, all over the world, the focus in terms of competition outcomes has tended to be on the

---

28 W. Grimes, 'Perspectives on Franchising: When Do Franchisors Have Market Power? Anti-Trust Remedies for Franchisor Opportunism' (1996), 65 *Antitrust L.J.* 105 at 124–5.

supply side – in other words, the focus has been on firms.'[29] For this reason there is less in the way of settled theory to explain franchisee.

**Psycho-social Motivations**

A franchisee's reasons to purchase the licence to operate a franchised business are not the same as the franchisor's in deciding to franchise. Rarely are a franchisee's motivations purely financial and rather encompass a complex mix of practical and emotional, personal, social, and financial considerations.[30] On a psychological level, franchising combines values of entrepreneurial individualism and independence with the cooperative appeal of a communal/team enterprise. Franchising is seen as a path to independence and economic security that can offer as much promise to ambitious young men and women starting out as to mothers with school-aged children and retirees. They are all, for different reasons, attracted to the flexibility and independence of the structure, and to the idea captured in the slogan, 'in business for yourself, but not by yourself'. For many, franchising represents an opportunity to realize goals such as autonomy, independence, material rewards, entrepreneurship, creativity and flexibility, but with perceived levels of risk that are lower than starting a new business independently. Independence and autonomy coexist, sometimes precariously, with financial and employment security.

**Franchisor Marketing**

The motivations of prospective franchisees are familiar to the franchisors who market to them. In many countries, the advantages of buying a franchise are disseminated by franchisor industry groups as well as individual franchisor systems. Many of a franchisee's reasons to franchise are based on perceptions that are generated and reinforced through franchisor

---

29 Louise Sylvan, 'Consumer Regulation – How do we know it is effective?' (Speech delivered at National Consumer Congress, Melbourne, 15 March 2004) <http://www.accc.gov.au/content/item.phtml?itemId=508102&nodeId=612a6307df40a30e1d22f49ddff4f69a&fn=2004%20March%2015%20National%20Consumer%20Congress%20speech.pdf> at 16 December 2009.

30 See, eg, Deloitte Touche Tohmatsu, 'Franchisee Satisfaction Survey Benchmark 2004' (2004) Deloitte <http://www.deloitte.com/dtt/cda/doc/content/franchise_survey_lo-res.pdf> at 16 December 2009; Kaufman and Stanworth, 'The Decision to Purchase a Franchise: A Study of Prospective Franchisees' (1995) 33 *Journal of Small Business Management* 22; Stanworth and Curran, 'Colas, Burgers, Shakes and Shirkers: Towards a Sociological Model of Franchising in the Market Economy' (1999) 14(4) *Journal of Business Venturing* 323.

marketing. The following list of claims has been posted on one national industry association website. The left hand column lists the claims while the right hand column provides comments about relevant information the association does not provide.

This self-described 'short list' conveys a sense of the benefits for a franchisee. They derive from the alliance with the franchisor's system that provides to a greater or lesser extent:

- Use of the franchise system intellectual property;
- Trademark-related benefits such as high levels of brand awareness;
- Business partnership that allows a franchisee to share franchisor expertise and that of its staff including, for example:
    - track record that helps assess prospects for performance,
    - training, management support, and technical assistance,
    - advice on location decisions and help with negotiating, and
    - help with finance and better cooperation from lenders;
- Economies of scale in purchasing; collective marketing and advertising; and
- Shared skill, experience and information from other franchisees.

At the same time a franchisee expects to reap the advantages of owning his or her own business, requiring less capital to start, and protected from competition by defined territories.

Because of these many potential benefits, franchises are promoted as being more likely to succeed than independent small business. The risk is claimed to be lower than an independent business because the brand is tested and proven and the existing successful name and reputation of the franchise system increase a franchisee's chances of success.[31] In fact franchising is often claimed to be 2.5 times more likely to succeed.[32] A franchisee's perception of the reduced risk of a franchised business is probably one of the most important components of the promise of franchising.

The high probability of success, however, is not entirely supported by academic research:

---

[31] See US Federal Trade Commission 'Buying a franchise: a consumer guide' (2008) <http://www.ftc.gov/bcp/edu/pubs/consumer/invest/inv05.pdf> at 16 December 2009.

[32] Frontline Recruitment Group, 'Franchising benefits' (2009) <http://www.frontlinerecruitmentgroup.com/index.php?site_id=6&page_id=271> at 16 December 2009.

> [T]he data contradict that investing in a franchise is a risk-free or very low-risk endeavour . . . failure rates suggest that joining a young or new franchise system is probably more risky than starting one's own business.[33]

While a franchisor is in franchising because it is efficient, saves costs, and shifts risk to franchisees, franchisees are in franchising for many reasons, with reduced risk not least among them. What is not clear is how, if a franchisor is shifting risk to franchisees, franchisees can be reducing their risk through this business form. Of course, when things are going well in business, everybody can share in the profit and there is no issue of allocating risk. The issue of risk is really only important when there is not enough to go around, or worse, when there are losses to be suffered.

Consider once again the claims made by the trade association in Table 2.1. Items 1 and 7 repeat essentially the same benefit, training. Items 7, 5, 11, 12, 13, 16 and 18 also overlap, each enumerating an aspect of franchisor support. Item 12 is a general repetition of items 10, 11, 13 and 14. As the comments in the second column suggest, many of these reasons, though they are strenuously asserted by franchisors and repeated so often as to seem axiomatic, are unsupported by the reliable data.

Franchisees are subject to assiduous marketing efforts not only by franchise systems, but also by trade associations, that are geared to appeal to prospective franchisees' financial interests, as well as to their psychological and social motivations. Information exchange is critical at this stage, but may not be candid, as each party seeks to make the best impression possible. A franchisor wants to make the sale and each party wants to secure a strong bargaining position in the subsequent negotiation stage. Enthusiastic franchisees often fail to adequately screen prospective franchisors to their cost. '[K]ey findings suggest that a lack of due diligence is associated with the formation of unrealistic expectations which increases the potential for future relational conflict.'[34] Despite, or perhaps because of, the fact that most prospective franchisees are pro-active, capable people, they are sometimes too confident in their prospects. Table 2.1 underscores some of the dangers of franchisee over-optimism. Mystery fuels a romance, but a lasting relationship requires candour. Franchisees' misconceptions often lead to disappointment when the reality of franchising fails to match its promise.

---

33 Blair and Lafontaine, *The Economics of Franchising* (2005) 44.

34 Weaven, Frazer and Giddings, 'How Can Regulation be Enhanced? New Perspectives on the Causes and Continuation of Franchising Conflict in Australia' (Paper presented at 23rd Annual International Society of Franchising, San Diego, 12–14 February 2009).

*Table 2.1 Franchise trade association promotions claims*

| The Industry Association Claims[a] | Information the Industry Association does not provide: |
|---|---|
| 'There are countless benefits to becoming a Franchisee, which is why Franchising is one of the fastest-growing sectors of the Australian economy. Here is a short list of eighteen advantages of Franchising over stand-alone forms of small business:' | The initial premise here deserves closer examination. The FCA presents franchising as alternative to starting your own business. More research is needed to provide a better understanding of how franchising actually compares with independent small business ownership. According to Blair and Lafontaine, 'In reality, owning a franchise is not at all the same as independent small business ownership.' Blair and Lafontaine note a common misperception about the nature of franchising that is perpetuated by franchisor claims that this business structure provides the opportunity for a franchisee to 'be your own boss'. They stress that a franchisee must see the arrangement as a contractual agreement of fixed duration. A franchisee is contracting for the right to use a particular trademark in a particular location for a particular time period; it should not see itself as establishing its own independent business that can be fully transferable. Franchising, therefore, is not comparable to independent small business ownership. This view is not cultivated by franchisors, however, because it would change the attitude of franchisees toward the enterprise, requiring different contractual and other devices to manage a franchisee. |
| '1. The Franchisor provides detailed training.' | This claim is true in some systems. The quality and extent of this training varies widely from system to system as do the costs that the franchisor charges to a franchisee for this service. |
| '2. The Franchisee has the incentive of owning their (sic) own business with the additional benefit of continuing assistance from the Franchisor.' | Again, the quality and extent of this assistance varies widely from system to system as do the costs that the franchisor charges to a franchisee for franchisor support. |

*Table 2.1* (continued)

| The Industry Association Claims[a] | Information the Industry Association does not provide: |
|---|---|
| '3. The Franchisee benefits from operating under the name and reputation (brand image) of the Franchisor, which is already well established in the mind and eye of the public.' | The franchisor's trademark/brand is indeed important but the quality varies significantly. Not all brands are well-established, and it can be hard to quantify and ensure maintenance of the brand, as this is left to the discretion of the franchisor. Also, the franchisee may lose this benefit and be left without legal recourse in the case of franchisor sale of the system or insolvency. |
| '4. The Franchisee will usually need less capital than they would if they were setting up a business independently because, through their pilot operations and buying power, will have eliminated unnecessary expense.' | A franchisee may in fact need more capital than to set up an independent small business. It must pay the franchise fee, its franchisor's as well as its own legal costs, and other upfront charges to a franchisor. |
| '5. The Franchisor provides the advice and/or help in identifying suitable trading locations or operating territories for the Franchisee.' | A franchisee may benefit from such advice and/or help but its interests are not the same as those of the franchisor. |
| '6. The Franchisor helps the Franchisee obtain occupation rights to the trading location, comply with planning (zoning) laws, prepare plans for layouts, shopfitting and refurbishment, and provide general assistance in calculating the correct level and mix of stock for the opening launch of the business.' | Depending on the nature of the property rights in the premises and who holds them, a franchisor may provide these services, but will charge a fee, for example 25 percent of the total for franchisor management of shop fit-out. |
| '7. The Franchisor trains the Franchisee (and very often, the Franchisee's staff as well) in all areas of the business such as; manufacture, preparation, accounting, business controls, marketing, promotion and merchandising.' | A franchisor may or may not offer these services. If so, the franchisor in most instances charges for them, usually at a profit to franchisor. The training of a franchisee and its staff can be a hidden expense, one not incurred in independent small business. |

*Table 2.1* (continued)

| The Industry Association Claims[a] | Information the Industry Association does not provide: |
|---|---|
| '8. The Franchisor may negotiate better rates of finance, or more favourable conditions, for Franchisees with financial institutions.' | Anecdotal evidence from franchisees indicates that this may not be as easy or as beneficial to the interests of a franchisee as the franchisor might claim. There are also privacy issues; the franchisee may find that the franchisor is privy to information that the franchisee had disclosed only to its bank. |
| '9. The Franchisee receives the benefit on a national scale (if appropriate) of the Franchisor's advertising and promotional activities at a lower cost than if they were to attempt such marketing themselves.' | This claim is true, but a franchisor has discretion to advertise and offer promotions that may cost the franchisee but may not benefit it or may even accrue to its detriment. (See discussion of advertising spending in Chapter 5.) |
| '10. The Franchisee taps into the bulk purchasing power and negotiating capacity made available by the Franchisor by reason of the size of the franchised network.' | This claim is true, but there is also the risk that franchisor receives kickbacks from suppliers and other businesses in the franchisor's network. Again, this can add to a franchisee's cost. |
| '11. The Franchisee can call on the specialised and highly-skilled knowledge and experience of the Franchisor's head office organisation, while remaining self-employed in their business.' | The accessibility and availability of assistance varies in different systems. This claim also raises the question of what it means to be 'self-employed' and still under the control of the franchisor. |
| '12. The support and benefits provided by a Franchise system greatly reduce a Franchisee's business risks.' | Not proven, in fact Blair and Lafontaine assert that the opposite is often true in the case of new systems.[b] |
| '13. The Franchisee has the services of the field operational staff of the Franchisor who are there to assist with any problems which may arise from time to time in the course of business.' | This claim is true, but here, too, the interests of the franchisor and a franchisee are different. The role of field staff is primarily to ensure compliance and productivity of the franchisee. |

*Table 2.1* (continued)

| The Industry Association Claims[a] | Information the Industry Association does not provide: |
|---|---|
| '14. The Franchisee has access to use of the Franchisor's patents, trade marks, copyrights, trade secrets, and any secret processes or formulae.' | This claim is true; this is what a franchisee is essentially paying for, as Lafontaine points out, but only for the time specified in the contract at the unit premises. The franchisee needs to understand what it owns and what it can sell at the end. |
| '15. The Franchisee has the benefit of the Franchisor's continuous research and development programs, which are designed to improve the business and keep it up-to-date and competitive.' | This claim is true to the extent the system has such programs. But the franchisor and franchisee have conflicting goals. Not all of the franchisor's new programs will benefit the franchisee. |
| '16. The Franchisor provides a knowledge base developed from their (sic) own experience, as well as that of all the Franchisees in the system, which would otherwise be impossible for a non-franchised business to access.' | The franchisor has such knowledge, but is not required to provide it to the franchisee. A franchisee has no right of access to information about the franchise system in which it participates. |
| '17. Defined territories of operation within the Franchise can help protect the Franchisee from competition.' | The franchisee may be protected from competition from other franchisees within the system, but not against franchisor encroachment or against competition from other competitors. A franchisee may be subject to contractual restraints while vulnerable to franchisor encroachment. Because the franchisee cannot trade outside its scope, but the franchisor can develop its business as it likes, the protection from competition accrues mostly to the franchisor. |
| '18. A Franchisee can always speak to their Franchisor or a fellow Franchisee to discuss their business challenges or problems – something a non-franchised business can almost never do.' | This may be true, however, dissatisfied franchisees are often told that problems are their fault. They may be required to repeat training. They also may be threatened with defamation for communications with other franchisees, despite Code provisions that prohibit the franchisor from stopping franchisee association, and there |

*Table 2.1* (continued)

| The Industry Association Claims[a] | Information the Industry Association does not provide: |
|---|---|
| | is the potential of anti-trust violations if franchisees try to act collectively in a way that impacts the franchisor.[c] |

*Notes:*

[a] Franchise Council of Australia, 'Advantages of the franchising system' (2008) <http://www.franchise.org.au/lib/pdf/aboutfranchising/AdvantagesBrochure.pdf > at 16 December 2009. See also Franchise Council of Australia, 'Advantages of the franchise system' (2008) <http://www.franchise.org.au/scripts/cgiip.exe/WService=FCAWWW/ccms.r?PageId=10110> at 16 December 2009; Franchise Council of Australia, 'Disadvantages of the franchise system' (2008) <http://www.franchise.org.au/scripts/cgiip.exe/WService=FCAWWW/ccms.r?PageId=10111> at 16 December 2009.

[b] Blair and Lafontaine, *The Economics of Franchising* (2005) 44.

[c] See Warren Pengilley, 'Trade associations and collective boycotts in Australia and New Zealand: a mistranslation of the Sherman Act down under' (1987) 32 *Antitrust Bulletin* 1019.

## INFORMATION ASYMMETRY

It is difficult for prospective franchisees (as well as for researchers and regulators) to make accurately informed judgments and decisions about franchising because there is a lack of balanced, reliable information about the sector and very often a lack of information about the particular franchise system.

A prospective franchisee needs information about franchising generally with respect to the structure, economics and performance of the sector. Because reliable information about franchising is not plentiful, however, it is difficult for a prospective franchisee to form an unbiased view of the nature of this business form and how the franchise sector operates. A survey of Australian franchisees asked, 'Has the reality of owning a franchise lived up to the promise?'[35] This survey pre-selected for positive responses, as it only included the most satisfied of franchisees, those still in business; former franchisees that had left the sector were not included

[35] The 'promise' is not defined by survey design; the mystery of what comprises the 'promise' of franchising persists. 'Deloitte Franchisee Satisfaction Survey (2004)' http://www.deloitte.com/dtt/press_release/0,1014,sid%253D5527%2526cid%253D83960,00.html 15 August 2005.

in the survey.[36] Even so, the survey reported that only 52 percent of franchisees believe that 'the reality of owning a franchise has lived up to the promise'.[37] For a slight majority of franchisees still operating, the survey suggests that their experience with franchising meets expectations. It is less encouraging that for almost half of franchisees still in operation it does not.

There are several reasons for the lack of balanced, reliable and accurate information about franchising. The most fundamental reason is that the sources of information about the sector are limited and the available information is dominated by franchisors' interests. Franchisors' interest in the dissemination of information only about the sunnier aspects of the sector is due not only to their motivation to avoid further scrutiny and intervention by regulators, but also, and perhaps more importantly, to their interest in marketing franchising to potential franchisees. This interest generally prevails over the need to analyse the sector through an objective lens in order to ensure and improve the quality of franchising generally.

The early stages of the market interaction are characterized by franchisor control over the system, the interaction and information. There are several potential sources of conflict in the relationship in the market interaction:

- An insufficient supply of qualified franchisees can create problems where franchisors are less concerned with franchisee qualification.
- Intense marketing by franchisor systems and by trade associations can involve misrepresentation by both sides as well as by third parties.
- Recruitment professionals can increase the miscommunication between franchisor and franchisee.[38]
- There is pressure on franchisees to commit.
- There is confirmation bias; franchisees want to believe in the promise of franchising.

---

[36] Forty-eight percent of those franchisees surveyed; the survey did not include failed franchisees that are no longer in operation. 'Deloitte Franchisee Satisfaction Survey (2004)' http://www.deloitte.com/dtt/press_release/0,1014,sid%253D5527%2526cid%253D83960,00.html 15 August 2005.

[37] The study report does not list the range of responses to this question, nor is it known how the franchisees were chosen who participated in this franchisor-funded survey. 'Deloitte Franchisee Satisfaction Survey (2004)' http://www.deloitte.com/dtt/press_release/0,1014,sid%253D5527%2526cid%253D83960,00.html 15 August 2005.

[38] '. . . the role of third parties and market conditions appear to exacerbate dissatisfaction in most franchise systems'. Weaven, Frazer and Giddings, 'How Can Regulation be Enhanced? New Perspectives on the Causes and Continuation of Franchising Conflict in Australia' (Paper presented at 23rd Annual International Society of Franchising, San Diego, 12–14 February 2009).

- Most franchisees cannot afford, or think that they cannot afford, extensive legal and professional advice.
- A franchisee is often encountering franchising for the first time while the franchisor is experienced.
- A franchisee is focused on one franchisor while a franchisor has many franchisees.

Not only at the beginning, but throughout the relationship, franchisors and franchisees have conflicting interests. A master franchisor wants to maximize system revenue, while a master franchisee will want to maximize territory or unit revenue, and a franchisee wants the best unit profits.[39] A franchisor seeks growth in sales, while for a franchisee sales growth may be undesirable if it comes at the expense of profits. A franchisee may want to take profits while a franchisor wants them reinvested, for example in capital assets and local advertising.

Due in part to these conflicts, the parties do not always share information as readily as an outside observer might expect. Threats of defamation suits and concerns about competition law provisions against boycotts can be of concern for franchisees that may wish to communicate to others their experiences with franchising. Also, franchisees may risk being found to have acted outside the parameters of good faith. Finally, it can be difficult to garner evidence from dispute processes. In Australia, for example, the Code-mandated dispute resolution procedure, mediation, is a confidential process, so no information is available to those outside the dispute.

It is said that information is power. A franchisee has less control and less information. Imbalance of control and information are both justified by the need for uniformity. This is why uniformity is another critical feature of the franchise relationship, as it informs the interaction between franchisor and franchisee from beginning to end.

## THE ROLE OF UNIFORMITY IN FRANCHISE SYSTEM OPERATION

Franchising is about intellectual property and 'the brand'. Without this intellectual property, a franchisor has nothing to sell. In order to maintain and protect the brand, a franchisor requires uniformity in the implementation of the system and the operation of each unit. Uniformity is critical to

---

39 B. Elango and Vance H. Fried, 'Franchising Research: A Literature Review and Synthesis' (1997) 35(3) *Journal of Small Business Management* 68, 73.

franchise systems not only for the sake of trademark protection and brand maintenance, but also because it reduces strategic risk and risk related to externalities and moral hazard. Uniformity also helps to control transaction costs and protects a franchisor against franchisee claims of unfair and discriminatory practices.

There are important advantages of uniformity for the franchisor in operating its system. The main advantages are that uniformity is crucial to brand maintenance, reduces risk, contains transaction costs and protects a franchisor against claims of unfairness. Each of these advantages is explained in more detail in the sections that follow:

**Uniformity is crucial to brand maintenance**

Traditionally in franchising, uniformity (in products, levels of service, cleanliness and other standards) has been considered the key to a successful operation. Blair and Lafontaine write:

> The strength of franchise systems does not lie in the *absolute* quality of the products offered. Instead, it resides largely in the capacity of the franchised chain to offer a *uniform* product at reasonable prices.[40]

Box 2.2 reproduces a thread posted on the American Bar Association (ABA) Forum on Franchising listserv where Michael Seid, the author of *Franchising for Dummies*, provides an insight into the zeal with which franchisors and their consultants defend the principle of uniformity.[41]

As the court recognized in a noted Canadian case:

> [I]t is vital to the integrity and success of the entire franchise system that the standards be uniform and that they be enforced. Uniformity must be central to the identity of the system. And maintenance of identity and uniformity must be central to continued operation of the system for all.[42]

Power asymmetry in the franchise relationship stems in part from the strict control over the system that a franchisor exercises in the name of the need for uniformity in franchise contracts. It is the essence of franchising

---

40 Blair and Lafontaine, *The Economics of Franchising* (2005) 117.

41 Enquiry posted on the ABA Forum on Franchising Listserv 1 February 2005 and replied to by Michael H. Seid 2 February 2005. Forum available at <http://mail.abanet.org/scripts/wa.exe?A0=FRANCHISING> at 16 December 2009.

42 *Coordinated Corporate Services Ltd v National Video Inc* (1984) 2 CPR (2d) 251, 755. The case also acknowledges the difficulties that can be encountered by franchisors in dealing with franchisees who may be in breach and who, by continuing to operate, may be damaging the goodwill of the franchise.

BOX 2.2 THE IMPORTANCE OF UNIFORM SYSTEM STANDARDS

**Enquiry to listserv:** 'Can anyone cite me to the case (if it wasn't just someone's hypothetical) where a franchisor attempted to enforce system standards against a franchisee who was exceeding system standards by serving fresh squeezed real orange juice instead of reconstituted stuff out of a container, which led to complaints by other franchisees?'

**Seid's Reply:** 'They had not exceeded system standards. For example, a McDonald's franchisee deciding to have less fat in their burgers would change the taste and texture. Changing the brixing on Coca Cola could make it sweeter or less sweet. Putting bigger desks in a Marriott Courtyard might make the working area bigger but the living area smaller. Adding moisture content in cheese used for pizza might cause the bread to burn or the pepperoni to cup because the melt time and temperature needs to change. They had not exceeded system standards – they had *violated* the system standards.'

that the brand be clearly identifiable and that franchisees conform to a franchisor's branding formula. In order to protect uniformity franchisors take pains to ensure that they maintain absolute authority over the terms of the relationship.

> Franchising is ultimately an extremely competitive industry. . . . To succeed, a franchisor must constantly watch its backside for approaching competitors, as well as learn how best to gain on the competitor in front of it. To win, or even be in, the race, a franchisor must have an absolute right to respond to market changes and set the direction of its system – right or wrong. It must be free to take all varieties of risks without a concern that the wisdom of its decision might be second-guessed in a courtroom.[43]

### Uniformity reduces risk

Risks for a franchisor include operating risk as well as strategic and reputational risks.

---

43 William L. Killion, 'Putting Critical Decision-Making Where It Belongs: Scouring the Franchise Agreement for the "D" Word' (2005) 24 *Franchise Law Journal* 228, 230.

Operating risk is defined as 'the risk of loss resulting from inadequate or failed internal processes, people and systems, or from external events'.[44] The choice to franchise decreases a franchisor's operating risk over that of a company-owned store, as a franchisee assumes the operating risk for the unit.

The addition of a franchisee, however, can increase a franchisor's strategic and reputational risks to the extent that a franchisee is able to exercise discretion in both the operation of the unit and the use of resources.[45] To contain these franchisee-related risks a franchisor imposes tight controls on the exercise of discretion by a franchisee. A franchisor relies on uniformity to help contain this risk.

Uniformity in the system also reduces the negative impacts of externalities within the system. Economists view voluntary exchange as mutually beneficial to both parties, but consumption and production often have external effects that can lead to moral hazard. Franchisors are concerned with a form of moral hazard known as 'free-riding' where a franchisee shirks on the trade name or brand. In the case of a particular franchise unit, when repeat customers accrue to the benefit of that particular franchisee, the externality is low and there are positive incentives for that franchisee to cultivate his customers.[46] A McDonald's unit located in a local shopping centre may see a high percentage of repeat customers, and so that franchisee will be interested in offering high quality service to those customers, as it will directly benefit from the repeat business. But where a franchise unit has a high number of non-repeat customers or its repeat customers accrue to the benefit of other franchisees in the system, such as in the case of a McDonald's unit located at a busy metropolitan highway interchange, high externalities may tempt a franchisee to free-ride and under-invest in its operation.[47]

A franchisor employs a variety of means to protect the brand against the

---

44 Basel Committee on Banking Supervision, 'International Convergence of Capital Measurement and Capital Standards ("Basel II")' Bank of International Settlements, §644 <http://www.bis.org/publ/bcbs128.pdf> at 16 December 2009.

45 Phillip H. Phan, John E. Butler, and Soo H. Lee, 'Crossing Mother: Entrepreneur-Franchisees' Attempts to Reduce Franchisor Influence' (1996) 11 *Journal of Business Venturing* 370. The Basel II definition in the previous note includes legal risk, but excludes strategic risk, namely the risk of a loss arising from a poor strategic business decision. This definition also excludes reputational risk.

46 James A. Brickley, 'Incentive Conflicts and Contractual Restraints: Evidence from Franchising' (1999) 42 *Journal of Law and Economics* 745, 749.

47 For examples of high-, intermediate- and low-externality industries see James A. Brickley, 'Incentive Conflicts and Contractual Restraints: Evidence from Franchising' (1999) 42 *Journal of Law and Economics* 745, 755–6.

risks of franchisee free-riding. Franchisee temptation to free-ride can be reduced through the use of incentives or a franchisor can step up its monitoring. Alternatively, in the case of demand externality, where the high price at one outlet decreases demand at all outlets, a franchisor may impose uniform pricing, further eroding a franchisee's local control. Franchisors may also respond to externalities through choice of organizational form. High externalities can signal a need for greater vertical integration, as franchisee free-riding leads a franchisor to prefer to run the unit as a company-owned store and hire a manager, whose compensation may not be tied as directly to the performance of that particular unit.[48]

**Uniformity contains transaction costs**

The franchise form exists largely to save transaction costs. Uniformity in drafting of contracts contains the transaction costs of entry into the relationship. A franchisor's costs would soar if each franchisee were governed by a different contract with its own individually-negotiated terms and provisions. Repetition of the same documents, processes and procedures with every franchisee in the system creates economies of scale in the preparation of the contract documents, administration and regulatory compliance. If a franchisor negotiates a different term, not only will a franchisor have to draft and monitor different franchise contracts, but also it will have to prepare different disclosure documents for each franchisee. Disclosure is considered onerous by franchisors even without this added burden.[49]

After the contract is signed, uniformity leads to ease of administration that also keeps transaction costs down. 'If there is not a high degree of uniformity, there can be difficulties for a franchisor in administering the system.'[50] Lower agent service levels, particularly lack of compliance with the system and failure to pay fees, correlate with higher monitoring costs,

---

48 See Francine Lafontaine and Margaret E. Slade, 'Incentive Contracting and the Franchise Decision' in Kalyan Chatterjee and William F. Samuelson (eds), *Game Theory and Business Applications* (2001) 146–57.

49 See James V. Jordan and Judith B. Gitterman, 'Franchise Agreements: Contract of Adhesion?'(1996) 16 *Franchise Law Journal* 1, 42: 'franchise agreements are often drafted as form contracts because of the constraints imposed on franchisors by state legislatures. For example, under the California Negotiated Sales Rule, the initial offer to a franchisee must be the offer that has been registered with the Department of Corporations. If the franchisor negotiates a change with a franchisee, the [Uniform Franchise Offering Circular] must be amended to disclose the negotiated terms. Additionally, the franchisor must attach all notices of negotiated sales within the past twelve months to the offering circular.'

50 Andrew C. Selden, 'The Negotiated Franchise: A Trap for the Unwary' (1983) 7 *International Franchise Legal Digest* 2.

as a franchisor must spend more to ensure compliance.[51] Generally, a franchisor seeks to contain these costs through unilateral governance and strict, uniform standards that are imposed through the contract as well as other documents supporting the relationship. Uniformity is therefore a key tool for a franchisor to maintain the system standards, to keep costs down, and to control externalities.

### Uniformity protects a franchisor against claims of unfairness

Finally, uniformity in the form of a franchisor's consistent treatment of franchisees can be an indication of fairness.[52] Negotiating the terms of the deal with each franchisee could leave a franchisor open to claims of favouritism and unfair treatment or discrimination.[53]

The need for uniformity explains why a franchisor takes pains to contractually protect its discretion to set standards, policies and rules. The following clause, taken from a franchise agreement in Australia, illustrates this point:

> The Franchisee acknowledges that it is imperative the standards of quality and uniformity of the Franchisor System be maintained. Accordingly, the Franchisee agrees that the Franchisor has the right to set such standards of quality and to make such policies and rules from time to time, as the Franchisor may determine. The Franchisee agrees to abide by and be bound by all such standards, policies and rules and any non-compliance shall constitute a breach of this agreement . . .

## The Price of Uniformity

While uniformity is essential for a franchisor and the brand, it does come at a cost. The disadvantage of the emphasis on uniformity is that, as it underpins the standard form and the discretion of franchisors, it also reinforces power asymmetry, sets up conditions of moral hazard and leads to conditions of uncertainty and risk for franchisees. Moral hazard arises, for example, where responsibility for risk is assigned to one party, but the

---

51 Deepak Agrawal and Rajiv Lal, 'Contractual Arrangements in Franchising: An Empirical Investigation' (1995) 32(2) *Journal of Marketing Research* 213.

52 Trade Practices Act 1974 (Cth) s 51AC.

53 In Australia the Trade Practices Act 1974 (Cth) s 51AC codifies this concern. The problem is that s 51AC equates consistency with fairness. Consistency and fairness are two distinct and not necessarily compatible concepts. For a discussion on the connection between unconscionability and balance of power see Daniel D. Barnhizer, 'Inequality of Bargaining Power' (2005) 76 *University of Colorado Law Review* 139.

other party still has control over relevant risk factors,[54] such as when a franchisee makes contributions to advertising funds which a franchisor can spend at its discretion and where a franchisor has discretion to require a franchisee to purchase from a supplier whose products are more expensive, but who will pay a franchisor a commission. A franchisor benefits but will not bear the costs, as a franchisor's royalty is calculated on franchisee gross turnover, not franchisee net profit.

A franchisor is also vulnerable to opportunistic behaviour on the part of a franchisee, such as free-riding, as well as cheating, inaccurate reporting, and withholding of information; or appropriation of intellectual property. Unlike a franchisee, however, a franchisor is able to limit opportunistic behaviour of a franchisee through contractual terms such as accounting and reporting requirements, minimum performance requirements, vertical restraints, and shifting of risk to a franchisee. This option of using the contract to contain the other party's opportunistic behaviour is unavailable to a franchisee because a franchisee neither drafts nor is able to negotiate contract terms. Moral hazard is thus a problem that only a franchisor can control through contract, crafting uniform contract terms to protect against risks, often by shifting them to franchisees.

As neither a franchisee nor a franchisor can predict future circumstances, a franchisee has to trust its franchisor and hope that a franchisor will act in a franchisee's best interests. Unfortunately, given the many conflicts of interest in the relationship, this is not always the case.[55] In the interests of uniformity a franchisor enjoys the ability to accord high levels of discretion to itself and high risk to a franchisee through the standard form. In this way the contract facilitates franchisor opportunism.

## The need for Uniformity from a Franchisee's Perspective

Because of the cardinal principal of uniformity a franchisee owns his or her own business, but does not enjoy control over it. Because of uniformity, a franchisee is subject to franchisor dictates, including unilateral changes at any time. Uniformity is a legitimate interest, but a franchisee needs to understand the nature of the relationship. Franchisees tend to accept the situation, rather than asserting their own interests, for a variety of reasons including franchisee individualism, optimism and naïveté; disparities in

---

54 The classic example of this type of moral hazard is insurance contracts.

55 The franchise contract binds a franchisee over a period of years. The franchisee is not free to transfer its rights and obligations under the contract without franchisor approval. Franchisors are not subject to such constraints under the typical standard contract.

legal representation; lack of resources; a general sense of subordination as the consumer and as the less experienced party; and even a sense that a franchisee is less sophisticated, less educated and less substantial than its franchisor. There may be ways, however, without compromising the brand, to involve franchisees collectively so that their needs are better met and that risks are not so easily shifted to them without understanding and consent.

## THE MARKET INTERACTION – THE TONE OF THE RELATIONSHIP

The market interaction sets the tone of the relationship. The dynamics of the franchise relationship at the market 'layer' of interaction comprise a complex mix of motivations and expectations. A franchisor chooses to franchise primarily for financial reasons, such as capital efficiency and containment of transaction costs. In the early stages of the business a franchisor develops the franchise system, a process that is critical to the future success of the enterprise. Once this is done, a franchisor can begin the process of recruiting franchisees. If there is an adequate supply of qualified franchisees, a well-run franchise structure benefits from the financial and human capital of its franchisees, successfully facilitates the rapid recruitment and training of management, allows for rapid expansion over geographically dispersed markets, and facilitates intra-organizational information-sharing and innovation. The franchise model allows a franchisor to significantly reduce its business risk through the use of franchisee capital and franchisees' responsibility for the success of the business at the unit level.

The motivations behind franchisees' choice to participate in franchising include franchisees' psychological, social and financial aspirations. The purchase of a franchise secures for a franchisee the licence to use the franchise system intellectual property. A prospective franchisee believes that it is much more than that, however, and the franchisor's marketing materials support the belief that a franchisee will benefit from a business partnership that includes sharing franchisor expertise and that of its staff in training and support, advice on location decisions and help with negotiating, and help with finance as well as in other areas as the need may arise.

A franchisee is also often led to expect economies of scale in purchasing and shared promotions, as well as shared skill, experience and information from other franchisees. A franchisee believes she will enjoy all the advantages of owning her own business, but one that needs less capital to start and is protected from competition by defined territories. The underlying theme of promotions to franchisees by franchisors is that franchisees can start a business with a significantly higher chance of success than through independent business ownership.

It appears then that a significant measure of the motivation of both franchisor and franchisee to be in the franchise relationship is to reduce risk. The possibility that the alliance can reduce risk for both is the promise of franchising as it is meant to be. If there are times when one party must bear the cost, however, a franchisor has full control not only over the brand and a franchisee's business, but also over information. The market layer of governance is characterized by an imbalance of control and asymmetry of information. The reason that these conditions persist is the need for uniformity. Uniformity is the cardinal principle in franchising and it is the underlying justification for the imbalance of power and information throughout the relationship. So, though both parties may be in the deal to reduce their risk, if there is any discrepancy in who bears the risk, the smart money is on the franchisee. Franchising can reduce risk and offer a better business model for all involved, yet at the same time there is the potential for highly opportunistic behaviour which threatens the security of franchisees. Perhaps it is this dynamic that motivated Professor Andrew Terry to observe that:

> Good franchising is very good. It is undoubtedly the most efficient, effective distribution system ever invented. It is the greatest invention of Western capitalism since the invention of the corporation. Good franchising is so much better than independent small business operation but bad franchising is so much worse.[56]

Franchisors operate franchise systems for many years and see many franchisees come and go, sometimes from the same locations. Franchisees are typically in business and hope for entrepreneurial success in shorter time frames. Though it varies according to many factors, it is typically around 5 to 10 years. In the period of a franchisee's tenure there will be issues that arise between franchisor and franchisee. Misguided franchisee motivations are a source of misunderstanding about franchising and, 'when expectations are set unrealistically, conflict almost invariably arises'.[57]

The question is how the parties will deal with the bumps in the road and what will be the terms of that commitment. To meet the expectations

---

[56] Andrew Terry cited in House of Representatives Standing Committee on Industry, Science and Resources, 'Finding a balance: towards fair trading in Australia'(1997) 83 <http://www.aph.gov.au/house/committee/isr/Fairtrad/report/contents.htm> at 16 December 2009.

[57] Blair and Lafontaine, *The Economics of Franchising* (2005) 221–2.

of both parties the ideal formula is one in which the legal arrangements are structured in such a way that *both* contracting parties can reduce risk. The next chapter explains the nature of the franchise contract and the importance of the role it plays in the allocation of risk and in the development of the relationship between franchisor and franchisee, the franchise relationship.

# 3. The contract as private regulation

## THE IMPORTANCE OF THE CONTRACTUAL RELATIONSHIP

Regulation by contract is a method of self-regulation as part of the control over the relationship by the parties themselves; such control is achieved through the form and terms of the agreements that govern the relationship. In the case of franchising, the relationship often involves multiple, interrelated contracts governing a wide range of dynamic issues, including trademark licences, real estate leases, financing arrangements, supply agreements, cooperative advertising agreements and so on. The most important of these is the franchise agreement. Chapters 3 and 4 deal with the nature of this contractual agreement which governs the franchisor–franchisee relationship.

Every franchisee needs to, 'recognize his contract for what it is. It is not an opportunity to develop a business and invest in developing a brand in partnership with a franchisor, but rather a short-term licence from which the franchisee must derive short-term benefits . . . it makes sense to think of a franchise contract as a rental contract over an intangible asset, namely the brand, with the terms of the franchise contract clearly defining the relationship'.[1]

A franchisee is not establishing its own fully-transferable, independent business, but rather is contracting for the right to use a particular trademark in a particular location for a particular time period. However, in the sales process, the relationship is often not presented this way. If it were, franchisees would no longer consider themselves as owners of their own businesses. This could threaten franchisee effort and commitment and increase agency costs. Different contractual and other non-legal devices to manage a franchisee would then be required.[2]

---

1 Blair and Lafontaine, *The Economics of Franchising* (2005) 221.

2 These may include 'extra franchise rights and expectations within the contract: verbal promises to the franchisee about future prospects should never suffice from the franchisee's perspective (they are not worth the paper they are written on!), especially in light of the frequent use of integration clauses . . . ': Blair and Lafontaine, *The Economics of Franchising* (2005) 292.

It is most important for a prospective franchisee to read and understand not only the terms of the contract, but the very nature of the contract itself. There are different species of contracts. Lawyers know this, but laymen have less appreciation for the implications.

A franchise contract is both standard form and relational. The standard form and relational characteristics of the franchise contract independently impact upon the relationship between the parties, and these impacts are reinforced by the interaction between these contractual qualities.

Courts and regulators also need to understand this interaction. Best practice in regulatory process requires a comprehensive understanding of the context of regulation. The context of regulating franchise contracts is, as Gillian Hadfield observed in 1990, that such contracts 'are long-term, standard-form contracts'.[3]

Two features are common to standard-form contracts: unequal bargaining power and the lack of negotiation. Relational contracts can also be defined by two features: incompleteness and longevity.

Both standard form and relational qualities of contract are designed to reduce transaction costs. Standard-form contracts stress contract formation and the formalities of the contract. Relational contracts emphasize flexibility, reciprocity and the trust that develops over time.

While the qualities of standard form and relational contracts have been treated as separate issues in the academic literature,[4] the franchise contract presents an instance where these two contractual qualities co-exist. In the franchise context, it is important to understand not only the nature of these contracts independently, but also the interaction of the standard form and relational qualities.

For a franchisee, the unequal bargaining power and lack of negotiation of the standard form combine with the relational contract's reliance upon flexibility and trust to reinforce an imbalance of power and uncertainty, so that the franchise contract reflects and reinforces the asymmetries in the franchise relationship already put in place by the market interaction.

The relational and standard form qualities of the contract, independently and in combination, enhance the power of a franchisor and allow a franchisor to shift risk to franchisees, increasing uncertainty and risk for

---

[3] G Hadfield, 'Problematic Relations: Franchising and the Law of Incomplete Contracts' (1990) 42 *Stanford Law Review* 927, 946. Having made this observation, Hadfield focused the balance of her analysis primarily on the incompleteness of the contract rather than the standard form or the combination of the two.

[4] See, eg, Poppo and Zenger, 'Do Formal Contracts and Relational Governance Function as Substitutes or Complements?' (2002) 23 *Strategic Management Journal* 707.

franchisees and depriving them of the capacity to manage risk through contract. Prospective franchisees characteristically lack experience with this business form and are often unaware of this increased risk.

This chapter outlines the effects on the franchise relationship of this interaction with a focus on the non-drafting party to such contracts, which in the case of franchising, is the franchisee.

Through its analysis of the interaction of the standard form and relational qualities of the franchise contract, this chapter suggests the importance of the interaction of these qualities should be recognized at all the layers of governance discussed in Chapter 1, including market and contract, as well as court interpretation and government intervention.

## THE STANDARD FORM QUALITIES OF THE FRANCHISE CONTRACT

Standard-form contracts are prevalent across many species of contracting relationships, including contracts for airline tickets, computer software, mobile phones, insurance contracts and a range of financial agreements. In 1971, W. David Slawson estimated that, 'Standard-form contracts probably account for more than ninety-nine percent of all the contracts now made.'[5]

The standard form:

> is not individually negotiated by the parties but is instead drafted by one party who uses a contract containing the same terms for all transactions of that type. The drafting party may be in the superior bargaining position and may offer the contract on a take-it-or-leave-it basis. . . . the party in the inferior bargaining position who wishes to contract must adhere to what is demanded by the party in the superior position, there being no room to negotiate.[6]

The essential defining elements of such contracts are the lack of negotiation of terms and unequal bargaining power, or 'The ability to get a large share

---

[5] John A. Burke, 'Reinventing Contract' (2003) 10(2) Murdoch University Electronic Journal of Law [22] <http://www.murdoch.edu.au/elaw/issues/v10n2/burke102.html> at 16 December 2009; see also D. Slawson, 'Standard-form Contracts and Democratic Control of Law Making Power' (1971) 84 *Harvard Law Review* 529.

[6] Nygh and Butt (eds), *Butterworth's Australian Legal Dictionary* (1997). Note that the distinction between standard form and adhesion contracts is not clear; many writers and legal resources use the terms interchangeably. This article will use the term 'standard form' because of the negative connotations of the term 'contract of adhesion'. See F. Kessler, 'Contracts of Adhesion – Some Thoughts about Freedom of Contract' (1943) 43 *Columbia Law Review* 629.

of the possible joint benefits to be derived from any agreement.'[7] Generally in business-format franchising, power asymmetry and lack of negotiation are inherent in the franchise relationship due to the need for uniformity. The imbalance of power in the relationship from the outset, combined with the fact that franchise contracts are non negotiable, means that most franchise contracts do satisfy the elements of the standard-form contract.

**Imbalance of Power**

The standard-form contract is typically entered into between unequal bargaining partners.[8] The weaker party to the contract has little voice in setting its terms.[9] In the franchising context, the main factor in the bargaining position equation is the need for franchisor control in the interests of brand maintenance, system administration, and the containment of transaction costs and negative externalities. Uniformity is the main reason why franchisors do not negotiate contracts with franchisees and is also the justification for the concentration of control in the hands of a franchisor.

Factors that contribute to the imbalance include an inequality of economic resources, business sophistication and the 'size' of the parties. As prospective franchisees are often new to franchising, if not to business ownership altogether, franchisee inexperience contributes to a franchisee's relative lack of power throughout the relationship.[10] Monopoly power and a franchisee's consumer status, often characterized by individualism, optimism and naïveté, also contribute to the disparity in the franchise relationship. A franchisee is relying largely on perceptions created by the assiduous marketing efforts of franchisors and on the 'trust us' aspect of the relationship that franchisors require for the sake of control and uniformity. A franchisee's role is to agree in advance to go along. The contract terms are written to add up to this and there is sometimes a collective agreement

---

[7] J. Black, *A Dictionary of Economics* (2002).

[8] Nygh and Butt (eds), *Butterworth's Concise Legal Dictionary* (3rd ed, 2004), 406.

[9] *Cubic Corp. v. Marty* 229 2d 828 (Cal. App., 1986); *Standard Oil Co. of California v. Perkins* 396 F 2d 809 (9th Cir., 1969).

[10] A successful, experienced businessperson is not the prototypical purchaser of a franchisor's product, which is all about the 'tried and tested system' and being 'in business for yourself, but not by yourself'. A 2004 survey showed that only one in five franchisees in Australia make over $100,000 per year: Deloitte Touche Tohmatsu, 'Franchisee Satisfaction Survey Benchmark 2004' (2004) Deloitte <http://www.deloitte.com/dtt/cda/doc/content/franchise_survey_lo-res.pdf> at 16 December 2009.

clause in the contract that explicitly states that a franchisee will abide by collective decisions or decisions made by the franchisor.

Disparities in legal representation may also contribute to the imbalance. Lawyers representing sellers shift risks in contract to buyers.[11] Franchisor's solicitors may include terms they know or suspect to be unenforceable because a franchisee is likely to believe that they are enforceable or because such clauses may be useful to a franchisor in conflict management.[12] Risk to a franchisor is minimal due to the low probability that the issue will lead to litigation. A busy franchisor may not even be aware of the problem or it may be that he or she leaves these concerns to a solicitor. The contract comes to represent not so much a franchisor's business judgment and experience, but rather a franchisor's solicitor's skill and zeal in shifting risk to a franchisee. The potential result is that the contract is no longer an instrument of the true intentions of either the franchisor or franchisee. Franchisees, generally, need thorough legal advice because they are inexperienced in owning and operating a business, but often franchisees do not obtain such advice. Furthermore, franchisees may not fully utilize legal advice as this is often a time when they do not want to hear about 'the downside'. Many franchisees are unaware of the need for quality advice, and others are unable to secure the quality of advice they need. In contrast to franchisors, for whom many deals riding on the drafting of one contract make paying top dollar for legal advice a necessity, franchisees often feel that legal advice is an unjustifiable expense.

Even if a franchisee does understand, as a franchisor does, that the terms of the contract are crucial to the power in the relationship, a franchisee may lack sufficient resources to engage a solicitor with relevant experience or a solicitor that does not have a conflict of interest.

Where a franchisee is perspicacious and financially capable of hiring the best legal advice, the experienced and zealous solicitor acting for a franchisee may still have difficulty negotiating due to the importance of uniformity across the system and its contracts. Even the most prudent franchisee might fail to see the reason to allocate resources to negotiation of a contract that is not negotiable.

While it is sometimes true that a franchisee can be more profitable and influential than its franchisor, such situations are less common, occurring

---

11 John A. Burke, 'Reinventing Contract' (2003) 10(2) Murdoch University Electronic Journal of Law [51] <http://www.murdoch.edu.au/elaw/issues/v10n2/burke102.html> at 16 December 2009.

12 John A. Burke, 'Reinventing Contract' (2003) 10(2) Murdoch University Electronic Journal of Law [51] <http://www.murdoch.edu.au/elaw/issues/v10n2/burke102.html> at 16 December 2009.

most frequently in cases of multi-unit franchisees. Many franchisors prefer the perceived advantage of keeping franchisees in a subordinate position, not only at the time of negotiation of the contract but throughout the stages of the relationship, to maintain uniformity and control, system standards and to limit transaction costs.

## No Negotiation

It is widely accepted within the sector that franchise contracts are not negotiated. Some minor adjustments may be countenanced, but in general the contract is part of the product that a franchisee can choose to purchase or not; it cannot be customized or 'tailor-made' for each and every franchisee. Gillian Hadfield observed:

> [There is] a clear ethic of non-negotiation, not merely to boost the bargaining power of a franchisor, but also to define what, fundamentally, it is that the franchisee is purchasing. In other words, franchisors use the standard-form contract to signal aspects of the relationship that the franchisee can expect . . . The clear message is that the refusal of a franchisor to negotiate – the superior position of a franchisor – is a hallmark of the relationship that the franchisee is purchasing.[13]

As with the imbalance of power, franchisee inexperience, franchisee psychology and disparities in legal representation help explain the lack of negotiation of the franchise contract. In addition, the timing of the presentation of the contract also affects a franchisee's negotiating position. Franchise contracts are confidential, often only provided to prospective franchisees at a relatively late stage in the negotiation process. A franchisee is asked to sign the contract at a time when entrepreneurial individualism and optimism are near their peak, not a time when a prospective franchisee is interested in collective action or the need for caution.[14] A franchisee who thinks the deal is almost done may be afraid to 'make waves' and avoid bargaining with a franchisor to avoid a perception of mistrust against the franchisor or being the 'wrong kind' of franchisee, one who does not expect to be successful.[15]

---

[13] G. Hadfield, 'Problematic Relations: Franchising and the Law of Incomplete Contracts' (1990) 42 *Stanford Law Review* 927, 961.

[14] These psychological conditions are discussed in S.K. Ripken, 'The Dangers and Drawbacks of the Disclosure Antidote: Toward a More Substantive Approach to Securities Regulation' (2006) 58 *Baylor Law Review* 139.

[15] G. Dent, 'Lawyers and Trust in Business Alliances' (2002) 58 *Business Lawyer* 45.

## How the Standard Form Impacts the Franchisor/Franchisee Relationship

Standard terms offer consistency and a degree of anonymity. Standard form contracts are credited with helping to 'democratize the marketplace' because they afford access to market interactions for participants who might otherwise be excluded.[16] The appeal of standard form contracts for franchisor's lies in their potential to reduce transaction costs by eliminating the cost of, and time associated with, drafting new contracts for similar transactions; reducing the cost of contract negotiations; containing a franchisor's administrative costs throughout the course of the performance of an agreement, and ensuring uniformity in a franchisor's ongoing dealings with every franchisee.

Despite its benefits, however, the standard form nature of a franchise contract raises concerns about fairness. In its 2008 report, the Productivity Commission in Australia found that 'Unfair terms appear to be commonplace in standard-form contracts,'[17] and that:

> terms of the kind described as unfair . . . are common in many contracts across many industries . . . their existence is widespread globally where regulatory mechanisms do not discourage this. . . . In Europe, prior to the introduction of measures against them, market studies revealed the ubiquity of unfair terms in standard-form contracts.[18]

The first implication of the prevalence of standard form contracts is the loss of bargained-for-exchange. Standard-form contracts are enforceable, but to the extent that the standard form deprives the contract of information exchange and consent, there may be no 'meeting of the minds'. 'Bargained-for-exchange' becomes largely irrelevant and consent, once considered an essential element of a valid contract, is lost.

Deprived of the many benefits of negotiation and consent, the contract becomes less reliable as an accurate reflection of the intentions of both parties. The standard-form contract becomes a vehicle for the exploitation

---

[16] John A. Burke, 'Reinventing Contract' (2003) 10(2) Murdoch University Electronic Journal of Law [46] <http://www.murdoch.edu.au/elaw/issues/v10n2/burke102.html> at 16 December 2009.

[17] Australian Government Productivity Commission, Commonwealth, Review of Australia's Consumer Policy Framework: Productivity Commission Inquiry Report No.45 (30 April 2008), 430 <http://www.pc.gov.au/__data/assets/pdf_file/0008/79172/consumer2.pdf> at 16 December 2009.

[18] Australian Government Productivity Commission, Commonwealth, 'Review of Australia's Consumer Policy Framework: Productivity Commission Inquiry Report No.45' (30 April 2008), 430 <http://www.pc.gov.au/_data/assets/pdf_file/0008/79172/consumer2.pdf> at 16 December 2009.

of unequal power relations and may encourage the imposition of unjust or inefficient terms. Ultimately, these conditions can negatively impact the parties' willingness to perform under the relevant contract.[19]

In the absence of bargained-for-exchange and negotiation, contract loses its function as a process. The contract becomes part of the product the franchisor is selling. Though formal rules of interpretation are applicable in the context of standard form contracts, formal rules for determining validity such as offer, acceptance and consideration are less relevant because the contract has become a product rather than a process. Some even suggest that there may be insufficient 'meeting of the minds' and effectively no valid consent, so that some standard-form contracts may not qualify as contracts at all.[20]

The standard form 'commodifies' the contract such that a franchisee's role is analogous to that of a consumer with a need for consumer protections. The commodification of the contract and a franchisee's role as a consumer raises problems with interpretation and regulation. Courts and regulators treat commercial transactions, such as the franchise contract, as business relations between equals. This presents a problem because there are significant inconsistencies in the standards and criteria employed by the courts in their approaches to the inequality of bargaining power in such relationships.[21] While traditionally courts have treated commercial agreements with a presumption of equal bargaining power, this is not always appropriate, particularly in the franchise sector. In the franchise context, for example, the assumption is not a legitimate one because of the consumer attributes of these contracts and the 'gross bargaining disparity' between the parties.[22] Though the role of a franchisee is analogous to that

---

[19] 'As a distinct legal concept, the doctrine of inequality of bargaining power is a relatively recent invention. Its provenance lies in the late 19th Century social and economic reactions to the perceived abuses of laissez-faire economic regulation . . . In the 1940s and 1950s, bargaining power became entrenched in contract law, particularly after adoption of Uniform Commercial Code (U.C.C.) 2-302 which expressly authorized courts to assess the parties' bargaining power under the rubric of unconscionability.' D.D. Barnhizer, 'Inequality of Bargaining Power' (2005) 76 *University of Colorado Law Review* 139, 194–5.

[20] Burke asserts that the standard-form contract is not so much a means of governance as a commodity. See John A. Burke, 'Reinventing Contract' (2003) 10(2) Murdoch University Electronic Journal of Law [51] <http://www.murdoch.edu.au/elaw/issues/v10n2/burke102.html> at 16 December 2009.

[21] D.D. Barnhizer, 'Inequality of Bargaining Power' (2005) 76 *University of Colorado Law Review* 139, 197.

[22] J.V. Jordan and J.B. Gitterman, 'Franchise Agreements: Contract of Adhesion?' (1996) 16 *Franchise Law Journal* 1, 16.

of a consumer, the regulatory approach is geared more toward a business and investor relationship to which minimal, if any, consumer protection is applied.

Collins has argued that the standard form need not cause problems where a contract is highly reflexive.[23] While he acknowledges that reflexivity caters solely to the needs of drafters, he claims that the qualities of the standard form are counter-balanced by markets for terms and fair dispute resolution procedures, unfair contracts legislation and democratic self-regulation within market sectors.[24] However, the factors Collins suggests save the standard form from the dangers of abuse are, generally, absent in the franchise context.[25] Collins' sanguine view of the use of the standard form in franchising also fails to acknowledge the effects of the standard form combined with relational contract characteristics.

## THE RELATIONAL QUALITIES OF THE FRANCHISE CONTRACT

Classical contract theory emphasizes the freedom of parties to contract, underscoring societal values of individualism and self-determination. There is, however, a body of research on the inadequacy of classical contract theory to address commercial relationships of extended duration.[26] Such extended contractual relationships can be labelled relational, incomplete or long-term contracts.

'Two features largely define what lawyers mean by a relational contract: incompleteness and longevity.'[27] The longer the term of the contract, the harder it becomes to predict all the conditions, preferences and requirements of the parties. Contracts are incomplete when they fail to outline all the possible situations in the course of dealings of the parties, thus creating gaps where the parties' obligations are not specified.

---

23 Collins, 'Regulating Contract' in C. Parker, C. Scott, N. Lacey and J. Braithwaite (eds), *Regulating Law* (2004) xxxv.

24 Collins, 'Regulating Contract' in C. Parker, C. Scott, N. Lacey and J. Braithwaite (eds), *Regulating Law* (2004) xxxv.

25 Collins, *Regulating Contracts* (1999) 244.

26 See, eg, E. Schanze, 'Symbiotic Contracts: Exploring Long-Term Agency Structures between Contract and Corporation' in C. Joerges (ed), *Franchising and the Law: Theoretical and Comparative Approaches in Europe and the United States* (1991) 67, 78–90.

27 A. Schwartz, 'Relational Contracts in the Courts: An Analysis of Incomplete Agreements and Judicial Strategies' (1992) 21 *Journal of Legal Studies* 271.

> A contract is relational to the extent that the parties are incapable of reducing important terms of the arrangement to well-defined obligations. Such definitive obligations may be impractical because of inability to identify uncertain future conditions or because of inability to characterize complex adaptations adequately even when the contingencies themselves can be identified in advance.[28]

As a practical matter, the use of the relational contract, like that of the standard form, is motivated largely by transaction costs. The information costs of contracting can be divided into *ex ante* transaction costs that include the costs of anticipating future contingencies and writing a contract that specifies outcomes and *ex post* enforcement costs that include the costs of monitoring and enforcement. In seeking to avoid both *ex ante* and *ex post* contracting costs, contracting parties write incomplete contracts.[29] Such contracts reduce transaction costs because they provide an efficient strategy for contracting parties to accommodate the relational conditions of incompleteness and longevity. Relational contracts economize on the *ex ante* negotiation of terms and permit the parties to determine the contours of the agreement incrementally over time.[30]

As relational contracts are defined by features of incompleteness and longevity,[31] it is impossible to specify terms for unforeseen future contingencies in relational contracts at the time the parties enter the contract. Parties do not know what conditions will be in five or ten years and, even if they did, they may not know how they would respond to them. Relational contracts therefore must be flexible, sometimes to the point of being vague. One or both parties must sacrifice efficiency and certainty for the unpredictable exigencies of the longer-term relationship.[32]

There is often a high level of discretion accorded to the parties, so that such contracts rely heavily on reciprocity and trust that develops over time between the contracting parties.[33] Relational contracts are designed

---

[28] C.J. Goetz and R.E. Scott, 'Principles of Relational Contracts' (1981) 67 *Virginia Law Review* 1091.

[29] R.E. Scott and G.G. Triantis, 'Incomplete Contracts and the Theory of Contract Design' (Working Paper No 23, University of Virginia, 2005).

[30] For more on the calculus of *ex ante* versus *ex post* contracting costs see I. Ayres and R. Gertnert, 'Strategic Contractual Inefficiency and the Optimal Choice of Legal Rules' (1992) 101 *Yale Law Journal* 729.

[31] Ronaldo Porto Macedo Júnior, 'Relational Contracts in Brazilian Law' (1997) Latin American Studies Association <http://bibliotecavirtual.clacso.org.ar/ar/libros/lasa97/portomacedopor.pdf> at 16 December 2009.

[32] C.J. Goetz and R.E. Scott, 'Principles of Relational Contracts' (1981) 67 Virginia Law Review 1089, 1091.

[33] I. Macneil, 'Contracts: Adjustment of Long-Term Economic Relations under the Classical, Neo-classical, and Relational Contract Law' (1978) 72(6)

to allow the parties latitude to maintain a dynamic balance between their shifting interests:

> The terms of exchange are open and substantive clauses are replaced by . . . clauses to regulate the continuous negotiation process, determined both by promissory relations and non-promissory links . . . such as status (e.g. weaker party protection), trust and economic dependence. [34]

The relational contract therefore 'assumes processual scope . . . [it] includes terms which establish . . . processes by which change and adjustment will be specified in the course of contractual performance or fulfillment'.[35]

The role of the relational contract is not to precisely define the rights and obligations of the parties, but to provide the framework, procedures and the points of departure for fair contract negotiation and adjustment over time. The fundamental nature of relational contracts is inconsistent with the standard form because, unlike the strict formality required by the standard form, relational contracts support 'the primacy not of the narrow contract provisions but of the wider franchise relationship'.[36]

In a discrete contract the subject matter of the contract is relatively independent of the parties' relationship. While discrete contracts are 'one-shot deals',[37] where each contract is an isolated, independent and autonomous act,[38] relational contracts create continuous and long-term relationships. Discrete contracts are impersonal and instrumentally-oriented, whereas relational contracts 'involve complex relations . . . in which . . . solidarity, trust, and cooperation relations are determinants'.[39]

Applying these characteristics outlined in the literature, franchise

---

*Northwestern University Law Review* 854. Such contracts in franchising are described in W. Dixon, 'What is the Content of the Common Law Obligation of Good Faith in Commercial Franchises?' (2005) 33(3) *ABLR* 207.

34 Ronaldo Porto Macedo Júnior, 'Relational Contracts in Brazilian Law' (1997) Latin American Studies Association <http://bibliotecavirtual.clacso.org.ar/ar/libros/lasa97/portomacedopor.pdf> at 16 December 2009.

35 Ibid.

36 A. Terry, 'Franchising, Relational Contracts and the Vibe' (2005) 33(4) *ABLR* 289.

37 W. Dixon, 'What is the Content of the Common Law Obligation of Good Faith in Commercial Franchises?' (2005) 33(3) *ABLR* 207.

38 Eisenberg, 'Relational Contracts' in J. Beatson and D. Friedmann (eds), *Good Faith and Fault in Contract Law* (1995) 291. See also Ronaldo Porto Macedo Júnior, 'Relational Contracts in Brazilian Law' (1997) Latin American Studies Association <http://bibliotecavirtual.clacso.org.ar/ar/libros/lasa97/portomacedopor.pdf> at 16 December 2009.

39 Ronaldo Porto Macedo Júnior, 'Relational Contracts in Brazilian Law'

contracts are relational. Yet, while it is a concept that has been accepted for many years in the academic community,[40] courts have not rushed to embrace the concept.[41] Perhaps this is because '[w]hile the categorisation of franchising as a relational contract seems straightforward, the legal consequences that follow . . . are highly controversial'.[42]

Because relational contracts accommodate uncertainty by leaving terms unspecified and providing high levels of discretion, these documents often fail to provide clear and specific answers in case of dispute. Relational contract theory holds that every transaction is embedded in complex relations, and that contextual analysis produces a more complete and accurate analytical product.[43] Such a prescription, however, may be little comfort to a judge seeking to arrive at such an 'analytical product'.[44] In deciding whether to enforce the contract, and in what ways to fill gaps with default obligations, courts may be reluctant to embrace a theory of interpretation that highlights the importance of the context of the relationship when the context can be challenging to discern, especially in the case of franchising where there are significant difficulties in obtaining reliable information.[45]

---

(1997) Latin American Studies Association <http://bibliotecavirtual.clacso.org.ar/ar/libros/lasa97/portomacedopor.pdf> at 16 December 2009.

[40] See G. Hadfield, 'Problematic Relations: Franchising and the Law of Incomplete Contracts' (1990) 42 *Stanford Law Review* 927. Professor Hadfield wrote that the franchise contract is incomplete because of the 'uncertain and long-term nature of the relationship' and because it 'fails to address a franchisee's problem of controlling franchisor opportunism'.

[41] A. Terry, 'Franchising, Relational Contracts and the Vibe' (2005) 33(4) *ABLR* 289 citing the New Zealand High Court's expression in *Dymocks Franchise Systems (NSW) Pty Ltd v. Bilgola Enterprises Ltd* (1999) 8 *TCLR* 612, 652.

[42] A. Terry, 'Franchising, Relational Contracts and the Vibe' (2005) 33(4) *ABLR* 289.

[43] F.G. Snyder, 'Relational Contracting in a Digital Age' (2005) 11(2) *Texas Wesleyan Law Review* 675–6; The Common Law of Contracts as a World Force in Two Ages of Revolution (Panel discussion at the Central Gloucester Initiative, Gloucester, England, 7–8 June 2004).

[44] The solution Hadfield proposed was that courts should imply a term of good faith in franchise contracts. G. Hadfield, 'Problematic Relations: Franchising and the Law of Incomplete Contracts' (1990) 42 *Stanford Law Review* 927.

[45] See Eisenberg, 'Relational Contracts' in J. Beatson and D. Friedmann (eds), *Good Faith and Fault in Contract Law* (1995) 291; Morten Hviid, 'Long-Term Contracts and Relational Contracts' in Boudewijn Bouckaert and Gerrit De Geest (eds), *Encyclopedia of Law and Economics, Volume III. The Regulation of Contracts* (2000) [631]; Scott and Triantis, 'Incomplete Contracts and the Theory of Contract Design' (Working Paper No 23, University of Virginia, 2005).

## Relational and Standard-form Contracts are Inconsistent and Therefore Deprive the Contract of its Intended Meaning

Relational contracting stresses shared values and interests and 'possesses a necessarily moral character . . . [rendering it] closer to the ideal partnership contract than to the classical sale and purchase contract'.[46] The standard form, however, brings it closer to the latter where the contract becomes commodified as product rather than process. Relational aspects, such as trust and cooperation upon which the franchisee depends, risk being vitiated by the uniform formalities of the standard form. The 'contract as commodity' of the standard form as opposed to 'contract as relationship' of the relational quality of the franchise contract creates conflict where the standard form prevails. Rather than an equal party to negotiation of terms, a franchisee as non-drafting party takes on qualities and vulnerabilities of a consumer, but without consumer-protections.[47] Representation of the franchisee as a consumer (of the franchise product, the intellectual property, the system, the brand) in regulatory process is therefore a critical aspect of establishing fair conditions in the sector.

## Standard Form and Relational Contracts Synergistically Erode Bargained-for-exchange

Independently of each other, both the standard form and the relational qualities of the contract erode the element of bargained-for-exchange. The standard form is characterized by an imbalance of power and lack of negotiation of contract; there is no 'promise for a promise', and parties may thus be deprived of a complete understanding of contractual terms. The lack of a negotiated process for arriving at agreed terms makes the standard form susceptible to the imposition of onerous terms that a franchisee might not fully understand or to which it does not genuinely consent. 'The result is that franchisees are constantly in peril of non-compliance.'[48]

---

[46] Ronaldo Porto Macedo Júnior, 'Relational Contracts in Brazilian Law' (1997) Latin American Studies Association <http://bibliotecavirtual.clacso.org.ar/ar/libros/lasa97/portomacedopor.pdf> at 16 December 2009.

[47] John A. Burke, 'Reinventing Contract' (2003) 10(2) Murdoch University Electronic Journal of Law [51] <http://www.murdoch.edu.au/elaw/issues/v10n2/burke102.html> at 16 December 2009.

[48] *E.S. Bills Inc v Tzucanow* 780 F.2d 1028 (9th Cir., 1995) per California Supreme Court Justice Stanley Mosk cited in James V. Jordan and Judith B. Gitterman, 'Franchise Agreements: Contract of Adhesion?' (1996) 16 *Franchise Law Journal* 1, 41.

The relational contract is about accommodating uncertainty by building in flexibility, reliance upon trust and contextual interpretation. Relational contracts further erode the bargained-for-exchange because parties must leave the terms of the contract unspecified to accommodate uncertainty. Where the relational contract is also a standard-form contract, where a franchisor drafts the contract but does not negotiate, flexibility is given not reciprocally, but to one party, a franchisor.

The result is that the standard form and relational characteristics of the contract synergistically deprive the franchise contract of the essential element of bargained-for-exchange. The interaction of the two qualities means that a franchisor can take on greater risk and manage risk more effectively through drafting and contractual risk-shifting, while a franchisee is not similarly able to manage risk through contract. The franchise contract, as it is both standard form and relational, accords the weight of its flexibility and discretion to a franchisor. A franchisee is faced with the choice to unqualifiedly accept the risk assigned to it by a franchisor's contract or to decline to enter the relationship altogether.

The loss of bargained-for-exchange that results from its standard form and relational qualities thus erodes the meaning of the contract for a franchisee and can reduce its commitment to perform, often under conditions that are likely to test that commitment. Trust is undermined, the need for franchisor monitoring increases, and the efficiency of the system is compromised.

### Standard Form and Relational Contracts call for Conflicting Interpretation by Courts and Regulators

The interaction of the standard form and relational contract characteristics creates conflict between an emphasis on formation as opposed to an emphasis on the performance of the contract. The contractual balance in relational contracting must be understood as it develops over the entire course of performance. 'The very concept of balance . . . is no longer defined '*a priori*', but rather '*a posteriori*'.'[49]

Regulation of the sector tends to rely on regulatory tools directed toward contract formation, such as disclosure, with little attention given to the relational aspects of the contractual arrangement and problems that arise during the course of performance. Of the 30 countries that

---

[49] Ronaldo Porto Macedo Júnior, 'Relational Contracts in Brazilian Law' (1997) Latin American Studies Association <http://bibliotecavirtual.clacso.org.ar/ar/libros/lasa97/portomacedopor.pdf> at 16 December 2009.

have franchise-specific regulation, that regulation is directed primarily at contract formation and relies heavily on disclosure.

Similarly, when courts interpret franchise contracts, formal interpretation required by the standard form conflicts with contextual interpretation appropriate to a relational contract. The formal interpretation for the standard form seems to prevail; formal rules and express contract terms, which a franchisee often does not understand because it did not draft or negotiate those terms, trump contextual interpretation.

This incompatibility of modes of interpretation of standard form and relational contracts by courts and regulators further deprives the contract of the essential element of bargained-for-exchange because it diminishes fundamental precepts of contract law such as consent and intention. Franchisors understand how courts and regulators interpret and regulate these arrangements; franchisees less so. The 'freedom of contract' that courts go to such lengths to protect is, in the context of franchising, largely a myth.

### Standard Form and Relational Contracts Result in Greater Discretion to a Franchisor and Increased Uncertainty and Risk to a Franchisee

Where a contract is both in a standard form and is relational, power and certainty are linked; and that link is *discretion*. Discretion is 'the power or right to decide or act according to one's own judgment; freedom of judgment or choice'.[50] A franchisor's discretion to act equates to a 'right of action'.[51]

The justification for discretion to a franchisor in franchise contracts is that it enables a franchisor to ensure uniformity and brand maintenance as well as the ability to change the system in order to take advantage of changes or opportunities in the marketplace. The disadvantage is that the party that concedes the discretion, a franchisee, bears the uncertainty and, with it, increased risk.

The interaction of the relational and standard form qualities of contract means that a franchisor is able to dictate and strictly control the terms, which involve high levels of franchisor discretion due in part to a franchisor's legitimate need for flexibility and discretion in operating the system. A franchisee grants discretion for a variety of reasons, not least because of the standard form aspect of the contracting process.

---

50 *Random House Unabridged Dictionary* (2006).

51 William L. Killion, 'Putting Critical Decision-Making Where It Belongs: Scouring the Franchise Agreement for the "D" Word' (2005) 24 *Franchise Law Journal* 228.

Standards for the exercise of a franchisor's discretion (for example in franchisor training, support or promotional activities) are rare in franchise contracts. Franchisor obligations are typically open-ended and written in permissive terms. Examples of the language used include, 'the Franchisor may grant other Franchises' and 'Franchisor may provide merchandising, marketing and advertising research data and advice'. Because of the uncertainty in the relationship over time, when they do occur, performance standards are generally not specific and rather rely on standards of reasonableness. Franchisee obligations, on the other hand, are typically subject to strict standards, schedules and minimum performance criteria, which may be set or changed at the sole discretion of a franchisor. If a franchisee fails to meet its obligations, a franchisor can often terminate for breach of contract.

As neither a franchisee nor a franchisor can predict future circumstances, a franchisee has to trust its franchisor and hope that a franchisor will act in a franchisee's best interests. A franchisor's discretion should, and often does, accrue to the benefit of all parties to the relationship. However, a franchisor can exercise its discretion to benefit itself solely or at the expense of a franchisee, and so in some instances the reduction of a franchisor's risk is mirrored by an increase in risk to a franchisee. A franchisor's ability to accord high levels of discretion to itself and high risk to a franchisee through the standard form means that the contract facilitates franchisor opportunism.

One way to address the problem is to contractually provide for reciprocal flexibility and discretion. Goddard observed that a relational contract may be more effective where the contract contains reciprocal commitments to help develop trust.[52] Symmetry in discretion permits the parties to balance threats of opportunism and free-riding on each side.[53] Symmetry in discretion, however, is not a common feature of franchise contracts primarily because, while a franchisor requires discretion to ensure it can maintain uniformity and protect the brand, a franchisee cannot make a similar claim.

The balance lies in preserving a franchisor's legitimate rights to modify and improve the system and a franchisee's expectations that any changes imposed by a franchisor will benefit the franchisee and the system as a whole. Franchisors, however, cannot be expected to place the interests

---

52 Goddard, 'Long-Term Contracts: A Law and Economics Perspective' [1997] *New Zealand Law Review* 423.

53 See Collins, 'Discretionary Powers in Contracts' in D. Campbell, H. Collins and J. Wightman (eds), *Implicit Dimensions of Contract: Discrete, Relational and Network Contracts* (2003) 226–31.

of one franchisee over and above the needs of the system or franchise network. A franchisor has a duty to the franchise system to establish effective means of control to protect the brand. There will be instances where individual franchisees will be disadvantaged in the process of refinements toward a better system, and evidence suggests that franchisors do tend to address these particular circumstances, often in the form of compensation or preferential treatment for a period of time. Many franchisors appear to utilize their discretionary powers for change with due regard for the consequences for the franchisees, particularly when improving the franchise system. Nonetheless, there will also be some franchisors who will be tempted to misuse their power and/or who seek to exploit their power advantage to the fullest.

It is at this level that the often-used analogy of comparing a marriage to a franchise is most apt:

> If one partner holds a consensual authority over the other, then that partner has an obligation to consider every decision in light of the highest and best good of the 'weaker' partner.

The analogy helps understand why franchisees have deep feelings of anger and betrayal when they perceive that a franchisor has misused its discretionary powers; it is perceived as a repudiation of a relationship of trust, not 'just business'. In a relational contract the subject matter of the contract is the relationship. One party taking unfair advantage in the negotiation or performance of the contract has the potential to undermine the relationship. While the opportunistic party may believe it is making a better deal for itself, it may also sacrifice reciprocity and erode trust.

Education to help franchisors understand the importance of trust in the relationship might help to curb opportunism. Franchisees need to better protect themselves before entering into the franchise through pre-investment education and external advice. Franchisees' needs for protection at the time of contracting are meant to be addressed in part by disclosure and other pre-contractual regulatory measures. As this book examines these regulatory tools, however, it demonstrates that they are often unlikely to function as effectively as intended.

One point worth noting here is that many of the issues that arise during the actual operation of the franchise unit are typically not covered in the franchise agreement. The franchise agreement is a legal document that sets the platform for the formal relationship between the parties. Operational issues are commonly found in supplementary documentation, such as 'operations manuals'. It would be unusual for a prospective franchisee to be allowed access to such sensitive and confidential operational information during any pre-investment investigations. Consequently, it is difficult for a financial adviser to independently assess the strengths or weaknesses of the business model unless he or she has prior experience with that particular system. The non-provision of operational documentation also makes it impossible to fully understand the implications of the franchise contract. At best, an adviser can identify the areas of potential power imbalance rather than *actual* requirements that might influence the purchase decision.

Pre-investment risks that a franchisee must make efforts to discover include extraordinary rebates to a franchisor from a supplier; a franchisor's inadequate investment in brand; inadequate franchisor support, training or technical assistance, including advice on site suitability (which is often a conflict because a franchisor wants visibility, while a franchisee wants access); franchisor misrepresentation of financial data, including misleading silence; and the risks of encroachment on physical territory or through the Internet. It may be because franchisees do not foresee these risks that they do not protect themselves. A franchisee's only real pre-investment protection is the ability to walk away from the deal. Prospective franchisees rarely have the ability to shift risk to a franchisor as part of the contract.

Risks for a franchisor include franchisee free-riding (lack of incentives due to high externalities), franchisee appropriation of intellectual property, monitoring issues and difficulties of exercising control over the franchisee,[54] inaccurate reporting, and exposure to liability for franchisee actions. A franchisor can plan for these risks and can reduce its exposure through contractual provisions such as performance standards, reporting requirements, constraints on the use of intellectual property, and clauses that shift liability to franchisees.

Franchisees need to understand from the outset that a franchisor uses the contract form and its terms to protect the brand, but also to protect itself against the risks of conflict and/or failure in the relationship. While franchisees are often unable to adequately identify or assess their risks, a franchisor is better positioned to do so, and is able to shift risk to franchisees. A franchisee is therefore more vulnerable not only to external risks inherent in business, but also to franchisor discretion under the contract.

**Contract terms**

If contracts do represent a meeting of minds, it is a meeting that reflects a balancing of competing interests, an exercise in compromise between

---

[54] For how higher monitoring costs equate to lower franchisee service levels, see D. Agrawal and R. Lal, 'Contractual Arrangements in Franchising: An Empirical Investigation' (1995) 32(2) *Journal of Marketing Research* 213.

franchisor and franchisee. The following sections give an overview of how franchise contracts are drafted to address competing interests. The sections describe contract clauses dealing with scope of grant; brand maintenance; training and support; minimum performance and reporting requirements; supply; unilateral amendment and collective agreement clauses; and clauses governing exit from the franchise relationship such as duration and right of renewal; transfer by franchisee; termination by franchisor; and post-termination and post-contractual restraints of trade. These sections are based primarily on information obtained from a survey of Australian contracts conducted from 2004 to 2005. While an effort has been made to survey experience in other jurisdictions, most of the examples are based on Australian contracts.

## Scope of Grant/Encroachment

The scope of grant clause defines the scope of the licence a franchisor grants to a franchisee to use intellectual property rights and sets the limits on that use.[55] This term, like all contract terms, reflects the contractual balance struck between the competing interests of the parties, a balance where a franchisor's interests often prevail. A franchisee wants to maximize the extent of the rights it is buying from a franchisor. It generally prefers an exclusive right to use the system intellectual property as extensively as possible in order to ensure that it will benefit from efforts to develop its business and that its investment is secure from franchisor encroachment.[56] A franchisor, on the other hand, wants to protect its flexibility and options to expand and develop the system and brand awareness to the fullest extent possible.

Encroachment is a common concern for franchisees because their rights are limited. Both franchisors and franchisees make major investments in the development of the system and of franchised units.[57] These investments

---

[55] For a general overview of grants clauses in intellectual property see Donald M. Cameron, 'The Grant Clause' (1997) JurisDiction <http://www.jurisdiction.com/grant.htm> at 19 December 2009.

[56] Encroachment is defined as 'the act of entering gradually or stealthily into the possessions or rights of another'. 'Merriam-Webster's Dictionary of Law', Dictionary.com <http://dictionary.reference.com/browse/encroach> at 19 December 2009.

[57] The size of the investment is not always indicative of the risk a franchisee might experience. See, for example, Personalised Chocolates 4U franchisor misled and deceived franchisees: Federal Court (Press Release, 2 December 2009) <http://www.accc.gov.au/content/index.phtml/itemId/904336?pageDefinitionItemId=16940> at 19 December 2009.

can be vulnerable. A franchisee may not understand that there is a contractual clause that ensures a franchisor's rights to use the intellectual property and to sell more units, sometimes to a franchisee's cost.

Typically, franchise contracts provide for a non-exclusive grant to a franchisee and/or to explicitly reserve a franchisor's rights to sell in other channels, in order to allow a franchisor to respond to market conditions.

Encroachment can take a variety of forms, such as franchisor development of alternative distribution channels and acquisition of a competing brand, which includes sharing information with franchisees from the other brand.[58] 'Virtual encroachment' can occur when a franchisor offers goods or services from outside a franchisee's area into his market through the use of the Internet.[59]

Franchisors who move into Internet or other e-commerce activities often struggle to strike the right balance with existing franchisees occupying a fixed location especially when it comes to the referral of enquiries from within the franchisee's territory. Similarly, franchisors might find it difficult to effectively control franchisees' use of web pages or e-commerce sites, and a lack of awareness of trade practices law on the part of franchisees can lead to price-fixing violations.

Perhaps the most common form of encroachment involves a franchisor placing a competing unit close to an existing unit. Franchisors may refuse to grant exclusive territories, recognizing the need for flexibility in responding to market conditions. As franchise agreements commonly last for 5 years or more, there will often be significant changes to the marketplace that limit the attractiveness of a fixed and exclusive territory over such a time frame, particularly in urban areas.

Where franchisors do grant exclusive territories to franchisees, the contract provision often covers only the unit premises. Contracts typically provide very limited, if any, restraints on a franchisor's use or further grant of the intellectual property beyond a franchisee's premises. Given that the grant to the franchisee is limited, any rights not expressly granted (such as marketing by Internet) will remain at the discretion of the franchisor.

---

[58] Co-branding involves a franchisor owning multiple franchise systems and brands, or franchisors agreeing to market together. Co-branding increases royalty revenue for the franchisor, but, like other forms of encroachment, can dilute the value of the brand to the franchisee. *Concise Legal Dictionary* (3rd ed, 2004).

[59] A 2003 survey carried out in the US showed that 24 percent of franchisees had been 'threatened, encroached upon or coerced into unwanted expansion by their franchisor'. Paul Steinberg and Gerald Lescatre, 'Beguiling Heresy: Regulating the Franchise Relationship' (2004) 109 *Penn State Law Review* 105, 185.

Franchisors have an interest in selling franchise units,[60] because initial entry fees can be a critical source of franchisor income and each new unit adds to brand awareness, which enhances the value of the franchise system in principle. Franchisees, however, do not always share a franchisor's enthusiasm for opening new stores. Take, for example, a franchisee operating a unit that grosses $10,000 per week. Its franchisor decides to open another store in the near vicinity but not so close as to breach the contractual obligations of the franchise agreement as to the franchisee's exclusive area. Within a few months the new unit might gross $7,000 per week. For a franchisor, two stores each making $7,000 per week is preferable because a franchisor receives royalties on $14,000 rather than $10,000. But to the extent that the second unit does pull $3,000 in business from the first, the first franchisees' profit margins decline.[61] The first franchisee has been disadvantaged and the second franchisee may never be as profitable as it might have been in another location.

Assuming that a franchisor has drafted the terms to protect and maximize its right to fully exploit its market, as long as this right is exercised reasonably, any detriment to a franchisee is unlikely to amount to misconduct by a franchisor.

The grant of an 'exclusive' right at the premises may give the illusion of greater protection of its rights than a franchisee actually enjoys. A franchisee with an 'exclusive' licence at its premises has little assurance that a franchisor will not grant another franchise (or supply a competitor) in the vicinity. As long as a franchisor has due regard for the potential impact upon the franchisee's business, it is free to open a new unit nearby, even if this will have a negative impact upon the franchisee's financial position.[62]

Some contracts, however, do include limits on a franchisor's licensing of the intellectual property in the franchisee's territory, and even a duty on a franchisor to protect a franchisee's territory. The franchisee should ensure it understands the potential scope for encroachment in the franchise system before committing to purchase.

---

[60] Lorelle Frazer (Griffith University), 'Are Franchisees Potential Competitors? A Study of Franchisees Who Exit the System but Continue Operating' (Paper presented at the 18th International Society of Franchising Conference, Las Vegas, 6–7 March 2004).

[61] This is particularly of concern to franchisees in low margin industries such as quick-serve restaurants. Paul Steinberg and Gerald Lescatre, 'Beguiling Heresy: Regulating the Franchise Relationship' (2004) 109 *Penn State Law Review* 105, 310.

[62] See *Scheck v. Burger King Corp.* (756 F. Supp. 543 (S.D. Fla. 1991)) for a 'common sense approach'.

Keeping a franchisor's options open is a justifiable discretion to the extent that it benefits the system and all franchisees; it may be less justifiable where it adversely affects the rights of individual franchisees to conduct business. To the extent that a franchisor retains the right to use and sell the intellectual property, notwithstanding any rights sold to a particular franchisee, then that franchisee may be receiving correspondingly less value for its investment in the right.

Franchise contracts that contain language reserving a franchisor's right provide a substantial legal basis for franchisor encroachment. A franchisee that is faced with franchisor encroachment is often forced to rely on a vague standard such as the principle of good faith.[63]

**Franchisor Obligations with Respect to Brand Maintenance**

Maintenance of the brand is a critical aspect of the success of any franchise system, and centralized brand maintenance for the system can help to curb franchisee free-riding. Franchisee participation in promotional funding is often mandatory and promotions are usually paid for with funds a franchisor collects from franchisees, although extra or 'top up' contributions by a franchisor are not uncommon.

A franchisor may allocate funds at its discretion for advertising and promotions.[64] Advertising and promotions is one of the few explicit contractual 'obligations' of a franchisor found in most franchise agreements,

> 'You agree to participate in any national advertising campaign or national promotion that we undertake . . . Whilst we will consult you regarding major elements of our advertising and promotion, all decisions relating to this advertising and promotion will be made by us and you will be bound by these decisions . . . You will pay us the marketing levy . . . we are not responsible for the effectiveness or success of such advertising, promotion or marketing expenditure . . .'

Another contract provides,

> 'Franchisor on behalf of its franchisees will establish an advertising fund to cover the costs of carrying out such advertising, promotion and/or marketing as the Franchisor decides, in its sole discretion, to be appropriate or desirable to promote the System.'

---

63 Jenny Buchan, 'Who is the franchisee contracting with and does it matter anyway?' (Paper presented at the 51st ICSB World Conference, 2006, Melbourne, Australia). There are few cases in franchising where a court has held in favour of a franchisee on a claim of unconscionable conduct.

64 Rupert M. Barkoff and Andrew C. Selden (eds), *Fundamentals of Franchising* (1997) 60.

There is usually no contractual provision to ensure franchisor spending on promotions is acceptable to its franchisees. If a franchisor's circumstances are such that promoting the brand becomes a lower priority, either for a franchisee's territory or for the entire franchise system, a franchisee has little recourse. To expect a franchisor to spend a franchisee's contributions solely in a particular franchisee's area is counterproductive to the group marketing goal. There will always be circumstances where certain franchisees are contributing more to an advertising fund than they benefit. The collective franchisees' interests, however, are also vulnerable.

For example, a franchisor might offer 35 percent off all products in a state-wide promotion. In such a situation volume increases but profit margins are reduced. The franchisor gains because its royalties are based on volume. Franchisees, whose remuneration is based on profits, often lose money. In these situations, a franchisor may assure franchisees that the decline in profit margins will be made up in volume, but franchisees report that in reality this is often not the case, and that those paying high royalties are particularly burdened.

What is striking here is that this obligation, one of the few stated franchisor obligations in franchise agreements, is stated in permissive terms, to be undertaken at a franchisor's discretion. Franchisor obligations regarding promotion typically state that the franchisor 'shall', 'will' or 'must' engage in some promotions or brand maintenance, but the obligation is qualified with permissive language to the effect that a franchisor may engage in advertising and promotion as it determines to be 'reasonably necessary', 'as it deems appropriate', or it will apply reasonable endeavours or efforts. Such drafting establishes little in the way of real obligation on the part of a franchisor and no contractual right in a franchisee.

Situations where one party provides an asset that is spent at the discretion of the other party presents a classic example of opportunistic risk. Problems arise either when a franchisor does not have sufficient funding to undertake advertising in their preferred medium or when financial pressures upon a franchisor make the advertising fund an inviting source of extra revenue to prop up the system. If a franchisor's circumstances are such that promoting the brand becomes a lower priority, either for a franchisee's territory or for the entire franchise system, a franchisee usually has little recourse under the contract. If a franchisor is rapidly expanding, for example, or if a franchisor is in a cost-cutting phase, a franchisee may lose franchisor brand support.[65]

---

[65] Interview with Nick Heys, National Manager, Franchising and Small Business, Australian Competition and Consumer Commission (telephone interview), 2004.

Marketing funds controlled by franchisors may be regarded as a form of trust. Ideally, franchisor promotional activities build and reinforce brand and trademark, but contractually, franchisors' contractual obligations are often so vague that franchisees can be forgiven for seeking additional assurance that franchisors will fulfil this crucial obligation in good faith.

### Franchisor Obligation to Provide Training and Support

Issues of training are integral to the concept of the value of the system. Training and support terms vary among jurisdictions and with local practice.[66] Australian contract terms impose an obligation on the part of a franchisor to provide training as and when a franchisor reasonably determines. This term usually includes a corresponding obligation on the part of a franchisee to attend training, often for an additional fee,

> 'We will provide training sessions at times and places reasonably selected by us. You and the specified person in item 13 and where necessary, your employees, must attend these training sessions at your cost.'[67]

Complaints about inadequate training are common.[68] Franchisees will often expect to receive full training in the concepts of the system, the use of the intellectual property and the operation of the business on a day to day basis. In other words, franchisees expect to receive a full 'business format' training. A British article advising franchisees about entering franchise agreements states:

> It is a *sine qua non* of franchising that franchisors must have an unequivocal obligation to train franchisees in how to operate the franchised business and this obligation to train must continue beyond initial training so that franchisors

---

66 For example, in the US franchisors usually do not charge for training of new franchisees and a certain number of its employees. This is also the case in some Australian franchises but more common that the franchisee is required to attend training at its sole cost. Barkoff and Selden, *Fundamentals of Franchising* (2nd ed, 2004).

67 This term usually includes a corresponding obligation on the part of a franchisee to attend training, often for an additional fee, such as that in the following clause taken from an Australian franchise contract, 'We will provide training sessions at times and places reasonably selected by us. You and the specified person . . . and where necessary, your employees, must attend these training sessions at your cost.'

68 Such complaints can be found in many Court claims, usually connected with an allegation of misleading or deceptive conduct.

are obliged to provide continuing and further training to franchisees during the subsistence of the franchise agreement.[69]

The reality is that the operation of many franchise systems is limited to one or two processes and the running of the actual business is left completely in the hands of the franchisee, which can be unfortunate where a franchisee has little or no experience in operating a small business and/or little or no experience in the industry.

Somewhat ironically, the 'operations manual' that may be so closely guarded by a franchisor prior to entry into the franchise system may have limited value in actually conducting business operations. Issues such as book-keeping, staff management and marketing, which are critical to any small business, may be assumed knowledge and receive nothing more than a token acknowledgement even when they are included.

Often the buoyant marketing terms in advertising the franchise can give rise to an impression that training sufficient to conduct the *business*, as opposed to the *system*, will be made available to the new franchisee. For a franchisor the management of expectations in training is crucial. If a franchisee is fully aware of the nature of the training to be provided, if any, then there is less scope for future dispute.

During the performance of the contract, as a franchisee matures in its role, the focus of a franchisor contribution to the relationship often shifts from training and support to the coordination of the franchise system and the services provided, most importantly brand maintenance.[70] A franchisee continues to pay the costs of the franchise but this may be with a decreasing appreciation of the benefits of the relationship and a franchisor may rely more on its powers and discretion as provided in the contract to ensure control.

### Minimum Performance and Reporting Requirements

While franchisees must guard against franchisor opportunism, franchisors must guard against franchisee free-riding. 'Best efforts' clauses and reporting requirements are used by a franchisor to address free-riding and inaccurate reporting by franchisees.

---

69 See Manzoor Ishani, 'Franchising – what should franchisees expect?' (2006) Business Solutions <http://boptions.sitc2.myzen.co.uk/article/art_44.pdf> at 19 December 2009.

70 Phillip Phan, John Butler and Soo Lee, 'Crossing Mother: Entrepreneur-Franchisees' Attempts to Reduce Franchisor Influence' (1996) 11 *Journal of Business Venturing*, 370, 402.

A franchisor takes measures to ensure franchisee performance through accounting procedures; minimum performance clauses; specific benchmarks; reservation of right of inspection;[71] and restrictive covenants that may require a franchisee to devote its effort exclusively to the operation of the franchise or set minimum hours or impose restrictions on passive ownership.

A franchisor reduces its risk that an unsuccessful franchisee will damage the system through its ability to terminate the agreement if a franchisee does not meet certain minimum performance standards. A franchisor may impose performance requirements with little or no consultation with a franchisee.[72] Such provisions should be considered carefully by the prospective franchisee as they may permit a franchisor to terminate the franchise on the basis of unilaterally imposed performance requirements that are vague, overly burdensome or unfair.

Failure to meet certain performance criteria may also trigger a right for a franchisor to require further training for the franchisee or assume the management of the unit at the franchisee's expense.

Franchisee obligations are typically subject to precise standards, schedules, and targets, often to be set and/or changed at the sole discretion of a franchisor. It is not uncommon that franchise contracts impose requirements on a franchisee that fail to clearly specify the nature of the contractual obligation. Minimum performance is one example where the contractual term allows a franchisor to unilaterally impose and vary exact requirements upon franchisees. With respect to certainty of contractual obligations, those assumed by a franchisee are often unclear, subject to change by a franchisor through the operations manual, technical and training manuals and other documents, as well as by relying on the collective agreement clause, or on provisions in the contract that accord to a franchisor broad discretion. Minimum performance terms in franchise contracts are also used to impose specific obligations on a franchisee, giving a franchisor grounds to terminate or to impose further requirements. Performance standards are less about process that includes franchisees than about a franchisor unilaterally setting standards which *can* provide grounds for termination. They provide another example of how discretion to a franchisor, however justified in principle, creates uncertainty for franchisees.

---

[71] Rupert M. Barkoff and Andrew C. Selden (eds), *Fundamentals of Franchising* (1997) 61–2.

[72] More than one system in Australia required master franchisees to open a certain number of new stores, but none of the master franchisees were able to meet the target number, leading to complaints that the targets were not realistic.

The maintenance of standards in the system relies heavily on a franchisor's ability to access the performance data and business practices of the franchisee. Without good reporting practices a franchisor may unnecessarily increase its exposure to franchisee bad debt and allow damage to the system that affects the sales of future franchises. A franchisor is obliged to act in circumstances where it becomes aware of a franchisee in financial difficulty.[73]

A franchisor is vulnerable to a franchisee's information advantage about the operation of the local franchise unit. Franchisor access to a franchisee's business premises and computer systems is often expressly guaranteed in the contract, along with penalties for inaccurate reporting. Some contracts may allow a franchisor access to all franchisee computers and business records, with no qualification that they be related to the franchise operation. Such terms raise issues of privacy because they provide such a broad licence for a franchisor to enter a franchisee's operation.

At its heart a franchise is intended to accelerate the acquisition and application of specific business knowledge. As the franchisee accumulates the experience and confidence of operating the franchise business, it may reach a point of surpassing its franchisor at a local level. This increased confidence may reduce a franchisee's dependence upon a franchisor and render a franchisee less cooperative with a franchisor across a range of issues. Information flowing from a franchisee to a franchisor becomes more important as the franchisee operation matures.

Franchisors impose various types and levels of reporting requirements ranging from providing annual tax returns to the daily downloading of information from an electronic till in the franchise store. Franchisors have a vested interest in ensuring that reporting is accurate and timely, especially where a franchisor's revenue is based on sales by the franchisee. In such situations a franchisor may consider sales volume as the most important indicator of the franchise unit performance, while a franchisee being more concerned with profit margins may be tempted to inflate costs (or a franchisee may for some reason lack incentive to control costs).[74] Even where royalties are not derived from franchisee sales, it is incumbent upon a franchisor to have an understanding of the financial position of its franchisees so as to guard itself against a franchisee bringing the system into disrepute through poor financial practices.

---

73 In some circumstances, a franchisor who has allowed a franchisee to accumulate a large trading debt may be more willing to allow the franchisee to continue to trade (in the hope of being paid) than should otherwise be the case.

74 Antony W. Dnes, 'A Case-Study Analysis of Franchise Contracts' (1993) 22 *Journal of Legal Studies* 367.

## Supply

Supply requirements vary with the type of franchise business. Franchises that involve sales of products often involve supply and product-tying requirements where any variation by a franchisee is subject to franchisor approval.[75] A franchisor may be a supplier or one of several approved suppliers, and will negotiate supply and distribution contracts to which it may require franchisees to commit to certain levels of purchases. A typical term might read as follows:

> 'Franchisee shall maintain in sufficient supply, and use and/or sell at all times, only such Products and Supplies as meet (franchisor) standards and specifications (Franchisee shall not deviate without franchisor's prior written consent) and as are expressly approved for use and/or sale in writing by franchisor. The Franchisee shall sell or offer for sale all types of Products and services specified by Franchisor.'

Tiered supply arrangements allow a franchisor to prevent franchisees' use of sub-standard products, as well as to provide for approved suppliers who meet a franchisor's requirements. Here, again, a franchisor's legitimate need to preserve uniformity creates risks to a franchisee. There is no requirement of reasonableness in a franchisor's supply requirements, which can be set regardless of whether local conditions warrant such levels. A franchisor can require a franchisee to supply from a franchisor or its designate, which sets prices and controls quality but a franchisor's product purchase requirements may also erode franchisee profit margins. Tying franchisees to vendors reduces franchisee flexibility in supply, threatens competition and can cause franchisees to have to pay higher prices, thus reducing franchisee profit margins. Thus, if franchisees must purchase products solely from a franchisor, or its designated suppliers, the determination of a franchisee's gross margin lies in the hands of a franchisor.[76] Such practices may be inherently anti-competitive but franchising often gets around this issue with a 'one-product exception' or by asserting the need to maintain standards and protect the brand.

Supply requirements also pose a risk where there may be secret rebates to franchisors. Kickbacks, promotional fees and commissions paid to a

---

[75] Antony W. Dnes, 'A Case-Study Analysis of Franchise Contracts' (1993) 22 *Journal of Legal Studies* 367, 393.

[76] E-mail from David Newton, Director of the Office of the Mediation Adviser, to Elizabeth Spencer, 10 February 2003. The particular concerns here involve quality, price or delivery time of goods.

franchisor reduce franchisee profit margins.[77] A franchisor has discretion to require a franchisee to purchase from a supplier whose products are more expensive, but who pays a franchisor a commission. Some franchise contracts expressly protect a franchisor's right to make deals with such suppliers. Rebates or other benefits may or may not be shared with the franchisees.

Circumstances can occur where an approved supplier is unable to provide a particular product to a particular store. Unless a franchisor permits the franchisee to use an alternate supplier (which may be at a franchisor's sole discretion) the franchisee may find itself unable to conduct business. Furthermore, the cost of freight to franchises in regional areas may make the cost of the product unviable in the local market.

Franchisor discretion with respect to supply has attracted some interest in the case of one master franchisor's recent changes to its pricing policies in Australia. Though it has not been tested in the courts, it would appear that the language of the contract provides the franchisor not only with the discretion to impose a reported 30 percent increase in prices over two months, but also,

> 'Effective January 1st 2009 [franchisor] will monitor the cost pricing and change the pricing on a monthly basis. This will then have the impact of a floating price structure that will move on a monthly basis – up or down dependent upon the cost pricing structure dictated by the US at time the stock leaves US shores . . . In addition to the pricing changes there will be a change to the look of your distributor invoice from January, 2009. The distributor delivery copy will come with "no prices" (allow some time for the distributors to make this change). In the event that it does (by accident) come with prices you should ignore the prices as they will not be correct. The [supplier] will email you a copy of the invoice with prices within 3 business days. If you need to raise a credit claim you may do so without pricing. Please be patient as we introduce this new system of invoicing and pricing – there may be some initial challenges as we begin this new process.'[78]

The discretion of the franchisor in this case equates to a level of uncertainty for franchisees that seriously compromises effective business operations and management at the unit level.

### Unilateral amendment and collective agreement clauses

The use of permissive language such as 'franchisor may provide' . . . training, advertising, advice, and so on commonly reinforce franchisor latitude

---

[77] The American Franchise Association, 'The Problems Franchisees Face' (2009) The American Franchise Association <http://www.franchisee.org/Buying%20a%20Franchise.htm#problem> at 19 December 2009.

[78] See http://www.bluemaumau.org/baskin_robbins_australia_allied_brands_shifts_ foreign_exchange_risk_to_franchisees at 4 May 2009.

for discretion, as does the use of reasonableness standards for franchisor performance rather than the specific standards of performance that typically apply to franchisee obligations.[79]

Another method to reinforce discretion is the use of phrases such as 'sole control' or 'absolute discretion' to characterize franchisor rights under the contract, 'Franchisee further acknowledges and agrees that (franchisor) shall have sole control and discretion over the development of the System and the designation of the Products and services to be offered in the Store, and that Franchisee will comply with franchisor's requirements in that regard.' Another contract provides that, 'The consent of the Franchisor may be granted or withheld at the Franchisor's absolute discretion and on such conditions as the Franchisor shall determine.'

Some contracts include a franchisor's right to unilaterally amend the contract, 'Standard franchise agreement means the standard terms and conditions pertaining to the grant of a franchise by us as amended by us from time to time in our absolute discretion.'

A collective agreement clause, also known as an 'agree to agree' or 'come along' clause binds a franchisee to cooperate with any decisions of the majority, whether or not it agrees. The following is a sample of the language used in a collective agreement clause:

> 'Come along: You will abide by any decision of the majority even if you are not one of the majority.'[80]

These clauses can be effective in ensuring that a system is not held to ransom by a small number of disaffected franchisees. Although such

---

[79] Franchisee obligations are typically subject to precise standards, schedules, and targets, often to be set and/or changed at the sole discretion of a franchisor (see Minimum Standards). Some argue that discretion offers insufficient protection for a franchisor, 'there is general agreement among the courts about one thing – the (implied covenant of good faith) requires that parties to an agreement exercise discretion "reasonably".' In order to avoid even this requirement to act reasonably a franchisor is counselled to, 'go hunting for the "D" word' replacing it with 'the (franchisor's) "right". . . Better yet, make clear somewhere in the agreement that whenever the franchisor is reserving a right, it has the uncontrolled or unfettered right. . .Almost all courts agree that the covenant of good faith and fair dealing does not trump an express right.' See William L. Killion, 'Putting Critical Decision-Making Where It Belongs: Scouring the Franchise Agreement for the "D" Word' (2005) 24 *Franchise Law Journal* 228, 229–30.

[80] Changes with respect to supply requirements, pricing, fit out requirements, and computer systems and many others regarding operations can also be imposed through the operations manual rather than by any change to the franchise agreement or formal contractual documentation.

clauses may be regarded with suspicion by franchisors as a limitation on their power to do what they want, they can help to ensure that the contribution of franchisees to the development and improvement of the system is valued and supported.

In sum it is not the inherent discretion of a franchisor to unilaterally impose change that creates problems. Though the old adage that 'power corrupts' does come to mind, from a practical perspective it would be virtually impossible to govern any franchise system by consensus. What is important with respect to these contractual provisions granting discretion is that there are mechanisms in place to curb the perception of misuse of franchisor discretion.

## Exiting the Franchise Relationship[81]

The franchise relationship can end in many ways, including expiry of the franchise term, transfer of the unit by a franchisee with franchisor approval, termination of a franchisee by a franchisor, franchisor sale of system, and insolvency of franchisee or franchisor.

At this final stage of the relationship, difficult issues must be resolved regarding the approval of a successor by a franchisor, additional fees and costs, ownership of goodwill and other property of the franchise. On transfer, for example, a franchisor may want to benefit the next franchisee by keeping entry costs low or may want to receive another franchise fee for unit. The current franchisee, however, will want to get the highest sale price possible.[82]

In recent times there has been an increased realization of the potential risks for a franchisee at exit, including compensation for goodwill and franchisee vulnerability in renewals, sales and termination.

## Duration and Right of Renewal

The duration of the contract, the ability to extend the term and the conditions placed upon renewal, are important considerations for both franchisor and franchisee.

A franchisee should seek a long enough duration in the initial contract to

---

[81] Franchise unit operations in Australia last an average of eight years. See Beluba Group, 'Franchises' (2006) Beluba Functional Design <www.beluba.com.au/ww3/franchise.htm> citing the Franchise Council of Australia at 19 December 2009.

[82] Gillian Hadfield, 'Problematic Relations: Franchising and the Law of Incomplete Contracts' (1990) 42 *Stanford Law Review* 927, 988–9.

allow it to recoup its initial investment and to achieve a reasonable return on its original capital investment. A franchisor typically prefers shorter contract duration with a conditional option to renew so that risks and returns can be maximized in each unit. In situations where the duration is extended or renewed, the conditions of renewal give franchisors the opportunity to impose additional operating requirements, to require franchisees to upgrade premises and/or to undertake additional obligations.[83] The conditions of renewal can also provide the franchisor the opportunity to discontinue relationships with underperforming or free-riding franchisees.

Established systems, larger territories and master franchise arrangements often involve longer contract durations, usually due to the larger investments by franchisees and longer time frames required to achieve reasonable returns. Another reason for longer terms is that well established and mature systems are less likely to require further changes to the operational requirements of the business. For example, it is common that McDonald's contracts run for twenty years and typically do not offer a right of renewal. Longer duration contracts are less likely to carry with them automatic rights of renewal due to higher risk exposure if franchisees do not perform or relations break down. However, it is worth noting that even well established systems, such as the McDonald's and Burger King restaurant chains, must still be able to react to changes in the market place and social trends. Even though the licence to conduct the franchise business may extend to many years, issues such as renovation, upgrades to plant and equipment and changes to product or services are still very much in the control of a franchisor.

The term 'right of renewal' is a misnomer to the extent that the term does not spell out a right of a franchisee as much as it outlines conditions and ensures franchisor discretion not to grant renewal. Even if it does not operate for a subsequent term, the franchise is not necessarily 'renewed', that is, the same terms are not carried forward. Most franchisors will require a franchisee to renew the relationship by 'signing the then current version of the franchise agreement, which may be on substantially different terms' to the current agreement. Issues of fairness and good faith may arise as it is difficult to expect an existing franchisee with a significant investment in their business to reject the terms of the 'renewal' agreement.

Contract terms vary among industries and can be expected to vary

---

[83] Jeff Elgin, 'Ready to Commit? About to buy a franchise but intimidated by the license agreement? We explain what to look for before you sign on the dotted line' (2005) Entrepreneur.com <http://www.entrepreneur.com/franchises/buyingafranchise/franchisecolumnistjeffelgin/article77946.html> at 19 December 2009.

among jurisdictions. In Australia, the initial contract duration is most commonly between five and ten years and many contracts contain a 'right of renewal' clause. In Europe, most franchisee agreements run for a period of between five and ten years but pan-European agreements are usually longer, between ten and 25 years, in order for the franchisee to obtain a decent return on its investment. There is commonly an option to renew for one term of the same length as the initial term but rarely any further option to renew. Some provisions may be made for 'holding over', the month-to-month continuation of the business after the expiration of the initial term.

To address franchisor concern that the 'right of renewal' might create a property right in a franchisee, most contracts include extensive conditions to prevent a franchisee from acquiring such rights. These conditions allow a franchisor to refuse to grant renewal where a franchisor may have an interest in limiting the power and influence of existing franchisees, for example in major or geographically extensive markets, or where a potentially strong franchisee seeks to 'bend the rules' and threaten a franchisor's control.

If the contract were to reflect a balance of power between the parties, the contract duration should be calibrated to allow recovery of a franchisee's specific investment while safeguarding a franchisor from franchisee free-riding.[84] It is not clear whether the commonly-used five-year initial term with five-year right of renewal creates such a balance. In saying that, it could be suggested that a franchisee can expect that a franchisor has turned their attention to this issue before offering the franchise as it is clearly an essential component of any system.

It is difficult for a prospective franchisee to assess the scope of a franchisor's discretion to renew the contract. Long-term contracts are, in theory, associated with uncertainty, but in practice give greater assurance that a franchisor views the relationship as viable in the long term. Shorter contract duration can create uncertainty for a franchisee and may increase financial pressures, especially if a franchisee has an expectation that the contract will be renewed. Not only is a franchisee in this situation giving discretion to a franchisor over the period of the initial term, but also a franchisee is subject to a franchisor's conditions, often exercised with a franchisor's discretion, at the expiration of the initial term. For example, a common renewal condition is to require a franchisee to update the physical plant of the business to the current basis for new units opening in the

---

84 Janet Bercovitz, 'An Analysis of the Contract Provisions in Business Format Franchise Agreements' (2000) International Society for New Institutional Economics <http://www.isnie.org/ISNIE00/Papers/Bercovitz.pdf> at 19 December 2009.

system, a potentially major investment.[85] As franchisees approach the expiration of their term they may be subject to franchisor pressure to conform to conditions of renewal.[86]

**Transfer by Franchisee**

Transfer refers to the assignment of the franchise unit by a franchisee. A franchisee has less latitude to sell its interests relating to the franchise system than a franchisor. The 'right' of a franchisee to transfer the franchise is usually subject to certain requirements of a franchisor because franchisors tend to derive less benefit from a franchisee transfer of the franchise than they do from selling a franchise unit.

This contract term consists primarily of identifying franchisor conditions before consenting to a franchisee transfer. Franchisors use constraints on a franchisee's right to transfer to protect a franchisor's interest in brand maintenance and to ensure the level of quality of system franchisees.[87] A franchisee cannot usually transfer his franchise unit without the prior written consent of a franchisor, allowing the franchisor to evaluate a prospective transferee's expertise and capacity to add value to the system. Most systems also require a payment of a transfer fee by the outgoing franchisee to alleviate the loss a franchisor suffers in retraining the new franchisee and losing the opportunity to re-sell the unit itself.

Finally, there is the issue of ownership of goodwill. A franchisee's rights regarding the goodwill at transfer are often unclear. Does the franchisee actually own any goodwill capable of being transferred to an incoming purchaser or is the goodwill solely owned by a franchisor? A franchise has been described as a 'wasting asset'.[88] As Blair and Lafontaine point out, a franchisee who contracts for a licence to use a franchisor's intellectual

---

[85] See Jeff Elgin, 'Ready to Commit? About to buy a franchise but intimidated by the license agreement? We explain what to look for before you sign on the dotted line' (2005) Entrepreneur.com <http://www.entrepreneur.com/franchises/buyingafranchise/franchisecolumnistjeffelgin/article77946.html> at 19 December 2009; The American Franchise Association, 'The Problems Franchisees Face' (2009) The American Franchise Association <http://www.franchisee.org/Buying%20a%20Franchise.htm#problem> at 19 December 2009.

[86] Paul Steinberg and Gerald Lescatre, 'Beguiling Heresy: Regulating the Franchise Relationship' (2004) 109 *Penn State Law Review* 105, 116.

[87] Note also that a franchisor is concerned with the nature of franchisee organization (individual, partnership, corporation, trust), in order to ensure that all individuals signing the agreement will be personally liable.

[88] Paul Steinberg and Gerald Lescatre, 'Beguiling Heresy: Regulating the Franchise Relationship' (2004) 109 *Penn State Law Review* 105, 116.

property needs to understand that it is purchasing something that it can never sell (though it often does!). In theory, the benefit in using a franchisor's system is to advance the business rapidly through establishment phases to profitable trading by taking advantage of the brand recognition and operational processes of a franchisor. As these elements will generate almost all of the goodwill in the business (leaving aside any personal goodwill that may have been established by the franchisee), the only real value that a franchisee can sell is the benefit of the franchise agreement, which is for a limited duration.

A franchisor may require as a condition of completing the sale that the selling franchisee sign a release form which provides that the outgoing franchisee will give a franchisor a general release of any claims they may have accrued.[89] Conversely, obligations of ongoing confidentiality regarding the system and personal restraints of trade are frequently imposed upon the outgoing franchisee. Restraints of trade are discussed in more detail in the post-termination section of this chapter.

**Termination by Franchisor**

Termination rights enable a franchisor to deal with under-performing or non-compliant franchisees. While a franchisor's right to terminate is important to a franchisor in maintaining uniformity and the quality of the brand, misuse of the power is a frequent area of complaint.

Efficiency in the termination of a franchise agreement is difficult to measure, especially when trying to quantify the negative impact on a franchisor's brand. Perhaps this is why '[c]ourts have traditionally applied the rule of termination at will to exclusive agency and distributorship agreements'.[90] This tradition has carried over into the franchise relationship and franchisors defend the right to terminate if a franchisee performs poorly or breaches the contract as a crucial aspect of maintaining the brand. A franchisee, however, must be regarded as having a relationship more than simply as an agent or distributor if for no other reason than the extent of its investment in the franchisor's brand.

A franchisor generally has wide latitude to exercise its rights to terminate. Franchisors argue that courts should demand only good faith and reasonable notice for termination because of their need to protect the

[89] The American Franchise Association, 'The Problems Franchisees Face' (2009) The American Franchise Association <http://www.franchisee.org/Buying%20a%20Franchise.htm#problem> at 19 December 2009.

[90] George Dent, 'Lawyers and Trust in Business Alliances' (2002) 58 *The Business Lawyer* 45, n247.

brand and that they are unlikely to terminate profitable franchisees. There are reasons, however, that a franchisor might wish to terminate, even when a franchisee is profitable. For example, where a franchisor feels the franchisee has too much power or independence or in the case of conflicts over leases or finance.

Termination of a franchise often leaves the franchisee exposed to ongoing commitments, that they are unable to service without the franchise, such as borrowings, leases or hire contracts. A franchisee's other related contracts and rights to dispute resolution may also be compromised.[91]

There is no assurance of reciprocity with respect to termination in franchise contracts. Termination by a franchisee is rarely addressed at all in franchise contracts. Some contracts in Australia, however, give a franchisor 30, 60 or 90 days to remedy any alleged defaults. This has arisen as a direct result of the ability of a franchisee to issue a Dispute Notice under the Franchising Code specifying the nature of the dispute, the action required by the complainant to resolve the dispute and a time frame within which the dispute is to be remedied. The downside to this approach is that most franchise agreements, representing a one-way transfer of rights from a franchisor to the franchisee, do not contain significant obligations which could give rise to a franchisee's claim of breach of the contract. Hence many cases under this heading relate to the breach of an 'implied' term, such as good faith in the termination process.

### Post-termination and Post-contractual Restraints of Trade in Franchise Agreements

Franchisees are often surprised to find that their entitlements at transfer or termination do not meet expectations. A franchisee intends the franchise to continue for a term long enough to recoup its investment, provide an opportunity to sell upon exiting the arrangement and not be subject to franchisor hold-up.

Even after the relationship has ended, legal issues arise with respect to post-contractual restraints of trade, insolvency and liability under contract and tort. A franchisor seeks to control these issues through contractual provisions including restrictive covenants. As a term in franchise agreements some restrictive covenants are quite abbreviated while others contain lengthy restraint of trade clauses. These clauses are

---

91 Paul Steinberg and Gerald Lescatre, 'Beguiling Heresy: Regulating the Franchise Relationship' (2004) 109 *Penn State Law Review* 105, 124–5.

often stepped to ensure a franchisor the maximum protection that the law will allow. [92]

Restrictive covenants protect a franchisor's intellectual property, information and brand identity against franchisee duplication and competition. Restrictive covenants are used to address information asymmetry where control over a resource, including a system or process, is separate from control over information relevant to efficient use of the resource.[93] Such problems are addressed through signalling regarding commitment to perform. This signalling function, along with its limited bargaining position generally, helps explain franchisee willingness to accept restraint of trade clauses. It also explains why there is no reciprocity of franchisor obligation here, for example, in the form of limitations on a franchisor's right to encroach.

In jurisdictions where a franchisee owns the goodwill of the franchise unit, as in the US, restrictive covenants effectively create a penalty for franchisee failure over the life of the contract. This is due to the fact that the value of local goodwill increases over time, while physical asset value may decline.[94] In other jurisdictions it may be that a franchisee does not own the goodwill, though a franchisor may permit a franchisee to include the value of goodwill in the value of the franchise at transfer.

Some franchisees argue that they should be allowed to engage in a similar business provided that they discontinue use of a franchisor's trademarks and trade secrets and return all confidential operating materials to a franchisor.[95] It is not often likely that there will be an issue about brand awareness at the location because in many cases a franchisor exercises some form of control over the premises so that a franchisee exiting the system cannot remain in the same location.[96]

Franchisees argue that their position is more analogous to that of employees than business owners in the interpretation of such restraints.

---

[92] A franchisee makes the choice to enter the agreement and may be required to specifically and separately acknowledge that the terms of any restraint are reasonable to protect a franchisor's legitimate interests.

[93] David Goddard, 'Long-Term Contracts: A Law and Economics Perspective' (1997) *New Zealand Law Review* 423, 438.

[94] Antony W. Dnes, 'A Case-Study Analysis of Franchise Contracts' (1993) 22 *Journal of Legal Studies* 367, 388.

[95] See, e.g., The American Franchise Association, 'The Problems Franchisees Face' (2009) The American Franchise Association <http://www.franchisee.org/Buying%20a%20Franchise.htm#problem> at 19 December 2009.

[96] Jenny Buchan, 'Who is the franchisee contracting with and does it matter anyway?' (Paper presented at the 51st International Council of Small Business World Conference, Melbourne, Australia, 18–21 June 2006).

Once a franchisee learns to run a computer repair business or a cake shop, effectively these clauses prohibit a franchisee from continuing to trade after the expiration of the franchise licence.

The restraint of trade doctrine is traditionally concerned with protecting personal liberty rather than competition generally in the market. At common law, any restraint of trade is *prima facie* contrary to public policy and void unless the restraint is reasonably necessary to protect legitimate interests. Whether a restraint of trade is reasonable depends on a number of 'market' factors including geographical area; the scope of the activities restrained; the period of the restraint; and the degree to which the restraint is necessary to protect goodwill, confidential information, customs and practices within the particular industry.[97]

Franchisors have successfully argued that restrictive covenants in franchising agreements, such as the grant of an exclusive territory to a franchisee, are pro-competitive and consequently fall outside the purview of the doctrine against restraints of trade. Australian case law is indicative of the difficulties faced by a franchisee wishing to challenge these clauses.[98]

**Market and the contract interaction spell imbalance in the franchise relationship**

Franchise contracts reflect and reinforce asymmetries already inherent in the franchise relationship. The relational and standard form qualities of the contract, independently and in combination, contribute to greater power to a franchisor and greater uncertainty and risk for a franchisee. This state of affairs between the parties is established at the formation of the contract and influences the balance throughout the duration of the contractual relationship.

Not only are there synergistic effects of the interaction between the standard form and relational contract, but there is also conflict due to the inconsistencies between these contract characteristics. A relational contract is meant to create an evolving long-term relationship that relies on flexibility, reciprocity and trust and requires contextual interpretation. The standard form, however, with its focus on contract at formation and formality, frustrates the essential nature of the relational contract. Franchisees that characteristically lack experience with this business form

---

97 Different tests for reasonableness of restraint apply depending upon jurisdiction. In *Smith v. Ward* [1999] NSWSC 138 there was a conflict between jurisdiction where common law applies and jurisdiction where legislation addresses defects in common law.

98 See: *Stained Glass Overlay Australasia Pty Ltd & Ors v. Kevin James Rea & Anor* [1998] WASC 325; *Sureslim Australia v. Mansell* [2002] NSWSC 945.

may not be aware of the interaction of these contractual qualities and cannot effectively manage risk through negotiation of the contract. As this chapter has outlined, the terms of franchise agreements are contractual evidence of the imbalance in favour of a franchisor.

While a franchisor's greater power does not necessarily equate to unfairness, franchisees, even those who have received independent legal advice, are potentially vulnerable to the abuse of franchisor discretion. The interpretation and regulation of the contractual relationship should comprehend the nature of this interaction in a way that is consistent with the balance of individual freedoms against state interests in regulating. Every jurisdiction in the world must determine that balance between the rights and responsibilities of its citizens to make their own choices and to protect themselves and the role of government in taking over those choices. There is always asymmetry in relationships and there is no right answer in determining the appropriate role for government in protecting weaker parties. While some argue for greater protection in standard form and consumer contracts, the matter is still the subject of debate. Between weaker and stronger, each has a stake in freedom to contract. As it is impossible to ignore the content of the contract, it may be that the only way to protect the weaker party's freedom is to limit that of the stronger.[99]

Achieving the correct balance in a new economic era demands revised approaches to governance. As discussed in Chapter 1 regulation is not only government intervention by legislative means; regulation happens from market to contract, as well as by courts, legislators and administrators. Currently, the parties to a franchise contract cannot rely on self-regulation through market and contract due primarily to the interaction of the standard form and the long-term nature of the contract.

Though there are some measures to improve the governance of the relationship at these levels, such as reputation, education, collective negotiation and shared knowledge of contract terms, other layers of governance can help to address these concerns. Complementary regulatory measures may be required to ensure that the contract serves stakeholders efficiently and equitably. Such measures should ensure that the contract provides two sorts of balance, a balance of values of freedom of contract against public policy values in favour of good faith and fair dealing, and a balance of

---

[99] See, eg, Olha O. Cherednychenko, *Fundamental Rights, Contract Law and the Protection of the Weaker Party: A Comparative Analysis of the Constitutionalisation of Contract Law, with Emphasis on Risky Financial Transactions* (2007); Peter Edward Nygh, *Autonomy in international contracts* (1999).

specificity of terms against flexibility and discretion to accommodate the uncertainty of the long term.

Court interpretation and effective legislative intervention have a role to play, but the interaction of the standard form and relational characteristics of the franchise contract may require that courts rely less upon the traditional *pacta sunt servanta*, formal interpretation and more on relational modes of contract interpretation, perhaps placing a greater emphasis on good faith.

With respect to regulation it may be necessary to supplement or improve the effectiveness of self-regulatory measures such as disclosure and mediation. These measures require balanced processes in which both parties have capacity to participate effectively, as the relationship imbalance diminishes that effectiveness. In addition there is a range of other tools with the potential to reduce the risk of abuse. Chapters 4 through 7 survey and discuss the application of these tools.

# 4. Purpose and scope of franchise-specific regulation and the UNIDROIT Model Law

## OBJECTIVES OF FRANCHISE-SPECIFIC LEGISLATION

Chapter 2 outlined how the parties regulate their interaction privately at the level of the market. Chapter 3 described in detail the nature and terms of franchise contractual agreements. These are private layers of governance. Private layers of governance through the market interaction and contract fail to address certain problems and inefficiencies in the relationship, such as imbalances of power and uncompensated allocations of risk. It is the perception that these important problems remain unaddressed through self-regulation that lead to legislative intervention. The focus of the remaining chapters will be on legislative intervention in the franchise sector, franchise-specific legislation.

A study of the regulation of franchising is a study of the ecology of the franchise sector. Legal concepts such as self-regulation and autopoiesis are borrowed from biological sciences. In biological terms systems regulate themselves through a range of inputs and feedback cycles. Each system is quite unique but what they all have in common is process.

When the Institute for the Unification of Private Law (UNIDROIT) adopted its 'Model Franchise Disclosure Law', the stated purpose was, 'to provide inspiration and guidance to national legislators in implementing legislation with respect to franchising' and 'to encourage the development of franchising as a vehicle for conducting business'. In generating this 'pro-commerce document', UNIDROIT recognized that franchising offers the potential of increased economic development, especially among countries seeking access to know-how.[1]

Instead of stating the harms that franchising regulation is intended to

[1] International Institute for the Unification of Private Law (UNIDROIT), Model Franchise Disclosure Law (2002) UNIDROIT, 10 <http://www.unidroit.org/english/modellaws/2002franchise/2002modellaw-e.pdf > at 19 December 2009.

address, UNIDROIT advises municipal governments to consider a long list of factors in determining the need for and nature of legislative intervention. The list includes the following; whether it is clear that there is a problem, what its nature is, and what action, if any, is necessary; whether prospective investors are more likely to protect themselves against fraud if they have access to truthful, important information in advance of their assent to any franchise agreement; whether economic and social interests are best served by legally requiring a balance of information between the parties to a franchise agreement; whether there is a pattern of abusive conduct; the nature of the evidence of abuse; whether existing laws address the concerns and whether they are adequately applied; and whether an effective system of self-regulation exists. UNIDROIT also recommends that governments consider the financial burden the new legislation will place upon franchisors and investors; the effect of proposed legislation on entry to franchisors, and on job-creation and investment; and the views of interested organisations.[2]

This chapter addresses the purpose of the legislation as enunciated by some jurisdictions. This chapter also considers a related aspect, the definition of franchising which determines the scope and application of the legislation. Table 4.1 provides examples of the stated purposes of franchise legislation:

The regulation of franchising is varied, but, given that eight countries list at least 17 different purposes for the statutory regulation of the franchising sector, one might expect even greater variation in the resulting legislation.[3]

The stated purposes of franchise-specific regulation represent the two principal goals of most regulatory intervention, economic efficiency and social welfare objectives. Economic objectives include promoting fair competition or business development (e.g. Republic of China and South Korea), reduction of the costs of disputes, reduction of risk, stimulating economic growth, and increasing certainty (e.g. Mexico and Australia). A common theme is the idea of promoting the development and/or maintaining the economic health of the franchise sector, as outlined in the purpose of legislation in Kazakhstan and Australia. Some economic efficiency objectives, such as addressing imbalance of power also serve social welfare objectives.

Social welfare objectives are generally about protecting the interests of

---

[2] International Institute for the Unification of Private Law (UNIDROIT), Model Franchise Disclosure Law (2002) UNIDROIT, 10 <http://www.unidroit.org/english/modellaws/2002franchise/2002modellaw-e.pdf> at 19 December 2009.

[3] Some jurisdictions do not state the purpose in the legislation itself; though the purpose may be found in explanatory notes, impact statements or the like.

*Table 4.1 Purposes of regulating franchising*

| | |
|---|---|
| Mexico | The purpose of the law is to establish conditions of legal certainty among the parties in the operation of franchises, as well as to guarantee non-discriminatory treatment for all franchisees of the same franchisor. |
| The United States | The Federal Trade Commission (FTC) concluded after nine years of investigation in October 1979 that the abuses in franchise selling practices were attributable to informational imbalance between franchisor and franchisee, usually also accompanied by economic disparity between the parties, and therefore the legal response has been aimed largely at franchising selling practices and on the formation of the agreement.[a] |
| France | The law is directed toward the improvement of the economic, legal and social environment for targeted enterprises. Its purpose is to make information known to the potential licensee/franchisee prior to executing the contract to ensure an informed decision. |
| Italy | The purpose of the law is to introduce a clear definition and a general regulation of franchising in Italy and to grant a higher degree of transparency of the contractual relationship, by way of a preliminary disclosure of documents and information. |
| Spain | The law provides guidelines for 'good commercial practices' that establishes a framework for the relationship between a franchisor and the intended franchisee. The Decree was amended in 2006 for the purpose of improving the registration system to allow potential franchisees to obtain reasonable information and help them make an informed decision whether or not to invest and to allow the Registry to better foster transparency in franchising and act more efficiently as an informative body. |
| People's Republic of China | The legislation is intended to strengthen the regulatory management of commercial franchising, and to maintain order in the franchising market. |
| Republic of China | The guidelines are specially adopted to ensure fair competition in franchise business and to avoid concealment by franchisors of important information during recruitment of franchisees in such a way as to affect the trading order with respect to franchising operations. |
| Indonesia | The regulation was considered to be necessary to enhance business order by means of franchising as well as to increase national business opportunities. |
| Japan | The Act, which is competition law, aims to promote the democratic and wholesome development of the national economy as well as to assure the interests of general consumers, 'by prohibiting private monopolization, unreasonable restraint of trade and unfair trade practices, by preventing excessive concentration of economic power |

*Table 4.1* (continued)

| | |
|---|---|
| | and by eliminating unreasonable restraint of production, sale, price, technology, etc., and all other unjust restriction on business activities to promote fair and free competition, to stimulate the creative initiative of entrepreneurs, to encourage business activities, to heighten the level of employment and actual national income'. |
| Kazakhstan | The law is directed to the development and promotion of franchise activities. |
| South Korea | The purpose of the legislation is to promote the welfare of consumers and further develop the national economy in a sound manner by instituting a fair and rational transaction system for franchises and ensuring mutually complementary and balanced development of the franchise relationship on an equal footing. |
| Australia | The Regulatory Impact Statement for the Franchising Code of Conduct (the Code) lists the 'objectives of government action' as raising standards of conduct in the franchising sector without endangering the vitality and growth of franchising, reducing the cost of resolving disputes in the sector, reducing risk and generating growth in the sector by increasing the level of certainty for all participants, and addressing the imbalance of power between franchisors and franchisees.[b] Part One, Article 2 of the Code states only that, 'The purpose of this code is to regulate the conduct of participants in franchising towards other participants in franchising.' |

*Notes:*

[a] Barkoff and Selden, *Fundamentals of Franchising* (2nd ed, 2004).

[b] Trade Practices (Industry Codes – Franchising) Regulations 1998 (Cth) Explanatory Statement.

participants, particularly franchisees. They include non-discrimination for franchisees, to protect rights, to improve standards of conduct, and to promote the interests of franchisees. Some laws state these goals generally, in terms of protecting both franchisors and franchisees as in South Korea; the People's Republic of China; and, in Australia, to 'protect participants'. Others focus on the protection of franchisees' interests for example in terms of protecting franchisees from unfair practices, discrimination, information imbalance (the US) and power imbalance (Australia). The Republic of China aims through its legislation to protect prospective franchisees.

Other stated objectives can be administrative or they may deal with best practice in regulation, such as to establish a definition, to provide transparency, to provide for disclosure, and/or to standardize practices. Some of these purposes seem to be conclusory, such as providing for disclosure, instead of identifying a harm to be addressed. Others, such as providing transparency, suggest a cut-and-paste approach rather than a more integrated approach to revising regulatory process toward one which by its nature would be transparent. These miscellaneous purposes can sometimes be unclear about the fundamental objectives and about whether standardizing practices is more about ensuring fairness or economic efficiency.

Purposes seem quite general and broad; the difficulties in getting baseline measurements and in gauging performance of the legislation pose challenges for the accurate assessment of the effectiveness of legislation. To facilitate assessment it is important to increase specificity in the enunciation of purpose. To that end it would be worthwhile to implement a process that would be effective in taking measurements and identifying the harms. Only after these steps are taken is it appropriate in any given jurisdiction to consider the range of regulatory options to address these harms.

The regulation of the franchise sector is in general intended to enhance the operation of the sector and to protect participants. When a purpose is stated in the regulation, most acknowledge the importance of the relationship and the need to ensure its efficient function. Effective regulation can help to ensure a favourable image of the sector and so contribute to the success of this business form which depends to a large extent upon a favourable public image. As a British Franchise Association analysis concludes, 'The biggest threat to good franchising is bad franchising.'[4]

## SCOPE OF THE LEGISLATION: DEFINING A FRANCHISE

The purpose of the regulation informs its intended scope which in turn informs the definition of franchising used in the legislation. The definition sets out who is to be regulated, the nature of the activity and the interaction of the participants. It also sets out who and what will be excluded from the scope of the regulation.

The legislation of most jurisdictions states a definition of franchising and/or describes the nature of the relationships it is intended to address. Regulating franchising is regulating the relationship between franchisor and franchisee; what is and is not franchising is determined by how that relationship is characterized. The intention of a definition is not to explain, but rather to circumscribe the parameters of the particular business practice that the legislation is intended to address. George Fletcher writes of the

---

[4] British Franchise Association, 'The Franchise Magazine' (2008).

German concept of *definitionsmacht*, the power to define the world, 'The power to decide becomes the power to define.'[5] And vice versa.

A definition can be narrowly focused on a specific type of business or it may be broadly drafted in order to capture a range of business models. The relation between a franchisor and franchisee in its most common form, unit franchising, is generally the focus of franchise-specific regulation. Even within this category, however, there is wide scope for variation. The franchise relationship has been compared to a joint venture, employment, investment, distributorship, marriage, and sharecropping to name a few.

This diversity within franchising complicates the task of defining and governing the sector. As Professor Hadfield has observed, 'Such an odd-shaped beast tangles in many areas of the law',[6] sometimes with grotesque results. Professor Terry notes that the definition must be 'broad enough to encompass franchising in all its forms yet restrictive enough to avoid the unjustified inclusion of other ways of doing business'.[7]

The UNIDROIT Model Law defines franchising as,

> the rights granted by a party (the franchisor) authorizing and requiring another party (the franchisee), in exchange for direct or indirect financial compensation, to engage in the business of selling goods or services on its own behalf under a system designated by the franchisor which includes know-how and assistance, prescribes in substantial part the manner in which the franchised business is to be operated, includes significant and continuing operational control by the franchisor, and is substantially associated with a trademark, service mark, trade name or logotype designated by the franchisor. It includes the rights granted by a franchisor to a sub-franchisor under a master franchise agreement; the rights granted by a sub-franchisor to a sub-franchisee under a sub-franchise agreement; and the rights granted by a franchisor to a party under a development agreement.[8]

Table 4.2 summarizes the elements of the definition of franchising provided in the scope and definitions of franchise-specific legislation.

Among the 30 countries that regulate 'franchising', eight do not use a

---

5 George Fletcher, *Basic Concepts of Legal Thought* (1996), 50–51.

6 Gillian Hadfield, 'Problematic Relations: Franchising and the Law of Incomplete Contracts' (1990) 42 *Stanford Law Review* 927, 928.

7 A.Terry, 'A Census of International Franchise Regulation' (Paper presented at 21st Annual International Society of Franchising Conference, Las Vegas, Nevada, 24–25 February 2007).

8 For the purposes of the definition 'direct or indirect financial compensation' does not include the payment of a bona fide wholesale price for goods intended for resale. The UNIDROIT Model Law applies both to new agreements and renewals. Note, however, exemptions at UNIDROIT Model Franchise Disclosure Law (2002) Art 5.

*Table 4.2 Definitions used in franchise regulation worldwide*

| | Grant of a right | System / marketing plan/assistance / information-sharing / support | TM/IP/Brand | Fee or pmt – direct or indirect | Other [e.g. Sub- or Master Franchising | Exemptions |
|---|---|---|---|---|---|---|
| North America | | | | | | |
| Canada | √ | Significant and continuing operational control | √ (TM, brand) | √ (direct or indirect) | √ | Yes, see text |
| United States | √ | Franchisor exercises significant control and offers significant assistance to Franchisee | √ (brand, TM) | √ | √ | |
| Central & South America | | | | | | |
| Brazil | √ | System | √ (TM, patent) | √ (direct or indirect) | √ | No exemptions but the law provides that franchising is not an employment relationship |
| Mexico | √ | Transfer of knowledge and assistance | √ (TM) | Not required | √ | No |
| Europe | | | | | | |
| Albania | | Jointly conducting services | | Not mentioned | | |
| Belarus | √ | | √ (TM, IP, trade secrets) | √ | | |
| Belgium | √ | Transfer of know-how and assistance | √ (common sign, TM) | √ (direct or indirect) | | |
| Estonia | √ | Franchisor know-how | √ (TM, commercial identity) | Not mentioned | | |
| France | √ | | √ (TM, shop sign) | Not mentioned | √ | |

*Table 4.2* (continued)

| | Grant of a right | System / marketing plan/assistance / information-sharing / support | TM/IP/Brand | Fee or pmt – direct or indirect | Other [e.g. Sub- or Master Franchising | Exemptions |
|---|---|---|---|---|---|---|
| Italy | √ | Know-how, assistance, part of franchising network | √ (IP, TM, shop signs, ©. . .) | √ | √ | No |
| Lithuania | √ | | √ (TM, other firm rights/ info) | √ | | |
| Moldova | √ | Reciprocal contribution and info-sharing | √ (TM) | √ | | |
| Romania | √ | Collaborative marketing system | | Not mentioned | √ | No |
| Russia | √ | Franchisee use of commercial expertise | √ (TM, service mark) | √ | | |
| Spain | √ | Communication of know-how and continuous assistance | √ (common name or sign, or other IP rights) | √ (direct and/or indirect) | √ | No exceptions but the law does not apply to partnerships, trademark licenses, wholesale distributor arrangements, credit card arrangements or specific industries if they do not contain the definitional elements of the franchise (not limited to retail franchises as the title of the legislation might suggest) |

*Table 4.2* (continued)

| | Grant of a right | System / marketing plan/assistance / information-sharing / support | TM/IP/Brand | Fee or pmt – direct or indirect | Other [e.g. Sub- or Master Franchising | Exemptions |
|---|---|---|---|---|---|---|
| Sweden | √ | Franchisee uses Franchisor's business system | √ (TM or other IP rights) | √ | | |
| Eurasia | | | | | | |
| Ukraine | √ | Franchisee can use Franchisor's commercial experience and business reputation | √ (IP e.g. TM, commercial secrets) | √ | | |
| China | | Franchisor must be able to provide operational guidance, support and training to Franchisee | | | √ | No exemptions, but note that only a corporation, not an individual, can be Franchisor . . . a partnership trademark wholesale distribution and similar arrangements may be deemed a franchise if they fall under definition |
| Republic of China | √ | Know-how, assistance and guidance offered to Franchisee | √ (TM) | √ | √ | |
| Indonesia | | Available sustainable support | √ (IP rights) | | √ | No |

*Table 4.2* (continued)

| | Grant of a right | System / marketing plan/assistance / information-sharing / support | TM/IP/Brand | Fee or pmt – direct or indirect | Other [e.g. Sub- or Master Franchising | Exemptions |
|---|---|---|---|---|---|---|
| Kazakhstan | √ | Marketing technology provided by Franchisor | √ (TM) | Not mentioned | | |
| South Korea | | | | | √ | No |
| Kyrgyzstan | √ | | √ (TM, patent) | √ | | |
| Malaysia | √ | Franchisor has control, and must provide Franchisee with assistance (e.g. supply, marketing, materials, training) | √ (mark, trade secret, IP) | May be required | √ | No exemptions – any contract / agreement made for purpose of 'direct selling' as per the Direct Sales Act 1993 |
| Vietnam | √ | System controlled by Franchisor | √ (TM, business logos, slogans) | Not required | | |
| Oceania | | | | | | |
| Australia | √ | System controlled by Franchisor | √ (TM, commercial symbol) | √ | | |

term that translates directly to the term 'franchise'. Belarus, Lithuania, Russia, and Ukraine instead opt for the term 'commercial concession'. Kazakhstan uses the term 'integrated business licence'; Kyrgyzstan uses the term 'complex business licence'; Belgium uses the term 'commercial partnership'; and Italy uses the term 'commercial affiliation'. In all these cases, it is accepted that the legislation is intended to cover franchising, despite the use of these various other terms. In France the law is not exclusive to franchising per se, but instead relates to the development of 'commercial and artisanal enterprises'.

Common elements of the various definitions of franchising are a right

(27 jurisdictions); a system or marketing plan (20 jurisdictions); a trademark (26 jurisdictions); a payment (20 jurisdictions); 'directly or indirectly' (in UNIDROIT and followed in seven others); control or 'significant control' (six jurisdictions); collaboration or community of interest;[9] and sharing of information (Moldova).

It appears that the proposed Uniform European Union Franchise Disclosure Law, like the UNIDROIT Model Law, will be franchise-specific and exclude other types of business arrangements. The definition under this proposed law is proposed to consist of three statutory elements, similar to that of the European Franchising Federation and the US Federal Trade Commission. The three elements are: 1) a franchisor granting a franchisee the right to sell under a marketing plan or system subscribed in significant part by the franchisor; 2) goods and services substantially associated with franchisor's trademark, trade name, service mark or other business identifier; and 3) the payment of a franchise fee, either directly or indirectly.

One of the principal issues in defining a franchise for the purposes of regulation is whether the regulation should be inclusive or exclusive of franchisor associates, masters, and sub-franchisors. The jurisdictions that expressly include master/sub-franchising within the definition of franchise or otherwise provide that the laws also extend to master franchise arrangements are Brazil, Belarus, Italy, Lithuania, Romania, Spain (requires registration of master franchises), Sweden, Ukraine, People's Republic of China, the Republic of China, Indonesia, South Korea, Malaysia, Vietnam, Australia and also the UNIDROIT Model Law.

In Alberta, Canada the definition of a franchise includes master franchising and the Franchise Act applies also to the grant by foreign franchise or of the master franchise, while in Ontario the master must provide disclosure to a prospective subfranchisee. In France if a franchisor is a party to a franchise agreement or other contract in connection with franchising there may be a requirement to provide disclosure to the prospective subfranchisees. In Japan it appears that the master franchise does entail a duty of disclosure under the law. In Australia, as in many other countries, the legislation applies to master franchising and master franchise agreements in essentially the same way as it applies to franchise agreements, and, since March 2008 it also applies to a master franchise with one subfranchisee in Australia.

---

[9] Several US states have a 'community of interest' element in the definition of franchising.

**Exemptions**

It has also been recommended that the law should include exemptions for certain arrangements, such as where the franchise agreement merely adds a similar product to the franchisee's product line and where such additional product accounts for less than 20 percent of the total sales.[10]

Many jurisdictions make exemptions from the scope of the legislation generally or with respect to particular regulatory tools, e.g. disclosure or registration. Exemptions acknowledge that the size, financial strength and/or experience of prospective franchisees may be such that these parties do not require the types of protections provided in the legislation. Exemptions are also made on the basis of expected turnover of the intended business (as in Australia's short form disclosure) as well as circumstances, such as renewal. The range of exemptions from the definition of a franchise law is quite varied.

The UNIDROIT Model Law specifies several exemptions from the obligation to make disclosure. Types of exemptions include fractional franchises, sophisticated investor franchisees, and transfer, renewal or extension of a franchise under particular conditions. The US disclosure regime under the revised FTC Rule also exempts fractional franchises and large investments, large investors and 'insiders'. In France there is the possible exemption if the arrangement does not satisfy the element of exclusivity as well as a possible exemption where the contract is not in writing.

Exemptions in the Canadian provinces of New Brunswick, Alberta, Ontario, and Prince Edward Island are (a) the grant of a franchise by a franchisee; (b) the grant of a franchise to a person who has been an officer or director of the franchisor for at least six months; (c) the renewal, extension, or additional grant of a franchise; (d) the grant of a franchise by an executor, receiver, trustee in bankruptcy or guardian; (e) the grant of a franchise to a person to sell goods or services within a business if the sales are not expected to exceed 20 percent of the total sales; and (f) the grant of a franchise where the prospective franchisee is required to make a total annual investment not exceeding $5000 CDN.

In Australia, legislation provides that certain relationships do not in themselves constitute a franchise agreement such as an employer-employee relationship, a partnership, landlord-tenant, mortgage or mortgagee, lender-borrower, or a relationship between members of a cooperative. The

---

10 Jon K. Perala, Franchise Disclosure Laws in the European Union (2007) Jon K. Perala, Attorney & Counselor at Law <http://peralaw.com/EU_Franchise_Disclosure.html> at 19 December 2009.

code also exempts agreements for the supply of goods and services that are substantially the same as those supplied by the franchisee for at least two years immediately prior to entering the agreement and if sales under the agreement are not likely to produce more than 20 percent of a franchisee's gross turnover for the first year.

Ultimately, of course, it is for each jurisdiction to determine what is involved in the type of arrangement that is sought to be regulated. Whatever the scope of the legislation, it is important that there be sufficient clarity for participants in the sector to determine whether or not they are caught by the legislation as lack of clarity leads to uncertainty and inefficiency. There is a concern over the issue of 'unintentional franchising' where licenses and distributorships and other business forms run the risk of being deemed to fall under the definition of a franchise, and so incur considerable expense in compliance in order to avoid liability. Such expense could be avoided with greater precision in defining what is intended to be regulated.

In Australia, for example, litigation on the definitional issue has tended to centre on when a licence or a distributorship is likely to be deemed a franchise.[11] A dependency requirement has been implied along with the standard elements of a trademark and a system. According to this model regulation should apply only when the overall business of a franchisee is substantially related to the trade mark of a franchisor; and the overall business of a franchisee operates under a system prescribed by a franchisor; and where there is an overall dependency of a franchisee on a franchisor.[12]

Franchising is often subject to particularized regulation by governments, while licensing and distributorship are largely left to private regulation by the parties through contract. The definitions of franchising offer clues as to why this is so, as they explain what is different about this business form that causes it to be regulated.

As outlined above, among the main elements of the definition of franchising are a right, usually a licence, to use intellectual property; often trademark is specified. Payment for the right is usually part of the definition of franchising, and control by a franchisor (and concomitant dependence and subordination of a franchisee) often appears as part of the definition. Other aspects of the definition include a system or a marketing system, and may include guidance, assistance, training, and/or

---

11 A.Terry, 'A Census of International Franchise Regulation' (Paper presented at 21st Annual International Society of Franchising Conference, Las Vegas, Nevada, 24–25 February 2007).

12 Warren Pengilley, 'What is a franchise agreement?' (Paper presented at Bond University and UNSW School of Business and Taxation Franchise Law Colloquium, Gold Coast, Australia, 20 November 2008).

control. Significant investment by a franchisee is often an element because of the value of the trademark, brand and uniformity. But there are other elements of these definitions that help to clarify the motivations behind legislation and to inform its intended scope. These include the consumer-like attributes of a franchisee; the nature of the contract which implies little negotiation, imbalance of power, reduces bargained-for-exchange and commodification the contract. Also included are elements of the ongoing relationship, which is long-term and relational, characterized by extensive discretion to a franchisor and dependence and subordination of franchisee as well as risk and uncertainty for a franchisee. These elements suggest that the definition and scope should be more focused on the system, support, information-sharing, and dependence of the franchisee on a franchisor.

## AN INTRODUCTION TO THE TOOLS USED TO ACHIEVE THE OBJECTIVES OF LEGISLATION

Before embarking on the next chapter's survey of tools employed in regulation in each jurisdiction, a brief introduction to different types of tools used in franchise-specific legislation is provided here along with an introduction to the UNIDROIT Model Franchise Disclosure Law, which was adopted in 2002 as a guide to countries considering implementing such legislation. This section is merely an introduction to the tools used; the chapters after the survey will provide a more detailed analysis.

Legislation is sometimes categorized as procedural, prescriptive, or performance-based. Procedural provisions require that the regulated parties comply with a certain procedural standard. Disclosure and registration are procedural requirements; so, too, are many legislative interventions with respect to dispute resolution, transfer and termination. Procedural tools tend to be used where performance and/or compliance are hard to measure or where government agencies lack the necessary motivation or support for a more hands-on approach.

Procedural tools used in franchise-specific legislation include disclosure, registration, negotiation procedures, cooling off and review periods, all used at the stage of pre-sales and entry into contract. Continuous disclosures, dispute resolution, and procedures in case of breach of contract are procedural tools used during conduct/performance of the relationship. At the exit stage procedural regulation is used to ensure fairness of procedures for termination, procedures for franchisor approval of transfer and procedures for assignment.

Prescriptive provisions involve the setting out in the regulation of a certain standard or set requirements method, prescribed technology, etc.[13] Note that voluntarism tends to work less effectively with highly prescriptive standards, because these standards restrict firms' responses, whereas voluntarism is flexible. However, voluntarism and prescription may work together in sequence.[14]

Prescriptive tools used include confidentiality, and miscellaneous requirements for franchisor such as to provide licences/intellectual property, and miscellaneous requirements for franchisee used at the stage of pre-sales and entry into contract.

Prescriptive tools used during conduct/performance of the relationship include:

- Mandatory contract terms; freedom of franchisees to associate; limitations on validity of restrictive covenants with respect to performance such as vertical restraints, pricing, and supply; competition law (not usually part of franchise-specific legislation); confidentiality; and prohibitions on encroachment and on general indemnity provisions.
- Miscellaneous requirements for a franchisor include requirements to provide training and technical assistance; to provide instructions, information and updates; to protect intellectual property rights from third parties; and to treat all franchisees equally.
- Miscellaneous requirements for a franchisee include requirements to use trade name; ensure quality standards; follow instructions; provide customers with additional services; conclude a certain number of sub franchises; and to pay royalties.

While many of these tools apply to the conduct/performance of the relationship, there are also prescriptive tools applied regarding exit from the relationship. These include proscription against unilateral termination, protections for franchisee right of renewal, validity of restraints of trade and confidentiality requirements.

Performance standards define a regulatee's responsibility in terms of problem to be solved or goal to be achieved. They are outcome focused.[15] This approach complements most forms of command and control,

---

[13] Neil Gunningham, Peter Grabosky and Darren Sinclair, *Smart Regulation: Designing Environmental Policy* (1998), 432–3.

[14] Neil Gunningham, Peter Grabosky and Darren Sinclair, *Smart Regulation: Designing Environmental Policy* (1998), 434.

[15] Neil Gunningham, Peter Grabosky and Darren Sinclair, *Smart Regulation: Designing Environmental Policy* (1998), 424.

especially when the goal is to move 'beyond compliance'.[16] Performance tools used include pre-sales standards for franchisors, for example, the 'two plus one' rule and pre-sales standards for franchisees used at the stage of pre-sales and entry into contract.

## A Model for Franchise-Specific Legislation: The UNIDROIT Model Law

On 25 September 2002 the Governing Council of the International Institute for the Unification of Private Law (UNIDROIT) adopted the 'Model Franchise Disclosure Law' (the Model Law).[17] The Model Law is a presale disclosure law, requiring disclosure to be provided in writing at least 14 days before the earlier of the signing by the prospective franchisee of any agreement relating to the franchise, with the exception of agreements relating to confidentiality of information delivered or to be delivered by the franchisor; or the payment to the franchisor or an affiliate of the franchisor by the prospective franchisee of any fees relating to the acquisition of a franchise that are not refundable.

Article 6 prescribes the content of the disclosure document to be provided by the franchisor, but does not set out a prescribed format for disclosure.[18] There is no requirement to disclose 'all material facts'. Instead, it follows the format of most US jurisdictions, including the FTC, by stipulating the various items required to be disclosed as the drafters felt that inserting an open-ended requirement was inconsistent with what already existed in most states, and created an unacceptable level of uncertainty for franchisors.

The Law is accompanied by an Explanatory Report that includes an explanation of the purpose of each provision. It states that the Law does not regulate the relationship. Article 8 provides the remedies under the law. Article 10 provides that no waivers are permitted.

### Objectives, scope and tools are the foundations of legislation

The objectives for franchise-specific regulation include both economic efficiency and social welfare objectives. The UNIDROIT Model Law,

---

[16] Neil Gunningham, Peter Grabosky and Darren Sinclair, *Smart Regulation: Designing Environmental Policy* (1998), 432–3.

[17] International Institute for the Unification of Private Law (UNIDROIT), Model Franchise Disclosure Law (2002) UNIDROIT <http://www.unidroit.org/english/modellaws/2002franchise/main.htm> at 22 December 2009.

[18] Siskinds, the law firm, Canada and the UNIDROIT Draft Model Franchise Law (2009) Siskinds <http://www.franchiselaw.ca/pdf/Canada%20and%20the%20UNIDROIT%20Draft%20Model%20Franchise%20Law.pdf> at 22 December 2009.

which was adopted in 2002 serves as a guide for municipal governments in structuring their own franchise-specific legislation to achieve their particular ends. There is a range of tools that can be employed toward these ends. The next chapter surveys municipal legislation, which, like the Model Law, exhibits a pattern of emphasis on disclosure, but otherwise seems to go its own way, or more accurately, in several different directions. Perhaps this is due in part to the fact that, of the 30 states that have adopted legislation, about 20 did so prior to the adoption of the Model Law.

# 5. Worldwide survey of franchise-specific regulation

This chapter surveys each jurisdiction that has adopted franchise-specific legislation of which there are about thirty. It is important to keep in mind that this book addresses franchise-specific regulation only. It does not encompass all regulation that may apply such as laws governing commercial relationships generally, laws regulating intellectual property, competition law, and many other areas of the law that may impact or apply to franchising.

This chapter reviews each country's regulation. Each section begins with population and Gross Domestic Product (GDP) estimates and some information about the economic importance of franchising in that jurisdiction to provide context. Then franchising regulation is summarized according to two broad categories of regulatory measures. The first category includes measures directed toward negotiation and contract formation such as disclosure, registration and other legislation targeted toward pre-sales negotiation and contract formation. The second includes measures targeted toward performance and toward the end of the relationship, as well as measures that deal with dispute resolution. Also noted is the presence, if any, of a statutory requirement of good faith.

## REGULATION OF THE FRANCHISE SECTOR IN THE AMERICAS

### Barbados

Barbados' population is estimated at approximately 285000 and its GDP is around US$3.6 billion.[1] Barbados is a common law jurisdiction. The franchise sector is subject to the Franchises (Registration and Control) Act 1974 as amended, Cap 179A (the FRCA). The Act provides for the

[1] <http://www.cia.gov/library/publications/the-world-factbook/geos/bb.html> and <http://www.state.gov/r/pa/ei/bgn/26507.htm> at10 January 2010.

licensing, registration, control and orderly development of franchised business.

The FRCA provides that the franchise licence application must be in writing addressed to the Minister in the form the Minister requires. The Minister upon receipt of an application must cause a notice inviting objections to the issue of a licence to be published in the Official Gazette.[2] A licence may be issued upon payment of the prescribed fee and shall be in the form determined by the Minister. It is not transferable, shall be valid for a period not exceeding one year, and is renewable.[3] There is a Register of Licences indicating the name and address of each person to whom a licence is issued, the type of business in respect of which a licence is issued, the number of the licence and the address at which the business is conducted. The Register is open to inspection by the public.[4]

A public officer assigned as an inspector may enter premises where a business is being operated pursuant to a licence granted under the FRCA, to examine the licence.[5]

A person who contravenes certain provisions of the FRCA or uses any mark, product, service, technique, device, copyright, industrial design, or invention that so nearly resembles a mark, product, service, technique, device, copyright, industrial design, or invention, as to be likely to mislead the public is guilty of an offence. There are further penalties prescribed for offences against an inspector or authorized person in the performance of his functions.[6]

## Brazil

As of the time of writing Brazil's population was estimated at approximately 198 million.[7] With a GDP of around US$ 1.6 trillion, Brazil's economy is ranked among the top ten in the world.[8] Brazil has the largest domestic market in Latin America,[9] the second largest economy in the

---

2 Franchises (Registration and Control) Act 1974, Section 3.

3 Franchises (Registration and Control) Act 1974, Section 5.

4 Franchises (Registration and Control) Act 1974, Section 6.

5 Franchises (Registration and Control) Act 1974, Section 13.

6 Franchises (Registration and Control) Act 1974, Section 16.

7 Central Intelligence Agency, 'The World Factbook – Brazil' (2009) Central Intelligence Agency <http://www.cia.gov/library/publications/the-world-factbook/geos/br.html> at 22 December 2009.

8 Central Intelligence Agency, 'The World Factbook – Brazil' (2009) Central Intelligence Agency <http://www.cia.gov/library/publications/the-world-factbook/geos/br.html> at 22 December 2009.

9 Embassy of Brazil, 'GDP, Growth and Employment' (2009) Embassy of

Americas after the United States, and the second largest economy in the developing world after China.[10] There are about 1013 franchise networks, with more than 62 500 franchised outlets. Based on number of franchised units Brazil is one of the most important franchising countries in the world.[11]

Brazil is a civil law jurisdiction. On 15 December 1994 Brazilian Law No. 8.955/94 relating to franchising contracts was adopted. This summary of the provisions of the legislation is based on a translation provided by the Brazilian Franchise Association.

Article 2 of the Brazilian Franchise Law defines franchising as 'the system by which a franchisor grants to franchisee the right of trademark or patent use, associated to the right to exclusive or semi-exclusive distribution of products or services and, eventually, also the right of use of technology of implantation and administration of business or operational system developed or detained by franchisor against direct or indirect remuneration, however, without characterising an employment relationship'.[12]

The Brazilian law applies to franchising contracts and franchise systems established and operated on Brazilian national territory and to master franchises.[13] The franchise law makes no distinction between Brazilian and foreign franchisors; the requirement of delivery of the document, as established in Article 3, is mandatory for all franchisors intending to operate in Brazil.[14] International franchise agreements, even those governed by foreign law and electing foreign jurisdiction, are advised to comply with the local law.[15]

Brazil's law requires pre-sales disclosure. Article 4 requires that a disclosure document be provided to a prospective franchisee at least ten days prior to the execution of the franchise agreement or 'preliminary franchising

---

Brazil in London <http://www.brazil.org.uk/economy/gdp.html> at 22 December 2009.

10 Embassy of Brazil, 'GDP, Growth and Employment' (2009) Embassy of Brazil in London <http://www.brazil.org.uk/economy/gdp.html> at 22 December 2009.

11 Candida Ribeiro Caffe, 'Franchising in Brazil' (2008) Franchising World <http://findarticles.com/p/articles/mi_hb6537/is_200803/ai_n25900403> at 22 December 2009.

12 The Franchise Law (Law 8.955) 1994 (Brazil) Article 2.

13 The Franchise Law (Law 8.955) 1994 (Brazil) Articles 8 and 9. See UNIDROIT, 'Legislation and Regulations Relevant to Franchising: Brazil' (1999) <www.unidroit.org/english/guides/2007franchising/country/brazil.htm> at 22 December 2009.

14 The Franchise Law (Law 8.955) 1994 (Brazil) Article 3.

15 The Franchise Law (Law 8.955) 1994 (Brazil) Article 8.

agreement', or the payment of any fee by the prospective franchisee to the franchisor or any company or individual related to the franchisor.[16]

Article 3 states that a franchisor should provide to a prospective franchisee a Circular Letter of Offer of Franchising, in clear and accessible terms in Portuguese. It specifies 16 items of information that a franchisor should provide the franchisee in 'clear and comprehensible language'.

Failure by a franchisor to supply the disclosure document at least ten days prior to the execution of the agreement or payment by a franchisee of any amount renders the agreement voidable by a franchisee and may result in a franchisor being required to refund all amounts paid by a franchisee in connection with the franchise plus damages.[17] This sanction is applicable also to a franchisor that includes false information, without barring applicable criminal sanctions.[18]

The franchise law contains no requirement with respect to filing or registration of disclosure. The executed franchise agreement must be registered with the National Institute of Industrial Property, however, if it is to be enforceable as to third parties.[19] Parties may adopt the English language to document the agreement, as long as the Brazilian party acknowledges that fluency in English. A certified translation into Portuguese is necessary for submission of the agreement to the Institute of Industrial Property. [20] That submission must also include a list of trademarks the franchisee is authorized to use under the franchise agreement and a copy of the franchise agreement.[21]

---

[16] The Franchise Law (Law 8.955) 1994 (Brazil) Article 4. A 'preliminary franchising agreement' includes a letter of intent or option to purchase franchise rights in Brazil, or the payment of any fee in connection with such a letter or intent or option. See Bryan Schwartz and Leandro Zylberman, 'Franchise Symposium Materials: International Franchise Regulation' (2008) 8 *Asper Review of International Business and Trade Law* 317, 322.

[17] The Franchise Law (Law 8.955) 1994 (Brazil) Article 4; Candida Ribeiro Caffe, 'Franchising in Brazil' (2008) Franchising World <http://findarticles.com/p/articles/mi_hb6537/is_200803/ai_n25900403> at 22 December 2009.

[18] The Franchise Law (Law 8.955) 1994 (Brazil) Article 7.

[19] Candida Ribeiro Caffe, 'Franchising in Brazil' (2008) Franchising World <http://findarticles.com/p/articles/mi_hb6537/is_200803/ai_n25900403> at 22 December 2009.

[20] Candida Ribeiro Caffe, 'Franchising in Brazil' (2008) Franchising World <http://findarticles.com/p/articles/mi_hb6537/is_200803/ai_n25900403> at 22 December 2009.

[21] Brazilian Law no. 9279 and Normative Act no. 135/97. See also <http://www.cesa.org.br/arquivos/guialegal_en04.pdf> at 27 December 2009 which further notes that if the franchisee is a foreign party, it has to be registered in the Central Bank in order to permit the remittance of the payments foreseen in the contract, and tax deduction of such payments.

Agreements must be executed by the parties and two witnesses.[22] The signature of the foreign party must be notarized and legalized at the Brazilian Consulate; and the agreement must specify the complete name and title of the representatives of the parties, as well as place and date of execution. If the representative is an attorney, a copy of the power of attorney duly notarized and legalized at the Brazilian Consulate is also required.[23]

## Canada

With a population of about 33 million and GDP for 2008 of about US$ 1.5 trillion[24] Canada's franchise sector is estimated to account for approximately 10 percent of GDP.[25] Canada operates under a federal system which comprises both civil and common law.

The Canadian Constitution confers exclusive jurisdiction to each province over property and civil rights and the administration of justice in each province. Franchise-specific legislation therefore can only arise at the provincial level, as private contracts are subject to the exclusive jurisdiction of provincial governments.[26]

The Canadian federal government has, through the Uniform Law Conference of Canada, developed a Uniform Franchises Act to provide a framework for consistent legislation at the provincial level. The final version of the Uniform Act which was adopted in 2005 contains sections under the headings of defining a franchise, application of the model legislation, fair dealing, freedom to associate, franchisor obligations to disclose, right of rescission, damages for misrepresentation, failure to disclose, dispute resolution, joint and several liability, prohibition of derogation of rights, prohibition of attempts to affect jurisdiction, prohibition of waiver of rights, burden of proof, and regulations.

Of the ten provinces in Canada, four have enacted franchise-specific

---

22 The Franchise Law (Law 8.955) 1994 (Brazil) Article 6.

23 Candida Ribeiro Caffe, 'Franchising in Brazil' (2008) Franchising World <http://findarticles.com/p/articles/mi_hb6537/is_200803/ai_n25900403> at 22 December 2009.

24 Stanley St Labs, 'Canada Economic Statistics and Indicators' (2009) Economy Watch <http://www.economywatch.com/economic-statistics/country/Canada/> at 16 December 2009.

25 Canadian Franchise Association, 'Fast Franchise Facts' (2009) Canadian Franchise Association <http://www.cfa.ca/Publications_Research/FastFacts.aspx> at 16 December 2009.

26 Andrew P. Loewinger and Michael K. Lindsey (eds), *International Franchise Sales* Laws (2006). Note that competition law and intellectual property fall under federal jurisdiction in Canada.

regulation. These are Alberta, New Brunswick, Ontario, and Prince Edward Island. Alberta enacted franchise legislation in 1972; this legislation was substantially revised in 1995. In Ontario the offer and sale of franchises has been subject to regulation under the Arthur Wishart Act since 2001. The New Brunswick and Prince Edward Island Acts came into effect in 2007 and 2008 respectively. The provinces of British Columbia and Manitoba have considered regulation of the sector, but have not to date enacted franchise-specific legislation.

At the federal level the Uniform Act defines a franchise as the right to engage in a business where the franchisee is required to make a payment (or series of payments) to a franchisor, directly or indirectly, in the course of operating the business or as a condition of acquiring the business, where the franchisor either grants the franchisee the right to sell or distribute products associated with a franchisor's trade mark or other commercial symbol, and exercises significant control over the franchisee's business operations or offers significant assistance; or the franchisor grants the franchisee distribution rights, while offering the franchisee location assistance.[27] The Uniform Act provides that the legislation should be applicable to a franchise agreement, or extensions or renewals thereof, entered into on or after the Act came into force, operated partly or wholly in the respective provincial jurisdiction.[28] All provincial franchise Acts define a franchise in a manner similar to the definition in the Uniform Act.[29]

The Uniform Franchise Act includes obligations to disclose, as do all four provincial acts. None of the provinces' franchise statutes prescribe the form for disclosure but they all prescribe content. Documents must contain all 'material facts'. The 'material facts' definition varies slightly among the

---

27 Uniform Franchises Act, SC 2005, s 1(1).

28 Uniform Franchises Act, SC 2005, s 2(1).

29 Franchises Act, RSA 2000, c. F-23, s 1(1); Franchises Act, SNB 2007, c. F-23.5, s1(1); Arthur Wishart Act (Franchise Disclosure), 2000, SO 2000, c. 3, s 1(1); Franchises Act, RSPEI 1988, c. F-14.1, s 1(1). The Alberta Act applies to the sale of a franchise made on or after 1 November 1995, if the business is to be operated partly or wholly in Alberta and the franchisee is an Alberta resident or has a permanent establishment in Alberta as prescribed by the Alberta Corporate Tax Act. The Act also applies to the sale of a franchise, operated partly or wholly within the province, made before 1 November 1995, if the franchisee was a resident of the province or had a permanent establishment there as prescribed by the Alberta Corporate Tax Act. Franchises Act, RSA 2000, c. F-23, s 2. The 'Application' sections of the New Brunswick, Ontario and Prince Edward Island Acts respectively are similar to the 'Application' section as prescribed by the Uniform Act. Franchises Act, SNB 2007, c. F-23.5, s2(2); Arthur Wishart Act (Franchise Disclosure), 2000, SO 2000, c. 3, s 2(1); Franchises Act, RSPEI 1988, c. F-14.1, s 2(1).

provinces, but it is generally defined as any information about the business operations' capital, or control of the franchise or its associates, or about the franchise system that would reasonably be expected to have a significant effect on the value or price of the franchise or the decision to acquire the franchise. All the provinces require a franchisor's financial statements to be included with disclosure.[30]

There are standards for disclosure. The Uniform Disclosure Documents Regulation directs that financial statements to be disclosed to a prospective franchisee must be prepared in accordance with accounting principles and auditing standards set out in the Canadian Institute of Chartered Accountants Handbook.[31] The Alberta, Ontario, and Prince Edward Island Regulations have adopted provisions relating to the preparation and disclosure of financial statements similar to those of the Uniform Disclosure Documents Regulations.[32] The New Brunswick Act states that the Lieutenant-Governor in Council may make regulations prescribing and governing financial statements to be disclosed to a potential franchisee.[33]

Registration is no longer a feature of franchise-specific legislation in Canada. The Uniform Franchise Act does not include registration, and in no province in Canada is registration a requirement of franchise-specific regulation.[34]

There is some franchise-specific legislation targeted toward performance in Canada. The Uniform Act provides that a franchisor cannot interfere

---

[30] According to Weinberg the New Brunswick bill is centred on three key principles and is based on the Ontario, Alberta and Prince Edward Island legislation. These three key principles are as follows: 1) the regulation permits the use of wrapped around documents which provide supplemental information to aid disclosure document prepared in accordance with the laws of another jurisdiction; 2) a requirement that in order for franchisors to be exempt from including financial statements in disclosure documents they must not have had any judgment order or award made in Canada against them in the five years preceding the date of the disclosure document relating to fraud, unfair or deceptive practices, or a law regulating franchises; 3) substantial compliance with the disclosure document requirements are sufficient in determining whether a franchisee may rescind the contract.

[31] Uniform Franchises Act Disclosure Documents Regulations, SC 2005, s 9.

[32] Franchises Regulation, Alta. Reg. 240/1995, s 3; Arthur Wishart (Franchise Disclosure) Regulation GENERAL, O Reg. 581/00, s 11(2); Franchises Act Regulations, PEI Reg. EC232/06, s 5.

[33] Franchises Act, SNB 2007, c. F-23.5, s 14.

[34] In 1995 the new Alberta Franchises Act, RSA 2000, Chap. F-23 eliminated the registration and governmental review process that had been in place since 1972. The current regulation provides for a standard form of disclosure document to be prepared by a franchisor, but does not require any government filing, review or approval.

with, prohibit or restrict the franchisee's right of association; nor can it penalize the franchisee or threaten to do so for exercising any such rights.[35] Any agreement purporting to limit the franchisee's rights of association is void. Furthermore, a waiver by the franchisee or prospective franchisee of a right conferred by the Act or regulation, or a release of an obligation imposed on a franchisor will be void.[36]

All provincial franchise Acts, with limited exceptions, have provisions similar to those of the Uniform Act with respect to the performance of the agreement.[37] The Alberta Act does not hold 'interference' by the franchisor as a contravention of the franchisee's right to associate; nor does it state that a provision in an agreement purporting to restrict the franchisee's right to associate is void and will give rise to an action for damages.[38] The New Brunswick and Prince Edward Island Acts are the only two that extend the 'Waiver of Rights' provisions to prospective franchisees.[39] All provincial franchise Acts provide that the right to associate applies retroactively to franchise agreements entered into before the legislation came into force.[40]

There is in Canada no substantive regulation targeted toward the end of the relationship, but there is a procedural requirement of disclosure with respect to events leading to the end of the relationship. Specifically, the Uniform Act requires that the disclosure document provided to a prospective franchisee contain a description of all contractual provisions dealing with the termination, renewal or transfer of the franchise business.[41] In the event of rescission by the franchisee, the Uniform Act prescribes the obligations and certain conduct of the parties, such as refund of money received from the franchisee, except money paid for inventory, supplies and equipment, repurchase of inventory, supplies and equipment sold to the franchisee and compensation of the franchisee for any losses incurred in acquiring, setting up and operating the business.[42]

---

[35] Uniform Franchises Act, SC 2005, s 4. If a franchisor contravenes the provision, the franchisee has a right of action.

[36] Uniform Franchises Act, SC 2005, s 12.

[37] Franchises Act, RSA 2000, c. F-23, ss 8, 18; Franchises Act, SNB 2007, c. F-23.5, ss 4, 12; Arthur Wishart Act (Franchise Disclosure), 2000, SO 2000, c. 3, ss 4, 11; Franchises Act, RSPEI 1988, c. F-14.1, ss 4, 12.

[38] Franchises Act, RSA 2000, c. F-23, s 8.

[39] Franchises Act, SNB 2007, c. F-23.5, s 12; Franchises Act, RSPEI 1988, c. F-14.1, s 12.

[40] Manitoba Law Reform Commission, 'Consultation Paper on Franchise Legislation' (2008) 8 *Asper Review of International Business and Trade Law* 181.

[41] Uniform Franchises Act Disclosure Documents Regulations, SC 2005, s 4(1) y).

[42] Uniform Franchises Act, SC 2005, s 6.

Provincial franchise Acts and Regulations contain provisions similar to the Uniform Act regulations regarding disclosure with respect to events leading to the end of the relationship.[43] However, the New Brunswick Act does not require that the disclosure document contain a description of the contractual provisions dealing with termination, renewal, or transfer.

The Uniform Franchises Act provides for confidential dispute resolution through mediation, which is mandatory once initiated by a party to a franchise agreement. A party may deliver a notice of dispute to another party setting out the nature of the dispute and the desired outcome. The parties must attempt to resolve the dispute within 15 days after delivery of the notice. If they fail to resolve it, a party may deliver a notice to mediate to all other parties who must then proceed according to the regulations respecting mediation.[44] At the provincial level the Alberta Act makes no mention of mediation or other dispute resolution process. The New Brunswick Act provides for rules and procedures for a confidential dispute resolution process similar to the one prescribed by the Uniform Act.[45] The Regulations enacted under the Ontario and Prince Edward Island Regulations stipulate that the disclosure documents provided to prospective franchisees must state whether mediation or another alternative dispute resolution process is to be used in resolving disputes arising from the franchise relationship. It must also include details such as the circumstances in which the process may be invoked (in the Ontario Regulation) and the location or venue of the process (in the Prince Edward Island Regulation).[46]

There is a duty of good faith in Canadian legislation. At the federal level the Uniform Franchises Act includes a general obligation of fair dealing, which equates to a duty to act in good faith and in accordance with reasonable commercial standards.[47] At the provincial level none of the Acts imposes a duty of fair dealing in the negotiation of an agreement,[48] but all provincial franchise Acts impose a duty of fair dealing in the performance

---

43 Franchises Act, RSA 2000, c. F-23, ss 13–14; Franchises Regulation, Alta. Reg. 240/1995, s 17; Franchises Act, SNB 2007, c. F-23.5, s 6; Arthur Wishart Act (Franchise Disclosure), 2000, SO 2000, c. 3, s 6; Arthur Wishart (Franchise Disclosure) Regulation GENERAL, O Reg. 581/00, s 6(18); Franchises Act, RSPEI 1988, c. F-14.1, s 6; Franchises Act Regulations, PEI Reg. EC232/06, s 15.

44 Uniform Franchises Act, SC 2005, s 8.

45 Franchises Act, SNB 2007, c. F-23.5, s 8.

46 Arthur Wishart (Franchise Disclosure) Regulation GENERAL, O Reg. 581/00, s 5; Franchises Act Regulations, PEI Reg. EC232/06, s 16.

47 Uniform Franchises Act, SC 2005, ss 3(1), 3(3).

48 Manitoba Law Reform Commission, 'Consultation Paper on Franchise Legislation' (2008) 8 *Asper Review of International Business and Trade Law* 181.

and enforcement of the franchise agreement.[49] All Acts, except the Alberta Act, interpret the duty of fair dealing to include a duty to act in good faith and in accordance with reasonable commercial standards. All Acts, except Alberta's, provide that a party has a right of action for damages against another party who breaches the duty of fair dealing. The Acts also provide that the duty of fair dealing applies retroactively.[50]

The Civil Code of Québec at Article 1375 states that parties must conduct themselves in accordance to the principles of good faith both at the time the obligation is created, and at the time it is performed.[51] There is also a duty of pre-contractual disclosure in adhesion contracts, as franchise agreements are defined under Québec legislation which is distinct from the duty of good faith under Article 1375. Disclosure requirements are unilaterally imposed on the franchisor, who also bears the burden of proof to show that the franchisee had knowledge and consented to the provisions of the contract.[52]

The Uniform Act provides for time-limited rights of rescission if pre-sale disclosure by the franchisor is omitted or non-compliant. The franchisee may rescind the contract by delivering to the franchisor a written notice of rescission, as prescribed by the franchise agreement, no later than 60 days after receipt by the franchisee of the disclosure document or no later than two years after the grant of the franchise.[53] In the event of a misrepresentation contained in the disclosure document, the franchisee is deemed to have relied on the misrepresentation and has a statutory right of action for damages. However, the franchisor is not liable for damages if the franchisee was aware of the misrepresentation at the time of purchase.[54] All the provincial franchise Acts contain provisions similar to those prescribed by the Uniform Act with respect to the administration and enforcement of the franchise agreement.[55]

---

[49] Franchises Act, RSA 2000, c. F-23, s 7; Franchises Act, SNB 2007, c. F-23.5, s 3; Arthur Wishart Act (Franchise Disclosure), 2000, SO 2000, c. 3, s 3; Franchises Act, RSPEI 1988, c. F-14.1, s 3.

[50] Manitoba Law Reform Commission, 'Consultation Paper on Franchise Legislation' (2008) 8 *Asper Review of International Business and Trade Law* 181.

[51] Civil Code of Quebec, SQ 1991, c. 64. 2.

[52] Bruno Floriani, 'The impact of the Civil Code of Quebec on franchising' (1994) Lapointe-Rosenstein LLP Attorneys <http://www.lapointerosenstein.com/fichier/listelibrary/29/Bfl-impact.pdf> at 21 December 2009.

[53] Uniform Franchises Act, SC 2005, s 6.

[54] Uniform Franchises Act, SC 2005, s 7.

[55] Franchises Act, RSA 2000, c. F-23, ss 9, 13–14; Franchises Act, SNB 2007, c. F-23.5, ss 6, 7; Arthur Wishart Act (Franchise Disclosure), 2000, SO 2000, c. 3, ss 6, 7; Franchises Act, RSPEI 1988, c. F-14.1, ss 6, 7.

## Mexico

Mexico's population is estimated at about 108 million and its GDP is about $1.1 trillion. Franchising in Mexico generates over 800 000 jobs and represents approximately 6 percent of GDP. The sector has strengthened considerably in the past few years, positioning Mexico as the eighth leading nation worldwide in franchise development.[56]

Mexico is a civil law jurisdiction. Franchising became regulated in Mexico in 1991. The Mexico Industrial Property Law and regulations enacted in 1991 and 1994, respectively, require franchisors to disclose information to prospective franchisees and to file an executed franchise agreement with the Mexican Institute of Industrial Property.[57] On 25 January 2006 a Decree (the 2006 Decree) was adopted to amend provisions on franchising of the Law on Intellectual Property (Articles 142*bis*–Article 142*bis* 3).[58]

Article 142 of the 2006 Decree focuses solely on franchising and begins by defining a franchise, 'A franchise shall exist, when simultaneously with the license of a trademark, granted in writing, technical knowledge is transferred or technical assistance is provided to a person, in order for the latter to be able to manufacture or sell goods, or to provide services in a uniform manner and with the operational, commercial and administrative methods set forth by the holder of the trademark, with the purpose of maintaining the quality, reputation and image of the products or services distinguished by said trademark.'

The law in Mexico has since 1991 required disclosure. The 2006 Decree requires a franchisor to provide a potential franchisee with ten items of information about the franchise as dictated by the Regulations at least 30 business days before the date of execution of the franchise agreement.[59]

The Mexican Institute of Industrial Property is the regulatory authority responsible for administering franchise law.[60] Administrative infringements include failure to provide a franchisee with the information required

---

56 Franchise Emporium, 'Maui Wowi Hawaiian Adds Mexico to Growing List of International Master Franchises' (2008) <http://www.franchiseemporium.com/franchise-news-100608.asp> at 22 December 2009.

57 Industrial Property Law (of June 25, 1991 as last Amended by the Decree of December 26, 1997).

58 The commentary provided here is based on translations from the WIPO Database of Intellectual Property Legislative Texts and a translation of the 2006 Amendment from Gonzales Cavillo, SC Copyright 2006.

59 Industrial Property Regulations 1994 (Mexico), Article 65 and Decree (2006) Article 142.

60 Bryan Schwartz and Leandro Zylberman, 'Franchise Symposium Materials:

to be disclosed and unauthorized use of intellectual property confusingly similar to other protected by this Law.[61] 2006 Decree Article 142 provides that any lack of accuracy in disclosure shall entitle the franchisee to demand the nullity of the agreement and, additionally, to claim the payment of any damages and losses. The latter right may be exercised by the franchisee for only one year from the execution of the agreement.

The filing of information about the franchisor and registration of the transmission of trademark rights to the franchisee are required. The provisions of the Chapter on Licenses and the Transfer of Rights apply to the registration of franchises.[62] Upon execution of a franchise agreement, the franchisor must file a registration application with the Mexican Institute of Industrial Property.[63] Transmission of rights is to be registered at the Ministry of Commerce and Industrial Development.[64] The disclosure document itself does not have to be filed. Article 142*bis* requires that the franchise agreement must be in writing and must include certain information.[65]

---

International Franchise Regulation', (2008) 8 *Asper Review of International Business and Trade Law* 317.

61 The use of such operational and image elements in the above mentioned manner constitutes unfair competition in terms of paragraph I of this article.

62 Decree 2006 Article 142.

63 The application must attach an original or certified copy of the franchise agreement and comply with the following requirements, among others: (1) all copies must be duly signed; (2) official forms must be used; (3) all documents written in a foreign language must be translated into Spanish; (4) all foreign documents must be legalized; and (5) the franchisor's and franchisee's names, corporate domiciles, and nationalities must be provided.

64 Decree 2006 Article 143.

65 The geographical zone in which franchisee shall mainly perform the activities which are subject matter of the agreement; The location, minimum size and investment characteristics of the infrastructure, relating to the premises in which the franchisee shall carry out the activities deriving from the agreement; The politics of inventories and marketing and advertising, as well as the provisions related to the merchandise supply and the engagement with suppliers, if applicable; The politics, procedures and terms for any reimbursements, financings and other considerations under the respective responsibility of the parties in the terms established in the agreement; The criteria and methods applicable to determine franchisee's commissions and/or profit margins; The characteristics of the technical and operational training of franchisee's personnel, as well as the method or manner in which franchisor shall provide technical assistance; The criteria, methods and procedures of supervision, information, evaluation and grading of the performance and of the quality of the services under the respective responsibility of franchisee and franchisor.

To establish the terms and conditions to sub-franchise, in the event it is agreed by the parties; The termination causes under the franchise agreement. The assumptions under which the parties may review, and if such is the case, may mutually agree to amend the terms or conditions related to the franchise agreement; Unless

With respect to regulation targeted toward performance of the agreement the 2006 Decree enumerates certain prohibited practices. Article 1 states that a franchisor may be involved in the organization and operation of franchisee only to guarantee the compliance with the administration and image standards of the franchise according to the provisions of the agreement.[66] Article 142*bis* 2 establishes that both during and after the duration of the franchise relationship, the franchisee must keep all information about the franchise confidential.

The 2006 Decree also targets the end of the relationship. Article 142*bis* 3 provides that a franchisor and franchisee may not unilaterally terminate or rescind the agreement, unless the parties had agreed to an undetermined term for the agreement, or there is a justified cause to terminate or rescind the agreement, and in any case requires parties to abide by the causes and procedures set forth in the agreement. In the event of a breach the advanced termination made by either the franchisor or the franchisee shall result in the payment of the conventional penalties agreed upon by the parties in the agreement, or in indemnification for any loss caused by such advanced termination.

## The United States

The United States has a population of 307 million and represents the largest national economy in the world with a GDP estimated at about $14.3 trillion. Franchised businesses produce goods and services worth about $881 billion per year, or 4.4 percent of private-sector output in the United States. Franchised businesses are estimated to be the cause of $2.31 trillion of annual output, or 11.4 percent of all private-sector output in the United States.[67]

The US is a common law jurisdiction under a federal system. The federal

---

otherwise agreed, franchisee shall not be bound to sell its assets to franchisor or franchisor's designee, upon the termination of the franchise agreement. Unless otherwise agreed, franchisee shall in no event be bound to sell or transfer the shares of its company to franchisor, or to make franchisor a partner of such company.

[66] It shall not be considered as franchisor's involvement in the event of a merger, split-up, transformation, bylaws amendment, transfer or encumbrance of partnership interests or shares of franchisee, when with any such action, the personal characteristics of franchisee which were considered in the agreement as a determining factor of franchisor's will to execute the agreement with such franchisee, are modified.

[67] International Franchise Association, 'Economic Impact of Franchised Businesses' (2005) <http://www.buildingopportunity.com/impact/index.aspx> at 22 December 2009.

government has jurisdiction to pass laws governing franchise contracts. States can also pass laws that are consistent with federal law; federal power pre-empts state power to the extent that it conflicts. At the federal level the franchise sector is governed by Title 16 – Commercial Practices; revised as of January 1, 1986, Chapter I, Federal Trade Commission, Subchapter D – Trade Regulation Rules, Part 436 – Disclosure Requirements and Prohibitions Concerning Franchising and Business Opportunity Ventures (the FTC Rule).[68] At the state level it may be governed by franchise, business opportunity and/or relationship statutes.

At the federal level in the US 'franchise' means any continuing commercial relationship whereby a franchisee sells/distributes goods/services which are identified by a trademark or required to meet the quality standard imposed by a franchisor; and the franchisor has significant authority over the business operations by the franchisee or the franchisor offers significant assistance to the franchisee. At the state level there may be other definitions of franchising:

- In the states of California, Indiana, Illinois, Maryland, Michigan, North Dakota, Oregon, Rhode Island, Virginia, Washington, and Wisconsin a franchise is an agreement where the franchisee is granted right to sell/distribute goods under a marketing plan prescribed by the franchisor, associated with the trademark of the franchisor and the franchisee must pay a fee (a minimum amount may or may not be specified in the legislation).
- Minnesota designates an agreement similar to the one defined by California; or a contract/lease/other agreement whereby the franchisee is authorized to sell motor vehicle fuel under the franchisor's trade name; or sale/lease of any products for the purpose of enabling the franchisee to start a business where the franchisor will assist in finding a location, or the franchisor represents that it will purchase all products made using wholly/in part the products sold to the franchisee, or the franchisor guarantees that the franchisee will derive from the business more income than what it paid to the franchisor; or the contract/agreement where a manufacturer selling security systems through distributors requires royalties for products purchased by the distributor.
- New York is similar to California, with the exception that there must be a marketing plan prescribed by franchisor AND payment of fee;

---

68 The 1979 Federal Trade Commission (FTC) rule on disclosure requirements and prohibitions concerning franchising and business opportunity ventures was replaced with a new FTC Rule in 2007, effective 1 July 2008.

OR product associated with franchisor's trade mark AND payment of fee.

- In Hawaii franchising involves an agreement where one person grants another the right to use a trademark, in which there is a community interest in selling the good/service and the franchisee must pay fees to the franchisor.
- South Dakota defines a franchise as an agreement where the franchisee is granted right to sell products associated with the franchisor's trademark, in which the franchisee and franchisor have a community of interest in the marketing of the products and the franchisee is required to pay a fee to the franchisor.

The FTC Rule establishes at the federal level minimum standards of disclosure, but states are free to require more stringent regulation. Uniform Franchising Offering Circulars (UFOCs) are required to be updated on an annual basis or when material changes occur, and financial statements of the franchisor must meet US Generally Accepted Accounting Principles, normally necessitating the formation of a US entity for foreign-based systems.[69]

At the state level, California adopted franchise sales legislation requiring disclosure in 1970. Since then Hawaii, Illinois, Indiana, Iowa, Maryland, Michigan, Minnesota, New York, North Dakota, Oregon, Rhode Island, South Dakota, Virginia, Washington, and Wisconsin have also adopted franchise sales legislation requiring disclosure. Generally, the same disclosure document can be used to satisfy both state and federal disclosure requirements.

Registration is not a feature of franchise-specific legislation at the federal level in the US. The FTC Rule does not require registration filing or approval by the FTC or any federal agency; it does not, however, pre-empt state laws establishing a registration duty since registration provides more protection to prospective franchisees and therefore does not conflict with federal law. Fifteen states require registration of disclosure documents. California, Hawaii, Illinois, Indiana, Maryland, Michigan, Minnesota, New York, North Dakota, Oregon, Rhode Island, South Dakota, Virginia, Washington, and Wisconsin all have some franchise registration obligation. These range from Michigan's simple requirement that a franchisor file a one-page notice identifying the franchisor and his agent for service of process before offering or selling franchising in the state, to

---

69 David E. Holmes, 'Franchise Law Developments and Current Status United States' (Paper presented at the International Bar Association 2006 Conference, Chicago, 22 September 2006).

more complicated requirements, for example in Hawaii and South Dakota, where the franchisor must file state application forms annually and where franchise applications remain subject to review and stop order at any time.

Most states require a franchisor to submit a franchise registration application, consent for service of process, and the disclosure document with exhibits, with a filing fee. State reviews generally take 30 to 60 days per state; these can be conducted concurrently. In states other than the 16 registration states, if the offering falls under the definition of a 'business opportunity' and is not subject to any exemption, filing may be required.

All registration states except Virginia require identification or registration of selling agents. All except Hawaii, Illinois, Indiana, Michigan, Virginia and Wisconsin require promotional material to be submitted to the state administrator for review.

The FTC Rule is a disclosure law only. While there are industry-specific federal laws governing relationships in various business fields (such as the petroleum distribution and motor vehicle sales industries), there is no federal law governing franchisee-franchisor relationships.[70] At the state level, however, approximately 20 US states and territories have 'relationship statutes' that govern various aspects of the franchise relationship such as unjust termination, right of renewal, right to assign, encroachment, restriction of right of free association among franchisees, discrimination, and unreasonable standards of performance on franchisees.[71] The substance of some of these state relationship laws is briefly summarized here:

- Ten states in the US prohibit franchisors restricting the right of free association among franchisees for any lawful purpose. These states are Arkansas, California, Hawaii, Illinois, Iowa, Michigan, Minnesota, Nebraska, New Jersey, and Washington.

---

[70] David E. Holmes, 'Franchise Law Developments and Current Status United States' (Paper presented at the International Bar Association 2006 Conference, Chicago, 22 September 2006).

[71] The states with relationship laws are: Arkansas, California, Connecticut, Delaware, Hawaii, Illinois, Indiana, Iowa, Michigan, Minnesota, Mississippi, Missouri, Nebraska, New Jersey, Rhode Island, Washington and Wisconsin. The District of Columbia, Puerto Rico and the Virgin Islands also have statutes that govern the termination of franchises. South Dakota and Virginia's statutes do not directly address termination but they arguably restrict a franchisor's discretion in refusing to renew a franchise. The remaining states do not have franchise relationship statutes, but may have industry-specific (ie petroleum or auto dealer) statutes. See Michael J. Lockerby, 'A World Wide Web of Potential Franchise Law Violations' (1999) 6 Rich. J.L. & Tech. 4 <http://law.richmond.edu/jolt/v6i1/lockerby.txt> at 21 December 2009.

- Five states in the US prohibit discriminating that is unreasonable or arbitrary among franchisees in business dealings. These states are Hawaii, Illinois, Indiana, Minnesota, and Washington.
- Five states prohibit the imposition of unreasonable standards of performance upon a franchisee. These states are Hawaii, Minnesota, Nebraska, New Jersey, and Washington.
- Four states prohibit franchisors requiring or prohibiting a change in management of the franchisee except for reasonable cause. These states are Arkansas, Minnesota, Nebraska, and New Jersey.
- Three states prohibit a franchisor receiving kickbacks, except under certain conditions, including disclosure. These states are Hawaii, Indiana, and Washington.
- Four states in the US prohibit requiring a franchisee to supply from designated sources unless reasonably necessary for a lawful purpose justified on business grounds. The states are Hawaii, Indiana, Iowa, and Washington.
- Four states prohibit a franchisor from establishing a similar business or granting a franchise for the establishment of a similar business within the franchisee's exclusive territory, if any. These states are Hawaii, Indiana, Minnesota, and Washington.
- Two states require that arbitration or litigation be conducted outside the state. These states are Michigan and Washington.
- Two states prohibit enforcing any unreasonable covenant not to compete after termination of the franchise relationship. These states are Indiana and Minnesota.
- At least one state outlaws each of the following practices:

    - providing for a term of less than three years (Connecticut).
    - substantial modification of the franchise agreement by franchisor without consent in writing of the franchisee (Indiana).
    - limiting litigation brought for breach of the agreement in any manner (Indiana).
    - requiring franchisee to participate in marketing at an indeterminate expense or an expense determined by a third party or by a formula unless the franchise agreement specifies a maximum amount that the franchisee may be required to pay (Indiana).
    - selling, renting or offering to sell to franchisee at more than a fair and reasonable price (Washington).
    - requiring a transfer fee in excess of the amount necessary to compensate franchise or for expenses incurred in the transfer (Washington).

- substantially changing competitive circumstances of a dealership agreement without good cause (Wisconsin).[72]

About 22 states have laws regulating the offer and sale of a business opportunity with which franchise offerings may be required to comply, and many states also have industry-specific relationship statutes, governing industries such as petroleum, motor vehicles, mobile homes, farm and industrial equipment and alcoholic beverages.

About 35 states have some form of regulation that is directly applicable to the franchise relationship. About 15 states have franchise statutes; 23, business opportunity statutes; and 17, relationship statutes.

Regarding regulation of the end of the relationship, 18 states have relationship statutes that provide protections against wrongful termination.[73] These states are Arkansas, California, Connecticut, Delaware, Hawaii, Illinois, Indiana, Iowa, Michigan, Minnesota, Mississippi, Missouri, New Jersey, Nebraska, South Dakota, Virginia, Washington, and Wisconsin.[74] Most such statutes were enacted in response to perceived unequal bargaining power and the use of 'adhesion contracts' and were designed to protect licensees against indiscriminate termination.[75] The District of Columbia, Puerto Rico and the US Virgin Islands also have statutes that govern the termination of franchises. The remaining states do not have franchise relationship statutes, but some have industry-specific statutes.

There is no requirement regarding dispute resolution at the federal level, but the FTC Rule does refer to disclosure of methods of dispute resolution by arbitration or mediation.[76] In addition there is a range of state laws with

---

[72] Rupert M. Barkoff and Andrew C. Selden, *Fundamentals of Franchising* (1997).

[73] Such protections override the terms of the franchise or distributorship agreement. Also note the distinction between rights to renew (and good cause for failure to renew) under the agreement and a straight expiration of the contract where there is no renewal right provided for, at least in those states that distinguish between the two. See *Wright-Moore Corp. v. Ricoh Corp.*, 980 F.2d 432 (7th Cir. 1992) (Indiana).

[74] The South Dakota and Virginia statutes do not directly address termination but may restrict a franchisor's discretion in refusing to renew a franchise.

[75] Similarly, the Petroleum Marketing Practices Act 15 USC §2801-2806 was enacted because Congress was concerned that threats of arbitrary termination or non-renewal were being used against franchisees to exact unfair concessions. For a summary of provisions of the various relationship statutes in the US see Appendix C in Barkoff and Selden, *Fundamentals of Franchising* (2nd ed, 2004), 325.

[76] However, the Arbitration Fairness Act of 2009 introduced in the House of Representatives on 12 February 2009, at s 2, would make any pre-dispute arbitration agreement invalid or unenforceable that requires the arbitration of a franchise agreement. This Act has not yet passed into law. The Arbitration Fairness Act of

*Table 5.1 US state franchise, business opportunity, and relationship statutes*[a]

| State | Franchise Statute | Business Opportunity Statute | Relationship Statute |
|---|---|---|---|
| Alaska | | √ | |
| Arkansas | | | √ |
| California | √ | √ | √ |
| Connecticut | | √ | √ |
| Delaware | | | √ |
| Florida | √[b] | √ | |
| Georgia | | √ | |
| Hawaii | √ | | √ |
| Illinois | | | √ |
| Indiana | √ | √ | √ |
| Iowa | | √ | √ |
| Kentucky | | √ | |
| Louisiana | | √ | |
| Maryland | √ | √ | |
| Michigan | √ | √ | √ |
| Minnesota | √ | √ | √ |
| Mississippi | | | √ |
| Missouri | | | √ |
| Nebraska | | √ | √ |
| New Hampshire | | √ | |
| New Jersey | | | √ |
| New York | √ | | |
| North Carolina | | √ | |
| North Dakota | √ | | |
| Ohio | | √ | |
| Oklahoma | | √ | |
| Oregon | √ | | |
| Rhode Island | √ | | √ |
| South Carolina | | √ | |
| South Dakota | √ | √ | |
| Texas | | √ | |
| Utah | | √ | |
| Virginia | √ | √ | |
| Washington | √ | √ | √ |
| Wisconsin | √ | | √ |

*Notes:*

[a] See Barkoff and Selden, *Fundamentals of Franchising (*2nd ed, 2004).

[b] Limited to prohibiting misrepresentations in the sale of franchises, no disclosure or registration duty.

respect to arbitration and mediation.[77] See also the Uniform Arbitration Act (1956 Act or 2000 Act).

There is no filing of the disclosure with the Federal Trade Commission and the FTC does not normally review disclosure. The courts have uniformly held that there is no federal private right of action by a franchisee for a violation of the FTC Rule; this lack of a private right of action for FTC violations is the main difference between state and federal remedies.[78]

The dual levels of regulation of franchise sales in the US have brought a corresponding complexity to the issue of enforcement. Generally, the registration states' statutes provide for enforcement. Remedies for statutory violations are available both to state officials and to franchisees adversely affected by the franchisor's failure to comply with applicable state laws. A franchisee's remedies are typically either for damages or rescission. State officials can sue on behalf of the franchisee to require rescission or the payment of damages. States may also impose civil and criminal penalties, as well as seek injunctive relief.[79]

## REGULATION OF THE FRANCHISE SECTOR IN EUROPE

### Albania

Consumer and economic conditions are reported to be favourable for franchising in Albania, a country with a population of about 3.2 million and a GDP of about $13 billion.[80] Albania is a civil law jurisdiction.

---

2009 is to amend Title 9 of United States Code with respect to arbitration of commercial contracts.

[77] For a full list of State mediation and arbitration legislation visit: Just Law Links.com, Arbitration & Mediation <http://www.justlawlinks.com/PRACTICE/ctarib.htm> at 21 December 2009; Cornell University Law School, 'Uniform Arbitration Act (1956 Act or 2000 Act)' (2003) <http://www.law.cornell.edu/uniform/vol7.html#arbit> at 21 December 2009.

[78] Rupert M. Barkoff and Andrew C. Selden (eds), *Fundamentals of Franchising* (1997).

[79] See Philip F. Zeidman, 'Franchising and Other Methods of Distribution: Regulatory Pattern and Judicial Trends' (Paper presented at the 42nd Annual Advanced Antitrust Seminar: Distribution and Marketing, California, January 2003) 536.

('Both the state and the injured franchisee may institute actions. The state, for example, typically may bring an action for injunctive or declaratory relief, or seek civil penalties or criminal penalties consisting of fines and/or jail sentences.').

[80] Population information throughout this book is from the United Nations

Franchise-specific legislation is found in Chapter XX of the Civil Code of the Republic of Albania at Articles 1056 to 1064.[81] The discussion here is based on a computerized translation of the Albanian legislation.

In Albania a franchise contract is understood to be one that contains ongoing obligations of independent business entities to promote and develop trade, jointly conduct services, and implement specific obligations. During pre-contractual negotiations the parties have to exchange information on matters of relevance to the business of franchising, particularly their respective obligations. The information exchanged during contract negotiations must be kept confidential even if the contract is not concluded. Violations may result in liability to pay damages for up to three years. Parties may receive damages if the contract is not completed due to the deliberate conduct of the other party.

The franchise contract must specify, *inter alia*, the mutual obligations of the parties, contract duration and other elements at its core. The text of the contract must contain a full list of each party's obligations.

With respect to performance of the agreement a franchisor must make available to a prospective franchisee the rights to non-standardized materials, models, drafts, ideas, marketing and knowledge appropriate for the development of trade, and further is obliged to protect this program against all violations of obligations by third parties, to continually develop it, and to support its implementation by franchisees. A franchisee has the right to reduce remuneration to the franchisor in the event that the rights do not exist or if the franchisor violates contractual obligations. A franchisor may be entitled to compensation for damage caused by the infringement of the contractual obligations on the part of the franchisee, in particular by the inadequate implementation of the program by a franchisee.

While there may not be a duty of good faith per se, the parties must perform their obligations according to principles of trust.[82] They also have a reciprocal obligation to compete fairly, which allows a ban on local competition for up to a year. If the prohibition of competition results in a reduction of professional activity, the franchisee may be entitled to financial compensation.

In the case of contracts of indefinite duration or with a term of more than

---

and GDP information is from the IMF 2008 estimates. See also *Doing Business in Albania: 2008 Country Commercial Guide for US Companies.*

[81] Law No 7850 Civil Code 1994 (Republic of Albania) Chapter XX-Franchising (Articles 1056–1064).

[82] Law No 7850 Civil Code 1994 (Republic of Albania) Chapter XX – Franchising, Article 1058.

ten years, early termination of the contract must be made by notice to the other party one year in advance.

## Belarus

Belarus' population is approximately 9.7 million with a GDP estimated at about $60 billion. Belarus is a civil law jurisdiction. Franchise-specific legislation is found in Chapter 53 of the Civil Code of Belarus.[83]

Like Lithuania and Ukraine, Belarus follows the Russian example of implementing legislation regarding 'commercial concession agreements' to govern franchising contracts. A franchise agreement is a 'complex licence' according to which a contract must include a right granted to the user (a franchisee) to use the trade name and information of the right-holder (a franchisor).[84]

Master franchise agreements are permitted, but the duration of the sub-franchise agreements may not extend beyond that of the master agreement. A franchisee remains accountable to the franchisor for the actions of the sub-franchisees unless otherwise provided by the contract. The legislative rules applicable to contracts of franchise are equally applicable to contracts of sub-franchise, unless otherwise provided by the legislation.[85]

The franchise contract must be concluded in written form.[86] It must be registered with the National Centre of Intellectual Property; unregistered contracts are null and void. Modifications to the agreement must also be registered. References to modifications to the franchise contract can only be made from the time of registration of the change.[87]

There is also regulation targeted toward performance of the agreement. A franchisor must transfer to a franchisee all technical and commercial documentation and other information necessary to exercise the exclusive rights granted under the contract, including issuing licences to a franchisee for the right to use the intellectual property provided for by the contract.[88]

Unless otherwise provided by the contract, the franchisor is obliged to render permanent technical and consultative assistance to the franchisee, including assistance in training the franchisee's staff.[89] It is the duty of

83 Law No 218-Z Civil Code 1998 (Republic of Belarus) Chapter 53.
84 Law No 218-Z Civil Code 1998 (Republic of Belarus) Article 910.
85 Law No 218-Z Civil Code 1998 (Republic of Belarus) Article 9102.
86 Law No 218-Z Civil Code 1998 (Republic of Belarus) Article 9101.
87 Law No 218-Z Civil Code 1998 (Republic of Belarus) Article 9107.
88 Law No 218-Z Civil Code 1998 (Republic of Belarus) Article 9103(1).
89 Law No 218-Z Civil Code 1998 (Republic of Belarus) Article 9103(2).

the franchisor to control the quality of goods being produced or services rendered by the franchisee.[90]

The legislation also outlines some franchisee obligations. For example, the remuneration payable to a franchisor may be in the form of fixed payments, a once-only payment, periodic payments calculated as a percentage of proceeds or in any other manner determined by the agreement.[91] A franchisee must use the franchisor's firm name when carrying out the activity provided for by the contract; must ensure that the quality of the goods produced or services rendered is as prescribed by the franchisor; comply with the directions of the franchisor, including instructions concerning the external and internal appearance of the commercial premises to be used; render to customers all additional services they would have received had they purchased from the franchisor directly; not divulge confidential information obtained from the franchisor, including trade secrets; and issue the stipulated quantity of sub-franchises, if such duty is provided for by the contract.[92]

The legislation expressly allows the parties to limit their rights under the contract. For example, a franchisee may require the franchisor not to grant to other persons similar exclusive rights on the territory allocated for the franchisee and to refrain from its own similar activity in this territory. Contracts may also require variously, the franchisor not to compete with the franchisee on the territory, a franchisee not to obtain similar rights from competitors or potential competitors of the franchisor, and a franchisee to agree with the franchisor on the location of the commercial premises to be used.[93] Limitations of the parties' rights under the contract are subject to judicial review under the country's anti-monopoly provisions.[94]

The regulation also addresses the end of the relationship. In the event of the death of the franchisor, and transfer of his rights and duties under the contract to the heir, the contract terminates, unless the heir is registered within six months as an individual entrepreneur in accordance with the procedure established by the legislation.[95] The exercise of the rights and performance of the duties of the deceased franchisor before the acceptance of these rights and duties by the heir and before registration of the heir as

90 Law No 218-Z Civil Code 1998 (Republic of Belarus) Article 9103(2).
91 Law No 218-Z Civil Code 1998 (Republic of Belarus) Article 910(4).
92 Law No 218-Z Civil Code 1998 (Republic of Belarus) Article 9104.
93 Law No 218-Z Civil Code 1998 (Republic of Belarus) Article 9105(1).
94 Law No 218-Z Civil Code 1998 (Republic of Belarus) Article 9105(2).
95 Law No 218-Z Civil Code 1998 (Republic of Belarus) Article 9108(2).

an individual entrepreneur is effectuated by the trustee manager appointed in accordance with the Code.[96]

Each of the parties to a franchise agreement for which the duration of the contract is not specified may terminate the contract upon notifying the other party six months in advance unless a longer period is provided for in the contract.[97]

Transfer to another person of any of his rights by the franchisor is not grounds for a change or dissolution of the contract. The new franchisor will become a party to the contract to the extent of the rights transferred.[98]

The franchise contract remains operational in the event of a change by the franchisor of its firm name, unless the franchisee requires the dissolution of the contract and compensation for losses. If the franchisee opts to continue with the operation of the contract, he may be entitled to demand a commensurate reduction in the fees payable to the franchisor. In the event of the termination of the rights to the firm name without replacing it by the new firm name, the contract will terminate.[99]

If the period of operation of the exclusive rights granted under the contract terminates while the franchise contract is still in operation, the contract remains operational, except for provisions relating to the terminated rights. Unless otherwise provided by the contract, the franchisee has the right to demand a commensurate reduction in the fees payable to the franchisor.[100]

Finally, in Belarus a franchisor is jointly and severally liable with a franchisee with respect to claims against a franchisee as the manufacturer of goods.[101]

## Belgium

Belgium's population is approximately eleven million and its GDP is estimated at about $506 billion. Annual sales turnover through franchise outlets is about €2.4 billion and accounts for about 6 percent of retail trade. Belgium is a civil law jurisdiction. Belgium's franchise-specific legislation, the Law relative to pre-contractual information in the framework of agreements of commercial partnership 2006 (Belgium), came into force

---

96 Law No 218-Z Civil Code 1998 (Republic of Belarus) Article 9108(3).
97 Law No 218-Z Civil Code 1998 (Republic of Belarus) Article 91011(2).
98 Law No 218-Z Civil Code 1998 (Republic of Belarus) Article 9108(1).
99 Law No 218-Z Civil Code 1998 (Republic of Belarus) Article 91010(1,2).
100 Law No 218-Z Civil Code 1998 (Republic of Belarus) Article 91010(1).
101 Law No 218-Z Civil Code 1998 (Republic of Belarus) Article 9106.

in February 2000.[102] Information provided here is based on a translation provided by the European Franchise Federation (EEF).[103]

The term 'franchising' is not defined by the legislation. The legislation instead refers to 'commercial partnerships', defined as agreements made between two parties whereby one party concedes to the other party, in exchange for a fee, the right to use a commercial formula in the sale of goods or services under a common brand, a common commercial name, the transfer of 'know-how', and/or the provision of commercial or technical assistance.[104]

The legislation is applicable to all franchise agreements irrespective of contractual terms to the contrary. The pre-contractual phase of the agreement is subject to the jurisdiction of the Belgian courts when the activity which is the object of the agreement is exercised principally in Belgium.

Belgium's law consists primarily of pre-sales disclosure. One month prior to the conclusion of the agreement, the franchisor must provide the franchisee with disclosure in two parts. The first part concerns the main provisions of the contract; nine items are listed in Article 4 that must be disclosed to convey the essence of the agreement. The second part is a document comprising eleven enumerated factors necessary for a correct appreciation of the agreement (see Appendix2 – Content of Disclosure). These documents must be provided in writing. No obligation may be undertaken and no payment may be asked for by the franchisor prior to the expiration of the one month period following the delivery of the documents. The legislation also allows the government to determine the form of the disclosure documents and to elaborate on the disclosure requirements.[105]

The terms of the franchise agreement and the elements provided in the disclosure document must be written in a clear and comprehensible manner. Any ambiguity is interpreted in favour of the receiving party.[106]

---

102 Law Relative to Pre-contractual Information in the Framework of Agreements of Commercial Partnership 2006 (Belgium).

103 European Franchise Federation, 'National Regulation by Country – Belgium' (2009) <http://www.eff-franchise.com/spip.php?rubrique21> at 16 December 2009.

104 Law Relative to Pre-contractual Information in the Framework of Agreements of Commercial Partnership 2006 (Belgium) Article 2.

105 Bryan Schwartz and Leandro Zylberman, 'Franchise Symposium Materials: International Franchise Regulation' (2008) 8 *Asper Review of International Business and Trade Law* 317, 329–31. See also Law Relative to Pre-contractual Information in the Framework of Agreements of Commercial Partnership 2006 (Belgium) Article 4.

106 Law Relative to Pre-contractual Information in the Framework of Agreements of Commercial Partnership 2006 (Belgium) Article 7.

A franchisee who does not receive disclosure as prescribed by the legislation may have the franchise agreement declared null and void at any time within two years following execution of the agreement. Agreement terms not properly described in the disclosure document will not be enforceable against the franchisee.[107]

Upon the conclusion of the franchise agreement the parties must keep confidential all information obtained; and they may not use the information, directly or indirectly, outside the franchise agreement.[108]

## Estonia

Estonia's population is approximately 1.3 million and its GDP is estimated at about $23 billion. Estonia is a civil law jurisdiction. Franchising agreements are regulated by the 2002 Law of Obligations Act at Chapter 19.[109]

The legislation defines a franchise contract as one where the franchisor grants the franchisee a set of rights and information to use in the economic or professional activities of the franchisee, including the right to the trade mark, commercial identifications and know-how of the franchisor.[110]

Under the law a franchisor must provide franchisees with instructions and permanent assistance for the exercise of the rights associated with the franchise.[111] A franchisee is under an obligation to use the commercial identifications of the franchisor; to ensure the quality of the goods manufactured or services provided are as prescribed by the franchisor; to follow the instructions of the franchisor and to provide clients with all additional services they would have expected to obtain had they contracted with the franchisor directly.[112] To ascertain compliance with its instructions the franchisor has the right to check the quality of the goods manufactured or services provided by the franchisee.[113]

Rules with respect to termination of contracts are prescribed by the Law of Obligations Act, as termination of a franchising agreement is not

---

[107] Andrew P. Loewinger and Michael K. Lindsey (eds), *International Franchise Sales Laws* (2006).

[108] Law Relative to Pre-contractual Information in the Framework of Agreements of Commercial Partnership 2006 (Belgium) Article 6.

[109] Law of Obligations Act 2002 (Estonia).

[110] Law of Obligations Act 2002 (Estonia) Article 375.

[111] Law of Obligations Act 2002 (Estonia) Article 376.

[112] Law of Obligations Act 2002 (Estonia) Article 377.

[113] Law of Obligations Act 2002 (Estonia) Article 378.

specifically regulated by the legislation. Renewal of the franchising agreement is not regulated by the law, and is subject to the agreement by the parties.[114]

With regard to claims brought against a franchisee as the manufacturer of the goods there is no joint liability; the liability is borne solely by the franchisee.

**France**

France's population is approximately 65 million and its GDP is estimated at about $2.87 trillion. Franchise annual sales are estimated to be about $34.1 billion, making it one of the largest and most developed markets for franchising in Europe. France has developed strong and predominantly home-grown systems, mostly in specialized retailing.

France is a civil law jurisdiction which in 1989 was the first country in Europe to adopt a law relating to franchising. The details of the Loi Doubin (Law No. 89-1008) are laid out in government decree No. 91-337 of 4 April 1991.

The law is not exclusive to franchising (though in effect it may be) as it relates to the development of commercial and artisanal enterprises and applies to the licensing of trademarks, trade names or logos in an exclusive or quasi-exclusive territory.[115]

The essence of the law is disclosure. All persons who make available a trading name, a trade mark, or a logo that requires entry into exclusive or quasi-exclusive obligations for the carrying on of its trading activities must furnish, prior to the execution of the agreement, a document giving all details to enable that person to enter into the contract with full knowledge.

When payment is required prior to execution of the contract, the undertaking must be in writing and it must mention the reciprocal obligations of the parties in the event of breach. The disclosure document as well as the

---

[114] International Franchise Lawyers Association, 'Franchising in Estonia' (2009) International Franchise Lawyers Association <http://www.franchiselawyers.de/reportestonia.htm> at 16 December 2009.

[115] While there are no exemptions, exclusions or exceptions with respect to franchises and other relationships that come within the scope of the law, there is the possibility that a licence may fall outside the scope of the law, for example due to the exclusivity aspect of Article 2. See Bryan Schwartz and Leandro Zylberman, 'Franchise Symposium Materials: International Franchise Regulation' (2008) 8 *Asper Review of International Business and Trade Law* 317. See also <http://www.europeanfranchising.com/> at 27 December 2009.

draft Agreement must be communicated at least 20 days before execution of the contract or, failing this, before payment.

Anyone who does not provide the required information as established by the legislation is liable to pay fines.[116] In order to render the agreement null and void a franchisee must demonstrate that it would not have entered into the franchise agreement if fully compliant disclosure had been made. If the agreement is declared null and void, the franchisee is entitled to be restored to the position it was in prior to the agreement, but it is not entitled to any loss of profits.[117]

## Italy

Italy's population is approximately 60 million people and its GDP is estimated at about $2.3 trillion. A civil law jurisdiction, Italy has adopted franchise legislation, Rules on the Regulation of Franchising 2004 (Italy). This summary is based on the unofficial translation of the legislation published by the EFF. [118]

The legislation defines a franchise agreement as an agreement between two economically independent legal parties, whereby a franchisor grants to a franchisee, for consideration, a series of industrial or intellectual property rights with the object of having the franchisee join a system consisting of a number of franchisees operating in the territory to market certain goods or services.[119] The legislative provisions relating to franchise agreements apply equally to master franchise agreements.[120]

Under Italian law, prior to commencing a franchising network, the franchisor must have tested its business concept in the market.[121] When

---

116 The Loi Doubin (Law No. 89-1008) are laid out in government decree No. 91-337 Article 2.

117 Parties are permitted to waive their rights under the Doubin law, but can do so only after execution of the agreement. See Field Fisher Waterhouse, 'Franchise Disclosure and Registration Requirements' (2008) International Franchising <http://www.europeanfranchising.com/how-we-can-help-you/disclosure-and-registration.aspx> at 21 December 2009.

118 (Unofficial Translation), European Franchise Federation, 'Italy: Law on "Commercial Affiliation" (Franchising)' (2004) <www.assofranchising.it/english/legislative_information.htm> at 21 December 2009. See also UNIDROIT, 'Legislation and Regulations Relevant to Franchising: Italy' (2005) <www.unidroit.org/english/guides/2007franchising/country/italy.htm> at 21 December 2009.

119 Law No 126 Rules on the Regulation of Franchising 2004 (Italy) Article 1(1).

120 Law No 126 Rules on the Regulation of Franchising 2004 (Italy) Article 2(1).

121 Law No 126 Rules on the Regulation of Franchising 2004 (Italy) Article 3(1–3).

it does begin to sell franchises, Italian law requires a franchisor to make disclosure. At least 30 days before the signing of a franchise contract, a franchisor must provide a prospective franchisee with a complete copy of the contract to be signed, together with annexes, except those for which objective and specific confidentiality requirements exist.[122]

Unless it is in writing, the franchise agreement is deemed null and void. Whenever the agreement is for a determined time, the franchisor must guarantee to the franchisee a minimum term sufficient to amortize the investment. This term cannot be less than three years, except for those cases where the agreement is terminated due to a breach by one of the parties. The agreement must also expressly indicate seven items (see mandatory terms discussion in Chapter 8).

There is a duty of good faith. In its dealings with franchisees, a franchisor must at all times behave with loyalty, fairness and in good faith, and must promptly provide a prospective franchisee with any information the franchisee deems necessary or useful in deciding to sign the franchise contract. A franchisor is not, however, under an obligation to furnish to the franchisee any objectively confidential information or to disclose information that would violate rights of a third party. Apart from the exempted information mentioned above, a franchisor must justify to a franchisee any failure to disclose the information requested by the franchisee.[123]

A prospective franchisee has an equal duty to act with loyalty, fairness and in good faith towards the franchisor; and to provide the franchisor with any information needed by the franchisor in deciding to sign the franchise contract, even if the information is not expressly requested by the franchisor.[124]

In the event of one party providing false information, the other party may ask for the annulment of the contract, as well as for damages, if due.[125]

The franchisee cannot transfer its registered office without the franchisor's prior consent. Also, the franchisee undertakes to respect and have respected by its own collaborators and personnel, even after termination of the contract, the confidentiality of the information subject to the franchise contract.[126]

---

122 Law No 126 Rules on the Regulation of Franchising 2004 (Italy) Article 4(1).

123 Law No 126 Rules on the Regulation of Franchising 2004 (Italy) Article 6(1, 2).

124 Law No 126 Rules on the Regulation of Franchising 2004 (Italy) Article 6(3).

125 Law No 126 Rules on the Regulation of Franchising 2004 (Italy) Article 8.

126 Bryan Schwartz and Leandro Zylberman, 'Franchise Symposium Materials: International Franchise Regulation' (2008) 8 *Asper Review of International Business and Trade Law* 317, 338.

There is also a process requirement for dispute resolution. It requires that in the case of a dispute over the franchise contracts, the parties can agree that before taking the case to the Courts or to arbitration, they must try to conciliate through the Chamber of Commerce and Industry where the franchisee's registered office is located.[127]

## Lithuania

Lithuania's population is approximately 3.4 million and its GDP is estimated at about $47 billion. A civil law jurisdiction, Lithuania follows the Russian example of implementing legislation regarding 'commercial concession agreements' as do Belarus and Ukraine. Franchise and sub-franchise agreements are regulated in Chapter XXXVII of the Civil Code of Lithuania, enacted in July 2001.[128]

A franchise agreement is one in which a franchisor grants a franchisee in exchange for remuneration the right to use the firm name, trade mark and protected industrial information belonging to the franchisor.[129] The provisions of Chapter XXXVII of the Civil Code are applicable to a contract of sub-franchise unless conditions of the sub-franchise provide otherwise.[130] The conditions of the sub-franchise contract have to be indicated in advance in the franchise contract or may be agreed later with the franchisor. [131]

The legislation does not deal with disclosure in a detailed manner, but Article 6.770 provides that the franchisor has the obligation to transfer technical and commercial documentation to the franchisee and provide other information necessary for the franchisee to exercise the rights granted to him under the franchise agreement.

A contract of franchise must be concluded in written form or it will be null and void.[132] If the subject matter of a franchise contract is protected by patent legislation, the contract must be registered. A contract of franchise may be invoked against third persons only if the contract is registered

---

[127] Law No 126 Rules on the Regulation of Franchising 2004 (Italy) Article 7.

[128] Bryan Schwartz and Leandro Zylberman, 'Franchise Symposium Materials: International Franchise Regulation' (2008) 8 *Asper Review of International Business and Trade Law* 317, 338.

[129] Civil Code 2000 (Republic of Lithuania) Article 6.766.

[130] Civil Code 2000 (Republic of Lithuania) Article 6.768(6).

[131] Bryan Schwartz and Leandro Zylberman, 'Franchise Symposium Materials: International Franchise Regulation' (2008) 8 *Asper Review of International Business and Trade Law* 317, 338.

[132] Civil Code 2000 (Republic of Lithuania) Article 6.767(1).

in the Register of Enterprises. If a franchisor is registered in a foreign state, the contract must be registered in the same register of legal persons where the franchisor is registered.[133]

The legislation provides for terms the contract must and/or may contain. The franchise contract must provide for the use of the exclusive rights, business reputation and commercial experience of the franchisor by establishing the minimum and maximum amount of use. The contract may also determine the applicable territory of use. A contract of franchise may provide for the right of the franchisee to enter into sub-franchising agreements.[134]

A sub-franchise contract may not be concluded for a period longer than that of the franchise contract. If a contract of franchise is null and void, a contract of sub-franchise upon which it is based will also be null and void.[135]

In the event of the dissolution of a franchise contract before the agreed time, the rights and duties of the sub-franchisee under the contract of sub-franchise pass to the franchisor if he agrees to accept the rights and duties under the sub-franchise contract, unless otherwise provided for by the contract. The same rules also apply in the event of the dissolution of a contract of indeterminate term.[136]

Remuneration may be as a fixed lump-sum, or payable in instalments, deductions being made from the receipts of the franchisee or calculated in any other way specified in the contract.[137]

A franchisor has a duty to transfer to the franchisee technical and commercial documentation necessary to implement the rights granted under the contract; train the franchisee and his employees with regard to the implementation of the transferred rights; issue to the franchisee licences provided for by the contract; render permanent technical and consultative assistance to the franchisee and execute control of the quality of goods or services provided by the franchisee under the contract. A franchisor is further obliged to ensure the registration of the contract.[138]

A franchisee must use the firm name and trade mark of the franchisor as specified in the contract; ensure the quality of the goods and services provided; comply with the directions of the franchisor with respect of the external and internal appearance of the business premises and any other

---

133 Civil Code 2000 (Republic of Lithuania) Article 6.767(2) and (3).
134 Civil Code 2000 (Republic of Lithuania) Article 6.768.
135 Civil Code 2000 (Republic of Lithuania) Article 6.768.
136 Civil Code 2000 (Republic of Lithuania) Article 6.768(4).
137 Civil Code 2000 (Republic of Lithuania) Article 6.769.
138 Civil Code 2000 (Republic of Lithuania) Article 6.770.

conditions specified in the franchise contract; provide customers any other additional services they would have expected had they acquired the goods or services directly from the franchisor; conclude a contract of sub-franchise if this is provided for in the contract; and inform customers that the franchisee is acting under a franchise contract.[139]

The franchise contract may limit the rights of the parties to the extent not prohibited by competition law. Conditions limiting the rights of the parties that are in breach of competition law are deemed void. [140]

A contract of franchise may be modified by agreement of the parties.[141] In the event of a change in the firm name or trade mark of the franchisor, which are subject to the franchise contract, the contract remains valid with respect to the new name or trade mark, unless the franchisee demands the termination of the contract and compensation for damages. If the contract remains valid, a franchisee has the right to require commensurate reduction of the remuneration owed to the franchisor, unless otherwise provided in the contract.[142]

There is also regulation targeted toward ending the relationship. A franchisee that has duly performed its duties under the contract, upon the expiry of the franchise contract has the right to conclude a new contract for a new term on the same conditions.[143] A franchisor has the right to refuse the formation of a new contract only if within three years from the date of expiry of the contract term he will not conclude a similar contract with other persons extending over the same territory. If before the expiry of the three-year time limit the franchisor wishes to grant the same exclusive rights to other persons, he is obliged to propose formation of a new contract to the franchisee or compensate the damages incurred by him. The

---

139 Civil Code 2000 (Republic of Lithuania) Article 6.771.

140 Prohibited limitations include the obligation of the franchisor not to grant similar rights to other persons for use on the territory of the franchisee; the prohibition of the franchisee to receive under a contract exclusive rights from competitors and potential competitors of the franchisor; the obligation of the franchisee to agree with the franchisor on the location and the external and internal appearance of the business premises of the franchisee. Competition law also limits a franchisor's right to determine prices or their lower limit of goods or services provided by a franchisee; and a franchisee's right to sell to a certain category of purchasers. Civil Code 2000 (Republic of Lithuania) 6.772(2)–(4).

141 But note that amendments to the contract may be invoked against third parties only if they have been registered in accordance to the procedure established by the Civil Code 2000 (Republic of Lithuania) Article 6.775.

142 Civil Code 2000 (Republic of Lithuania) Article 6.778.

143 Civil Code 2000 (Republic of Lithuania) Article 6.774(1).

conditions of the new contract may not be more onerous for the franchisee than the conditions of the previous contract.[144]

In the case of a franchise contract of indeterminate duration, each party has the right to repudiate the contract upon giving notice to the other party at least six months in advance.[145] The franchise contract will automatically terminate in the event of the franchisor losing his right to the firm name or trade mark, as well as upon bankruptcy proceedings being initiated against the franchisor or the franchisee.[146]

In the case of transfer the new franchisee becomes a party to the contract.[147] In the case of death of the franchisor or the franchisee, rights will pass to the heir.[148] In the event that the operation of the exclusive rights under the contract expires or is terminated upon any other grounds, the contract continues to be valid, except for the conditions relating to the terminated right. In such event the fact of concluding a contract shall be subject to re-registration unless the franchisor demands termination of the contract and compensation of damages. A franchisee will be entitled, unless otherwise provided by the contract, to commensurate reduction in the remuneration due to the franchisor.

The franchisor has subsidiary liability for claims brought against the franchisee concerning the quality of the goods or services provided by the franchisee.[149] The franchisee shall bear subsidiary liability towards the franchisor for the actions committed by sub-franchisees.[150]

**Moldova[151]**

The Republic of Moldova has a population of approximately 3.6 million. One of the poorest countries in Europe, Moldova's GDP is about $6 billion. The country has two instruments regulating franchising: Chapter

---

[144] Civil Code 2000 (Republic of Lithuania) Article 6.774(2).

[145] The dissolution of the contract is subject to registration as prescribed by the Civil Code 2000 (Republic of Lithuania) Article 6.776(1)–(2).

[146] Civil Code 2000 (Republic of Lithuania) Article 6.776(3) and (4).

[147] Civil Code 2000 (Republic of Lithuania) Article 6.777(1).

[148] The heir must be an entrepreneur and continue or start the business within six months from the date of opening the inheritance. Otherwise, the contract shall terminate. The effectuation of the rights and performance of the duties of the deceased under the contract before the acceptance of these rights and duties by the heir shall be executed by the property administrator appointed by the Civil Code 2000 (Republic of Lithuania) Article 6.777(2).

[149] Civil Code 2000 (Republic of Lithuania) Article 6.773.

[150] Civil Code 2000 (Republic of Lithuania) Article 6.768(5).

[151] UNIDROIT, 'Legislation Relevant to Franchising – Moldova' (2005)

XXI of the 2003 Civil Code and 'The Law of the Republic of Moldova on Franchising' No. 1335 (1997) (Law No. 1335).

The Civil Code defines a franchise contract as an instalment contract whereby the franchisor and franchisee agree to contribute reciprocally to distribute goods and services.[152] According to Law No. 1335 the franchising contract may be entered into at the suggestion of the franchisor or the franchisee. The proposal to enter into the contract must include the business plan specifying the provision of goods or services; the parameters of the production process; remuneration of employees; anticipated income; the amount and purpose of additional investments and any other clauses as requested by the franchisor or franchisee.[153]

The franchise contract must be in writing, contain a full description of the procedure for transfer and the obligations of the parties, state the term of the contract, contain any provisions regarding the termination or extension of the contract and other important elements.[154] The franchise contract also must specify the parties to the contract; the name, nature and area of business; the amount and terms of the payments to be made; the rights and obligations of the parties, including those following the termination/expiration of the contract; the commitment by the franchisor to provide assistance to the franchisee; the responsibility of each party in the event of non-execution or inadequate execution of the terms of the contract; the method of settling disputes; the territory where the franchisor's trademark will be used; the duration of the contract, as well as terms for its amendment, extension or termination; the address of the company's headquarters, bank details and signatures of the parties; and other clauses agreed upon by the parties, not contravening the legislation.[155]

The country's Intellectual Property State Agency collects and keeps information regarding existing and potential parties to a franchise agreement. The franchise agreement must be registered with the State Agency for the Protection of Industrial Property. There is a registration fee associated with the process, which is determined by the government.[156]

---

<http://www.unidroit.org/english/guides/2007franchising/country/moldova.htm> at 23 December 2009.

[152] Civil Code 2003 (Republic of Moldova) Article 1172.

[153] Law No 1335 with Respect to Franchising 1997 (Republic of Moldova) Article 8(1–2).

[154] Civil Code 2003 (Republic of Moldova) Article 1173.

[155] Law No 1335 with Respect to Franchising 1997 (Republic of Moldova) Article 9.

[156] Law No 1335 with Respect to Franchising 1997 (Republic of Moldova) Article 9(4).

Potential franchisors and franchisees may purchase information from the Agency.[157]

With respect to legislation targeted toward performance, the Civil Code prescribes that a franchisor must transfer to the franchisee the relevant intellectual property rights, trade marks, concepts of delivery and supply and other information necessary to adequately perform the franchise contract. The franchisor is further obliged to protect the franchise program from the intervention of third parties, to update the program continuously and to support the franchisee through training and information.[158] A franchisee may reduce the amount of money to be paid to the franchisor if the rights do not exist or if the franchisor does not perform its obligations.[159]

A franchisee has a duty to pay royalties, observe the business format prescribed by the franchisor, and, if provided by the terms of the contract, to purchase goods or services required from the franchisor or a person designated by the franchisor.[160] Both the franchisor and the franchisee are under an obligation of confidentiality.[161]

The rights of the parties are guaranteed by legislation. The property rights of the franchisor temporarily transferred to the franchisee are protected, and the legislation prohibits a third party from going after a franchisor's assets transferred to the franchisee.[162]

An unusual provision in the law assures a franchisors' right to associate in national or international associations to establish and ensure the protection of ethics for franchising. The legislation makes no mention of a right of association for franchisees.[163]

Moldova also has implemented regulation targeted toward end of relationship. The contract may be terminated as follows: if both parties agree, one of the parties breaches the agreement, one of the parties is in liquidation or bankrupt, the Court declares the formation documents invalid, the death of the responsible person who represented the parties at the

---

157 Law No 1335 with Respect to Franchising 1997 (Republic of Moldova) Article 8(3)–(4).

158 Civil Code 2003 (Republic of Moldova) Article 1174.

159 Civil Code 2003 (Republic of Moldova) Article 1179(2).

160 Civil Code 2003 (Republic of Moldova) Article 1175.

161 Civil Code 2003 (Republic of Moldova) Article 1176.

162 Law No 1335 with Respect to Franchising 1997 (Republic of Moldova) Article 16(3)–(4).

163 Law No 1335 with Respect to Franchising 1997 (Republic of Moldova) Article 17.

signing of the agreement, or any other situations as agreed by the parties or prescribed by law.[164]

The duration of the agreement is to be agreed by the parties. If the term is not specified in the contract and it exceeds ten years, any of the parties may terminate the agreement upon one year advance notice to the other party. If the termination right is not exercised the contract is prolonged in two-year increments.[165]

In Moldova the franchise agreement must contain a dispute resolution clause.[166] The protection of the parties' rights is effected by the economic courts, which may be international; or alternatively by commercial arbitration.[167]

## Romania

Romania's population is approximately 21.5 million and its GDP is estimated at about $200 billion. A civil law jurisdiction, Romania in 1997 enacted Government Ordinance No. 52/1997 regarding the Legal Status of Franchise which was approved and modified by Parliament in 1998.

Franchising is defined as a marketing channel based on a continual collaboration between persons or legal entities, financially independent, whereby a franchisor grants to a franchisee the rights to operate and develop a business, product, technology or service. A franchisor is a business person or legal entity that owns the rights of a registered trademark; grants the right to operate or develop a business, product, technology or service; ensures the franchisee receives initial training for the development of the trademark; and employs personnel and financial means to promote its trademark, research and development, and to ensure the development and viability of the product. A franchisee is a business person or legal entity, chosen by the franchisor, which adheres to the principle of uniformity of the franchise system, as defined by the franchisor.[168]

There are standards for disclosure. To enable a franchisee to make an informed decision a franchisor is required to provide certain information

---

164 Law No 1335 with Respect to Franchising 1997 (Republic of Moldova) Article 10(2).

165 Civil Code 2003 (Republic of Moldova) Article 1177.

166 Law No 1335 with Respect to Franchising 1997 (Republic of Moldova) Article 9(2)(g).

167 Law No 1335 with Respect to Franchising 1997 (Republic of Moldova) Article 16(6).

168 Ordinance No 52 Regarding the Franchise Legal Framework 1997 (Romania) Article 1(a–c).

in a disclosure document which must be submitted before a franchisee undertakes any legal obligations with respect to the proposed business.[169] A franchisor must provide the prospective franchisee with information allowing him to participate, with full knowledge, in the operation of the franchise contract. A franchisor must, *inter alia*, inform the prospective franchisee of the financial conditions of the contract, such as the initial fee and advertising fees, and how they will be calculated. A franchisor must also disclose whether the contract contains a contractual obligation to purchase clause and must also disclose information to allow the franchisee to forecast and to prepare its financial plan; as well as information on the objectives and scope of exclusivity granted; duration of the contract; and the conditions for the renewal, termination and assignment of the contract.[170]

The Law does not require filing or registration, but the Romanian State Office for Inventions and Trademarks may require registration of trademark licences and some franchise agreements may need to be filed with the Competition Council.[171]

There is in Romania other regulation targeted toward pre-sales and contract formation. The franchise contract must reflect the interest of the franchise network members, protecting the franchisor's industrial and intellectual property rights, through maintenance of the common identity and reputation of the franchise network.[172]

A franchisor must unambiguously define the obligations and responsibilities of each party and all other terms of collaboration.[173] Prior to the launch of the franchise network the franchisor must hold and exploit a business activity for a specified period, and must be the owner of the intellectual and industrial rights the subject of the contract.

A franchise contract must contain clauses with respect to the object of the contract; the rights and obligations of each party; the financial conditions of the contract; the duration of the contract; and the amendment, renewal and termination conditions. It must clearly state the conditions

---

169 Bryan Schwartz and Leandro Zylberman, 'Franchise Symposium Materials: International Franchise Regulation' (2008) 8 *Asper Review of International Business and Trade Law* 317, 340.

170 Ordinance No 52 Regarding the Franchise Legal Framework 1997 (Romania) Article 2(3).

171 Andrew P. Loewinger and Michael K. Lindsey (eds), *International Franchise Sales Laws* (2006).

172 Ordinance No 52 Regarding the Franchise Legal Framework 1997 (Romania) Article 3.

173 Ordinance No 52 Regarding the Franchise Legal Framework 1997 (Romania) Article 4(1).

governing the transfer of the franchise agreement, in particular the conditions for designation of a successor.[174]

A franchise contract must also comply with the following principles: the term of the contract shall be set to allow the franchisee to depreciate the franchise-specific investment; non-competition clauses shall be included in the contract, to protect know-how; financial obligations of the franchisee shall be clearly stated and shall be determined so as to facilitate achievement of common objectives; advertising materials, which give the financial forecast of a franchisee, shall be objective and verifiable.[175]

A franchisor may impose a non-competition and confidentiality clause, to prevent alienation of the transferred know-how during the exclusivity contract.[176] A franchisor has the obligation to create a franchise network that must be utilized so as to allow preservation of the franchise network's identity and reputation, for which the franchisor is guarantor.[177] A franchisor must select the franchisee that demonstrates proof of required skills, respectively: management skills and financial ability to develop the business.[178] In its capacity as creator and guarantor of the franchise network, a franchisor must ensure the preservation of the identity and reputation of the franchise network.[179]

A franchisor must provide its franchisees with initial training as well as permanent commercial support. A franchisor must ensure that the franchisee, through adequate advertising, makes known that the franchisee is a person or legal entity financially independent from the franchisor or other persons or legal entities.

A franchisee has an obligation to pay a fee to the franchisor, which authorizes it to use the trademark, know-how or other franchise special knowledge, as well as any other intellectual or industrial property rights, throughout the duration of the franchise contract.[180] A franchisee is

---

174 Ordinance No 52 Regarding the Franchise Legal Framework 1997 (Romania) Article 5.

175 Ordinance No 52 Regarding the Franchise Legal Framework 1997 (Romania) Article 6(1).

176 Ordinance No 52 Regarding the Franchise Legal Framework 1997 (Romania).

177 Ordinance No 52 Regarding the Franchise Legal Framework 1997 (Romania) Article 11.

178 Ordinance No 52 Regarding the Franchise Legal Framework 1997 (Romania) Article 15(1).

179 Ordinance No 52 Regarding the Franchise Legal Framework 1997 (Romania) Articles 10 and 15.

180 Ordinance No 52 Regarding the Franchise Legal Framework 1997 (Romania) Article 6(2,3).

under an obligation to develop the franchise network and to maintain its common identity, as well as its reputation; provide the franchisor any information likely to facilitate knowledge and analysis of the franchisee's performance and its real financial position, to ensure an effective management of the franchise; and not disclose to third parties the franchisor's know-how, throughout the duration of the contract, as well as subsequently.[181]

Some regulation in Romania is targeted toward end of the relationship. The terms of the franchise contract must state clearly the circumstances which may lead to termination without notice. In the event of breaches of contract, a franchisor must notify the franchisee, in writing of any such breaches and must allow it sufficient time to remedy them.[182]

Upon the termination of the agreement, post-contractual relations are based on fair competition rules. However, a franchisor is permitted to impose strict obligations on the former franchisee, to ensure the protection of the confidential nature of the business and, in particular, its know-how from being rendered ineffective by a competing network.[183]

Although there are no governmental remedies available in Romania for a franchisor's failure to comply with disclosure requirements, a franchisee may seek remedies, including damages resulting from any infringement or failure to comply with any of the legal requirements for the pre-contractual phase.[184]

## Russia

Russia's population is approximately 142 million and its GDP is estimated at about $1.68 trillion. Franchising as a business model first came to Russia, a civil law jurisdiction, in the early 1990s.[185] The Civil Code of the Russian Federation, which came into effect in 1996, regulates the relationship between the franchise parties, as the Code's reference to 'commercial

---

181 Ordinance No 52 Regarding the Franchise Legal Framework 1997 (Romania) Article 4(2,3).

182 Ordinance No 52 Regarding the Franchise Legal Framework 1997 (Romania) Article 6(1).

183 Ordinance No 52 Regarding the Franchise Legal Framework 1997 (Romania) Article 8.

184 Bryan Schwartz and Leandro Zylberman, 'Franchise Symposium Materials: International Franchise Regulation' (2008) 8 *Asper Review of International Business and Trade Law* 317, 340.

185 Anastasia Chukanova, 'Franchising in Russia: Main Trends' (2006) IND Franchising <http://www.ind-f.com/eng/?page=publications> at 28 December 2008.

concessions' includes franchising (similar terminology has been adopted in Belarus, Lithuania, and Ukraine). The Code translation on which this summary is based has been sourced from the International Institute for Law-Based Economy.

A franchise contract, referred to in the legislation as a 'contract of commercial concession', is one whereby a franchisor undertakes to grant to a franchisee, for a fee, the right to use certain exclusive rights belonging to a franchisor. The franchise contract provides for the use of the exclusive rights, with or without indication of the territory to which the agreement applies. A franchisor and franchisee may be commercial organizations and individuals registered as individual entrepreneurs.[186]

Though it does not require disclosure, Russian law requires transfer of the contractual document to the franchisee. The franchise contract is null and void, unless it is concluded in written form, and, unless provided otherwise by the contract, the franchisor must ensure the registration of the contract.[187] In relations with third persons the parties to the franchise contract have the right to refer to the contract only if registered.[188]

In Russia there are extensive provisions targeted toward performance. For example, a franchisee must pay a franchisor remuneration in the form of fixed lump sum or periodical payments, deductions from proceeds, mark-up on the wholesale price of goods supplied by the franchisor for resale, or in any other form stipulated in the contract.[189] A franchisor must transfer the technical and commercial documentation, and other information necessary for the franchisee to exercise his rights under the contract; must instruct the franchisee and his employees on the issues related to the execution of these rights; and must issue to the franchisee licences stipulated in the contract, having formalized them according to the established procedure. Further, a franchisor must render continuous technical and consulting assistance to the franchisee, including assistance in the training of employees. A franchisor must also supervise the quality of goods or services provided by the franchisee.[190]

A franchisee must use the franchisor's firm name and trademark when performing the activity stipulated by the contract; ensure quality

---

[186] Civil Code 1996 (Russian Federation) Article 1027(1–3).

[187] Civil Code 1996 (Russian Federation) Article 1031(2).

[188] The contract of commercial concession for the use of an object protected in accordance with the patent legislation must also be registered with the patent agency of the Russian Federation or the contract shall be deemed null and void. Civil Code 1996 (Russian Federation) Article 1028.

[189] Civil Code 1996 (Russian Federation) Article 1030.

[190] Civil Code 1996 (Russian Federation) Article 1031.

conformance of the goods or services provided; observe the franchisor's instructions, including directions with respect to the exterior and interior of the commercial premises; render customers all additional services the customers would have expected had they acquired the goods or services from the franchisor directly; ascertain the confidentiality of the franchisor's know-how and other commercial information; issue the specified number of sub-franchise contracts, if such a requirement is stipulated by the contract; and inform the customers of the existence of the franchise contract.[191]

The franchise contract may place limitations on the rights of the parties, such as a franchisor's obligation not to grant other persons similar exclusive rights to be used on the territory assigned to the franchisee or desist from performing on his own a similar activity on this territory; a franchisee's obligation not to compete against the franchisor on the territory specified in the contract; the prohibition against a franchisee's gaining similar rights from the franchisor's competitors or potential competitors; and a franchisee's obligation to coordinate with the franchisor the location of commercial premises used.[192]

Although limitations may be placed upon the rights of the parties, the limiting terms may be deemed invalid if the terms contradict antimonopoly legislation. For example, a franchisor does not have the rights to prescribe the price of the goods or services provided, or their upper or lower limit, and a franchisee is prohibited from rendering goods or services to a specific group of customers exclusively.[193]

Russia has also implemented legislation targeted toward end of the relationship. Either party has the right to recede from the contract at any time by notifying the other party six months in advance, unless the contract specifies an earlier date.[194]

The franchise contract remains valid in the event of all or some of the exclusive rights under the contract being transferred to another party. The transferee becomes party to the franchise contract to the extent of the rights received.[195]

In the event of the death of the franchisor his rights and obligations under the contract pass to his heir, provided that the heir is registered as

---

191 Civil Code 1996 (Russian Federation) Article 1032.

192 Civil Code 1996 (Russian Federation) Article 1033(1).

193 Civil Code 1996 (Russian Federation) Article 1033(2).

194 Bryan Schwartz and Leandro Zylberman, 'Franchise Symposium Materials: International Franchise Regulation' (2008) 8 *Asper Review of International Business and Trade Law* 317, 342.

195 Civil Code 1996 (Russian Federation) Article 1038(1).

an individual businessman; otherwise the contract terminates. The rights of the deceased franchisor are to be accordingly exercised and discharged by the administrator.[196] If a franchisor changes the firm's name or commercial designation, the franchise contract remains valid with regard to the new name or designation, unless the franchisee demands the dissolution of the contract and reimbursement for damages. If the contract continues to operate, the franchisee is entitled to demand a proportionate reduction of the remuneration due to the franchisor.[197] If the period of operation of exclusive rights granted under the contract terminates while the contract is still in operation, the contract remains operational except for provisions relating to the terminated rights. However, a franchisee, unless otherwise provided by the contract, has the right to demand a commensurate reduction in the fees.[198]

According to the Russian Civil Code, a franchisor is liable jointly with a franchisee concerning goods or services sold by the franchisee.[199]

**Spain**

Spain's population is around 45 million and its GDP is estimated at about $1.6 trillion. Spain is a civil law jurisdiction. Franchising, which has experienced steady growth in recent years, is governed by Article 62 of the Law 7/1996 on Retail Trade (the Retail Trade Act) and Royal Decree 2485/1998 dated November 26, 1998, amended by Royal Decree 419/2006. A franchisor coming to Spain ought to consider both the Royal Decree of 1998 and of 2006, as the latter complements the former.[200]

Franchising in Spain is defined and differentiated from other forms of distribution networks. The 2006 Decree introduces an extensive definition of a franchise in order to clarify certain aspects which permit a business to be qualified as a franchise as distinguished from an exclusive distribution agreement or a concession. The 2006 version applies to all types of franchising with the exception of 'industrial franchising' (essentially a franchise based on a patented process), and applies to all franchising companies, whether Spanish, foreign, or a master franchise.

According to the new Decree, franchise activity shall be understood to

---

[196] Civil Code 1996 (Russian Federation) Article 1038(2).

[197] Civil Code 1996 (Russian Federation) Article 1039.

[198] Civil Code 1996 (Russian Federation) Article 1040.

[199] Civil Code 1996 (Russian Federation) Article 1034.

[200] Bryan Schwartz and Leandro Zylberman, 'Franchise Symposium Materials: International Franchise Regulation'(2008) 8 *Asper Review of International Business and Trade Law* 317.

be the activity undertaken under an agreement by which the franchisor assigns to the franchisee, the right to operate a business in a given market in exchange for a direct, indirect, or mixed compensation, the franchisor having been engaged in said activity previously, with sufficient experience and success, selling certain types of products or services. The franchise shall include at least: (i) the use of a common denomination or sign or other intellectual or industrial property rights and a uniform presentation of the premises or transport media for which the agreement was signed, (ii) the franchisor provides the franchisee with its own technical know-how, which must be substantial and singular and (iii) the franchisor provides the franchisee with continual commercial and/or technical assistance for the duration of the agreement, all without prejudice to the power of supervision and business control which may be established by contract.

Under the new Decree and for registration proposes a distinction between consolidated and non-consolidated franchises was introduced. A consolidated franchise is any registered franchise that has been in operation for more than two years with at least two establishments or has appointed four franchise establishments, among them, two belonging to the franchisor. This distinction creates no legal consequences but rather is intended to provide eventual franchisees with more information.

Spanish law requires pre-contractual disclosure which targets trade and commercial enterprises and networks. A franchisor must disclose to a potential franchisee, in writing, at least 20 days prior to the signing of any franchise agreement or pre-agreement or prior to any payments related to the franchise, a truthful and non-misleading account of all necessary information to facilitate making a well-informed decision. A franchisor or master franchisee must disclose specified information, including a description of the franchised business including its structure, the nature of the system, and the essential terms of the franchise agreement and must certify that all information is accurate and truthful.[201]

The 2006 Amendments rectify inconsistencies among regional governments and difficulties in harmonizing information. Spain requires that all franchise systems (national or foreign) operating on its territory be registered in a national franchise registry. The Ministry of Economy and Finance is the Spanish regulatory authority responsible for administering portions of, and enforcing, Spanish franchise law.[202] This is intended to

[201] Bryan Schwartz and Leandro Zylberman, 'Franchise Symposium Materials: International Franchise Regulation' (2008) 8 *Asper Review of International Business and Trade Law* 317.

[202] Bryan Schwartz and Leandro Zylberman, 'Franchise Symposium Materials:

centralize data for franchisors operating in more than one state. Master franchises also need to be registered, while foreign franchisors are required to register in a separate registry.[203]

The principle of the Register ensures that a brand name must be recognized and validated on the Spanish market. A franchise system cannot be marketed on the basis of brands submitted to the Patents and Brands Office if the brand name has not been registered in the national or regional franchise register.

The following information must be registered with the Registry:

- Commercial and economic information of the franchisor.
- Denomination of industrial and intellectual property rights of the franchising contract and confirmation of the transfer of ownership or licences to use such rights.
- Description of the business: report of the activity, number of franchisees in the network, number of franchised and company-owned franchises, the length of time for which the company has been in the franchising business as well as the franchisees that have ceased to belong to the network in Spain during the last two years.
- A Master Franchisee must provide information of its franchisor company, the duration of the Master franchising agreement, as well as the assignment agreement entered by the original franchisor.

Companies registered through a representative must provide a certificate of agency. For registration with the Franchisors' Registry, foreign companies must submit the original documents together with their translations.[204]

All amendments of franchise or distribution contracts have to be in writing.[205] A franchising agreement may not provide for:

---

International Franchise Regulation' (2008) 8 *Asper Review of International Business and Trade Law* 317.

[203] Jon K. Perala, 'Franchise Disclosure Laws in the European Union' (2007) Jon K. Perala <http://peralaw.com/EU_Franchise_Disclosure.html> at 16 December 2009.

[204] Alberto Echarri, 'Franchising in Spain' (2007) Gomez-Acebo & Pombo <http://www.interlaw.org/newsite/Pubs/Docs/FranchisinginSpainG%F3mez.pdf> at 16 December 2009.

[205] Field Fisher Waterhouse, 'Publications – Spain: Draft law proposes compensation to franchisees' (2007) International Franchising <http://www.europeanfranchising.com/publications/alerts/compensation-payment.aspx> at 16 December 2009.

- Sales outside of the franchisee's locale;
- Restrictions on passive sales, such as the Internet and catalogues;
- Imposition of minimum prices, except in promotional activities. (Not included are the recommendation and imposing of maximum sales prices); and
- Restriction or prohibiting of the franchisee to sell or supply directly through other franchisees.

Otherwise, within the limits of the regulation, parties are free under the Civil and Commercial Code principles to enter into any contractual agreements they wish by stipulating the terms and conditions they think suitable, as long as those terms are not contrary to law, morality, or public policy.[206] Exclusive supply agreements are permitted when they are used to maintain the identity and reputation of the chain.

Spain's legislation targeted toward end of the relationship allows termination of franchise agreements against payment of liquidated damages equal to two years' earnings. Spanish courts will allow the premature termination of a franchise contract if, due to unforeseen circumstances, the economic means of the contract cannot be achieved.[207]

It is unclear when franchisees and distributors have the right to claim an indemnity, as the right to claim indemnity is limited to specific circumstances. The law does make it clear, however, that franchisees are entitled to the same indemnity payment as commercial agents.

The Regulation permits the agreement to continue in force for a year following the termination of the contract, if certain conditions are fulfilled. Non-compliance with the registry obligation may give rise to a fine; there may also be civil consequences.

The Courts regard a franchisor and franchisee as independent entities, each one assuming the individual responsibility for the success or failure of their business. A franchisor cannot expect to avoid liability for poor performance, however. If poor performance is due to lack of assistance, support or management from a franchisor, or if the problems have been caused by a lack of disclosure by a franchisor, it may be liable.

---

[206] Alberto Echarri, 'Franchising in Spain' (2007) Gomez-Acebo & Pombo <http://www.interlaw.org/newsite/Pubs/Docs/FranchisinginSpainG%F3mez.pdf> at 16 December 2009.

[207] See Field Fisher Waterhouse, 'Welcome to EuropeanFranchising.com' (2008) International Franchising <www.europeanfranchising.com> at 16 December 2009.

**Sweden**

Sweden's population is approximately 9.3 million and its GDP is estimated at about $485 billion. Sweden's legal system is part of the Scandinavian-German civil law tradition. Franchise legislation in Sweden was introduced in 2006 with the Law on the Duty of a Franchisor to Provide Information (Law No. 2006:484).[208] As indicated by its title, this brief Law which is modelled on the UNIDROIT Model Law, is based on pre-contractual disclosure.[209] The Law is a disclosure law; it imposes no other obligations upon franchisors and franchisees.

The Law on the duty of a franchisor to provide information applies to franchise and master franchise agreements.[210] The legislation states that well before a franchise agreement is entered into, a franchisor must give the franchisee, in writing, the information needed to make an informed decision with respect to the implications of the agreement and other conditions; it enumerates eight items of information that should be provided as a minimum. The information must be clear and understandable.[211]

A franchisor entering into a franchise agreement without having fulfilled his disclosure obligations may, with reference to that agreement and future agreements, be enjoined to give such information. The enjoinder may also be directed towards an employee or agent of the franchisor. Proceedings for enjoinders may be brought by a franchisee, an association of entrepreneurs, or another association which has a legitimate interest to represent entrepreneurs.[212] Under Section 6 an enjoinder in accordance with Section 4 shall be combined with a fine, unless this is not necessary for special reasons.

---

208 Law No 2006:484 Law on the Duty of a Franchisor to Provide Information 2006 (Sweden).

209 Bryan Schwartz and Leandro Zylberman, 'Franchise Symposium Materials: International Franchise Regulation' (2008) 8 *Asper Review of International Business and Trade Law* 317.

210 Swedish Franchise Association, Law on the Duty of a Franchisor to Provide Information (2006) <http://sff.chainformation.com/DownloadArea/Sweden%20-%20Franchise%20law%20Lag%202006-484%20_2_.pdf> at 21 December 2009.

211 Law No 2006:484 Law on the Duty of a Franchisor to Provide Information 2006 (Sweden) Article 3. The commentary on the draft law states that the omission of a standard time requirement was a conscious decision, as it was felt that the needs might differ from case to case, and that therefore the court should be free to decide if a period of time was adequate.

212 Law No 2006:484 Law on the Duty of a Franchisor to Provide Information 2006 (Sweden) Articles 4 and 5. Anyone who has a right to bring an action has the right to participate in the proceedings as intervener in accordance with Chapter 14 of the Book [Code] of Procedure.

**Ukraine**

Ukraine's population is approximately 46 million and its GDP is estimated at about $180 billion. Around 300 national and foreign franchises now operate in Ukraine,[213] a civil law jurisdiction. Rather than legislation with respect to franchising per se, Belarus, Lithuania and Ukraine instead follow the Russian model of implementing legislation regarding 'commercial concession agreements'.

The franchise agreement is a commercial concession agreement belonging to the category of payable and consensual agreements. The Ukraine Civil Code contains provisions on 'commercial concessions'. In accordance with the legislation both physical and legal persons may be parties to a franchise agreement. The Civil Code, however, authorizes the subjects of entrepreneurial activities only to conclude the franchise agreements; the successor of the franchisor is allowed to continue the fulfilment of the franchise agreement only if it is registered as the subject of entrepreneurial activities.

Under the Civil Code and Commercial Code of Ukraine there are two types of franchise agreements: single-unit franchise agreements and sub-franchise agreements.

Although the legislation does not impose any disclosure requirements, the law follows the Russian model generally. The franchise agreement should be registered by the body registering the franchisor if the latter is registered in Ukraine or by the franchisee if the franchisor is registered in any other country. The Civil Code provides that the procedure of registration and management of the respective registries are regulated by a separate law, but such a law has not yet been adopted. Until a law is adopted, a franchisor and franchisee can make a franchise agreement without any registration. Currently, Ukraine has no plans to adopt a law on registration that would apply to franchise agreements, which need merely to be made in writing and sealed with the parties' stamps. If a foreign legal person has no seal, only the Ukrainian party to the agreement need comply with the sealing requirement. The transactions under the legislation come into force from the moment of registration. Ukraine has cancelled the requirement for obligatory registration with the Patent Office.

The Civil and Commercial Codes require that the franchise agreement be made in writing, which includes those fixed in letters, telegrams exchanged

---

213 Franchise Association (Ukraine), 'Franchising in Ukraine' (2009) Franchise Association <http://www.franchising.org.ua/index.php?pageid=67> at 16 December 2009.

by the parties, or by teletype, electronic or any other technical type of communication. The Commercial Code also stipulates that the franchise agreement should be made as a single document. Non-compliance with this requirement shall result in the annulment of the agreement.

Ukraine also has implemented legislation targeted toward performance. Article 1120 specifies the obligations of franchisor, Article 1121 the obligations of a franchisee. Article 1122 indicates that the agreement may contain provisions regarding territorial exclusivity and non-compete clauses. It prohibits price-fixing and provisions limiting the operation of the franchisee to a certain area or to a specific category of clients (Article 1122(3)).

Ukraine has also implemented legislation targeted toward the end of the relationship. Article 1124 deals with the right of the franchisee to conclude an agreement for a new term upon the same conditions, Article 1125 deals with modifications to commercial concession agreements, and Article 1126 provides that the right to terminate the agreement belongs to both parties. Article 1127 deals with the preserving of the validity of the agreement when the parties change, and Article 1128 outlines the consequences of changes in the trademark of the titleholder.

Article 1129 deals with the consequences of termination of a right of which use has been granted; the agreement as such is not terminated, only the provisions affected by the right.

A party has a right to seek the annulment of an agreement in court if it was concluded on the basis of an error that affects its 'essential circumstances'. A party that acts imprudently and thereby contributes to the error will be liable to compensate the other party. Similar to its Russian equivalent, the Code requires the franchisor to assume joint and several liability for the franchisee's sale of goods and services. Note that franchising is also regulated by Chapters 35, 36, 38–44, and 46 of the Civil Code of Ukraine and special legislation with respect to intellectual property.[214]

## REGULATION OF THE FRANCHISE SECTOR IN ASIA

### People's Republic of China

The People's Republic of China has a population of about 1.3 billion and a GDP of about $4.3 trillion.[215] Chinese law represents a mix of

---

214 Anna Tsirat, 'Franchise Agreements in Ukraine' (2009) Jurvneshservice International Legal Services <http://www.jvs.com.ua/> at 16 December 2009.

215 Central Intelligence Agency, 'The World Factbook – China' (2009)

civil and socialist law. In 1997 China's Ministry of Internal Trade promulgated the Administration of Commercial Franchise Procedures, China's first regulation specific to the franchise sector. The Measures for the Regulation of Commercial Franchise (Franchise Measures) came into force in 2005, replacing the 1997 Measures.[216] In May of 2007, the Department of Commercial Reform and Development of Ministry of Commerce (MOFCOM) then replaced the 2005 Franchise Measures with the Regulations on the Administration of Commercial Franchises (Franchise Regulations). The Franchise Regulations, together with the MOFCOM-issued Administrative Measures for the Information Disclosure of Commercial Franchises (Information Disclosure Measures) and the Administrative Measures for Archival Filing of Commercial Franchises (Archival Filing Measures) currently govern franchising arrangements, providing for both disclosure and filing requirements. The measures are intended to respect the parties' own contractual arrangements.[217]

Article 2 of the Franchise Regulations states that the regulations are applicable to all investors engaged in commercial franchise operations in China but only if the franchise operations are conducted within the People's Republic of China (Hong Kong and Macau are covered by their own laws).

A 'commercial franchise' is defined in the Franchise Regulations as 'business activities whereby a franchisor, through execution of agreements, allows a franchisee to use operational resources, such as a trademark, logo, patent, know-how and others which are owned by the franchisor [refers to legal, not natural, persons], and the franchisee conducts business under the unified business model in accordance with the provisions of the contract and pays franchise fees to the franchisor'.[218]

---

Central Intelligence Agency <https://www.cia.gov/library/publications/the-world-factbook/geos/ch.html> at 16 December 2009.

[216] See also Philip F. Zeidman, Lee J. Plave and Tao Xu, 'New China Franchise Regulation to be Effective February 1' (2005) DLA Piper Rudnick Gray Cary <http://www.envoynews.com/piperrudnick/e_article000344455.cfm?x=b11,0,w> at 16 December 2009.

[217] The requirement that all franchising operations be conducted only by PRC entities has effectively removed the alternative measures being used by foreign franchisors for many years, including licensing arrangements and international franchising agreements. See Gregory M. Sy and Currie Lee, 'Guide to Franchising in China' (2009) Grandall Legal Group <http://www.hg.org/article.asp?id=5289> at 16 December 2009.

[218] Gregory M. Sy and Currie Lee, 'Guide to Franchising in China' (2009) Grandall Legal Group <http://www.hg.org/article.asp?id=5289> at 16 December 2009.

There are standards for disclosure in the People's Republic of China; the Franchise Measures require the franchisor to provide a prospective franchisee with 27 items of information 30 days prior to the signing of the contract.

In addition to disclosure, registration is an important feature of franchise-specific legislation in China. A franchisor must file with the relevant commercial authority (provincial or MOFCOM if they engage in franchising in multiple provinces) within 15 days after the execution of the initial franchise contract (i.e. selling the first franchise).[219] If the submitted documents satisfy all the requirements, the authority will record the agreement within ten days and will list the franchisor's name on the government website.[220]

A foreign direct enterprise is no longer required to obtain approval from the authority to engage in franchise activity. The new regulation now merely requires a 'record' of registration, which will apply equally to domestic and foreign franchisors.

A franchisor is required to report annually the status of each franchise agreement.[221] Additionally, a franchisor must, within 30 days of any change potentially impacting the filing, apply for an alteration of filings.

A franchisor petitioning for registration shall provide to the registering agency:

(1) A brief introduction of the franchise.
(2) A brief introduction of the distribution of all the franchised units in China.
(3) A copy of the franchisor's marketing plan.
(4) A copy of the franchisor's corporate business licence or other important documents evidencing eligibility.
(5) A copy of the registrations of the franchisor's trademarks, patents or other business resources related to the franchising operations.
(6) Documents provided by a commercial regulatory department in a city with administrative districts, evidencing a franchisor's compliance with Article 7 Section 2 of the Regulations; with respect to company-operated units located outside China, a franchisor shall

---

219 Administrative Measures for Archiving Commercial Franchises 2007 (People's Republic of China) Article 6.

220 Administrative Measures for Archiving Commercial Franchises 2007 (People's Republic of China) Article 10.

221 Administrative Measures for Archiving Commercial Franchises 2007 (People's Republic of China) Article 8. See also Gregory M. Sy and Currie Lee, 'Guide to Franchising in China' (2009) Grandall Legal Group <http://www.hg.org/article.asp?id=5289> at 16 December 2009.

provide documents evidencing same (including Chinese translation), which shall be notarized and certified by a Chinese Consulate located in the administrative region as such company-operated units.

(7) Sample Franchise Contract.
(8) Table of contents of the Franchise Operation Manual.
(9) With respect to franchising of services or products subject to pre-approval pursuant to relevant laws and regulations, franchisor must provide documents evidencing such approval by relevant government agency.
(10) Franchisor's affidavit, signed and sealed by legal agent of such franchisor.[222]

Completed filings may be cancelled if a Franchisor's business licence is cancelled by the competent registration authority because of illegal operations; or MOFCOM receives a court order regarding the cancellation of the filing due to illegal operations of the franchisor; or a franchisor was discovered to have failed to disclose material information or provided false information; and/or, franchisor itself cancels the filing.[223]

In addition to disclosure and registration, China has implemented a range of particular provisions targeted toward pre-sales negotiation and contract formation. For example, a franchisor must have a well-developed business model, and be capable of providing continued operational management, technical support, business training and other services to the franchisee.[224]

Franchisors must own at least two company-owned stores for a period of at least one year, but not stated as 'in China', so it appears not to disadvantage foreign franchisors that may commence franchising activities in China.[225] It is unclear whether both stores must have been operating for at

---

[222] Administrative Measures for Archiving Commercial Franchises 2007 (People's Republic of China) Article 5.

[223] Administrative Measures for Archiving Commercial Franchises 2007 (People's Republic of China) Article 11.

[224] Regulations for the Administration of Commercial Franchising Operations 2007 (People's Republic of China) Article 7.

[225] Regulations for the Administration of Commercial Franchising Operations 2007 (People's Republic of China) Article 7. See also Gregory M. Sy and Currie Lee, 'Guide to Franchising in China' (2009) Grandall Legal Group <http://www.hg.org/article.asp?id=5289> at 16 December 2009. The previous Measures required the franchisor's two direct-operation stores to be located in China. The new regulation is silent on this, which could mean that operating two stores anywhere will satisfy this requirement. It appears, based on MOFCOM statements,

least one year or whether a franchisor needs to have been in business for more than one year. The former is likely to be the case, since the purpose of the 'two plus one' requirement is to prevent fraud and illustrate a model to franchisees.[226] The 'two plus one' requirement does not apply to an existing franchisor.[227]

The Franchise Regulations also require the contract to contain a clause setting out the time period during which the franchisee may rescind the agreement (post-execution of the contract).[228] Where deposits or other fees are required prior to execution of the franchising agreement, provisions for the use and refund of the same must be expressly stated.

There are also mandatory contract terms that must be included in a standardized franchise form to stipulate the obligations and rights of franchisee and franchisor in a written agreement. The franchise agreement must be for a term of at least three years unless a franchisee expressly agrees otherwise.[229] Other required terms include basic information of both parties; content and term of franchise; types, amounts and payment methods of the franchise fee; contents and methods of operational, technical support and business training; quality and standards requirements; promotion and advertising for the products or service; arrangements for protection of consumer interests and compensation; amendment and termination of the franchise agreement; and liability for breach of the agreement and dispute resolution.[230]

The regulation requires a franchisor to provide the franchise operation manual and operational guidance, technical support and business training to the franchisee.[231] A franchisee must not disclose the franchisor's trade

---

that non-Chinese units operated by the franchisor (or its affiliate) may be used to satisfy this requirement.

[226] Minter Ellison, 'Legal Update – Intellectual Property Development in China' (2007) Minter Ellison <http://www.minterellison.com/public/connect/Internet/Home/Legal+Insights/Alerts/LU-IP+developments+in+china-May> at 21 December 2007.

[227] Minter Ellison, 'Legal Update – Intellectual Property Development in China' (2007) Minter Ellison <http://www.minterellison.com/public/connect/Internet/Home/Legal+Insights/Alerts/LU-IP+developments+in+china-May> at 21 December 2007.

[228] Regulations for the Administration of Commercial Franchising Operations 2007 (People's Republic of China) Article 12.

[229] Regulations for the Administration of Commercial Franchising Operations 2007 (People's Republic of China) Article 13.

[230] Regulations for the Administration of Commercial Franchising Operations 2007 (People's Republic of China) Article 11.

[231] Regulations for the Administration of Commercial Franchising Operations 2007 (People's Republic of China) Article 14.

secrets to others.[232] Advertising and promotional fees collected by the franchisor must be used specifically for stated purposes and accounting should be provided to the franchisee on a timely basis.[233] A franchisor must guarantee the quality of the products sold by its designated suppliers.

China is one of the only countries to include franchisee qualifications in the regulation. A franchisee must demonstrate that it has a lawfully established enterprise or other economic organization; and that it has financial resources, fixed premises and personnel.[234]

There is some regulation targeted toward end of the relationship. The franchisee must not transfer the franchise licence to others without the consent of the franchisor. Article 4 of the 2007 Regulations provides that all franchise operations shall be conducted in accordance with the principles of free will, good faith and fair dealing.[235]

Chapter 4 prescribes penalties for violation of the Regulations;[236] however, the Ministry's enforcement is expected to be confined to selected investigation of complaints.[237]

## Taiwan

Taiwan is a civil law jurisdiction. The original disclosure rules were issued in June 1999. In November 2003 the Fair Trade Commission of Taiwan amended its 'Guidelines on the Disclosure of Information by Franchisors'.

'Franchise operating relationship' refers to a continuing relationship in which an enterprise, through contractual means, licenses its trademarks or operating know-how for use by another enterprise and assists or offers

---

[232] Regulations for the Administration of Commercial Franchising Operations 2007 (People's Republic of China) Article 18.

[233] Regulations for the Administration of Commercial Franchising Operations 2007 (People's Republic of China) Article 17.

[234] Bryan Schwartz and Leandro Zylberman, 'Franchise Symposium Materials: International Franchise Regulation' (2008) 8 *Asper Review of International Business and Trade Law* 317, 351.

[235] Regulations for the Administration of Commercial Franchising Operations 2007 (People's Republic of China) Article 4. Standard-form contracts require the offering party to observe principles of fairness and to disclose provisions excluding or limiting the offering parties' liability or liabilities which must be explained upon request under Chinese contract law. Also the principal of *contra proferentum* in interpretation applies.

[236] Regulations for the Administration of Commercial Franchising Operations 2007 (People's Republic of China) Articles 24–28.

[237] Richard Wageman, 'China's New Franchise Rules' (2007) 2 Franchise Update Magazine <http://www.franchiselawnews.com/articles/316/> at 16 December 2009.

guidance to that other enterprise in its operations, and for which the other enterprise provides specific consideration.[238]

The law is a disclosure law. It requires a franchisor to provide written information on nine prescribed items of information ten days prior to entry into contracts with trading counterparts. Further, a franchisor is required to allow franchisees at least five days to review the contract.[239]

Concealment or delaying disclosure of important trade information that is clearly unfair to the trading counterparts and is sufficient to affect franchising operations violates Article 24 of the Fair Trade Act, and is subject to investigation or penalty by the Fair Trade Commission of Taiwan.[240]

While not part of the disclosure law, the Civil Code and fair trading laws generally require advance notice of termination and a reasonable period to cure the breach.[241]

## Georgia

Georgia's population is estimated at approximately 4.4 million and GDP is estimated at about $13 billion. Georgia is a civil law jurisdiction. The Civil Code of Georgia, (1997) Book Three, Title One, Chapter Seven deals specifically with franchising.[242]

Under the Code, 'A franchise agreement is a long-term relationship whereby independent enterprises reciprocally undertake, where necessary, to promote the production and marketing of goods and provision of services by performing specific obligations.'[243]

Both parties must openly and completely inform each other about the circumstances relating to the franchise, especially the franchise 'system', and communicate the information to each other in good faith. Contracts

---

238 Guidelines on the Disclosure of Information by Franchisors 1999 (Taiwan) Article 2.

239 Guidelines on the Disclosure of Information by Franchisors 1999 (Taiwan) Articles 4 and 5.

240 Guidelines on the Disclosure of Information by Franchisors 1999 (Taiwan) Article 6.

241 Andrew P. Loewinger and Michael K. Lindsey (eds), *International Franchise Sales Laws* (2006).

242 There is little information available at the time of writing about franchising and its regulation in Georgia. The information provided here is based primarily from UNIDROIT, Legislation and Regulations Relevant to Franchising: Georgia (2005) <http://www.unidroit.org/english/guides/2007franchising/country/georgia.htm> at 21 December 2009.

243 Civil Code 1997 (Georgia) Article 607.

must be in writing and must include provisions on termination 'and other essential clauses' and a description of the franchise system.[244]

Georgia has implemented regulation targeted toward performance. There are two categories of franchisor obligations, one providing the franchisee with intellectual property rights, samples and packaging, and information on the franchise system, and the other requiring a franchisor to protect the franchise system from third parties, to develop the system 'consistently' and to support the franchisee by, *inter alia*, providing training.[245]

The franchisee must pay the franchise fee, actively conduct the business with due diligence, and receive services and purchase goods through the franchisor if directly related to the objective of the agreement. If the franchisor breaches its contractual obligations, the franchisee shall be entitled to reduce the franchise fee as determined by an independent expert. There is a duty of confidentiality required of both parties even if the agreement is not executed.[246]

Georgia has implemented regulation targeted toward the end of the relationship. The term of the contract is to be determined by the parties but if the term of the contract exceeds ten years, either party is entitled to terminate the contract with a year's notice, or the contract is automatically renewed by two years. If the contract expires by lapse of time or by the initiative of one of the parties, 'then the parties shall try, observing the principles of mutual confidence, to continue the contract on the same or altered terms up until the time the business relationship is actually ended'. [247]

Post-term restraints of trade are permissible within a certain area and not exceeding one year. If the restraint jeopardizes the business of the franchisee, the franchisee shall receive appropriate monetary compensation even if the term of the contract has expired.[248]

A franchisor is generally liable for the rights and information provided to a franchisee.[249]

## Indonesia

Indonesia's population is estimated at approximately 231 million and GDP is estimated at about $512 billion. The law of Indonesia is based on the civil

---

244 Civil Code 1997 (Georgia) Article 611.
245 Civil Code 1997 (Georgia) Article 608.
246 Civil Code 1997 (Georgia) Article 610.
247 Civil Code 1997 (Georgia) Article 612.
248 Civil Code 1997 (Georgia) Article 613.
249 Civil Code 1997 (Georgia) Article 614.

law of Holland and the cultural law of Indonesia. Government Regulation No. 16/1997 requires disclosure and the registration of both the franchise agreement and the disclosed information with the Ministry of Industry and Trade.[250] In 2007 the Franchise Law was replaced by Government Regulation No. 42 ('GR 42'). GR 42 retained many of the original requirements from the Franchise Law and added some new requirements. This law has been supplemented by the 2008 Franchise Operations Regulations.

A franchise is an exclusive right of individuals or statutory bodies to a business system with specific business characteristics in the framework of marketing goods and/or services already proven successful and usable by other parties on the basis of a franchise agreement.[251]

A franchisor shall register the franchise-offering prospectus before making a franchise agreement with a franchisee.[252] An offering prospectus must contain data about identity of the franchisor, legality of business belonging to the franchisor,[253] history of business activity, organizational structure of the franchisor, financial statement in the last two years, quantity of business places, a list of franchisees, and rights and obligations of franchisor and franchise.[254] The procedure for registration of the franchise agreement and the issuing on the part of the government of a trade licence are provided in Articles 11 to 13 and are supplemented by the 2008 Regulations. The 2008 Regulations also provide that the prospectus and the agreement must be furnished to a franchisee no later than two weeks before signing the agreement.[255]

There is in Indonesia other legislation targeted toward pre-sales negotiation and contract formation. The franchise agreement must be in writing

---

250 Bryan Schwartz and Leandro Zylberman, 'Franchise Symposium Materials: International Franchise Regulation' (2008) 8 *Asper Review of International Business and Trade Law* 317.

251 Government Regulation 42/1997 Government Regulation on Franchise 1997 (Republic of Indonesia) Article 1.

252 Government Regulation 42/1997 Government Regulation on Franchise 1997 (Republic of Indonesia) Article 10.

253 A domestic franchisor must possess a franchised business registration certificate issued by the Ministry of Industry and Trade, or a business licence issued by another technical Ministry. A foreign franchisor must possess legal evidence from an authorised government agency in its country of origin, and this legal evidence must be acknowledged by the local official of the representative office of the Republic of Indonesia.

254 Government Regulation 42/1997 Government Regulation on Franchise 1997 (Republic of Indonesia) Article 7.

255 J. Mazero, 'Best Practices in Legal Services for your International Expansion', Paper presented at 49th Annual Convention, International Franchise Association, San Diego, CA (2009).

in accordance with Indonesian law in the English language and translated into Indonesian.[256] The legislation also sets some standards for a franchise system that include specific business characteristics; proven already profitable, a written standard of the offered service and goods and/or services, easy to teach and apply, available sustainable support, and registration of the intellectual property.[257]

There is also regulation targeted toward performance. For example, some mandatory contract terms are enumerated. The contract must include names and addresses of parties; kinds of intellectual property rights; business activity; rights and obligations of parties; assistance, facilities, operational counselling, training and marketing provided by the franchisor for franchisee; business area; valid period of agreement; procedures for the payment of compensation; ownership, change in ownership and rights of heirs; procedures for settlement of dispute; and procedures for extending, discontinuing and terminating agreement.[258] The duration of the agreement must be at least five years.[259] A franchisor shall provide training, management counselling, and research and development to a franchisee in a sustainable manner.[260]

A franchisor and franchisee must prioritize the use of domestic goods and/or services as long as they meet the quality standards of goods and/or services stipulated in writing by the franchisor. A franchisor must cooperate with small and medium-scale businesses in the local region as franchisees or suppliers of goods and/or services as long as they fulfil the requirements stipulated by the franchisor.[261] Franchising can be executed throughout the territory of Indonesia, however there are limitations regarding the locations in which franchising will be permitted.[262]

The government and regional governments shall foster franchising through the provision of franchise education and training, recommendations

---

[256] Government Regulation 42/1997 Government Regulation on Franchise 1997 (Republic of Indonesia) Article 4.

[257] Government Regulation 42/1997 Government Regulation on Franchise 1997 (Republic of Indonesia) Article 3.

[258] Government Regulation 42/1997 Government Regulation on Franchise 1997 (Republic of Indonesia) Article 5.

[259] Government Regulation 42/1997 Government Regulation on Franchise 1997 (Republic of Indonesia) Article 12.

[260] Government Regulation 42/1997 Government Regulation on Franchise 1997 (Republic of Indonesia) Article 8.

[261] Government Regulation 42/1997 Government Regulation on Franchise 1997 (Republic of Indonesia) Article 9.

[262] Government Regulation 42/1997 Government Regulation on Franchise 1997 (Republic of Indonesia) Article 2.

regarding marketing, recommendations to attend franchise exhibitions in the country and abroad, consultancy assistance through business clinics, awards to the best local franchisor, and/or capital fortification assistance.[263]

The Minister in charge of trade affairs shall supervise the implementation of franchising, and shall coordinate related institutions in executing the supervision.[264] The Minister, governors, regents/mayors in accordance with their respective authority can impose administrative sanction on franchisors or franchisees violating the provisions in Articles 8, 10 and/or Article 11. Sanction can take the form of written warning, fine, and/or revocation of certificate of registration of franchise.[265]

**Japan**

Japan's population is estimated at approximately 128 million and GDP is estimated at about $5 trillion. Japan has over 1000 franchisors operating over 198 000 outlets and generating an annual turnover of more than US$142 billion. The most popular types of franchises are convenience stores with 56 chains trading from over 36 000 stores.[266]

Japan's legal system is modelled after the European civil law system. In Japan a franchise is considered a 'technical assistance agreement'.[267] Franchise regulation is part of the fair trading legislation. Guidelines were first promulgated in 1983. In 2002 the Japan Fair Trade Commission (JFTC) published new guidelines comprised of the Medium-Small Business Promotion Act (the 'Act') and the Act Concerning Prohibition of Private Monopoly and Maintenance of Fair Trade (the 'Guidelines').[268] These two acts include a general description of franchising, provisions for the disclosure of information with the offer of a franchise, and prohibitions against vertical restraints.

---

263 Government Regulation 42/1997 Government Regulation on Franchise 1997 (Republic of Indonesia) Article 14.

264 Government Regulation 42/1997 Government Regulation on Franchise 1997 (Republic of Indonesia) Article 15.

265 Government Regulation 42/1997 Government Regulation on Franchise 1997 (Republic of Indonesia) Article 16(2)(a–c).

266 To see Japan Franchise Association 2006 statistics visit <http://jfa.jfa-fc.or.jp/pdf/2006_FC_Statistics.pdf> at 23 December 2009.

267 J. Mazero, 'Best Practices in Legal Services for your International Expansion', Paper presented at 49th Annual Convention, International Franchise Association, San Diego, CA (2009).

268 Bryan Schwartz and Leandro Zylberman, 'Franchise Symposium Materials: International Franchise Regulation' (2008) 8 *Asper Review of International Business and Trade Law* 317, 355.

Although the Act does not explicitly state that it applies to non-Japanese franchisors, the purpose of the Act is to protect Japanese medium- and small-sized businesses and thus would apply to non-Japanese franchisors.[269]

Disclosure must be provided to a prospective franchisee prior to signing a franchise agreement. The Act is loosely structured; it does not explicitly state a specified time period within which the disclosure document must be delivered. Nor does it prescribe exact items or form for disclosure. Rather, the guidelines list eight items as examples of the items to be disclosed. The guidelines also require that if a franchisor provides the franchisee with the projected sales or profits, such projection shall be made in a reasonable manner, on the basis of reliable data.[270] Under the Act disclosure is required of 22 categories of information.[271]

When a franchisor holds a dominant position, requirements in the franchise agreement or acts of the franchisor under it, such as restraints on sources of supply, quotas, coercion to dispose of the merchandise to enhance the royalty, requirements to offer services not prescribed in the agreement, or certain forms of non-competition clauses may not be permitted. In these cases a franchisor will be found to hold a dominant position if the franchisee would be faced with difficulties if the transaction with the franchisor were to be terminated. If vertical restraints imposed by a franchisor go further than necessary to duly operate the franchised business, they may be deemed to constitute an abuse of a dominant position.

If a franchisor requires a franchisee to purchase goods or materials from either itself or a designated supplier, such a requirement may, if there are anti-competitive effects, be found to constitute a 'tie-in' or a 'dealing on restrictive terms', both of which are listed as unfair trade practices.[272]

Where a franchisor supplies goods to a franchisee, the fixing of a retail price by a franchisor, rather than a suggested price, shall be illegal per se as resale price maintenance. If a franchisor is not itself supplying the goods,

---

269 Bryan Schwartz and Leandro Zylberman, 'Franchise Symposium Materials: International Franchise Regulation' (2008) 8 *Asper Review of International Business and Trade Law* 317, 355.

270 Ministerial Order No 100 Implementing the Medium-Small Retail Business Act 1973 (Japan) Article 11. Taken from www.unidroit.org/english/guides/2007franchising/country/japan.htm. (Contributed by Professor S. Kuka, Sophia University, Tokyo.)

271 J. Mazero, 'Best Practices in Legal Services for your International Expansion', Paper presented at 49th Annual Convention, International Franchise Association, San Diego, CA (2009).

272 Fair Trade Commission Public Notice No 15 1982 (Japan) Articles 10, 11, 13.

the practice may fall under the category of 'dealing on restrictive terms' subject to the rule of reason.[273]

According to the second part of the guidelines, the failure to provide necessary information shall constitute deceptive customer inducement, and shall be subject to a cease-and-desist order by the government fair trading agency. The aggrieved party is also entitled to bring suit for injunction.

## Kazakhstan

Kazakhstan's population is estimated at approximately 16 million and GDP is estimated at about $132 billion. The Republic of Kazakhstan, a civil law jurisdiction, has adopted a law on franchising, Law No. 330 of 24 June 2002 concerning the Integrated Business Licence (Franchise). The Law has 24 articles.

The subjects of franchise relationships are both physical persons and legal entities, and the legislation regulating investments shall apply to both of these categories, as shall the legislation regarding the State promotion of small entrepreneurship.[274] Different types of franchising are covered by the concept 'integrated business licence'.[275]

Information relating to the intellectual property rights of the franchisor is to be transmitted to the potential franchisee and is required to be kept confidential.[276] Intellectual property must be registered.[277] Articles 14 through 17 list the rights and obligations of franchisors and franchisees. Article 19 refers to the protection of other information which is transferred under the agreement.[278]Article 21 deals with accounting and financial

---

273 Fair Trade Commission Public Notice No 15 1982 (Japan) Articles 12, 13.

274 Law No 330 Concerning the Integrated Business Licence 2002 (Republic of Kazakhstan) Article 3.

275 Law No 330 Concerning the Integrated Business Licence 2002 (Republic of Kazakhstan) Article 20. Article 12 divides the participants in a franchise relationship into the parties to the contract and third parties such as banks and licence brokers, the latter of which are defined in Article 13.

276 Law No 330 Concerning the Integrated Business Licence 2002 (Republic of Kazakhstan) Article 18.

277 Law No 330 Concerning the Integrated Business Licence 2002 (Republic of Kazakhstan) Article 9.

278 Law No 330 Concerning the Integrated Business Licence 2002 (Republic of Kazakhstan) Article 19. It specifies in paragraph (4) that State bodies and their officials shall have no right to demand access to the confidential commercial information that is transferred under the agreement, except as regards data that is necessary for the fulfilling of the supervising, controlling, registration or other functions attributed to those bodies by legislation.

reports.[279] Article 24 deals with the settlement of disputes in accordance with the law of Kazakhstan.

Article 2 states that the legislation on franchising is based on the Constitution and a ratified international treaty which conflicts with the provisions of the Law shall prevail. Article 4 provides principles that shall apply to the promotion of franchise relationships by the State, including the co-ordinated interaction of State bodies when they promote franchise relationships. Article 5 lists the measures that the State bodies may take to promote franchising.[280]

Article 22 deals with the supervision of compliance with legislation concerning franchising, and Article 23 with responsibility for its infringement.

## South Korea

South Korea has a population of 48 million and a GDP of about $947 billion. Korea's contract law is based on the Japanese civil law of contract. Korea introduced franchise legislation in 2002, with the Act on Fairness in Franchise Transactions, together with the Presidential Decree to Implement the Act on Fairness in Franchise Transactions (the 'Act'). Korea implemented extensive enhancements to its legislation in 2007 with a purpose to protect the welfare of consumers and to place the relationship on an equal footing. 2007 amendments to the Act include a new registration requirement, additional disclosure requirements, an escrow requirement, a 'cooling-off' period that applies to all franchisors, franchisee territorial protections, and 'just cause' requirements for non-renewal and termination requirements.[281]

---

279 Taken from: UNIDROIT.org, 'Legislation and Regulations Relevant to Franchising' (2002) UNIDROIT.org <www.unidroit.org/english/guides/2007 franchising/country/kazakhstan.htm> at 16 December 2009.

280 The elaboration and implementation of programs for the development and promotion of franchise relationships, the elaboration and improvement of regulatory legal acts dealing with the development and promotion of franchise relationships, and the providing of consulting services for the carrying out of franchise activities. Article 6 provides for compensation for damage suffered by the subjects of franchise relationships as a result of the issuing by State bodies of acts that are inconsistent with the legislation of the Republic, and as a result of illegal actions or omissions on the part of the officials of those bodies. Article 8(1) states that the subjects of franchise relationships shall have the right to become acquainted with the legal acts, court decisions and other acts pertaining to the exercise of the franchise.

281 Hyung-Sang Youn and Brendon Carr, 2003–2004 'Franchise Law Review and Forecast' (2008) Franchise Update Media Group <http://mobi.franchise-update.com/news/feature/564/> at 16 December 2009.

The regulations implemented under the Act require franchisors to provide necessary information about the franchise business to prospective franchisees.[282] The Act requires that a disclosure document be provided at the earlier of five days before the date that the prospect (a) pays any type of fee; or (b) signs a franchise agreement. Annual updates of disclosure information and a 14-day cooling-off period are also required.[283]

2007 amendments mandate that franchisors prepare and register a detailed disclosure statement containing information similar to that prescribed by the US at the federal level. Disclosure statements may be subject to review and approval by the Korean Fair Trade Association. Franchisors must deliver disclosure statements to all prospective franchisees (not only to prospective franchisees who make written requests for disclosure statements).

The disclosure document must be a single document in book form and may be provided in any one of three ways: (i) the prospective franchisee may inspect it at the franchisor's offices; (ii) the franchisor may give it directly to the prospective franchisee; or (iii) the franchisor may make it available for the applicant to download from the Internet.[284]

Article 5 of the 2007 Amendment sets procedures for Registration of the Uniform Franchise Offering Circular, Registration or Reporting Changes in the Uniform Franchise Offering Circular, Disclosure of the Uniform Franchise Offering Circular by The Fair Trade Commission, and Cancelling the Registration of the Uniform Franchise Offering Circular.

The June 2003 Enforcement Decree amendment established standards to accredit 'franchise consultants'.[285] Certified franchise consultants are officially approved to (i) advise on franchise business plans; (ii) draft and review franchise agreements and disclosure statements; (iii) counsel franchisors and franchisees regarding ongoing duties; and (iv) conduct franchisee-training workshops. Franchise consultants, once certified, must register

---

[282] Fair Franchise Transaction Act 2007 (South Korean) Article 7. See also Bryan Schwartz and Leandro Zylberman, 'Franchise Symposium Materials: International Franchise Regulation' (2008) 8 *Asper Review of International Business and Trade Law* 317, 358.

[283] Fair Franchise Transaction Act 2002 (South Korean) Articles 7 and 8.

[284] Presidential Decree No 17773 Enforcement Decree of the Fair Franchise Transaction Act 2002 (South Korean) Article 4 addresses 'Matters to be Included in the Uniform Franchise Offering Circular'.

[285] Presidential Decree No 17773 Enforcement Decree of the Fair Franchise Transaction Act 2002 (South Korean) Articles 31–32. Certified franchise consultants are officially sanctioned to (i) advise on franchise business plans; (ii) draft and review franchise agreements and disclosure statements; (iii) counsel franchisors and franchisees regarding ongoing duties; and (iv) conduct franchisee-training workshops. Franchise consultants, once certified, must register.

with the government agency. Franchise consultant certification resembles a quality-assurance mark rather than a professional licence. Franchise consultant certification does not constitute a licence and non-certified consultants are not prohibited from providing the sanctioned services. The 2007 legislation also addresses the conduct of the franchise consultants.

Article 5 provides for the duties of the franchisor and Article 6 for the duties of the franchisee. These are extensive and include a number of duties which in most other countries are left to the agreement between the parties. (see Article 5 for the duties of the franchisor and Article 6 for the duties of the franchisee).

The Presidential Decree to Implement the Act on Fairness in Franchise Transactions requires that franchisors not unreasonably require franchisees to purchase equipment or commodities from the franchisor or an approved source; not unfairly restrict a franchisee's dealings in commodities, services, or business activities; provide commodities, services, or assistance without rightful cause; and to obtain the franchisee's consent prior to imposing monetary burdens on the franchisee.[286]

A Franchise Dispute Mediation Council (the 'Mediation Council') was established by the Korea Franchise Association as an optional dispute resolution mechanism. Nine mediators are appointed to the council: three representing the public at large, three representing franchisor interests, and three representing franchisee interests. Under the 2007 legislation mediation proceedings are free of charge.

The Act lays down a general duty of good faith in the performance of the duties of the parties. [287]

**Kyrgyzstan**

Kyrgyzstan's population is estimated at approximately 5.5 million and a GDP of about $5 billion. Kyrgyzstan is a civil law jurisdiction which has since 1998 regulated franchising under its Civil Code, Chapter 44, Complex Business Licence (Franchising). [288]

Under a complex business licence contract, for a fee the complex

---

[286] Fair Franchise Transaction Act 2007 (South Korean) Article 12. See also Bryan Schwartz and Leandro Zylberman, 'Franchise Symposium Materials: International Franchise Regulation' (2008) 8 *Asper Review of International Business and Trade Law* 317, 358.

[287] Fair Franchise Transaction Act 2007 (South Korean) Article 4.

[288] DLA Piper, 'Executive Summary of Franchise Laws Around the World' (2008) DLA Piper <http://www.franchise.org/uploadedFiles/Files/Executive_Summary_Franchise_Laws_World.pdf> at 16 December 2009.

licensor shall provide the complex licensee with a set of exclusive rights which includes the right to use the firm name of the licensor and protected commercial information, as well as other exclusive rights provided by the contract in the licensee's business activities. The contract shall provide for the use of the licensor's licence set, business reputation and commercial experience. The parties to the contract can be only commercial organizations and citizens who are registered as businessmen. The complex business licence contract shall be respectively regulated by the rules of the Code on intellectual property, unless otherwise provided by Chapter 44 or by the essence of the contract.[289] The complex business sub-license contract is also addressed in the legislation.[290]

The licensor is required to transfer to the licensee technical and commercial documents and provide him with other information necessary for the licensee to exercise his rights, conferred on him under the contract, as well as give instructions to the licensee and his employees on issues which relate to these rights.[291]

A complex business licence contract must be entered into in writing; failure to comply will invalidate the contract.[292] A complex business licence contract may provide for restrictive (exclusive) conditions, but these may be rendered invalid, if they contradict anti-trust legislation. [293]

In addition to the transfer of information and instructions, the contract may provide for other licensor's obligations.[294] Considering the nature and specific features of the activities implemented by the licensee in accordance with a complex business licence contract, there are certain enumerated duties of the licensee in the legislation which also provides that the contract may provide for other licensee's duties. [295]

A complex business licence contract can be amended in accordance with rules of Chapter 22 of the Code.[296] Articles 875–878 cover the Termination of Complex Business Licence Contract, Maintenance of Contract of Complex Business Licence in Force in Case of Changing the Parties, Maintenance of the Contract of Complex Business Licence in Force in Case of Changing the Firm Name, and Consequences of Termination of Exclusive Right Included in Licence Set.

---

289 Civil Code 1997 (Kyrgyz Republic) Article 866.
290 Civil Code 1997 (Kyrgyz Republic) Article 868.
291 Civil Code 1997 (Kyrgyz Republic) Article 870.
292 Civil Code 1997 (Kyrgyz Republic) Article 867.
293 Civil Code 1997 (Kyrgyz Republic) Article 872.
294 Civil Code 1997 (Kyrgyz Republic) Article 870.
295 Civil Code 1997 (Kyrgyz Republic) Article 871.
296 Civil Code 1997 (Kyrgyz Republic) Article 874.

A licensor shall bear joint and several liability on claims against the licensee for damage caused by the activities carried out by the licensee under the supervision of the licensor, unless damage is inflicted by default or improper performance by the licensee of his contractual obligations.[297]

**Macau**

Macau, like Hong Kong, is a special administrative region of the People's Republic of China. Under a 'one country, two systems' formula it enjoys autonomy, with the exception of foreign relations and defence. Macau is a civil law jurisdiction. It regulates franchising through provisions of the Commercial Code 1999 (Macau), Law No 6 2000 (Macau), Decree-Law no. 40/99/M 1999 (Macau).

'A franchising contract is that by which one of the parties, against a direct or indirect payment, grants to the other, in a certain zone and in a stable manner, the right to produce and or to sell certain goods or services under his entrepreneurial image, according to his know-how, with his technical assistance, and subject to his control.'[298] Except if there is an agreement to the contrary, the use of sub-franchisees is not permitted.[299]

A franchise contract must be concluded in writing, and a franchisor 'is obliged to provide, in writing and with adequate advance, complete and truthful information to an interested party, so that the latter can form a balanced and informed assessment of the advantages and disadvantages of concluding the contract . . .' There are 12 categories of required information. A franchisor must also provide . . . with adequate advance, a model of the standard contract and any pre-contract with the complete text, including annexes.[300]

If no time limit is stated, the contract is presumed to have been agreed for an undetermined period of time; if a time limit is agreed, it cannot be less than three years.[301] Within the zone determined in the contract, the franchisee can neither manufacture nor sell goods nor render services in competition with those of the franchisor, nor can the latter, directly or indirectly, compete with the former, except if there is a written agreement to the contrary.[302]

---

297 Civil Code 1997 (Kyrgyz Republic) Article 873.

298 Commercial Code 1999 (Macau) Article 679.

299 Commercial Code 1999 (Macau) Article 685.

300 Commercial Code 1999 (Macau) Articles 680 and 681.

301 Commercial Code 1999 (Macau) Article 684 (Duration of contract) and Article 659.

302 Commercial Code 1999 (Macau) Article 683.

Chapter II on the rights and obligations of parties is divided into two sections, obligations of franchisor and franchisee. Articles 686 and 694 are general provisions that require franchisor and franchisee respectively to act in accordance with good faith. Each section also includes a detailed list of specific obligations. A franchisor is obliged to allow the franchisee the use of his industrial and intellectual property rights and other elements that identify his enterprise; to ensure peaceful enjoyment of the industrial and intellectual property rights authorized, and of the know-how provided to the franchisee; to ensure the constant updating of his know-how; to provide training to the franchisee and his auxiliaries; to ensure the advertising of the franchise network at regional and international levels; to supply or to ensure the supply of goods that, in the circumstances, are necessary to run the franchise; and to compensate the franchisee for the obligation of non-competition after termination of the contract.[303] A franchisor is also obliged to timely inform a franchisee of alterations introduced in the composition and presentation of the goods, in conditions of sale, or in the rendering of the service, or any others concerning the running of the franchise.[304]

A franchisor cannot, directly or indirectly, prohibit a franchisee from freely choosing the equipment, the installations and the suppliers of goods or services to be used in the assembly or in the functioning of the franchise, except to the strict extent to which it is necessary to protect his industrial and intellectual property rights or to maintain the common identity and reputation of the franchise network.[305]

Article 690 provides obligations of provision and of guarantee.[306] Article 691 requires a franchisor to effect a rigorous supervision of the franchise network, controlling and verifying performance. Article 692 requires a franchisor to adequately compensate the franchisee for new experience gained, in accordance with Article 697, in the running of the franchise.[307] Article 693 requires confidentiality.[308]

A franchisee is obliged to pay remuneration on the agreed terms; to

303 Commercial Code 1999 (Macau) Article 687.

304 Commercial Code 1999 (Macau) Article 688.

305 Commercial Code 1999 (Macau) Article 689.

306 Commercial Code 1999 (Macau) Articles 669 and 670 apply to the franchisor.

307 Commercial Code 1999 (Macau) Article 697. A franchisee is obliged to communicate to the franchisor any new experience gained in running the franchise that amounts to an improvement to its conditions of functioning and efficiency, as well as to grant both authorization to use such know-how and the right to allow its use by the other franchisees.

308 Commercial Code 1999 (Macau) Article 671 is applicable to the franchisor.

use the industrial and intellectual property rights and other elements that identify the enterprise of the franchisor; to follow the instructions of the franchisor regarding the equipment and the uniform presentation of the premises and/or means of transport mentioned in the contract; to produce, to sell, or to use exclusively goods that satisfy the minimum objective quality specifications set by the franchisor; not to change the location of the premises mentioned in the contract without the assent of the franchisor; and to observe, with the necessary adaptations, the provisions of subparagraphs b) to e) of Article 662.[309]

A franchisee cannot use the know-how for purposes other than running the franchise, nor disclose its content to third parties, without the franchisor's agreement in writing.[310] Article 698 requires a franchisee to attend, or to instruct his assistants to attend, periods of training organized by the franchisor, with the frequency mentioned in the contract. Article 699 requires that all advertising to be made by a franchisee must be previously approved by the franchisor. Article 700 requires a franchisee to inform the franchisor of any breach to the industrial and intellectual property rights that are the object of the franchise, which may come to his knowledge, and take action, or support the franchisor in any judicial proceedings against the infringer. A franchisee can be required to periodically sell a minimum quantity, or to acquire a certain quota of goods, or to reach a certain share of market penetration.[311] There are also statutorily imposed franchisee obligations of confidentiality and non-competition.[312]

There is in Macau also legislation targeted toward end of the relationship. Chapter III regulates the transfer by a franchisee. A franchisor can oppose the transfer *inter vivos* of the position of franchisee inherent in the sale of the respective enterprise.[313] A franchisor can also oppose temporary transfers of the enjoyment of the franchisee's enterprise.[314] A franchisor, or

---

309 Commercial Code 1999 (Macau) Article 695.

310 Commercial Code 1999 (Macau) Article 696.

311 Commercial Code 1999 (Macau) Article 701. Subject to Article 663.

312 Commercial Code 1999 (Macau) Article 702. Articles 629 and 630 are applicable to the franchisee, with the necessary adaptations.

313 In accordance with paragraph 1 of Article 672 of Commercial Code 1999 (Macau). Article 672 (Transfer of position of concessionaire) 1. A principal can oppose the transfer by an *inter vivos* act of the position of concessionaire inherent in the transfer of the respective enterprise, if the acquirer: a) does not correspond to the standards required of his new concessionaires; b) does not offer sufficient guarantees as to the performance of his obligations. 2. The previous paragraph applies, with the necessary adaptations, to temporary transfers of the enjoyment of a concessionaire's enterprise.

314 Commercial Code 1999 (Macau) Article 703.

a third party indicated by him, has a right of pre-emption in case of transfer of the franchisee's enterprise.

Chapter IV regulates termination of the contract and provides that termination of a franchising contract is regulated, with the necessary adaptations, by the provisions on termination of the commercial concession contract in all respects not especially provided for in this chapter IV. A franchise contract does not lapse as a result of the death of the franchisee or, in the case of a collective person, by its extinction, if the successor or the adjudicating associate continues the operation of the enterprise.[315] After termination of a contract, the franchisee cannot continue to use the industrial and intellectual property rights or the know-how authorized in the framework of the franchise contract. Certain obligations of a franchisor with respect to re-purchase of stock, continued use of intellectual property, and compensation for expenses in the event of termination of contract for reasons not imputable to franchisee are also outlined in Chapter IV. [316]

Article 686 requires a franchisor to act in accordance with good faith, in order to fully achieve the contractual aim, while Article 694 requires a franchisee to act in good faith and 'watch over the maintenance of the identity, image and good reputation of the franchise and develop adequate activities in order to fully achieve the contractual aim'.[317]

## Malaysia[318]

Malaysia's population is estimated at approximately 28 million and GDP is estimated at about $222 billion. The franchise sector has averaged an annual growth of around 10 percent contributing an estimated US$5 billion to GDP (over 12 percent). Malaysia's legal system is based on English common law; personal law based on Sharia law applies to Muslims. The Franchise Act No 590 1998 (Malaysia) is comprised of 61 articles in eight sections, dealing with the appointment of the Registrar of Franchises and registration requirements, the franchise agreement, the conduct of the parties, termination of the franchise agreement, the

---

315 Commercial Code 1999 (Macau) Article 705. In any of the cases mentioned in the previous paragraph, the franchisor can subject the transfer to the condition of successful attendance by the transferee of the training program to which he subjects the admission of new franchisees.

316 Commercial Code 1999 (Macau) Articles 704 to 707.

317 Commercial Code 1999 (Macau) Article 686.

318 Act 590 Franchise Act 1998 (Malaysia).

Franchise Advisory Board, offences, penalties and enforcement; and miscellaneous provisions.[319]

According to Article 4 the Act covers both unit franchises and master franchises, but only franchises operated within Malaysia.

Malaysia's law requires both disclosure and registration. The disclosure documents must be submitted to the prospective franchisee at least ten days before the agreement is signed. The documents given to the prospective franchisee are the same as those handed in to the Registrar as required by Article 7(1), 'A franchisor shall make an application to register his franchise by submitting to the Registrar the application in the prescribed form together with the complete disclosure documents with all the necessary particulars; a sample of the franchise agreement; the operations manual; the training manual; a copy of the latest audited accounts, financial statements, and the reports, if any, of the auditors and directors of the applicant; and such other additional information or documents as may be required by the registrar for the purpose of determining the application.' A person who fails to comply commits an offence. [320]

The Registrar of Franchises is a public officer appointed by the Minister entrusted with the responsibility for matters relating to franchises. Before a franchisor can make an offer, it is required to register the franchise with the Registrar. The application must be made on the prescribed form and must annex the complete disclosure documents.[321]

If the disclosure documents or the additional information or documents requested by the Registrar are amended, the amended documents must be filed with the Registrar, who may request additional information on the amendments.[322]

An application that is approved may be made subject to any such conditions as the Registrar may impose, and the Registrar may require the applicant to pay any amount of fees that may be prescribed.[323] The registration continues to be effective, unless the Registrar issues an order by written notice to the applicant or the franchisor to suspend, terminate, prohibit or deny the sale or registration of the franchise.[324]

---

319 The Miscellaneous Provisions of Part VIII (Articles 53–61) cover items such as the subjecting of the sale of a franchise to a non-Malaysian citizen to the approval of the Registrar (Article 53) and the sale of franchises by foreigners in Malaysia (Article 54).

320 Act 590 Franchise Act 1998 (Malaysia) Article 15(1).

321 Act 590 Franchise Act 1998 (Malaysia) Articles 6 and 7.

322 Act 590 Franchise Act 1998 (Malaysia) Article 11(1)–(3).

323 Act 590 Franchise Act 1998 (Malaysia) Article 8.

324 Act 590 Franchise Act 1998 (Malaysia) Article 10.

No indication is given of the reasons on which such decisions may be based, but if the Registrar proposes to suspend, terminate, prohibit or deny the sale or registration of a franchise, he is required to give the applicant or the franchisor written notice of his intention to do so, specifying the nature of the proposed action and the grounds on which he proposes to take such action. The applicant or the franchisor shall be given opportunity to make a written representation on the matter within 14 days from the date of the service of the notice.[325]

The legislation also provides for continuing disclosure. A franchisor must on the anniversary date of the registration submit a report to the Registrar in the prescribed form. It must contain updated disclosure documents, which the Registrar may review, and notify the franchisor if any additional information or modification is required or issue an order to suspend, terminate, prohibit or deny the sale or registration of the franchise in the public interest or for the purpose of protecting prospective franchisees until any deficiencies specified by the Registrar have been corrected.[326]

In addition to the registration of the franchisors themselves, the Act provides for the registration of franchise brokers. The registration of a franchise broker is effective for one year from the date of registration unless the Registrar determines otherwise.[327]

There is other legislation targeted toward pre-sales negotiation and contract formation in Malaysia. Article 18(2) provides a list of the items that the franchise agreement must contain. A cooling-off period of at least seven working days is required. If the franchise agreement is terminated in this cooling-off period, a franchisor may retain a sum of money from out of the initial franchise fees to cover the reasonable expenses it has incurred in the preparation of the agreement; the rest of the money must be returned to the franchisee.[328]

Where initial franchise fees are required, or where a franchisor requires the franchisee to make payment before signing a franchise agreement, a franchisor is required to state in writing the purpose of the payment and the conditions for the use and refund of the money. If a franchisee is required to pay any franchise fees or royalty to a franchisor, the rate of franchise fees or royalty shall be the rate as provided in the disclosure documents.[329]

---

325 Act 590 Franchise Act 1998 (Malaysia) Article 12.
326 Act 590 Franchise Act 1998 (Malaysia) Articles 16 and 17.
327 Act 590 Franchise Act 1998 (Malaysia) Article 14.
328 Act 590 Franchise Act 1998 (Malaysia) Article 18(4).
329 Act 590 Franchise Act 1998 (Malaysia) Articles 19 and 21.

Articles 25–28 provide that the franchise term shall be no less than five years, that information is to be kept confidential, for non-competition, and that parties are not permitted to waive compliance with the Act.

Regulation targeted toward performance is also part of the Malaysian regulatory regime. Where the franchisee is required to pay fees for the purpose of promoting the franchise, a special Promotion Fund is to be set up and any payments for promotional purposes are to be made to the fund.[330]

Finally there are provisions targeted toward end of the relationship. Article 31 specifies that no franchisor shall terminate a franchise agreement before the expiration date except for good cause.[331] Article 32 states that a franchisor commits an offence if it refuses to renew a franchise agreement, to extend a franchise term without compensating a franchisee, or to waive any portion of the franchise agreement which prohibits the franchisee from continuing to conduct substantially the same business under another mark in the same area subsequent to the expiration of the franchise agreement, or if it does not give the franchisee a written notice of its intent not to renew the franchise agreement at least six months prior to the expiration date of the franchise agreement.[332]

Earlier termination is admitted in certain circumstances. With respect to extension, at any time before the expiration of the franchise term, the franchisee shall (at its option) give written notice to the franchisor to extend the franchise term. A franchisor is obliged to grant the extension of the term to another period except where the franchisee has breached the terms of the previous agreement. The terms of the extended agreement shall contain conditions that are similar to, or not less favourable than, the conditions contained in the previous franchise agreement.[333]

Good faith is a duty imposed by statute. A franchisor and a franchisee are required to act in an honest and lawful manner and endeavour to pursue best franchise business practice of the time and place. In their dealings with one another they shall avoid substantial and unreasonable overvaluation of fees and prices; conduct which is unnecessary and unreasonable in relation to the risks to be incurred by one party; and conduct that is not reasonably necessary for the protection of the legitimate business interests of the franchisor, franchisee or franchise system.[334]

---

330 Act 590 Franchise Act 1998 (Malaysia) Articles 22 and 23.

331 Act 590 Franchise Act 1998 (Malaysia) Article 31(2) elaborates on the meaning of 'good cause'.

332 Act 590 Franchise Act 1998 (Malaysia) Article 32.

333 Act 590 Franchise Act 1998 (Malaysia) Articles 33 and 34.

334 Act 590 Franchise Act 1998 (Malaysia) Article 29.

A Franchise Advisory Board composed of 15 members who have wide knowledge and experience of franchising and whose selection is entrusted to the Minister will advise the Minister and the Registrar on matters concerning franchises and the administration and enforcement of the laws that relate to franchising. The Minister and Registrar are, however, not bound to act upon the advice of the Board.[335]

Part VI deals with offences and penalties, covering fraud and deceit, the obstruction of officers, a general penalty provision, offences by the body corporate, and the compounding of offences.[336] The Act includes provisions for investigation and enforcement.[337]

**Vietnam**

Vietnam's population is estimated at approximately 88 million and GDP is estimated at about $90 billion. Vietnamese law is based upon a combination of French civil law and communist legal conventions. Franchising regulations are set out in Decree No. 35/2006/ND-CP ('Decree 35') and Circular No. 09/2006/TT-BTM ('Circular 9'), both promulgated in 2006.[338] The Decree has 28 articles divided into three chapters: General Provisions; Franchising Activities; and Implementing Provisions.[339] The law regulates franchising activities between Vietnamese parties, a foreign franchisor that grants a franchise to a franchisee in Vietnam, or a Vietnamese franchisor that grants a franchise to a franchisee in a foreign country.

Franchising in Vietnam means a commercial activity whereby a franchisor authorises and requires a franchisee to conduct on its own behalf the purchase and sale of goods or provision of services. The purchase and sale of goods or provision of services is to be conducted according to the method of business organization specified by the franchisor and be associated with the trademark, trade name, business know-how, business mission statements, business logo and advertising of the franchisor. The franchisee accepts the franchisor's assistance and guidance in the conduct of the business.[340] The Decree further defines franchising to include master franchising and franchise development contracts.

---

335 Act 590 Franchise Act 1998 (Malaysia) Articles 35 and 36.

336 Act 590 Franchise Act 1998 (Malaysia) Articles 37–41.

337 Act 590 Franchise Act 1998 (Malaysia) Articles 42–52.

338 Decree No 35/2006/ND-CP Detailing the Provisions of the Commercial Law on Franchising 2006 (Socialist Republic of Vietnam).

339 Decree No 35/2006/ND-CP Detailing the Provisions of the Commercial Law on Franchising 2006 (Socialist Republic of Vietnam).

340 Decree No 35/2006/ND-CP Detailing the Provisions of the Commercial Law on Franchising 2006 (Socialist Republic of Vietnam) Article 2.

The law is principally a disclosure law. It requires a franchisor to supply copies of the franchise contract form and the written introduction of its commercial franchise to the intended franchisee at least 15 working days before signing the contract, unless otherwise agreed by the parties. Compulsory contents of the written introduction of commercial franchise shall be specified and promulgated by the Ministry of Trade.

There is ongoing disclosure in that a franchisor must promptly notify all franchisees of all important changes in the commercial franchise system, which may affect the latter's business activities by mode of commercial franchising.

Where the franchised commercial right is a common one, the secondary franchisor must in writing notify the intended franchisee of information on the franchisor that has granted commercial rights, contents of the common commercial franchise contract, and method of handling secondary commercial franchise contracts in case of termination of the common commercial franchise contract.[341]

The intended franchisee must supply the franchisor with information reasonably requested by the latter before deciding on the grant of commercial rights to the former.[342]

There is also a registration requirement. A franchisor must register a form of disclosure document prior to commencing franchising activities.[343] Other legislation targeted toward pre-sales negotiation and contract formation includes a qualification requirement. The business system intended for franchise must be in operation for at least one year in order for a trader to be permitted to grant commercial rights.[344]

Articles 11–13 provide that a commercial franchise contract may have certain principal contents.[345] Commercial franchise contracts must be

[341] Decree No 35/2006/ND-CP Detailing the Provisions of the Commercial Law on Franchising 2006 (Socialist Republic of Vietnam) Article 8.

[342] Decree No 35/2006/ND-CP Detailing the Provisions of the Commercial Law on Franchising 2006 (Socialist Republic of Vietnam) Article 9.

[343] Decree No 35/2006/ND-CP Detailing the Provisions of the Commercial Law on Franchising 2006 (Socialist Republic of Vietnam) Articles 17–23.

[344] Decree No 35/2006/ND-CP Detailing the Provisions of the Commercial Law on Franchising 2006 (Socialist Republic of Vietnam) Article 5. Where a Vietnamese trader is the primary franchisee of a foreign franchisor, such Vietnamese trader must conduct business by mode of commercial franchising for at least one year in Vietnam before sub-franchising.

[345] Decree No 35/2006/ND-CP Detailing the Provisions of the Commercial Law on Franchising 2006 (Socialist Republic of Vietnam) Article 11: 1. Content of franchised commercial right; 2. Rights and obligations of the franchisor; 3. Rights

made in Vietnamese; for franchises granted by Vietnamese parties overseas, the language of commercial franchise contracts shall be agreed upon by the parties.

The valid term of a commercial franchise contract shall be agreed upon by the parties. Legislation targeted toward end of the relationship provides that the agreement *may* contain provision for extension and termination of the contract.[346] A commercial franchise contract may be terminated ahead of the agreed time in the cases specified in Article 16.

The franchisee may transfer commercial rights to another intended franchisee when certain conditions are satisfied.[347] The franchisee must send a written request for transfer of commercial rights to the direct franchisor. Within 15 days after receiving such written request of the franchisee, the direct franchisor must reply in writing, clearly stating its consent to the transfer of commercial rights by the franchisee or its rejection of the transfer of commercial rights by the franchisee for the reasons specified in Clause 3. The direct franchisor may reject the transfer of commercial rights of the franchisee for certain enumerated reasons, but if it fails to reply in writing within 15 days, it shall be deemed as having consented to the transfer.[348] The transferor of commercial rights shall no longer hold the transferred commercial rights; all rights and obligations related to commercial rights shall be held by the transferee, unless otherwise agreed.[349]

Article 16 provides that a franchisee has the right to unilaterally terminate the commercial franchise contract in cases where the franchisor breaches its obligations specified in Article 287 of the Commercial Law. A franchisor has the right to unilaterally terminate the commercial franchise contract where the franchisee no longer holds the business licence, the franchisee is dissolved or goes bankrupt, commits serious violations of law,

---

and obligations of the franchisee; 4. Price, periodical franchise fee and mode of payment; 5. Valid term of the contract; 6. Renewal and termination of the contract, and settlement of disputes.

[346] Decree No 35/2006/ND-CP Detailing the Provisions of the Commercial Law on Franchising 2006 (Socialist Republic of Vietnam) Article 11.

[347] Decree No 35/2006/ND-CP Detailing the Provisions of the Commercial Law on Franchising 2006 (Socialist Republic of Vietnam) Article 15 prescribes the conditions for transfer.

[348] Decree No 35/2006/ND-CP Detailing the Provisions of the Commercial Law on Franchising 2006 (Socialist Republic of Vietnam) Article 15(3) enumerates permissible reasons for refusing the transfer of the franchise.

[349] Decree No 35/2006/ND-CP Detailing the Provisions of the Commercial Law on Franchising 2006 (Socialist Republic of Vietnam) Article 15.

or fails to remedy immaterial breaches in the contract within a reasonable time limit.[350]

Traders involved in commercial franchising that commit the following acts of violation shall, depending on the nature and seriousness of their violations, be administratively sanctioned according to the provisions of law on handling of administrative violations: conducting commercial franchising business without having fully satisfied the specified conditions; granting commercial franchises for goods or services banned from business; breaching the obligation to supply information in commercial franchising specified in the Decree; including in written introductions of commercial franchise untruthful information; violating regulations on registration of commercial franchising; violating regulations on notification in commercial franchising; failing to pay tax(es) according to the provisions of law, but not seriously enough for penal liability examination; failing to abide by requests of competent state agencies conducting examinations or inspections; and/or violating other provisions of this Decree. Those who violate the law may be liable to pay damages.[351]

As part of Decree 59/2007/ND-CP (2007) some goods and services are prohibited from circulation in Vietnam; or, if circulation is not restricted, necessary conditions for circulation must be satisfied.[352] Decree No. 11/2006/ND-CP of the Government Regulations on Cultural Activities and the Business of Public Cultural Services ('Decree 11') provides that a franchise program must not include contents contrary to certain enumerated state interests.

Article 11 states that the agreement may contain provisions for dispute resolution.[353]

Several other laws of Vietnam impact significantly on franchising. Contract law has been upgraded by the amended Civil Code (effective January 2006) and specific commercial transactions, including franchising, have been accommodated in the new 2005 Commercial Law (effective January 2006).[354] In 2005 the National Assembly enacted a new

---

[350] Decree No 35/2006/ND-CP Detailing the Provisions of the Commercial Law on Franchising 2006 (Socialist Republic of Vietnam) Article 16.

[351] Decree No 35/2006/ND-CP Detailing the Provisions of the Commercial Law on Franchising 2006 (Socialist Republic of Vietnam) Articles 24–26.

[352] Decree No 59/2007/ND-CP Detailing the Provisions of the Commercial Law on Franchising 2007 (Socialist Republic of Vietnam).

[353] Decree No 35/2006/ND-CP Detailing the Provisions of the Commercial Law on Franchising 2006 (Socialist Republic of Vietnam) Article 11.

[354] Under the Commercial Law anything which is commercial in nature but regulated by specialized laws will be governed by such specialized laws, and

Intellectual Property Law (effective July 2006) which is WTO TRIPS compliant and consistent with international best practice. A Competition Law was passed in 2004.[355] The 2005 United Enterprise Law and the Common Investment Law govern enterprises of both foreign and domestic investors and investment activities of foreign and local individuals and entities respectively.[356]

## REGULATION OF THE FRANCHISE SECTOR IN OCEANIA

### Australia

Australia's population is estimated at approximately 22 million and its GDP is estimated at about $1 trillion. Annual turnover in the franchise sector within Australia is around A$80 to 90 billion.

Australia is a common law jurisdiction in which franchising has been subject to a variety of regulatory regimes. From 1981 to 1987 it was subject to prescribed investment security provisions of the Corporations Law. After a period of deregulation from 1987–93 a voluntary code of practice was established in 1993.[357] However, a 1995 review of that code found that only about 50 to 60 percent of franchisors had chosen to register, and, widely viewed as ineffective, the code was allowed to lapse in 1996.[358]

The 1997 Review of Fair Trading identified a number of small business concerns with the franchising system, including unfair contract terms, complexity of documentation, lack of pre-contract disclosure, inadequacy of advice and education for small business, and the prohibitive costs of and long delays in legal action.[359] The 1997 Review gave rise to the adoption of the mandatory Franchising Code of Conduct (the Code) prescribed under

---

anything which is neither provided for by the commercial law nor any specialized law will be regulated by the Civil Code.

355 Law No. 27/2004/QH11 Law on Competition 2004 (Socialist Republic of Vietnam).

356 Andrew Terry, 'Asia's Next Franchising Frontier: Good Morning Vietnam!' (Paper presented at the 22nd Annual International Society of Franchising Conference, Saint-Malo, France; 20–21 June 2008).

357 Western Australia, 'Inquiry into the Regulation of Franchising', Background Paper (2007).

358 Manitoba Law Reform Commission, 'Consultation Paper on Franchise Legislation' (2008) 8 *Asper Review of International Business and Trade Law* 181.

359 Manitoba Law Reform Commission, 'Consultation Paper on Franchise Legislation' (2008) 8 *Asper Review of International Business and Trade Law* 181.

the Trade Practices Act 1974 (the TPA), Trade Practices (Industry Codes – Franchising) Amendment Regulations 2007 (No 1) (Cth). Modelled on the former voluntary code, Part 1 sets out purpose of the Code and definitions; Part 2 requires franchisors to create and maintain a disclosure document; Part 3 includes some conduct and relationship provisions; and Part 4 pertains to resolution of disputes.

Under the Code the elements of a franchise are a grant by a person to another person of the right to carry on the business of providing goods or services under a system determined or controlled by the franchisor; and the operation of the business must be substantially or materially associated with a trademark, advertising or commercial symbol owned or specified by the franchisor; and there must be a payment from the franchisee to the franchisor, e.g. an initial capital investment fee, a payment for goods or services, or a fee based on a percentage of gross or net income.[360] Effective 1 March 2008 the Franchising Code applies to overseas franchisors who grant only one franchise or master franchise in Australia.

The Australian legislation relies in large part upon pre-sales disclosure. It states that a franchisor that intends to enter into, extend or renew a franchise contract covered by the Code must provide to the prospective franchisee at least 14 days prior to signing the contract a copy of the Code, a copy of the franchise contract, and a disclosure document that provides information about contract terms. The Code comprehensively details a franchisor's obligations in relation to disclosure in Annexure One which prescribes 21 items to be disclosed. The disclosure process also requires a prospective franchisee to attest that it has consulted with legal and accounting professionals prior to signing the franchise contract or that it has been advised but has declined to seek such assistance.[361]

In addition to disclosure, with respect to pre-sales negotiation and contract formation, the Code mandates a seven-day cooling-off period for franchisees.[362] Further, a franchise agreement must not contain or require a franchisee to sign a waiver of any verbal or written representation made by the franchisor.

In regard to performance of the agreement the Code contains a handful of substantive provisions. There can be no general indemnity of franchisor

---

[360] Trade Practices (Industry Codes – Franchising) Regulations (No 162) 1998 (Cth) Clause 4.

[361] Trade Practices (Industry Codes – Franchising) Regulations 1998 (No 162) (Cth) Clause 10.

[362] Trade Practices (Industry Codes – Franchising) Regulations 1998 (No 162) (Cth) Clause 13.

by franchisee.[363] There can be no prohibition on franchisees' or prospective franchisees' freedom to associate with other franchisees.[364] Ongoing disclosure is required. A franchisor must update their disclosure document within four months after the end of each financial year. If a franchisee makes a written request for a franchisor's current disclosure document, the franchisor must comply within 14 days of the request. A franchisee can only make one such request in any 12-month period, not including a request made under a right of renewal. Also, a franchisor must on an ongoing basis also provide financial statements for marketing or other cooperative funds to which franchisees have made financial contributions.[365]

There are also a few provisions targeted toward end of the relationship, such as procedural requirements with respect to transfer and termination.[366]

There is a process requirement for dispute resolution. This aspect of the Australian legislation, along with procedures for transfer and termination, is second in importance to disclosure. Part IV of the Code states that if one party to a dispute requests mediation the other must attend and it prescribes procedures for the dispute resolution process. [367] The parties to mediation must act in good faith and, unless they agree otherwise, each party will be equally liable for costs associated with mediation or help to resolve the dispute.[368]

---

363 Trade Practices (Industry Codes – Franchising) Regulations 1998 (No 162) (Cth) Clause 16.

364 Trade Practices (Industry Codes – Franchising) Regulations 1998 (No 162) (Cth) Clause 15.

365 Trade Practices (Industry Codes – Franchising) Regulations 1998 (No 162) (Cth) Clause 17. Note that The Code applies concurrently with the Petroleum Retail Marketing Franchise Act 1980 (Cth) (PRMF Act); see Stephen Giles and Fiona Wallwork, 'Franchising and Co-operatives – The Franchising Code of Conduct' (2002) Australian Centre for Co-operative Research and Development <http://www.accord.org.au/social/infobriefs/franchising_code_of_conduct.html> at 23 December 2009. 2008 Amendments provide for auditing of marketing and other cooperative funds and the standardization of the audit period so that a franchisor must create a disclosure document within four months after the end of each financial year.

366 Trade Practices (Industry Codes – Franchising) Regulations 1998 (No 162) (Cth) Clauses 20–23 and Part 4.

367 Trade Practices (Industry Codes – Franchising) Regulations 1998 (No 162) (Cth) Part 4. See also Bryan Schwartz and Leandro Zylberman, 'Franchise Symposium Materials: International Franchise Regulation' (2008) 8 *Asper Review of International Business and Trade Law* 317, 347.

368 Trade Practices (Industry Codes – Franchising) Regulations 1998 (No 162) (Cth) Clause 31.

There is no statutory requirement of good faith applicable to franchising in Australia, except with the respect to mediation.[369]

The Australian Competition and Consumer Commission (the ACCC) is responsible for educating the public about the Code, as well as for proceeding against those suspected of breaching the Code. The ACCC can also apply for injunctions and for compensatory orders on behalf of individuals who have suffered loss as a consequence of another person's breach.[370]

The ACCC administers the Franchising Code as a 'Compliance' authority. Enforcement of the Franchising Code is not its preferred means of gaining compliance; instead the ACCC prefers to see franchisors adopting a best practice approach to ensure that they have systems in place to comply with the Code.[371]

A breach of the Code is a breach of Section 51AD of the TPA. The remedies available under the TPA include injunctions, damages, requirements for undertakings, corrective advertising, and other orders.

---

[369] There are numerous precedents for imposing or recognizing obligations of good faith in statutory contexts. These include the Trade Practices (Industry Code – Oilcode) Regulations 2006 (Cth) Clauses 32(6)–(9), the unconscionability provisions of the Trade Practices Act 1974 (Cth) (e.g. s 51AC), the Fair Trading Act 1999 (Vic) s 32W, and Native Title Act 1993 (Cth).

[370] Manitoba Law Reform Commission, 'Consultation Paper on Franchise Legislation' (2008) 8 *Asper Review of International Business and Trade Law* 181.

[371] Allan Fels, 'Administering the Franchising Code of Conduct' (Speech delivered at Hotel Sofitel, Melbourne, 1 September 1998) <http://www.accc.gov.au/content/item.phtml?itemId=97070&nodeId=b93c0749b0e0a4d7801b6b0a7353fa27&fn=Administering%20the%20Franchising%20Code%20of%20Conduct.doc> at 23 December 2009.

# 6. Summary of trends in franchise-specific legislation

Twenty years ago there would have been little to report in a global survey of franchise-specific legislation, but clearly there has been a trend toward an increase in legislation directed toward the franchise sector. In 1990 only four countries had implemented such legislation, but regulation has increased at a steady rate since the 1990s, so that today approximately 30 countries have adopted franchise-specific legislation, and others such as New Zealand and the province of Manitoba have been actively engaged in the process of investigating their options for implementing such legislation.

Certainly one reason for the growth in the regulation of the sector is the growth of the sector itself, as was outlined in the introduction to this book. For the purposes of this research into the operation of franchising and its regulation globally, the presence of McDonald's in any given country was adopted as a proxy for the presence of a franchising sector in the local economy.

While the reach of franchising is clear, given its extensive coverage, the growth of legislation seems, if anything, to have proceeded at a conservative pace. Figure 6.1 indicates the presence of franchise-specific regulation as well as that of a trade association in countries around the globe.

**The Americas:** Of approximately 36 countries in North, Central and South America, unofficial data indicate that there are 22 countries where McDonald's operates units. There would be about 14 in which McDonald's appears not to operate, generally very small Caribbean islands and the remotest and poorest of the larger countries such as Bolivia. Only five of the 22 countries where McDonald's operates have enacted franchise-specific legislation.

Canada, Mexico and the US have enacted franchise-specific legislation. Canada has put forward a model law at the federal level to guide provinces, and four provinces have enacted legislation, while a fifth, Manitoba, is considering legislation. The US has regulation at the federal and state levels (about 20 states). Thus, of the approximately 53 jurisdictions in the world that regulate the franchise sector, about half are in North America.

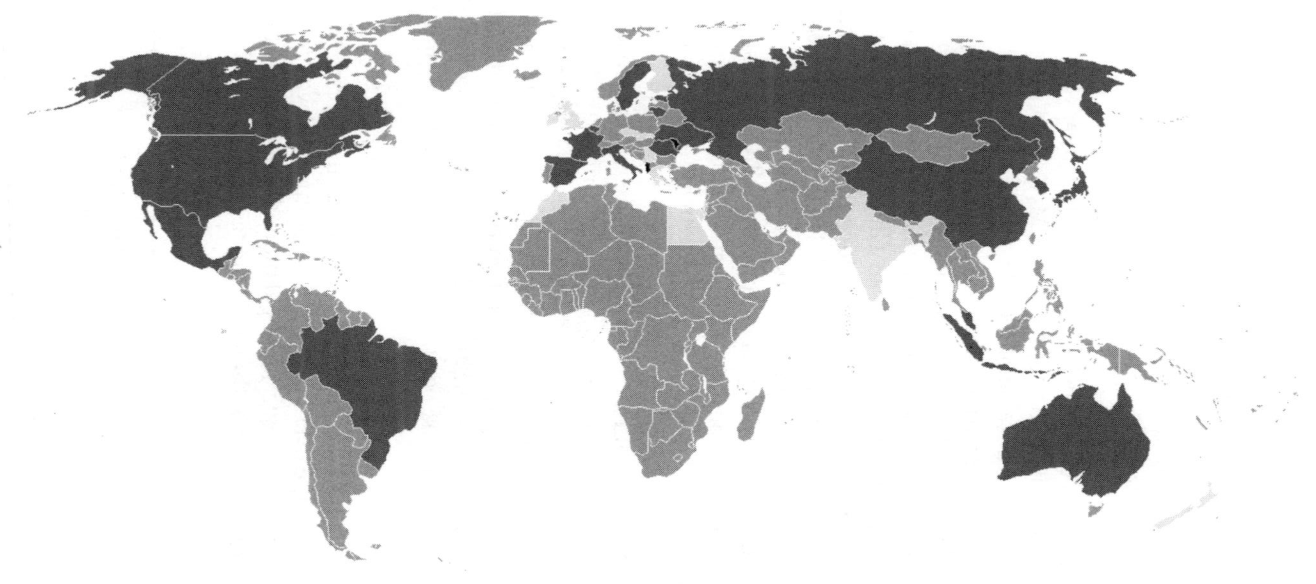

Key:
Darkest grey = legislation only
Dark grey = both a trade association and legislation;
Light grey = trade association only;
Medium grey = no association or legislation

*Figure 6.1 The presence of franchise-specific legislation and/or a trade association*

Of Caribbean countries only Barbados has passed franchise-specific legislation. Of the South and Central American countries only Brazil has done so. Though Venezuela is nearly on a par with Brazil in terms of the importance of franchising to its economy, and there is a franchise trade association in that country, Venezuela has not enacted legislation regulating the franchise sector.

**Europe:** There are about 43 countries in Europe; nearly all have at least one McDonald's. Interestingly, one country where McDonald's appears not to operate is Albania, which is one of the 13 countries in Europe that has enacted franchise sector regulation. There is in Europe a trend toward regulation at the municipal level, as the period since 2000 has seen the number of EU states with franchise-specific laws double from six to 12.

At the pan-European level the only European Union (EU) regulation specific to franchising is a block exemption regulation for franchise agreements under Article 81 of the Treaty of Rome.[1] There has also been a proposal for a Uniform European Union Franchise Disclosure Law. A draft chapter on franchising in the model European Civil Code contains pre-contractual disclosure provisions, as well as a number of provisions to regulate the franchise relationship throughout the term of the agreement.[2]

**Africa:** There are about 54 countries in Africa. Two are reported to have McDonald's operating in the country. No countries in Africa have enacted franchise-specific regulation, but some do have active franchise sectors. With over 500 franchise systems operating in the country, South Africa, for example, now claims a franchising sector that contributes approximately 12 percent of South Africa's gross domestic product.[3] Egypt, Morocco and South Africa have franchise trade associations that have Codes of Conduct or Ethics.

**Asia:** Of the approximately 48 countries in Asia, it appears that McDonald's operates in a little over half, about 29 countries. Eleven Asian countries have enacted franchise-specific regulation. Countries in which McDonald's does not report an operation are among these.

---

[1] See M. Mendelsohn, *The Guide to Franchising* (1999), 6th edn.

[2] Jon K. Perala, 'Franchise Disclosure Laws in the European Union' (2007) Jon K. Perala, Attorney & Counselor at Law <http://peralaw.com/EU_Franchise_Disclosure.html> at 22 December 2009.

[3] http://www.nixonpeabody.com/publications_detail3.asp?ID=2785 at 12 July 2009.

**Oceania:** Of the approximately 14 countries in Oceania, there are about four in which McDonald's operates. Australia is the only jurisdiction that currently regulates the sector. New Zealand has an active franchise trade association and has been considering legislation to regulate the sector.

## PATTERNS IN THE ADOPTION OF FRANCHISE-SPECIFIC LEGISLATION AND THE DISPOSITION TO IMPLEMENT LEGISLATION

The pattern of the growth of regulation of the sector has been uneven. Of the 30 countries that now regulate the sector, three jurisdictions adopted legislation between 1970 and 1980 (Barbados, the US and Alberta, Canada); two between 1980 and 1990 (France and Japan); 16 between 1990 and 2000 (Albania, Brazil, Mexico, Moldova, Romania, Russia, Spain, People's Republic of China, Taiwan, Georgia, Indonesia, Malaysia, Macau, Kyrgyzstan and Australia); and 13 since 2000 (Belarus, Belgium, Estonia, Italy, Lithuania, Sweden, Ukraine, Kazakhstan, Korea and Vietnam as well as three Canadian provinces, Ontario, New Brunswick and Prince Edward Island).

Two countries substantially revised their legislation between 1990 and 2000 (Mexico and Canada) and six have revised franchising legislation since 2000 (Mexico, Spain, China, Taiwan, Japan and the US). Some countries with already well-established regulatory regimes such as Australia and the US review and revise their legislation periodically. There seems to be no common standard regarding ongoing monitoring and review of legislation, which appears to take place more on an ad hoc basis. Best practice of course dictates that procedures should be in place for review on a routine basis, to avoid such review occurring only in response to political pressure.

There appears to be no rule of thumb about whether any given jurisdiction can be expected to regulate. It may be that a significant level of economic development in some cases serves as precondition for regulation of franchising to be considered a worthwhile and necessary measure. Many countries that have enacted franchise-specific regulation have emerging franchising sectors, but many, such as the US, Australia, France and Canada, have a solid history of franchising and mature franchising sectors. Seven of the countries that regulate franchising are among the top ten economies in the world by GDP (the US, China, Japan, Russia, France, Brazil and Italy). Seven more countries that regulate are among the top 20 (Mexico, Spain, Canada, Korea, Indonesia, Australia and Taiwan). Of the 30 countries that regulate, half are among the top 20 countries in the world by GDP.[4]

As Figure 6.2 below illustrates, civil law is the most common legal tradition in the world, and most countries that regulate the sector are civil law jurisdictions or are heavily influenced by civil law. There are only four common law countries that regulate the sector, Barbados, the US, Canada and Australia.

Increased legislative intervention in the sector globally can be attributed to several factors. First, the expansion and development of franchising as a global economic force and as an important driver of municipal economies brings with it an increased awareness of the risks of this business form. Secondly, the trend toward increased legislation may result in part from the evolution of theoretical principles underpinning regulation and the changing currents in approaches to best practice in regulation. Thirdly, in a post-global financial crisis era of global economic interaction, views of regulation as interference have been exchanged for a reinvigorated awareness of the value of regulation as governance as well as a renewed interest in its potential.

Regulation is always undertaken with a degree of caution, however. It is to be applied judiciously, and only where and to the extent it can be truly beneficial in improving the function of economies and in advancing social welfare objectives. So the question is, when and where will franchise-specific regulation be economically and socially beneficial?

While it is not possible to predict patterns of regulation into the future, it may be possible to identify some areas where further development can be expected. With the growth of franchising in South America, for example, it will be interesting to observe the trends in regulation on that continent, whether they follow a pattern of more extensive regulation, as in Brazil, or a less interventionist approach, relying more heavily on trade association codes as in Venezuela.

Western Europe is probably unlikely to see new franchise-specific regulation in countries with mature and vibrant franchise sectors that have for years avoided regulation, such as England, the Netherlands and Germany. Like South America, Eastern Europe appears likely to see strong growth of franchising as an emerging sector and one that will be of increasing importance economically, socially and politically. The shape of

---

4 Central Intelligence Agency (United States of America), 'The World Factbook: Country Comparison: GDP (purchasing power parity)' (2009) CIA <http://www.cia.gov/library/publications/the-world-factbook/rankorder/2001rank.html> at 22 December 2009.

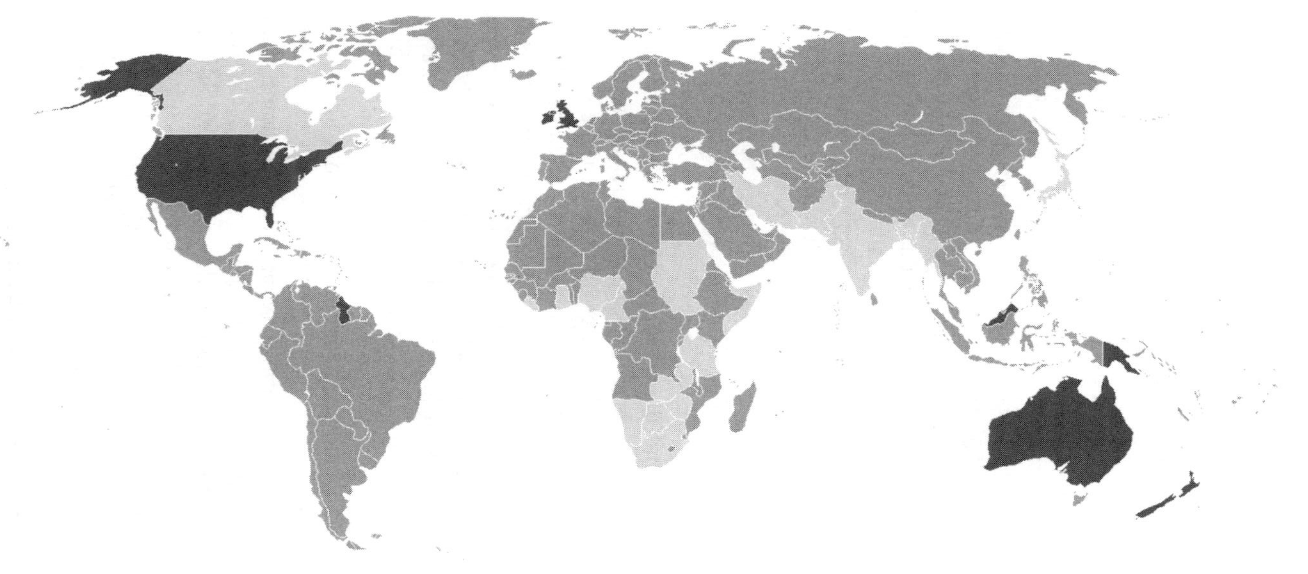

Key:
Dark grey = common law
Light grey = civil law or other legal system
Palest grey = mixed civil and common law
Because of the civil law jurisdiction of Quebec, Canada is shown as a mixed jurisdiction.
Some Middle Eastern countries are principally Sharia law.

*Figure 6.2* *Civil law and common law jurisdictions of the world*

regulation in those jurisdictions will be particularly interesting to watch as it develops.

## TOOLS USED IN FRANCHISE REGULATION

Information about patterns of regulation globally helps to inform a better understanding of commercial regulation and to identify the most promising approaches to regulating the sector. The various approaches to regulating and the tools used are the main focus of the next two chapters. Before getting to that more detailed analysis, however, the last part of this chapter provides a bird's-eye view of approaches and tools used by the 30 countries that regulate the sector, in order to orient the reader to the more detailed discussion in those chapters. Table 6.1 below summarizes the dates of implementation of legislation and the tools used in each jurisdiction, while the commentary after the table begins to identify patterns in the legislation. As the table indicates, many countries rely heavily on disclosure, but many also apply some other regulatory tools as each jurisdiction must assess and respond to its particular needs and objectives with a mix of tools to best serve its purposes.

From the survey it is clear that disclosure and other regulatory tools directed towards formation have emerged as the preferred means of legislative intervention, followed by measures addressing the end of the relationship. Of the 30 countries that have promulgated franchise-specific legislation 20 countries (about 67 percent) have regulated by means of disclosure requirements. (If you add to this the nine countries that require a franchisor to transfer information a franchisee needs to operate the franchised enterprise, the number requiring some disclosure of information would rise to 29, or almost 100 percent of the countries with franchise-specific legislation.)

Other pre-sales measures include registration, cooling-off, advice and warnings and standards. Approximately 17 countries (about 58 percent) have regulated by means of registration requirements of some kind. Registration appears to be a more important tool in the US at the state level, as many US states require registration, though, interestingly, no Canadian provinces require it. Approximately five countries (about 17 percent) have regulated by means of a pre-contractual cooling-off or review period, and approximately six countries (about 20 percent) have regulated by means of franchisor standards or qualifications. These are all measures directed toward the entry into and formation of the contract.

Measures employed to affect performance or conduct of the relationship are less common in franchise-specific legislation. Among these the most

*Table 6.1* *Tools used in franchise regulation worldwide*

| | *Year of franchise-specific legislation and years of revision* | Procedural pre-sales | | | Pres-criptive | Perf pre-sales | Procedural | | |
|---|---|---|---|---|---|---|---|---|---|
| | | *Statutory disclosure requirement* | *Registration requirement* | *Cooling-off or Review* | *Standards (for franchisors/franchisees systems)* | *Prescribed content of contract (incl min.term)* | *Dispute Resolution provisions* | *Termination provisions* | *Statutory requirement of good faith* |
| THE AMERICAS | | | | | | | | | |
| Barbados | 1974 | | √ | | | | | | |
| Brazil | 1994 | √ | √ | | | | | | |
| Canada | 1972–2008 | √ | | | | | | √ | √ |
| Mexico | 1991, 1994, 2006 | √ | √ | | | √ | | √ | |
| United States | 1979/2007 | √ | √ | | √ | | | √*** | √ √* |
| EUROPE | | | | | | | | | |
| Albania | 1994 | NI | | | | √ | | √ | √ |
| Belarus | 2005 | NI | √ | | | √ | | √ | |
| Belgium | 2006 | √ | | | | | | √ | |
| Estonia | 2002 | NI | | | | | | | |
| France | 1989 | √ | | | | | | | |
| Italy | 2004 | √ | √ | | √ | √ | | √ | √ |
| Lithuania | 2000 | NI | | | | | | √ | |
| Moldova | 1997 | √ | √ | | | √ | | √ | |
| Romania | 1997 | √ | √ | | √ | √ | | √ | |
| Russia | 1996 | NI | √ | | | √ | √ | √ | |
| Spain | 1996/2006 | √ | √ | | | | | √ | |
| Sweden | 2006 | √ | | | | | | | |
| Ukraine | 2004 | NI | √ | | | | | | |
| EURASIA | | | | | | | | | |
| People's Republic of China | 1997/2005/2007 | √ | √ | √ | √ | √ | √ | √ | |
| Republic of China | 1999/2003 | √ | | √ | | | | √ | |
| Georgia | 1997 | NI | | | | | | √ | |
| Indonesia | 1997 | √ | √ | | √ | √ | | | |
| Japan | 1983, 2002 | √ | √ | | | | | √ | |

*Table 6.1* (continued)

| | | Procedural pre-sales | | | Pres-criptive | Perf pre-sales | Procedural | | |
|---|---|---|---|---|---|---|---|---|---|
| | *Year of franchise-specific legislation and years of revision* | *Statutory disclosure requirement* | *Registration requirement* | *Cooling-off or Review* | *Standards (for franchisors/franchisees systems)* | *Prescribed content of contract (incl min.term)* | *Dispute Resolution provisions* | *Termination provisions* | *Statutory requirement of good faith* |
| Kazakhstan | 2002 | NI | √ | | | | | | |
| Korea | 2002 | √ | √ | √ | | | | √ | √ |
| Kyrgyzstan | 1998 | NI | | | | | | √ | |
| Macau | 1999 | √ | | | | √ | | √ | √ |
| Malaysia | 1998 | √ | √ | √ | | √ | | √ | |
| Vietnam | 2006 | √ | √ | | √ | | | | |
| OCEANIA | | | | | | | | | |
| Australia | 1998 | √ | | √ | | √ minor | √ | √ | |

*Notes:*
NI – franchisor must transfer information necessary for franchisee to exercise exclusive rights transferred under the agreement in Belarus, Georgia, Lithuania, Ukraine, Kyrgyzstan, Estonia, Albania and Kazakhstan. Russia requires delivery of the agreement
* but not in franchise-specific legislation
*** at the state level

frequently used measure is the imposition of some sort of form and/or content requirements of the contract. Such requirements allow regulators to influence performance, but through a low-intervention means that can be effected at contract formation.

Other performance-oriented measures include dispute resolution and good faith. Approximately nine countries (about 30 percent) have regulated in this way. Approximately six countries (about 20 percent) have regulated by means of a franchise-specific statutory requirement of good faith, though many countries require good faith or similar in non-franchise-specific laws applicable to commercial relationships. Approximately five countries (about 17 percent) address the subject of dispute resolution.

Finally, there are legislative measures that can be directed toward ensuring fairness and efficiency at the end of the relationship. These are commonly used, generally in minimally interventionist ways. Approximately 21 countries (nearly 70 percent) address termination in some way in the legislation. Five of these merely require disclosure of termination provisions. Fourteen countries (about 46 percent) have implemented some type of procedural requirement with respect to termination.

Of the 30 countries with franchise-specific legislation there are actually about 54 discrete jurisdictions that regulate, if one includes the approximately 20 US states and 4 Canadian provinces that regulate the sector within these two federated systems. Of these 54 jurisdictions that have promulgated franchise-specific legislation, approximately 40 jurisdictions (about 75 percent) have legislated by means of disclosure requirement. About the same number have implemented transfer, termination and/or renewal requirements. Approximately 32 jurisdictions (about 60 percent) have registration requirements, and about ten jurisdictions (a little under 20 percent) have regulated by means of a statutory requirement of good faith. Only about eight jurisdictions (about 15 percent) address the subject of dispute resolution.

## 'MODELS' OF FRANCHISE-SPECIFIC LEGISLATION

Patterns in franchise-specific legislation suggest that approaches to legislating are frequently borrowed or shared, and that there are several discernible 'models' of regulating franchising that can be identified, albeit in a very simple form, and subject to refinement as research continues. Most of the jurisdictions with franchise-specific legislation appear to fall under one of these models.

### Prescribed Disclosure

The first model, disclosure with extensive disclosure content requirements, can be labelled 'prescribed disclosure', disclosure with extensive disclosure content requirements. Countries that have adopted this model include the US, Australia, Canada, and Brazil. Legislation in countries with this model is similar in approach to the UNIDROIT Model Law. Such legislation relies principally on disclosure, with no registration requirements (except Brazil which requires registration of the agreement). There appears to be minimal government involvement; the focus is on the self-regulatory capacity of the parties through disclosure. There is also in Australia and Canada inclusion of provisions for dispute resolution, a tool that also emphasizes the parties' self-regulatory capacity in implementation. In some of these countries disclosure is also supplemented by miscellaneous substantive provisions, such as a cooling-off period and procedural requirements for termination.

Korea and, to some extent, Japan, seem to fit the 'prescribed disclosure' model as well. Korea requires about 19 items of information in disclosure with no registration requirement. Japan's legislation is a part of competition law and it, too, requires disclosure of about 19 items of information with no registration requirement.

Though the US is included in this category of prescribed disclosure, there are some general differences between the approach taken in the US *at the state level* and elsewhere in the world. Federal law in the US requires disclosure only. At the state level, however, there is significant variation among the 20 or so states that have implemented franchise, business opportunity, and relationship statutes. Many US states have implemented conduct and relationship laws. Fewer US states require good faith in franchise-specific legislation, and this may be due to its inclusion at the federal level under the UCC and the Restatement (Second) of Contracts. Similarly, registration seems to be favoured by a number of states, and may be in response to the lack of such a requirement at the federal level.

Finally, it seems that franchise-specific legislation in the US appears to make little attempt to regulate using dispute resolution. This may be due in part to the inclusion of dispute resolution in other state laws.

**Simple Disclosure**

A second model might be termed 'simple disclosure'. Here again the emphasis is principally on disclosure, but there are less extensive content requirements. As with 'prescribed disclosure' there is generally no requirement of registration of the disclosure document. Countries in this category include France, Belgium, Romania, and Sweden, which require only about ten to 15 items of information to be disclosed and no registration. Italy requires about 18 items of information with no registration requirement. Mexico requires about ten items of information with a requirement of registration of the agreement.

**Disclosure Plus Registration**

The third model, followed in several Southeast Asian countries can be termed 'disclosure plus registration'. It retains the emphasis on disclosure but with a greater emphasis on registration. Vietnam, Malaysia and Indonesia (with about six, seven, and five required items of disclosure respectively) fall into this category. The approach taken in this model seems to imply greater government involvement in the operation of the sector in these jurisdictions and concomitantly reduced emphasis on the self-regulatory capacities of the parties. Note that these jurisdictions also tend to have a more nascent sector in terms of development. It could be expected that the levels of sophistication of franchisees would be less consistent with an ability to carry out a role in self-regulatory measures such as disclosure and conflict resolution procedures.

**Civil Code-based**

A fourth model identified in the study might be labelled the 'civil code-based' model, characterized by the 'complex business licence' or 'commercial concession agreement' approach to legislation impacting the sector that is taken in Russia, Belarus, Georgia, Lithuania, Ukraine, Kyrgyzstan, Estonia, and Albania. Such legislation is usually part of a civil or commercial code rather than franchise-specific legislation. Kazakhstan has a dedicated franchise law, but otherwise seems to follow the 'complex business licence' model found in most of these jurisdictions.

In these jurisdictions the definition used to cover franchising is that of a 'complex business licence' or 'commercial concession agreement'. Regulation in these jurisdictions with the exception of Estonia requires transfer of intellectual property and information 'a franchisee needs to operate the business'. Some form of registration is generally required, with the exceptions of Albania, Estonia and Georgia. Most of these jurisdictions make some provision for itemized obligations and rights of the parties, effects of transfer, and give some detailed prescriptions regarding the role of the state.

Moldova, too, could be placed in this category, as it addresses franchising in its Civil Code, but it also has a separate, dedicated and extensive franchise statute. For this reason, Moldova might share a separate category with Romania. Both Romania and Moldova exhibit some particular adaptations such as increased government involvement in the registration of information with a state agency that makes registered information available for purchase.[5]

**Asia**

There is no single pattern of legislation in the People's Republic of China, Hong Kong, Macau, and Taiwan. The author regrets if this analysis, given

---

5 Innovations in legislation are sometimes criticized as aberrations; nevertheless it can also be the case that innovation, whatever its motivation, is worth monitoring for its potential to contribute to our understanding of the regulation of the sector.

its early stages, gives the impression of unnecessarily grouping some Asian jurisdictions together for the purposes of beginning to sort through their diverse characteristics.

The People's Republic of China is an interesting study in the regulation of the franchise sector, and there are several academics and practitioners writing excellent commentary and analysis in this area. Extensive disclosure is required. Twenty-seven items of information must be provided at least 30 days prior to entering the contract, and registration is also required, that must include extensive information about the franchise system. Changes to the system must also be registered and annual reporting is required. There is a significant level of government involvement in the regulation of the franchise sector in China. There are also specific franchisor requirements of a well-developed business model; a franchisor must have the capacity to provide the necessary management support training and other services; there is a 'two plus one' rule; and there are extensive mandatory contract terms requirements including a minimum duration of the agreement of three years. There is a requirement of fair dealing, honesty and trustworthiness imposed by the measures in addition to a similar requirement for standard-form contracts, and the principle of *contra proferentum* applies. Substantial penalties apply for violation of the measures. There are, however, no provisions with respect to required processes for resolving disputes.

As separate legal jurisdictions, Hong Kong and Macau are not covered by the regulatory measures for the People's Republic of China. Hong Kong does not have statutory regulation of the sector but there is an extensive code of conduct for the members of the franchise trade association in Hong Kong.

In contrast to Hong Kong, Macau does have extensive franchise-specific regulation. It requires prescribed disclosure 'with adequate advance' plus the contract and annexures. There is no registration requirement. Some of the provisions in the legislation may extend beyond contractual requirements, such as the obligation to compensate a franchisee for the costs incurred in fulfilling its noncompetition obligation. There is also extensive enumeration of franchisor and franchisee obligations that in most jurisdictions would be left to the contract, such as a franchisor's obligation to provide training and to supply goods. Other requirements of the legislation that might in other jurisdictions be part of the contractual agreement of the parties include requirements that all advertising by franchisee must be approved by the franchisor, that the franchisee must pay the franchisor, and that the franchisee must satisfy the quality standards of the franchisor. Macau is the only jurisdiction that expressly permits a franchisee to demand annulment of the contract in the case of non-performance by franchisor.

In Taiwan the disclosure requirements are briefer; there are only nine prescribed items required to be provided ten days before entry into the contract, but there is also a five-day review period. There is no registration, no dispute resolution requirement, and no mandatory contract terms.

What all these models have in common is that, with respect to particular tools, legislative intervention very often involves pre-sales measures. There is an emphasis on formation of contract with a heavy reliance upon disclosure and registration. Disclosure is the tool promulgated in the UNIDROIT Model Law, and so might be assumed to be well-suited to address the problems commonly encountered in franchising. There is little cost-benefit analysis or evidence of its efficacy, however.

There is less legislation aimed toward performance of the agreement. Compared with jurisdictions that embrace disclosure, fewer jurisdictions mandate contract terms, and/or require dispute resolution and procedural requirements with respect to termination and transfer and renewal. This apparent reluctance to apply regulatory tools toward the parties' performance of the agreement is unwarranted because, in franchising agreements, the relational nature of the arrangement requires greater emphasis on performance.

In addition to the focus on pre-sales and contract formation, there is also an emphasis on procedural tools, where the burden falls on the parties to carry out, monitor and enforce the regulation. Almost all of the tools used to regulate the relationship at pre-sales and contract formation including disclosure, registration, cooling-off and warnings, are procedural. Of the few tools directed toward performance, the most commonly-used are procedural, such as procedural requirements for termination and dispute resolution. Of the few tools directed toward performance, the most commonly used are procedural, for example, with respect to termination and dispute resolution, that also put much of the onus on the parties themselves, who are often not adequately equipped to fulfil this role. There is minimal use in a few jurisdictions of substantive and prescriptive tools such as standards and qualifications, and only one or two jurisdictions include qualifications of franchisees. Chapters 7 and 8 will explore these aspects of legislation in greater depth.

# 7. Legislation impacting upon negotiation and formation of franchise contracts

Following on from the summaries and overview of legislation in Chapters 5 and 6, the next two chapters analyse and discuss patterns of franchise-specific legislation globally. The two separate chapters reflect a significant point of delineation in the substance of the legislation as franchise-specific legislative measures fall into two categories, those that are directed towards the formation of the contract, and those that are directed toward performance of the terms of the contract and the end of the relationship.

The current chapter is devoted to legislation impacting upon negotiation and formation of franchise contracts. Regulation of franchising is regulation of the contractual agreement. Contract law is generally concerned with entry into the contract and procedural fairness. The assumption is that, where proper procedures ensure that parties enter into contracts voluntarily and with full understanding, the contract can be assumed to be fair and that the government's role thereafter is principally to ensure performance and to provide remedies where parties do not meet their obligations. Pre-sales regulation focuses on the parties' capacity to regulate their own interactions and in this way it ensures market efficiency. Consistent with the traditional attitude toward the role of government in contract, such legislation addresses contract formation.

The regulatory tools used typically include procedural measures such as disclosure and registration, as well as, though less commonly, cooling off, advice requirements and risk statements. Such legislation can also involve prescriptive standards such as qualifications and/or accreditation of participants in the transaction. This chapter describes both procedural and prescriptive pre-sales tools used in franchise-specific legislation. Chapter 8 will deal with measures that impact on the performance of and exit from the relationship.

## PROCEDURAL PRE-SALES MEASURES

### Pre-sales Disclosure Requirements

In 2002 disclosure was adopted as the centrepiece of the UNIDROIT Model Franchise Disclosure Law. Today, of the approximately 30 countries with sector-specific regulation of franchising, 19 countries include disclosure as a principal means of regulating the sector. They are Canada (the Uniform Franchise Act and four Canadian provinces that regulate the sector), the US (at the federal level under the FTC Rule and at the state level in 17 states), Brazil, Mexico, Belgium, France, Italy, Moldova, Romania, Spain, Sweden, People's Republic of China, Taiwan, Indonesia, Japan, Korea, Malaysia, Vietnam, and Australia.

Though not part of this survey of franchise-specific legislation, at least ten additional jurisdictions require disclosure because of a statutory duty of good faith in non-franchise-specific commercial or consumer law. Many European jurisdictions, for example, impose a disclosure requirement through the requirement of good faith in negotiation.

Belarus, Estonia, Georgia, Kyrgyzstan, Kazakhstan, Ukraine, Lithuania and Russia do not have a disclosure requirement for franchising along the lines of the UNIDROIT Model Law, but there is a disclosure requirement in these countries because a franchisor is required to transfer technical and commercial documentation and other information necessary to exercise rights to the system (including licences for the use of intellectual property). Most of these laws provide no listing of particular content requirements for prior disclosure information, but some require the franchise contract to cover certain specified information such as fees, territory, and renewal.

Many countries that have regulated the sector also have trade associations that require disclosure under Codes of Conduct. These include Canada, Japan, Korea and Malaysia. Other jurisdictions that have not enacted sector-specific legislation also have national trade associations with voluntary codes of conduct that require disclosure. These countries include Ireland, New Zealand, Egypt, Hong Kong, India, Israel and Venezuela. Further, the European Franchise Federation (EFF) Code of Ethics for Franchising also requires disclosure. EFF members include Austria, Belgium, Denmark, France, Germany, Hungary, Italy, the Netherlands, Portugal and the United Kingdom. Though they are not members of the EFF, Greece and Slovenia have adopted the EFF Code, as has the Baltic Franchise Association.

**Procedural requirements for disclosure**

While disclosure is itself a procedural regulatory tool, there are procedures contained within it, and these vary among jurisdictions. Procedures prescribed for disclosure may include whether or not the disclosure must be in writing and/or in a prescribed form; whether registration is required; delivery requirements, e.g. electronic delivery; where a franchisee must go to receive disclosure; and timing.

The first point to note about disclosure is by whom and to whom it is required. Generally, a franchisor must disclose to prospective franchisees, and in most countries a master franchisee must disclose to a sub-franchisee. A few jurisdictions make some provision that a franchisee must provide relevant information to a prospective franchisor. Korea in addition requires disclosure by brokers and agents.

Delivery requirements for disclosure are not common; only five jurisdictions, Macau, People's Republic of China (some parts of disclosure), Spain, Sweden and Vietnam expressly require delivery of disclosure in writing. The UNIDROIT Model Law also specifies that disclosure be in writing. Other jurisdictions such as Australia require disclosure in a certain form, and in this way they also require writing. Sector-specific legislation does not typically address the issue of electronic delivery of information, for example on computer disks, CD-ROMs, via emails, or Internet websites.

Several jurisdictions require disclosure in a prescribed form. Countries that provide for a prescribed disclosure format include Australia, Brazil, Canada (the Model Law and some provinces), Korea, Malaysia, the US (the FTC Rule at the federal level and some state laws), and Vietnam. This requirement facilitates comparison and in combination with a filing requirement facilitates the collection of data such as sector statistics.[1] Countries with a prescribed disclosure document generally require annual updates sometimes with notification required to franchisees of materially relevant factors.

As for timing of disclosure, UNIDROIT requires that disclosure be made at least 14 days before the earlier of the signing by the prospective franchisee of any agreement relating to the franchise or the payment of any fees relating to the acquisition of a franchise that are not refundable. The time period for disclosure is not specified in Indonesia, Japan or Kazakhstan, but in Romania disclosure must be made before a franchisee undertakes any legal obligations with respect to the proposed business.

---

[1] A Terry, 'A Census of International Franchise Regulation' (Paper presented at 21st Annual International Society of Franchising Conference, Las Vegas, Nevada, USA, 24–25 February 2007).

In Sweden the statutory command is simply ‘well before’ a franchise agreement is entered into. In those jurisdictions that do specify a time, the prescribed time varies from 5 days (Korea) to 30 days (Belgium, Italy, Mexico and People’s Republic of China). The US, Brazil, Taiwan, and Malaysia require disclosure to be made ten days prior to entering the agreement while France and Spain require 20 days. In Australia a franchisor is required to make disclosure 14 days before the prospective franchisee enters into a binding franchise agreement with, or pays any money to, the franchisor or any affiliate of the franchisor involved in the franchise sale. Canadian provinces all specify 14 days. Vietnam requires 15 days.

Registration of disclosure documents has been adopted only in Indonesia, Korea, and Malaysia as well as in about 14 US states (though ten countries require registration of the agreement).[2] Ontario, Canada has a certification requirement and Australia requires a receipt of delivery of the disclosure document.

**Disclosure content requirements**

Despite the almost universal requirement of franchisor prior disclosure in franchise-specific legislation, there is little uniformity in the extent and content of the required disclosures. The prescribed document regimes which are closely based on US disclosure requirements, such as Australia, are comprehensive, listing over 20 categories of required information. At the other extreme are those disclosure regimes which provide only a few specific disclosure obligations or rely on formulae such as ‘such information as is needed in the circumstances’ (Sweden) or ‘such information necessary to enable the franchisee to take part in a franchise agreement in full awareness’ (Romania).[3] Table 7.2 provides a summary overview of content requirements across all jurisdictions that require disclosure. The detail of the content of disclosure requirements in each jurisdiction is provided in Appendix 2.

As Figure 7.1 below illustrates that Canada (several provinces), the US, Brazil and Australia require the highest numbers of items of disclosure, between 20 and 30 items of information. Belgium, France, Italy, Sweden,

---

[2] Secretariat, Office of Small Business, Commonwealth of Australia, ‘Review of the disclosure provisions of the franchising code of conduct’ (October 2006) <http://www.innovation.gov.au/Section/SmallBusiness/Documents/Franchising_Code_Review_Report_2006_FINAL_0612072007020513425 0.pdf> at 22 December 2009.

[3] A. Terry, ‘A Census of International Franchise Regulation’ (Paper presented at 21st Annual International Society of Franchising Conference, Las Vegas, Nevada, USA, 24–25 February 2007).

*Table 7.1 Summary of disclosure requirements*

| | Disclosure | Franchisor must transfer all info necessary for franchisee to exercise rights | Timing of Disclosure (Number of Days) | Number of prescribed Items of information | Registration of Disclosure | Continuous Disclosure |
|---|---|---|---|---|---|---|
| THE AMERICAS | | | | | | |
| Brazil | √ | | 10 | 20–30 items listed | | |
| Canada | √ | | 14 | 20–30 items listed | | |
| Mexico | √ | | 30 | about 10 items listed | | |
| United States | √ | | 10 | 20–30 items listed | | |
| EUROPE | | | | | | |
| Albania | | | | | | |
| Belarus | | √ | | | | |
| Belgium | √ | | 30 | 11–20 items listed | | |
| Estonia | | √ | | | | |
| France | √ | | 20 | 11–20 items listed | | |
| Italy | √ | | 30 | 11–20 items listed | | |
| Lithuania | | √ | | | | |
| Moldova | √ | | | fewer than 10 items listed | | |
| Romania | √ | | | about 10 items listed | | |
| Russia | | √ | | | | |
| Spain | √ | | 20 | | | |
| Sweden | √ | | | 11–20 items listed | | |
| Ukraine | | √ | | | | |

*Table 7.1* (continued)

| | Disclosure | Franchisor must transfer all info necessary for franchisee to exercise rights | Timing of Disclosure (Number of Days) | Number of prescribed Items of information | Registration of Disclosure | Continuous Disclosure |
|---|---|---|---|---|---|---|
| EURASIA | | | | | | |
| People's Republic of China | √ | | 30 | 11–20 items listed | | |
| Republic of China | √ | | 10 | 11–20 items listed | | √ |
| Georgia | | √ | | | | |
| Indonesia | √ | | | fewer than 10 items listed | √ | |
| Japan | √ | | | 11–20 items listed | | |
| Kazakhstan | | √ | | | | |
| Korea | √ | | 5 | 11–20 items listed | √ | √ |
| Kyrgyzstan | | √ | | | | |
| Macau | √ | | | 11–20 items listed | | |
| Malaysia | √ | | 10 | fewer than 10 items listed | √ | |
| Vietnam | √ | | 15 | fewer than 10 items listed | | √ |
| OCEANIA | | | | | | |
| Australia | √ | | 14 | 20–30 items listed | | √ |

China, Taiwan, Japan, Korea and Macau require between 11 and 20 items of information. Mexico and Romania require 10 items of information. Moldova, Indonesia, Malaysia and Vietnam itemize fewer than ten items of information to be provided in disclosure.

The content required of disclosure in franchise-specific legislation

*Table 7.2 Disclosure content requirements*

| Classifications of prior disclosure information | Canada | the US | Brazil | Mexico | Belgium | France | Italy | Moldova | Romania | Spain | Sweden | China (PR) | Taiwan | Indonesia | Japan | Korea | Macau | Malaysia | Vietnam | Australia |
|---|---|---|---|---|---|---|---|---|---|---|---|---|---|---|---|---|---|---|---|---|
| From franchisor to franchisee | | | | | | | | | | | | | | | | | | | | |
| About franchisor | | | | | | | | | | | | | | | | | | | | |
| franchisor and any parents, predecessors and affiliates | √ | √ | √ | √ | √ | √ | √ | | | √ | | √ | √ | √ | | √ | √ | | √ | √ |
| financial statements | √ | √ | √ | | √ | √ | √ | | | | | √ | | √ | | | √ | | √ | √ |
| business experience | √ | √ | | | √ | √ | | | √ | √ | | √ | √ | √ | | √ | √ | | | √ |
| litigation | √ | √ | √ | | | | √ | | | | | √ | | | | √ | √ | | | √ |
| bankruptcy | √ | √ | | | | | | | | | | √ | | | | | √ | | | √ |
| About the franchise system | | | | | | | | | | | | | | | | | | | | |
| franchisee information | √ | √ | √ | | | √ | √ | | | | √ | √ | √ | | | | √ | | | √ |

| | | | | | | | | | | | | | | | | | | | | |
|---|---|---|---|---|---|---|---|---|---|---|---|---|---|---|---|---|---|---|---|---|
| franchisee financial statements | | | | | | | | | | | | | | | | √ | | | | |
| number of operational units | √ | √ | √ | | √ | √ | √ | | | √ | √ | √ | √ | √ | √ | | √ | | √ | √ |
| closures of franchisee or franchisor outlets | √ | √ | √ | | √ | √ | √ | | | √ | | | √ | | √ | | √ | | √ | √ |
| bank account information | | | | | | √ | | | | | | | | | | | | | | |
| lawsuits etc | | √ | √ | | | | | | | | | √ | | | | √ | √ | | | √ |
| Rights and obligations | | | | | | | | | | | | | | | | | | | | |
| initial fees | √ | √ | √ | √ | √ | √ | √ | | √ | | √ | √ | √ | | √ | | √ | √ | √ | √ |
| other fees | √ | √ | √ | √ | √ | √ | √ | | √ | | √ | √ | √ | | √ | | √ | √ | √ | √ |
| estimated initial investment | √ | √ | √ | | √ | √ | | | √ | √ | | √ | | | | | √ | | √ | √ |
| restrictions on sources of products and services | √ | √ | √ | | | | | √ | √ | | √ | √ | | | √ | √ | | | √ | √ |
| franchisee's obligations re financing | √ | √ | | | | | | | | | | | | | √ | √ | | | | √ |

*Table 7.2* (continued)

| Classifications of prior disclosure information | Canada | the US | Brazil | Mexico | Belgium | France | Italy | Moldova | Romania | Spain | Sweden | China (PR) | Taiwan | Indonesia | Japan | Korea | Macau | Malaysia | Vietnam | Australia |
|---|---|---|---|---|---|---|---|---|---|---|---|---|---|---|---|---|---|---|---|---|
| franchisor's assistance, advertising, computer systems and training | √ | √ | √ | √ | | | √ | √ | √ | √ | | √ | √ | √ | √ | √ | √ | √ | | √ |
| territory | √ | √ | √ | √ | | √ | √ | | √ | √ | | | | | | √ | | | | √ |
| trademarks | √ | √ | √ | √ | √ | | √ | | √ | √ | √ | √ | √ | | √ | | | | | √ |
| patents, copyrights proprietary information | √ | √ | √ | √ | √ | | √ | | √ | √ | √ | √ | √ | | √ | | | | | √ |
| obligation to participate in the actual operation of the franchise business | √ | √ | √ | | | | | | | | | | √ | | | √ | √ | | | √ |
| restrictions on what franchisee sells | √ | √ | | | | | | √ | | | | | | | | √ | | | | √ |

| | | | | | | | | | | | | | | | | | | | | |
|---|---|---|---|---|---|---|---|---|---|---|---|---|---|---|---|---|---|---|---|---|
| renewal, termination, transfer | √ | √ | √ | | √ | √ | √ | | √ | √ | √ | | √ | | √ | √ | | | | √ |
| public figures | | | | | | | | | | | | | | | | | | | | |
| financial performance representations | √ | √ | | | | | | √ | √ | √ | | √ | | | | | | | | √ |
| related agreements | √ | | | | | | | | | | | | | | | | | | | √ |
| duration of agreement | | √ | √ | | √ | | | | √ | √ | | | √ | | √ | √ | | | | √ |
| conditions for renewal | √ | √ | √ | | | | | | √ | | | | | | | | | | | √ |
| other end of term arrangements | | √ | √ | √ | √ | | √ | | | | √ | | | | | | | | | √ |
| dispute procedures | | | | | | | | | | | √ | | | | | | | | | √ |
| Other specified information | | | | | | | | | | | | | | | | | | | | |
| general sector info | | | | | | | | | | | | | | | | | | | | |
| information re development of the market | | | | | | | | | | | | | | | | | | | | |
| risk statements | √ | √ | | | | | | | | | | | | | | | | | | √ |
| payments to agents | | | | | | | | | | | | | | | | | | | | √ |

*Table 7.2* (continued)

| Classifications of prior disclosure information | Canada | the US | Brazil | Mexico | Belgium | France | Italy | Moldova | Romania | Spain | Sweden | China (PR) | Taiwan | Indonesia | Japan | Korea | Macau | Malaysia | Vietnam | Australia |
|---|---|---|---|---|---|---|---|---|---|---|---|---|---|---|---|---|---|---|---|---|
| a general requirement of relevant information | √ | | | | | | | √ | √ | | √ | | | | | | | | | √ |
| From franchisee to franchisor | | | | | | | √ | | | | | | | | | | | | √ | |

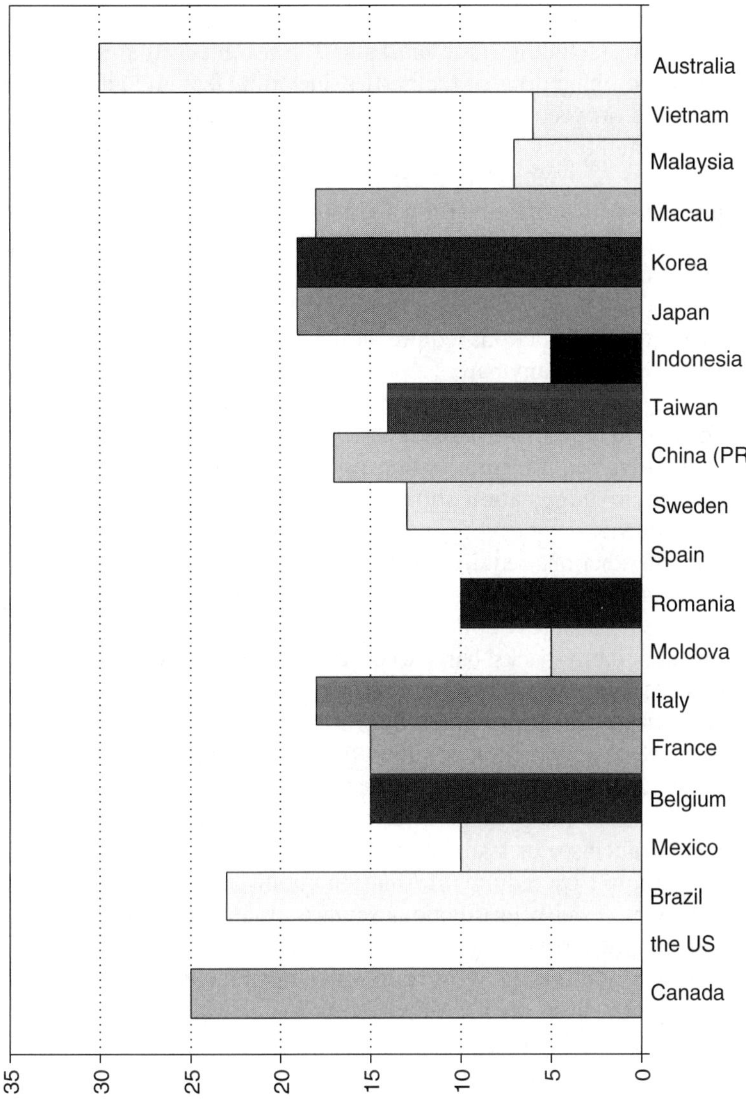


*Figure 7.1* *Number of items of disclosure required*

globally betrays little in the way of discernible patterns. Though the UNIDROIT Model Law has been available as a guide to countries implementing legislation since 2002, 14 of the 20 countries that currently require disclosure implemented legislation prior to 2002. The main categories of information to be disclosed are information about a franchisor; about the franchise system, including trade marks and other intellectual property; about rights and obligations of the parties, including fees and allocations of territory; and provisions for exit from the relationship. These are dealt with in more detail below.

- Information that must be provided from a franchisor to a prospective franchisee often includes information about the franchisor, such as the franchisor and any parents, predecessors and affiliates; financial statements; business experience; litigation; and bankruptcy.
  Seventeen jurisdictions require the disclosure of information about a franchisor, and any parents, predecessors and affiliate companies. Fifteen jurisdictions require financial statements. Sixteen require information about business experience of the franchisor. Eleven jurisdictions require information about litigation. Seven jurisdictions require information about franchisor history of insolvency or bankruptcy.
- Many jurisdictions require further information about the franchise system, such as franchisee financial statements; number of operational units; closures of outlets, including non-renewal, termination, transfer and buy-backs; bank account information; and information relating to dispute procedures filed against the franchisor.
  Fifteen jurisdictions require information about franchisees in the system. One jurisdiction requires franchisee financial statements. Sixteen jurisdictions require information about the number of operational units in the system. Twelve require information about closures a franchisee or franchisor outlets. Two require bank account information. Five require information about past lawsuits affecting the system. Twelve jurisdictions require disclosure of information regarding the territory.
- Information about the rights and obligations included in the franchise agreement as well as other rights and obligations which may not be expressed in the contract is often required, and usually specifies disclosure of fees; estimated initial investment; restrictions on sourcing of products and services; franchisee's financing obligations; franchisor's assistance, advertising, computer systems and training; territory; trademarks; patents, copyrights and proprietary information; obligation to participate in the actual operation of the franchise

business; restrictions on what the franchisee may sell; renewal, termination, transfer and dispute resolution; public figures; financial performance representations; related agreements; duration of the agreement; conditions for renewal; other end-of-term arrangements; and dispute resolution procedures.

Fifteen jurisdictions require information to be given regarding a franchisor's obligations to provide assistance, advertising, computer systems and infrastructure, and training.

Eight jurisdictions require disclosure regarding obligations to participate in the actual operation of the franchise business.

In addition to requirements to disclose some of the key contractual provisions, it is important also to consider mandatory contract terms; several countries mandate prescribed content of a franchise agreement (see Chapter 8).

- Fees are an important part of disclosure. About 20 jurisdictions require information about initial fees. Twenty jurisdictions require information about other fees. Twelve jurisdictions require information to be provided about the estimated initial investment. Seven jurisdictions require information to be provided regarding franchisee's obligations with respect to financing.
- Fifteen jurisdictions require disclosure regarding renewal, termination, and/or transfer; usually the requirement is that any processes and procedures be disclosed. Six require information regarding conditions for renewal. Five require information on other end-of-term arrangements.
- Other categories of information required to be disclosed include:

    - Intellectual property. Seventeen countries require information to be disclosed regarding franchisor trademarks. Eighteen require information to be provided regarding patents, copyrights and other proprietary information.
    - Restrictive trade practices: Eleven jurisdictions require information to be provided with respect to restrictions on sources of products and services. Eight jurisdictions require disclosure of non-compete provisions.
    - Three jurisdictions require information on dispute procedures.
    - Five jurisdictions require information regarding financial performance representations which is interesting to note as this is arguably the most important information to prospective franchisees.
    - Seven require information regarding the duration of the agreement.

  - One jurisdiction requires information to be disclosed regarding the development of the market for products or services relating to the franchise opportunity.
  - Two require risk statements.
  - Two require information with respect to payments to agents made in connection with the recruitment of a franchisee.
  - Only the US requires information to be disclosed about public figures involved with the franchise.

- There may be a general requirement of relevant information in addition to or instead of specific itemized requirements, sometimes referred to as 'closed' and 'open' disclosure respectively.[4] Several jurisdictions make a general requirement of relevant information. These include the Canadian Model Law and the provinces of Ontario, New Brunswick, and Prince Edward Island as well as Spain, Malaysia, Lithuania, Moldova, Romania, and Sweden. Some laws require 'open' disclosure of all 'material information' with no other specification, while other laws, such as those of Australia and the Canadian provinces, list detailed content requirements for disclosure as well as the additional requirement of all 'material information'. The Spanish law requires a franchisor to provide all information necessary to a franchisee to make its decision, but does not specify items to be required in disclosure. Malaysia's regulation resembles open disclosure, but it does specify disclosure of payments of fees and royalties. Some jurisdictions, such as the People's Republic of China, provide that the government agency has the authority to require additional disclosure information.

  The additional disclosure requirement of 'material information' or information a franchisee may need to make an investment decision may be preferred by franchisees as it seeks to provide more information, but it arguably imposes more onerous disclosure obligations and preparation costs on the franchisor and gives rise to disputes as to the 'materiality' of any information not provided.[5] It is not clear whether specification of items to be disclosed offers a

---

[4] A. Terry, 'Issues with Prior Disclosure as a Regulatory Strategy for Franchisee Protection' (Paper presented at 23rd Annual International Society of Franchising Conference, San Diego, CA, USA, 17–18 February 2009).

[5] A. Terry, 'Issues with Prior Disclosure as a Regulatory Strategy for Franchisee Protection' (Paper presented at 23rd Annual International Society of Franchising Conference, San Diego, CA, USA, 17–18 February 2009).

significant benefit relative to the cost of compliance with the different requirements in each jurisdiction.

- Finally, the content of disclosure sometimes extends to a requirement that other documents be included, such as the franchise agreement.

  - Three jurisdictions require information to be provided regarding related agreements, such as leases and licensing agreements. Financial documents may also be required.
  - Some prior disclosure regimes require a franchisor to provide the franchise agreement with disclosure. Italy requires a 'definitive draft' of the contract be provided. Australia has recently amended its legislation to provide that the contract must be provided in the form in which it is to be signed. Australia also requires that a copy of the Code of Conduct be provided with disclosure.
  - The operations manual is not often required to be provided with disclosure, probably due to its highly confidential nature, though it does contain information critical to an understanding of the system.

- Information can also be required to be provided from franchisee to franchisor, as is the case in Italy, Vietnam and Romania. In Italy, Article 6 requires a franchisee to provide a franchisor with any information and data necessary or appropriate for the purposes of the signing of the contract. In Vietnam, Article 9 provides that the franchisee supply the franchisor with information reasonably requested by the franchisor. In Romania, Article 4 requires a franchisee to provide the franchisor any information likely to facilitate knowledge and analysis of the franchisee's performance and its real financial position.

Discussion of the proposed Uniform European Union Franchise Disclosure Law suggests that the European Franchise Federation's Code of Ethics disclosure requirements should be updated following the Italian or Belgian franchise laws which require disclosure of details of all trademarks used in the franchise system; a summary of the franchise activities and operations; a list of franchisees currently operating in the franchise system; year-by-year details of the changes in the number of franchisees for the previous three years; a summary of any court or arbitral proceedings in the jurisdiction related to the franchise system, whether instigated by a franchisee, third party, or public authority; and copies of franchisor's balance sheets for the previous three years, or since start-up if less than three years.[6] Not recommended for inclusion are fees, territory, transfer, termination, renewal, and dispute resolution. Perhaps most significantly there is no requirement with respect to disclosure of information regarding the financial performance of the unit for sale.

**Revising and ongoing disclosure**

Requirements for revision and ongoing disclosure are not common. They may provide that a franchisor must update its disclosure document if there are significant changes relating to the franchisor and the franchise system or that disclosure must be updated on at least an annual basis (for example, in the US and Australia). Continuing disclosure during the course of the franchise relationship is required in Australia, China, Korea and Vietnam.

Ongoing disclosure serves a different purpose from that served by initial disclosure. While franchisees have onerous reporting requirements on an ongoing basis, and failure to comply can result in termination, franchisors in most jurisdictions have few, if any, reporting requirements to franchisees. It makes some sense that franchisors would owe some level of reciprocal reporting to franchisees. Franchisor reporting to franchisees can assist franchisees in understanding the business as it evolves, to understand the franchise system within which it operates, its patterns, and trends, changes in management and so on. It can help them with business planning, tax and other financial planning, budgeting, and staffing. It can also help franchisees to understand the franchisor's financial position and so to protect themselves against the risks of franchisor insolvency.

Without ongoing disclosure by franchisors to franchisees, franchisees are not able to fully participate in the operation of the franchise system. While this result may be what the operators of some franchise systems intend, it is based on an outdated model of command-and-control franchising. Without ongoing disclosure the system fails to maximize the contributions of franchisees for business planning purposes and in decisions regarding the operations of franchise systems.

Ongoing disclosure is, of course, also useful to franchisees considering whether or not to commit to renewal. Because of this some jurisdictions such as Australia also require disclosure at renewal of the agreement.

---

[6] Jon K. Perala, 'Franchise Disclosure Laws in the European Union' (2007) Jon K. Perala, Attorney & Counselor at Law <http://peralaw.com/EU_Franchise_Disclosure.html> at 22 December 2009.

## ANALYSIS OF DISCLOSURE

Disclosure is a form of informational regulation used to influence the flow of information in a market.[7] It enhances economic efficiency by addressing problems that arise because information is withheld, is misleading, is difficult to obtain or to evaluate, or cannot be used because of behavioural bias.[8] Disclosure has been a popular regulatory strategy in the US since its introduction in securities regulation in the 1930s, where it has been used to reveal risks to investors.[9] Disclosure is now favoured as a cost-efficient alternative to conventional regulatory approaches, not only to protect investors, but also consumers; notable examples are for insurance and home mortgage products. It has also been applied in environmental regulation to equip the public with information about the activities of companies and their potential risks to local communities.[10]

In principle disclosure can enhance the ability of franchisees to negotiate and/or to find alternatives in the market. By reducing information asymmetries and transaction costs disclosure facilitates bargaining, increasing fairness and reducing market volatility.[11] Disclosure is thought to 'level the playing field' and so promote trust and boost confidence in the market.

Among all the tools that can be employed by governments in the regulation of the sector, disclosure is by far the most common regulatory strategy. It is the principal regulatory tool in all of the different models of regulating identified in this survey.

Disclosure appears to be most heavily relied upon where the role of government is minimized and self-regulatory tools are preferred. Generally, of the countries that regulate franchising, the Eastern European countries place less emphasis on disclosure, where the greater emphasis is on the rights and obligations of the parties and the role of the state in such

---

7 Anthony I. Ogus, *Regulation: Legal Form and Economic Theory* (1994).

8 Organisation for Economic Cooperation and Development, 'Roundtable on economics for consumer policy: summary report' (June 2007) Directorate for Science, Technology and Industry, Committee on Consumer Policy, OECD < http://www.oecd.org/dataoecd/5/38/39015963.pdf > at 22 December 2009.

9 David W. Case, 'The Law and Economics of Environmental Information as Regulation' (2001) Environmental Law Institute <http://www.vanderbilt.edu/vcems/papers/ELRVersion2.pdf> at 22 December 2009.

10 Susanna Kim Ripken, 'The Dangers and Drawbacks of the Disclosure Antidote: Toward a More Substantive Approach to Securities Regulation' (2006) 58 *Baylor Law Review* 139.

11 Susanna Kim Ripken, 'The Dangers and Drawbacks of the Disclosure Antidote: Toward a More Substantive Approach to Securities Regulation' (2006) 58 *Baylor Law Review* 139.

commercial relationships. In these jurisdictions disclosure is only required of intellectual property and 'information a franchisee needs to operate the business'. Several Southeast Asian countries place greater emphasis on the registration and the role of the government in the registration process.

Disclosure in franchising is a procedural (rather than a prescriptive or performance-based) measure that requires relatively little administration by a regulatory body. As a low-intervention tool, where recipients of disclosed information remain responsible for their decisions, disclosure reduces costs to the regulator in both monitoring and enforcement.[12] Another benefit of the self-regulatory qualities of disclosure is the reduction of guesswork and the risk of obvious missteps by the regulator. Disclosure may also help to avoid the appearance of paternalistic approaches to regulating, a criticism commonly levelled at substantive regulation. The attractiveness of disclosure to regulators, then, is due largely to its self-enforcing qualities which are seen to offer an effective, low-intervention and cost-efficient alternative to conventional regulatory approaches in facilitating the efficient operation of markets. The question that remains unresolved, however, for this as for other regulatory tools, is whether the benefits are worth the costs.

## How Disclosure Works: Elements of Effective Disclosure

While cost-benefit analysis is beyond the scope of this book, it is possible to consider the appropriateness of this regulatory tool for franchising based on certain conditions that correlate with the optimal effectiveness of disclosure. Sunstein notes that because informational regulation relies on, 'market pressures . . . and public pressure to enforce . . . standards', it depends on the availability of reliable and 'useable' information. Informational regulation can only be effective if recipients have the ability to understand and use the information; also there must be alternatives in the market.[13]

Research in the area of environmental regulation has identified four separate 'functions' as necessary for the establishment of an effective information disclosure strategy, 1) to gauge the extent and magnitude of the particular risks; 2) to obtain reliable information; 3) to disseminate information in a form that is both useable by and accessible to the com-

---

[12] David W. Case, 'The Law and Economics of Environmental Information as Regulation' (2001) Environmental Law Institute <http://www.vanderbilt.edu/vcems/papers/ELRVersion2.pdf> at 22 December 2009.

[13] Cass Sunstein, 'Informational Regulation and Informational Standing: Akins and Beyond' (1999) 147 *University of Pennsylvania Law Review* 613, 618.

munity; and 4) to ensure options for the target audience to act upon the information.[14]

For the purposes of this analysis the second and third of these four functions are discussed together, collapsed into a framework of three conditions for effective disclosure. First, if informational regulation does not gauge the extent and magnitude of the risks, it cannot be designed to address these risks. Second, if it fails to ensure that reliable information is obtained and disseminated in an accessible and useable form, then franchisees as recipients of the information cannot rely upon or access or use the information. Third, if it does not ensure that recipients can act upon the information, then no matter how reliable, accessible and useable the information may be, it is ineffective. Because there is a transaction cost for the recipient to assimilate and use the information, if it does not meet these conditions, disclosure can even be counter-productive.[15]

Thus, the benefits of disclosure for franchising depend upon fundamental conditions relating to the quality of the information and the capacity of a franchisee as the recipient of the information. The benefits of disclosure also require reliability, accessibility and useability of the disclosed information and that the recipients of the information are able to act on that information.[16] These conditions are not always assured in the context of franchising, as the following sections explain.

### Limits on the effectiveness of disclosure related to failure of conditions of reliability, accessibility and useability

There are several limitations to the efficacy of disclosure with respect to the reliability, accessibility and useability of the disclosed information. The most obvious limitation is that the needed information may not always be provided. There are two sub-sets of such information, first about the specific franchise system, and second about the nature of the franchise business form and of the contractual arrangement generally.

With respect to information about the specific franchise system, depending on the jurisdiction, information may not be provided. This includes information with respect to prior disputes and nature of previous

---

[14] Tom Tietenberg, 'Disclosure Strategies for Pollution Control' (1998) 11 *Environmental and Resource Economics* 587.

[15] Hugh Collins, *Regulating Contracts* (1999) 284–5. See also Anthony I. Ogus, *Regulation: Legal Form and Economic Theory* (1994) 121–49.

[16] See Cass Sunstein, 'Informational Regulation and Informational Standing: Akins and Beyond' (1999) 147 *University of Pennsylvania Law Review* 613; Tom Tietenberg, 'Disclosure Strategies for Pollution Control' (1998) 11 *Environmental and Resource Economics* 587.

mediations involving other franchisees in the system; and information about franchisees who are, for one reason or another, no longer with the system. Also, the relational quality of the contract means that certain terms of the contract are left unspecified and therefore cannot be disclosed.

The second sub-set of information that should be provided, but often is not, is general information about the advantages and disadvantages of the franchise business form and the franchisor/franchisee relationship overall. Franchisees agree to the terms of the standard form contract, but because it is also relational, in entering the contract a franchisee reasonably expects to participate in a relationship of trust, flexibility and reciprocity. What franchisees often fail to understand is that, because franchisors require control for the sake of uniformity and because contracts are standard form, they have contracted out of such participation.

More research is needed in order to understand the content of disclosure and which formulations for this content are most useful and effective. What is appropriate depends on the relevance of the information to the franchisee and to what extent the benefits of the information justify the costs of providing it.

It is also important to acknowledge that the quality of the information can be compromised if there are deficiencies in monitoring and enforcement and/or where disclosure is not well-orchestrated with other legislation. The use of registration to support compliance with and quality of disclosure has been adopted in 14 US states, but has not been widely accepted internationally.

Finally, accessibility and useability of information are impacted by franchisee inexperience and psychological factors, as outlined in Chapter 3. Other factors that may negatively impact in accessibility and useability of information are the use of legalese, lack of sufficient expert advice and inappropriate presentation and timing of documents. Here, again, other regulatory measures can be considered to enhance and support the efficacy of disclosure, such as training, education and/or prescription of standards for participants.

**Limits on the effectiveness of disclosure related to recipients' inability to act**

With respect to recipients' ability to act on the information there are essentially two ways a franchisee can act on disclosed information; one is to use the information to negotiate and the second is to use it to inform a decision whether to accept the terms or to walk away and try to find a better deal elsewhere.

Negotiation is impaired in the franchise context because the standard form means that the franchisee has an inability to negotiate (see Chapter 3), and also because there are limited alternatives for contract terms among different franchise systems in the market. Further, a franchisee cannot negotiate to address specific aspects of the performance of the contract, because the relational quality of the contract means that terms are left unspecified, often subject to a franchisor's discretion (this phenomenon is also outlined in Chapter 3). It is important to note here also that the flexibility of the relational contract shifts the emphasis in the commercial relationship more toward reliance on trust and if so diminishes the perceived importance of pre-contractual due diligence on the part of the franchisee. The imbalance of negotiating power between the parties is unlikely to be adequately addressed by disclosure in a situation where one party writes the contract and is willing to engage in only limited negotiation of contract terms.

The franchisee's ability to find alternatives, a better deal, is also impaired in the franchising context. By providing market participants better access to information, disclosure is intended to help franchisees make better-informed choices among the alternatives in the market. Disclosure only works in this way, however, where the party to whom information is disclosed has options. In the franchising context the time and expense of finding alternatives in the market impacts effectiveness of disclosure. A prospective franchisee is not entirely analogous to an investor or a consumer, both of which can compare what is on offer in the market, and can generally find practical alternatives. For a franchisee there is often much greater time and psychological investment in the deal by the time disclosure is introduced, and less latitude for substitution of other products in the market, if indeed there are any comparable alternatives.

**Summary of the conditions of effective disclosure and the limits of disclosure**

The lack of information about franchising makes disclosure seem the perfect solution. Disclosure would appear to be able to reduce the mythology of franchising and so help re-balance the power in the relationship. It would appear to be able to reduce uncertainty for franchisees, and to alleviate franchisee misperceptions that might otherwise lead to conflict. The reality, however, may be quite different.

Reliance upon disclosure in the regulation of franchise relationships is ill-advised where it fails, as it often will, to meet the conditions for effective disclosure. Because of the limitations on the efficacy of disclosure with respect to the reliability, accessibility and useability of the disclosed information and the limitations on recipients' ability to act on the information, disclosure cannot function optimally as a tool of franchise regulation.

Disclosure is heavily self-regulatory in nature, and self-regulation has been an attractive option in the regulation of franchising. The US, Canada, Australia, Brazil, France and many other jurisdictions, as well as the UNIDROIT Model Law, all rely heavily on low-intervention, self-regulatory instruments. The appeal of such measures is strong; because of their low cost and their ability to engage the parties who understand best the needs for regulation, and because they can help to avoid unnecessary and costly involvement of government agencies in private affairs.

Nevertheless, regulators of franchising need to acknowledge that, despite these appealing features, informational regulation is not always the ideal regulatory strategy. Evidence of the limitations of disclosure from other applications has suggested that it has been 'at best, a blunt and unfocused instrument.'[17] In fact disclosure can generate problems if, for example, it provides inaccurate or incomplete information; fails to identify actual, existing concerns; promotes unjustified fears; produces a false sense of security; perpetuates misinformation; and/or promotes under- or over-reaction.[18] In the area of consumer protection some studies indicate wiser decisions being made based on less information.[19]

Though it is relatively low-cost from the point of view of the regulator, costs to participants of regulation through disclosure can be significant. Franchisors are able to pass these costs on to franchisees, but, whoever ultimately pays them, what is not known is whether the benefits are worth the costs. Because there is a transaction cost for a franchisee to assimilate and use the information and because there may be opportunity costs, the use of disclosure may actually be counter-productive, leading to the kind of cynicism about regulation that further decreases its efficacy.

## Registration

Registration is a regulatory tool used to ensure parties' rights and obligations and to monitor and enhance compliance. Registration can be used in several ways in the regulation of the franchise sector; the most commonly-used applications are registration of disclosure; registration of intellectual property; and registration of franchise systems, as well as of franchise consultants and brokers.

---

17 David W. Case, 'The Law and Economics of Environmental Information as Regulation' (2001) Environmental Law Institute <http://www.vanderbilt.edu/vcems/papers/ELRVersion2.pdf> at 22 December 2009.

18 Cass Sunstein, 'Informational Regulation and Informational Standing: Akins and Beyond' (1999) 147 *University of Pennsylvania Law Review* 613.

19 Organisation for Economic Cooperation and Development, 'Roundtable on economics for consumer policy: summary report' (June 2007) Directorate for Science, Technology and Industry, Committee on Consumer Policy, OECD <http://www.oecd.org/dataoecd/5/38/39015963.pdf> at 22 December 2009.

Table 7.3 below summarizes registration requirements. Thirteen of the 30 jurisdictions that regulate franchising have been omitted from the table because they have no registration requirement as part of the franchise law. These are Canada, the US, Albania, Belgium, Estonia, France, Italy, Romania, Sweden, Georgia, Japan, Macau and Australia. The UNIDROIT Model Law is a disclosure law and makes no provision for registration.

- Ten countries require registration of the franchise agreement. They are Brazil, Mexico, Belarus, Italy, Moldova, Russia, Ukraine, People's Republic of China, Indonesia and Malaysia.
- Registration of disclosure documents has been adopted in only three jurisdictions, Indonesia, Korea and Malaysia as well as in about 14 US states.[20]
- The US registration states as well as China, Indonesia, Malaysia, Spain and Vietnam also have an annual reporting requirement.
- A registration requirement for franchise systems in Alberta, Canada has been repealed. A requirement to register the system is still in place in Barbados, Mexico, Estonia, Vietnam, Malaysia, Spain and some US states.[21]
- Korea and Japan have registration requirements for franchise consultants or brokers.

Registration systems generally require the submission of franchise documentation, in particular the disclosure document and a sample or actual franchise agreement, but 'vary from full audit to mere recording

[20] Secretariat, Office of Small Business, Commonwealth of Australia, 'Review of the disclosure provisions of the franchising code of conduct' (October 2006) <http:// www.innovation.gov.au/Section/SmallBusiness/Documents/Franchising_Code_Review_Report_2006_FINAL_06120720070205134250.pdf> at 22 December 2009.

[21] State laws generally define franchising similarly to the FTC Rule, but differences between the states' definitions and exemptions can be crucial to determining whether a particular sale was or was not the sale of a franchise. California, Hawaii, Illinois, Indiana, Maryland, Michigan, Minnesota, New York, North Dakota, Oklahoma, Rhode Island, South Dakota, Virginia, Washington, and Wisconsin require a registration or notice filing before offering franchises for sale, and pre-sale disclosure through 20 items in a prescribed format called a Uniform Franchise Offering Circular (UFOC). Also, Oregon requires pre-sale disclosure without a governmental filing. See Mark Miller, 'Unintentional Franchising' (2005) 19(2) *St. Mary's Law Journal* 308.

*Table 7.3 Registration requirements*

| Registration requirements | Of the Franchise | Of disclosure | Of the franchise agreement | Of franchise intellectual property | Other |
|---|---|---|---|---|---|
| THE AMERICAS | | | | | |
| Barbados | √ | | | | |
| Brazil | | | √ * | | |
| Mexico | √ | | √ | Must register patents, know-how, trade names, etc – *Law on Industrial Property* | |
| United States | | √ at state level | | | California, Hawaii, Illinois, Indiana, Maryland, Michigan, Minnesota, New York, North Dakota, Oregon, Rhode Island, South Dakota, Virginia, Washington, and Wisconsin all have some franchise registration obligation. |
| EUROPE | | | | | |
| Belarus | | | √ | | Modifications to agreement must also be registered. |
| Estonia | √ | | | √ | |
| France | | | | | |
| Italy | | | √ | | Brokers and sales personnel utilized by franchisors must register with the Chamber of Commerce Register. |

| | | | | |
|---|---|---|---|---|
| Lithuania | | | If subject matter of contract is patent protected, fact of forming contract must be registered as per industrial property protection institution. | |
| Moldova | | √ | | Company formed as a result of entering into franchising agreement must be registered.<br>Must notify of cessation of activity. |
| Romania<br>Not in the franchise law, but other laws and agencies may require | | | If agreement contains trademark licences, the agreement must be filed with RSOIT for registration of trademark. | Certain franchise agreements must be filed with Romanian Competition Council for obtaining clearance (if market share of franchisor is more than 30% of market). |
| Russia | | √ | If subject matter of contract is patent/trade mark protected, then contract must be registered with the executive body re patents and trademarks. | |
| Spain | √ | | | Annual report.<br>All franchisors must register with the Registry of Franchisors; must update information each January. |
| Ukraine | | √ | | |

*Table 7.3* (continued)

| Registration requirements | Of the Franchise | Of disclosure | Of the franchise agreement | Of franchise intellectual property | Other |
|---|---|---|---|---|---|
| EURASIA | | | | | |
| People's Republic of China | √ | | √ | √ | See listing of requirements including other documents as required. |
| Taiwan | | | | | Under Taiwan Fair Trade Law if a transaction results in a company directly/indirectly controlling business operation of another, the transaction is deemed a business combination and a merger notification filing may be required. |
| Indonesia | √ | √ | √ | √ | |
| Kazakhstan | | | | √ | |
| Korea | | √ | | | Changes. |
| Kyrgyzstan | | | | | |
| Malaysia | √ | √ | √ | | Brokers, Report changes. |
| Vietnam | √ | | | √ | Annual report. |

*Note:* * Registration requirement not contained in franchise-specific legislation.

systems'.[22] The jurisdictions with extensive monitoring generally impose a comprehensive registration and audit process of disclosure documents, agreements, manuals, audited accounts, financial statements, auditor and directors' reports as well as 'any such additional information or documents as may be required by the Registrar for determination of the application' and the power of the Registrar to approve the application 'subject to any such condition as the Registrar may impose' (as in Malaysia). Jurisdictions with minimal monitoring include Vietnam and China under which documentation is processed rather than audited. While some of the 14 US registration states have onerous registration and audit regimes, the level of scrutiny from state to state and from franchisor to franchisor is reported to vary.

A requirement of registration of intellectual property is common, though it is important to note that many jurisdictions' requirements for the registration of intellectual property are contained in laws other than franchise-specific legislation. Brazil and Romania, for example, have registration requirements based on other laws, such as those relating to the protection of intellectual property and requirements of other agencies, such as competition law. The primary purpose of such laws is to ensure economic efficiency by protecting intellectual property rights; such laws are less directed toward protecting franchisees and/or ensuring balance in the franchise relationship.

A number of countries without franchise-specific legislation may have registration requirements that do apply to franchising, instead of or in addition to those that apply to intellectual property. An example of this is Greece where the franchising agreement must be filed with the tax authority of both the franchisor and the franchisee within ten days from the date the agreement was signed, or else it is unenforceable and void.

**Costs and benefits of registration**

The impact of the registration process in the US states that have adopted it has long been a matter of debate.[23] There is no consensus on whether the benefits of registration are worth the costs, 'The IFA considers mandatory registration to be archaic, costly and burdensome for both franchisors and government while providing no measurable public policy benefit to

---

22 A. Terry, 'Issues with Prior Disclosure as a Regulatory Strategy for Franchisee Protection' (Paper presented at 23rd Annual International Society of Franchising Conference, San Diego, CA, USA, 17–18 February 2009).

23 A. Terry, 'A Census of International Franchise Regulation' (Paper presented at 21st Annual International Society of Franchising Conference, Las Vegas, Nevada, USA, 24–25 February 2007).

prospective franchisees.'[24] In opposing registration the IFA suggests that there has been no data in the US to prove that franchise investors in states with registration requirements are more adequately protected from sales fraud. Of course, there is also little reliable data on the effectiveness of disclosure or other regulatory measures for franchising.

The cost of registration is the most common objection even though the cost of registration can be trivial in comparison to the overall cost of preparing and maintaining an accurate disclosure document. While disclosure can easily run to $25 000 (USD) and more initially, and potentially tens of thousands of dollars a year thereafter, the cost of registration is the filing fee and perhaps $500 to $1000 in other costs. Opponents also point to the burden of the information technology infrastructure that is used to run these systems, the cost of staffing requirements based on volumes; timelines and other internal guidelines for efficient processing.[25] Further, it has been suggested that there may be a time penalty if a process of review is required.

The principal benefits of registration are its potential to enhance compliance and to help to address the paucity of information available not only about individual franchise systems to prospective franchisees, but also about the sector as a whole. One important benefit of registration is that it can make this information available not only to prospective franchisees, but other interested parties. Information from registration is useful in at least two ways and to at least four different interests. It is useful for information about individual systems and information about the sector, and it is useful to franchisees, researchers, regulators, consumers, suppliers, and competitors. Understandably franchisors might resist providing more information to the benefit of these other stakeholders, but the greater benefit in enhancing competition can be weighed against this.

Costs and benefits are difficult to assess. Some argue that the poor quality of and poor compliance with disclosure means that investors suffer and is a sufficiently compelling reason to require registration. They argue that the costs of non-compliance are shifted to the public, in litigation and court costs, misallocated capital, and investment losses.[26]

By increasing transparency and allowing the possibility of comparison, registration supports collaborative processes at several layers of regulation, from a 'market for terms' to identifying problems. It also provides important baseline data about the sector as a whole. In the US, 'Using these documents has generated a volume of highly reliable data unmatched in any

---

24 Email from Stephen Giles to ABA listserv, 18/12/08.

25 Ibid.

26 Email from Andrew Selden to Elizabeth Spencer 19 December 2008.

prior survey-based studies.'[27] In other countries as well such information could prove invaluable in identifying the problems in the sector, formulating regulatory goals, and in selecting the appropriate tools to achieve them.

As Professor Andrew Terry notes, 'Because franchising is a method of doing business and not a separate industry group, franchising is not usually captured in government data collection systems and there is debate or uncertainty in many jurisdictions on fundamental sector statistics. . . . In the interests of better and more comprehensive sector data the filing of annual updated disclosure documents should be seriously considered.' If accurate, reliable data is made publicly available, it can help franchisees, researchers and others interested in understanding what is really happening in the sector. Having at least a filing requirement puts disclosure on the public record. This is most useful for researchers, investors who don't want to contact a franchisor to get disclosure or who cannot get disclosure, and competitors.

Finally, registration has potential to create healthier franchisors because of better transparency and investor confidence:

> There are a variety of studies that show that franchisors operating in registration states are more likely to survive over time than franchisors that do not . . . Franchisor survivors, those who continue to work and operate as a business entity, are 22 percent more likely to operate in a registration state than failures. Moreover, the benefits of operating in registration states increase with system size. These patterns strongly suggest that operating in a registration state makes it easier to attract franchisees because adherence to the registration requirements shows that you are not a fly-by-night operation.[28]

As long as franchisees benefit from buying franchises from franchisors who manage to stay around to support them in future years, registration requirements can provide some protection for franchisees. There is no precise data on whether 'franchise investors in states with registration requirements are more adequately protected from sales fraud than investors in states without registration', but some have concluded that registration does benefit franchisees sufficiently to justify the cost.[29]

---

27 Deacons Lawyers, 'Deacons on franchise legislation' (2006) Franchisebusiness.com.au <http://www.franchisebusiness.com.au/c/Deacons-Lawyers/Deacons-on-franchise-legislation-n858792> at 22 December 2009.

28 Scott Shane, 'Studies Show Registration Benefits Franchisors and Franchise Buyers' (2008) Blue MauMau <http://www.bluemaumau.org/studies_show_registration_benefits_franchisors_and_franchise_buyers> at 22 December 2009.

29 Scott Shane, 'Studies Show Registration Benefits Franchisors and Franchise Buyers' (2008) Blue MauMau <http://www.bluemaumau.org/studies_show_registration_benefits_franchisors_and_franchise_buyers> at 22 December 2009.

In Europe, problems in Spain with respect to the administration and execution of registration requirements have lead to scrutiny and criticism. In the US there has also been opposition to registration requirements in many states. This opposition has been based on the inconsistencies among the various state requirements and the cost of administration. While disclosure is self-regulatory, registration tends to be used more heavily in those jurisdictions where the government is more intrinsically involved in the day-to-day operations of administration of the business sector such as Malaysia and Indonesia.

Registration is not embraced by governments not only because of the added expense, about which there is little documented evidence, but probably more because there is a greater role that must be played by government in its implementation. Regulators may fear being left with smaller budgets and greater exposure to censure for poor implementation and administration, and with little certainty of a beneficial result, they choose the conservative position.

That said, registration is equally as or more important than disclosure in several jurisdictions, e.g. Mexico, Spain, Malaysia, Ukraine, Russia and Lithuania. In Russia, for example, failure to register voids the contract. Contrast this with Australia, for example, where even failure to disclose may not.

While disclosure has been widely accepted, what registration achieves is more controversial. Some argue that it has improved the quality of disclosure in those few jurisdictions which require it and that it achieves greater accountability. Anecdotal reports suggest it improves reliability of disclosure and there is significant evidence of its importance in providing a source of badly needed reliable information about the franchise sector and individual franchise systems.

Registration's principal benefits are to improve compliance with disclosure and to provide information about franchise business and the sector. If the information were in a public register, it might enable comparison shopping, with the caveat that each system would have legitimately different conditions, marketing strategies and requirements. Registration might help franchisees' position with respect to the duration of contract as comparisons and vetting of figures can help a franchisee to accurately assess return on investment upfront.

Registration provides a benefit of more and better information generally. This is less a provision for franchisee protection than it is a sensible provision to maximize productivity and optimal governance of franchising generally. It is perhaps for this reason that registration may seem a less compelling regulatory measure to regulators who are primarily concerned with protecting franchisees against franchisor opportunism. It is important to remember in this context, however, that information about the sector does empower and so benefits individual franchisees.

## OTHER PRE-SALES PROCEDURES

### Cooling-off and Review

A cooling-off or review period prior to the formalization of the contract is a procedural requirement that can further protect parties in the contracting process. Cooling-off periods are a popular regulatory tool in the protection of consumers from undue influence or duress in entering contracts. Such measures are relatively low-intervention and low-cost.

For franchising, the cooling-off period typically specifies a certain period of time during which the consumer (or in this case a franchisee) is entitled to terminate the agreement at no cost or only a nominal cost, but may allow the other party to retain a reasonable amount in expenses.

A cooling-off period is prescribed as part of the franchise-specific legislation in four jurisdictions, China (no exact time period stated in the legislation), Korea (14 days), Malaysia (seven working days), and Australia (seven days).

The regulation in Taiwan provides for a review period before the entry into contract, which states that a franchisor, before it signs up a written agreement involving the franchise operating relationship, shall endow its trading counterparts with a period of no less than five days to review the contract.

Australia requires that a franchisor advise a franchisee to seek advice prior to signing the agreement, and a franchisee must sign a document that it has received such advice, or has been advised to and has declined to do so.

A cooling-off period does not prevent franchisees from entering contracts, but it may save an occasional reluctant contracting party from making a precipitous or unwise commitment. The requirement that a franchisor obtain a signed statement from a franchisee regarding provision of advice does not ensure a remedy if it is not complied with, but again, it may result in the occasional prospective franchisee benefiting from such advice in entering into a contractual commitment.

### Risk Statements, Advice and Warnings

Australia and the US mandate 'warnings', which require a statement that, 'entering into a franchise agreement is a serious undertaking' (Australia) or 'buying a franchise is a complex investment' (the US) to be included in the first or cover page of the disclosure document. In Australia the Matthews Committee acknowledged the problems of lack of franchisee awareness of the risks involved in franchising. Item 3 recommended a requirement of franchisors to include a Risk Statement with the disclosure document.[30]

Warnings take many forms; some warnings simply provide information about the product while others state a specific prohibition. Some warnings are short, others long; some are directed at a general audience, others a specific one. A strong and direct connection between behaviour and its consequences is provided in some warnings; those consequences can be general or specific. One reason warnings vary in information content and take many forms is that they serve different functions. The same warning can serve as a means for alerting the consumer to potential hazards while also serving as protection against liability.

Empirical research suggests that warning messages increase recipients' awareness of potential risks, which in turn tends to increase the probability that recipients will take measures to protect themselves from potential risks. This research also suggests that the reasons for compliance appear to be associated more with the characteristics of the message recipient than with the form and content of the warning message. Warnings should be designed so that they will be noticed and examined and they should be understandable by as large a portion of their intended audiences as possible. The message should have persuasive elements to ensure correct beliefs and attitudes, and warnings should motivate people to comply. However, because warnings do not always lead to compliance, it is suggested the better approach wherever possible is to 'design out the hazard' using other means.[31]

---

[30] This recommendation was not agreed to by the government. Its statement, 'Decisions relating to the viability and associated risks of any business venture are ultimately the decision of the businesses themselves', seems to undermine the theoretical basis for the choice of disclosure as a principal tool of regulatory intervention in franchising. See Secretariat, Office of Small Business, Commonwealth of Australia, 'Review of the disclosure provisions of the franchising code of conduct' (October 2006) <http://www.innovation.gov.au/Section/SmallBusiness/Documents/Franchising_Code_Review_Report_2006_FINAL_061207200702051342 50.pdf> at 22 December 2009; Commonwealth of Australia Government, 'Australian Government Response to the Review of the Disclosure Provisions of the Franchising Code of Conduct (February 2007) <http://www.innovation.gov.au/Section/SmallBusiness/Documents/Response_to_Recommendations_(Final)06Feb0720070206091019.pdf > at 22 December 2009.

[31] Michael S. Wogalter and Kenneth R. Laughery, 'WARNING! Sign and Label Effectiveness' (1996) 5(2) *Current Directions in Psychological Science* 33–37.

Any use of warnings in regulation should include evaluation of their effectiveness in informing the consumer and/or changing behaviour. Form and content of warnings and the characteristics of the audience are important when evaluating their use as a regulatory tool. It may be that warnings could have the potential to help some franchisees with some of the issues that arise in the course of the franchise relationship. Research shows that education complements disclosure and it would seem to have some potential to help franchisees understand what they should be aware of. Warnings, might, for example, help a franchisee to understand what right of renewal is about. On the other hand, warnings are unlikely to stop problems such as encroachment as long as franchisors have the contractual freedom to engage in the activity.

## PRE-SALES PERFORMANCE REQUIREMENTS

### Standards and Qualifications

Standards, accreditation, and qualifications are performance-oriented pre-sales measures. These may apply to franchisors, franchisor sales agents and brokers, and they can also apply to franchisees.

Six jurisdictions have requirements with respect to franchisor qualifications. For example, in China a franchisor must have operated two stores for at least one year prior to selling franchises for the system. In Italy the franchise system must test its formula on market prior to selling franchises. In Romania a franchisor must operate the business for an unspecified period of time prior to expansion. In Indonesia a franchisor must own and manage at least one of the outlets. Also in Indonesia a business certificate must be obtained before franchising and international franchisors must have legal proof of country of origin. In Vietnam franchisors must hold a licence, while fiscal solvency requirements must be met before registering franchise offerings in the US state of Virginia.[32]

These measures are similar in effect to accreditation but the focus is on performance rather than procedure. Performance standards for franchising might also include Codes of Ethics and/or Practice. A similar requirement to the two plus one rule is included in some trade association codes

---

[32] <http://www.scc.virginia.gov/srf/> at 23 December 2009. The laws of individual US states are not considered in this table at the time of this writing, with this exception. For more information on this requirement, please refer to the Division of Securities and Retail Franchising, Virginia State Corporation Commission.

of conduct, such as that of the European Franchise Federation, Egypt, and Malaysia.

In Korea the June 2003 Enforcement Decree amendment established standards to accredit 'franchise consultants'. Malaysia requires registration of franchise brokers.

No standards or qualifications for franchisees are included in the legislation surveyed, but this may be a measure worthy of consideration. If franchisees are suffering some harm and/or are perceived to need protection, it makes sense to equip them to protect themselves to as great an extent as possible through education, training, strengthening their position to negotiate, and to find and meaningfully assess options and make choices among alternatives.

### Pre-sales Prescriptive Requirements

The US state of Washington outlaws selling renting or offering to sell to a franchisee at more than a fair and reasonable price.

## PRE-SALES MEASURES: A PART OF, BUT NOT THE FULL SOLUTION

Disclosure is the most important regulatory measure in franchise-specific legislation, not only because of the frequency of its use, but also because in many jurisdictions it is the principal or only means used to regulate the sector. In such cases, it is important that disclosure be designed to function effectively in the way that it is structured and delivered.

At its best, disclosure does help to redress the imbalance of information that impairs transparency and efficiency at all layers of interaction. But informational regulation should not be limited to a listing of certain enumerated items that must be provided by a franchisor to a prospective franchisee a certain number of days prior to signing the contract.

A range of measures can be applied to improve the efficacy of disclosure. Accessibility and useability of information can be improved through assurance of appropriate coverage in terms of the items that are disclosed, by giving a franchisee the right information. This involves better informing prospective franchisees about the nature of the sector and the nature of the franchising relationship generally, as well as the inherent risks for participants in the sector, particularly for franchisees. A franchisee needs a better understanding of the nature of this business form, the characteristics of the contractual relationship, and the nature of contract terms, including explanation of the risks involved with particular contract terms.

Such information would help a franchisee in making a decision about whether to purchase a franchise or to operate an independent small business. Further, it could have some influence on which franchise to purchase. This information could be provided through educational initiatives that involve franchisors, franchisees and the regulator on an ongoing basis, rather than being limited to the franchisor/franchisee interaction at the time of entering the contract.

There is also the related issue of the need for the right information to be provided about the particular franchise system. The risks must be identified in order to determine what information a franchisee needs to make its decision. Here, participative process can be used to better determine the nature and extent of the risks to both parties in the relationship and the best ways to address them.

Reliability of disclosure could be improved through registration of disclosure documents. Registration of disclosure documents is particularly valuable because of its potential as a source of information about the operation of the sector. A cost-benefit analysis might reveal other alternatives, such as posting the information on the Internet, that may be equally as effective and efficient. Another avenue to better disclosure is improved monitoring and enforcement procedures.

Accessibility and useability also can be improved through appropriate timing and presentation; and assistance with interpretation (at time of disclosure). Finally, because the language of disclosure in some cases may be confusing, further measures could improve franchisee access to legal advice. If franchisees are to understand the terms of a franchise contract without having to consult with a lawyer, a 'plain language' requirement could be included in the legislation.[33] Franchisors could be required to construct the documents so that they are intelligible to prospective franchisees that may be inexperienced in business and/or lack a legal background.

Improvement to disclosure is only one small measure towards better regulation, and it does not address many systemic problems. Measures to supplement disclosure should also be considered. Current theories of regulation and formulations of best practice require that regulatory process comprehend the dynamics and interactions among a versatile range of regulatory tools and that it take advantage of synergies among these tools to achieve regulatory objectives.[34] The next chapter provides a more in-depth

---

[33] Please refer to Chapter 7's overview of tools used to regulate the franchise sector in other jurisdictions, but the author is not aware of a plain language requirement in any other jurisdiction at the time of this writing.

[34] The work of Hugh Collins; Julia Black; Gunningham and Grabosky; Martin and Cave; and Baldwin, Scott and Hood; among others support Malcolm

discussion of performance-oriented legislation, but it is worth noting here some supplementary mechanisms with the potential to enhance disclosure.

The most significant tool to supplement disclosure is education. Education can be used to strengthen the parties' capacities to self-regulate at the market layer and contract layer and in legislative intervention such as disclosure and dispute resolution processes. Information should be as widely available and as comparable as possible so that the prospective franchisee is an informed participant in the transaction and so that the ensuing contractual relationship is one that meets the reasonable expectations of both parties, and so is more likely to be durable and profitable for both.

Disclosure is one form of investor or consumer-protection, and a franchisee does act like an investor and a consumer, but its role also resembles that of an employee and business partner. To the extent that a franchisee's role is analogous to these and other commercial relationships a franchisee needs the appropriate types of protection such as assistance in the negotiating process, collective negotiation and registration and enforcement of disclosure.

Depending on the nature and needs of the jurisdiction, measures may also include performance-based and prescriptive regulatory tools such as mandatory contract terms, warranties and/or requirement of a duty of care on the part of franchisor. As Chapter 8 will examine in more detail, many jurisdictions have already put in place measures with respect to registration, termination provisions, content requirements, good faith and dispute resolution. Instead of relying on a very limited number of tools whose efficacy is unproven, regulators seeking to ensure efficient and fair practices in the franchising sector should choose instead, through a participative process, to avail themselves of the full range of regulatory instruments that is available to them.

---

Sparrow's call for the expansion, diversification and improved calibration in the use of regulatory tools.

# 8. Legislation impacting upon the performance of and exit from the agreement

Legislation regulating the performance of the relationship is often referred to as 'relationship' or 'conduct' legislation. It establishes the rules that govern the franchisor/franchisee interaction after the contract has been signed. Such legislation typically alters the rights of parties, 'to freely contract among themselves, setting ground rules on aspects of the relationship such as termination, non-renewal, rights of franchisees to form associations, purchasing requirements, transfer rights, and system expansion'.[1]

While many countries rely heavily on disclosure, a significant number do apply a mix of regulatory tools. The use of such tools is occasionally in lieu of, but more often in addition to, disclosure. Table 8.1 summarizes the principal types of conduct regulation directed towards the performance of the franchise relationship. Such measures include control over the content of contracts, prescribed performance provisions, and procedural requirements for dispute resolution, transfer and termination.

## PRESCRIPTIVE LEGISLATION

Prescriptive legislation includes legislation directed towards the form and content of the contract, such as formal and language requirements, mandatory contract terms, consumer-protection legislation, and unfair contract terms legislation. It also includes prescriptive legislation with respect to particular issues such as confidentiality requirements, restrictive covenants, and protection for freedom of association for franchisees.

---

[1] Barkoff and Selden, *Fundamentals of Franchising* (2nd ed, 2004).

*Table 8.1 Conduct legislation worldwide*

| JURISDICTION | Year of franchise-specific legislation | Content control Prescribed content of contract (including minimum term of the agreement) | Dispute Resolution provisions | Termination provisions | Statutory requirement of good faith | Other conduct/ prescribed performance provisions |
|---|---|---|---|---|---|---|
| THE AMERICAS | | | | | | |
| Barbados | 1974 | | | | | |
| Brazil | 1994 | | | | | |
| Canada | 1972–2008 | | | √ | √ | |
| Mexico | 1991, 1994 2006 | √ | | √ | | √ |
| United States | 1979/2007 | | | √** | √ | √ |
| EUROPE | | | | | √* | |
| Albania | 1994 | √ | | √ | √ | √ |
| Belarus | 2005 | √ | | √ | | √ |
| Belgium | 2006 | | | √ | | √ |
| Estonia | 2002 | | | | | √ |
| France | 1989 | | | | | |
| Italy | 2004 | √ | | √ | √ | √ |
| Lithuania | 2000 | | | √ | | √ |
| Moldova | 1997 | √ | | √ | | √ |
| Romania | 1997 | √ | | √ | | √ |
| Russia | 1996 | √ | √ | √ | | √ |
| Spain | 1996/ 2006 | | | √ | | √ |
| Sweden | 2006 | | | | | |
| Ukraine | 2004 | | | | | |
| ASIA & OCEANIA | | | | | | |
| People's Republic of China | 1997/ 2005/2007 | √ | √ | √ | | √ |
| Republic of China | 1999/ 2003 | | | √ | | |
| Georgia | 1997 | | | √ | | √ |
| Indonesia | 1997 | √ | | | | √ |
| Japan | 1983, 2002 | | | √ | | |
| Kazakhstan | 2002 | | | | | √ |
| Korea | 2002 | | | √ | √ | √ |
| Kyrgyzstan | 1998 | | | √ | | √ |
| Macau | 1999 | √ | | √ | √ | √ |
| Malaysia | 1998 | √ | | √ | | √ |

*Table 8.1* (continued)

| JURIS-DICTION | Year of franchise-specific legislation | Content control Prescribed content of contract (including minimum term of the agreement) | Dispute Resolution provisions | Termi-nation provisions | Statutory require-ment of good faith | Other conduct/ prescribed per-formance provisions |
|---|---|---|---|---|---|---|
| Vietnam | 2006 | | | | | √ |
| Australia | 1998 | √ minor | √ | √ | | √ |

*Notes:*
* Not in franchise-specific legislation
** At the state level

## Contract Form and Language Requirements

Mexico, Vietnam, Korea, Spain and Indonesia all require that the franchise agreement must be in the local language. Ten jurisdictions, Albania, Belgium, Indonesia, Italy, Kyrgyzstan, Lithuania, Macau, Mexico, Moldova and Ukraine, expressly require that the contract be in writing. The writing requirement may be less necessary in those countries where the legislation calls for mandatory provisions as it does in Belarus, Romania and the People's Republic of China as the contract will already be in writing to demonstrate compliance. Nevertheless, given the significance of the franchise agreement as the ultimate reference point for defining the franchisor/franchisee relationship, it is surprising that not all jurisdictions expressly require the agreement to be in writing.[2] Australia, for example, provides that franchise agreement may be written, oral or implied.

## Content Control: Unfair Contract Terms Legislation

Content control legislation is a prescriptive regulatory tool used in several jurisdictions that regulate franchising. Content control has in large part

---

2 A. Terry, 'A Census of International Franchise Regulation' (Paper presented at 21st Annual International Society of Franchising Conference, Las Vegas, Nevada, USA, 24–25 February 2007).

been limited to consumer protection, and only rarely extended to the protection of commercial actors. It is commonly used to regulate standard form contracts, to protect the interests of the weaker party, which has not had the benefit of the process of negotiating contract terms, and in recognition of the overriding separation of parties' interests.[3] Perhaps this is why, though it is not common in commercial contexts, content control has been used in several jurisdictions that regulate franchising.

Unfair contract terms legislation is a form of content control that provides compulsory rules with respect to particular terms deemed to be unfair. It is most often applied to transactions with consumers in a particular trade or sector.[4] Such legislated contract terms typically cannot be contracted out of by the parties. Commonly used in consumer law applications in many jurisdictions, unfair contract terms legislation often applies to standard form contracts and may be appropriate for franchising because of the nature of a franchisee's role as a consumer requiring regulatory protection similar to that enjoyed by consumers. It is also consistent with the commonly-used, investor-oriented protection of disclosure, as disclosure is also widely used in consumer protection.

It is often argued that consumer-protective regulatory measures are not appropriate in the regulation of the franchise sector because a franchisee is a businessperson and not a consumer. A franchisee as a businessperson is viewed through a certain legal lens that sees little need for statutory protection. A franchisee as an investor is viewed differently, and it has been conceded in this context that a franchisee should have the benefit of a certain set of protections similar to those enjoyed by investors, for example, disclosure.

A franchisee also functions as a consumer of a franchisor's intellectual property, products and services. Because the standard form renders the consumer/commercial distinction less meaningful, in the case of the franchise relationship the 'contract as commodity' of the standard form suggests that a franchisee takes on qualities of consumer of product, rather than an equal party to negotiation of terms. The use of the standard form contract in franchising lends force to a franchisee's right as a consumer to reasonable quality, reasonable prices, and fair terms and justifies lawmakers' consideration of content control provisions for select terms.[5] The

---

3 Alessandra Arcuri, 'Product Safety Regulation' (1999) findlaw.com <http://encyclo.findlaw.com/5130book.pdf> at 27 December 2009.

4 Council Directive 93/13/EEC of 5 April 1993 on unfair terms in consumer contracts (where 'Council' means the Council of the European Communities). See also Hugh Collins, *Regulating Contracts* (1999) 236.

5 For more on fair terms in contracts see John Tillotson, *Contract Law in*

fact that a franchisor is selling a product, a licence, and a franchisee is the consumer of that product, suggests that there should be some minimum protections for the consumer of that product. No jurisdiction, however, is known to have instituted warranties for the sales of franchises.

The power imbalance that characterizes many franchise relationships, not only at formation, but also in the performance of the contract, needs to be addressed as regulatory intervention has done in the case of consumer and employment contracts.[6] The standard form contract is a fact of life; it is admittedly indispensable to the containment of transaction costs in repeated commercial transactions. Realizing this, and not wishing to stifle commercial activity, regulators exercise caution in dealing with its abuses. They should balance this caution, however, against the interests of parties unable to sufficiently protect themselves in commercial interactions.

The protection of a franchisee as consumer is on the horizon. In Australia franchisees were originally contemplated in the proposed unfair contract terms legislation which applied to standard form, non-negotiated contracts. South Africa's Consumer Protection Act will apply to franchising.[7] These two measures to protect franchisees as consumers represent a potentially important step in the development of the regulatory landscape. The development is toward a model of economic efficiency that is founded on the efficiencies to be gained from quality and trust among contracting parties. This philosophy may be extended not only to consumer relationships but also to commercial relationships in which one party plays a role with a strong consumer-like aspect such the contractual relationship between franchisor and franchisee.

There may be problems, however, that arise in the application of 'general purpose' unfair terms legislation to franchising relationships. The first potential problem lies in defining the meaning of 'unfair'. The issue here with respect to franchising is that many contract terms that would cause a significant imbalance in the parties' rights and obligations arising under a contract are necessary in order to protect the legitimate interests of the party who would be advantaged by the term. The terms of a franchise contract are always characterized by a significant imbalance and they are always or almost always reasonably necessary to protect the brand.

---

*Perspective* (3rd ed 1995) 121–4. For a discussion of content control in standard form contracts see John J.A. Burke, 'Reinventing Contract' (2003) 10(2) Murdoch University Electronic Journal of Law [51].

6 Phillip P. Blumberg, 'The Increasing Recognition of Enterprise Principles in Determining Parent and Subsidiary Corporation Liabilities' (1996) 28 *Connecticut Law Review* 295, 344.

7 Effective April 2010.

Wording such as that proposed in the Australian legislation, 'Reasonably necessary in order to protect the legitimate interests of the party who would be advantaged by the term', is too broad and vague to afford any real protection to franchisees. With a few minor exceptions, all terms in franchise contracts can pass this test (or they would all fail it).

Franchisor discretion is a legitimate interest for the sake of the uniformity of the brand which is in the interests of both contracting parties. What needs to be addressed is franchisor *abuse* of this legitimate discretion/power in ways that unduly harm the interests of individual franchisees with a more particular calculus of when the *use of power* is legitimate and when it is not. The best franchise systems use this power judiciously and such use generally accrues to the benefit of all parties. The question in each case is whether the harm to a franchisee in the use of the power afforded by the term can be justified by the benefit to a franchisor and or the brand, and also whether this harm is beyond the reasonable expectations of the parties, not only in entering the contract, but also, because these contracts are long-term, relational contracts, over the course of the contract performance.

The second potential problem lies in determining whether a term of a standard form contract is unfair and the factors that a court must take into account. Again, borrowing from the proposed Australian legislation, the wording, 'the extent to which it would cause, or there is a substantial likelihood that it would cause, detriment (whether financial or otherwise) to a party if it were to be applied or relied on', would appear to be helpful to an overall balancing, as is the extent to which the term is transparent; and 'the contract as a whole' is taken into account. It is debatable whether 'the contract as a whole' would mean the contract interpreted as a standard form contract, but also, in the case of franchising, as a relational contract.

The third potential problem arises in the examples of the kinds of terms of a standard form contract that may be unfair. In the Australian draft legislation there are many examples of terms that are common, virtually universal, in franchise contracts. They create cause for concern that the proposed legislation will either lead to a flood of litigation in franchising or that it will be almost entirely ineffectual. Table 8.2 lists some of the examples in the draft legislation with comments about how they relate to franchising.

Indeed, because of these problems or others, the inclusion of franchising in the Australian law has been abandoned. General unfair contract terms legislation is probably not going to cater to the issues particular to franchising. One further concern about the legislation applies not only to franchisees, but to consumers generally. It is that a litigation-based

*Table 8.2 Australia's proposed unfair terms legislation*

| Example in draft legislation from Australia | Nature of term in franchise agreements |
|---|---|
| (a) a term that permits, or has the effect of permitting, one party (but not another party) to avoid or limit performance of the contract; | Most franchise contract terms are written to bind franchisees but to ensure flexibility of franchisors; they specify performance of precise franchisee obligations, 'a franchisee must' while franchisor obligations are drafted in permissive terms, 'a franchisor may'. |
| (b) a term that permits, or has the effect of permitting, one party (but not another party) to terminate the contract; | Procedural requirements under regulations 21–23 of the Code of Conduct notwithstanding, a franchisor can terminate for a variety of reasons, while it is virtually impossible for a franchisee to terminate for franchisor breach because of the discretionary nature of franchisor contractual obligations. |
| (d) a term that permits, or has the effect of permitting, one party (but not another party) to vary the terms of the contract; | Franchisors commonly enjoy a right to unilaterally alter the terms of the contract. They can also effectively alter the nature of the contractual agreement through the operations manual and other means. |
| (e) a term that permits, or has the effect of permitting, one party (but not another party) to renew or not renew the contract; | Common in franchise agreements, because of the nature of franchisee investment and the convention of a lack of franchisee right of renewal. |
| (g) a term that permits, or has the effect of permitting, one party unilaterally to vary the characteristics of the goods or services to be supplied, or the land to be sold or granted, under the contract; | Franchisors almost universally enjoy a right to unilaterally alter the terms of supply under the contract. |
| (h) a term that permits, or has the effect of permitting, one party unilaterally to determine whether the contract has been breached or to interpret its meaning; | Franchisors commonly enjoy a right to unilaterally alter the terms of the contract. They can also effectively alter the nature of the contractual agreement through the operations manual and other means. |

*Table 8.2* (continued)

| Example in draft legislation from Australia | Nature of term in franchise agreements |
|---|---|
| (j) a term that permits, or has the effect of permitting, one party to assign the contract to the detriment of another party without that other party's consent. . . | Common in franchise contracts. |

enforcement approach may not be affordable for most consumers, and, even if it is, it will not assist other similarly situated consumers.[8]

Another disadvantage of unfair contract terms legislation is that it effectively removes an aspect of self-regulation as parties must conform to approved terms for the market sector. This may be another reason why it is not the most appropriate direction for the regulation of the franchising sector.

Though such legislation is an important development in the reform of consumer law, considering the realities of franchise contracting, in particular the legitimate interest of franchisors in the power and discretion accorded to them in franchise agreements, it is debatable whether such legislation is the most appropriate instrument to protect franchisees who are at risk of significant hardship on the occasions when there is abuse of that power.

Two further points might be made before moving from the subject of unfair contract terms. The first is that there are other approaches to regulating standard form contracts. One example is to include provisions in the laws of contracts or obligations, such as §42 of the Law of Obligations of Estonia which states that:

> a standard term is void if, taking into account the nature, contents and manner of entry into the contract, the interests of the parties and other material circumstances, the term causes unfair harm to the other party, particularly if it causes a significant imbalance in the parties' rights and obligations arising from the contract to the detriment of the other party or if the standard term is contrary to good morals.'[9]

---

8 See Larry Bates, 'Administrative Regulation of Terms in Form Contracts: A Comparative Analysis of Consumer Protection', (2002) 16 *Emory International Law Review* 1, 7.

9 There are many jurisdictions that have laws of general application which can include such provisions.

A related category of regulation is protection against unfair competition. Two examples of many are the Lithuanian Civil Code that provides that parties may provide conditions limiting competition only where not prohibited by the competition law, and Malaysia's proscription against the use of restrictive covenants. Competition law, like consumer law, however, falls outside the scope of this study.

**Content Control: Mandatory Contract Terms**

Unfair contract terms legislation prescribes or proscribes terms for a class of contracts; parties cannot usually contract around them. Another form of content control, mandatory contract terms legislation, directs the parties themselves to include certain terms and/or address certain issues in their contracts. In this way there may be a greater level of discretion left to the parties in accommodating such requirements. Approximately 13 countries include at least one or two such prescriptive provisions.

Mandatory terms deal with, *inter alia*, fees, term/duration of the contract, rights and duties under the contract, amendment and termination. Examples of mandatory terms are listed by implementing jurisdiction in Table 8.3 below.

Legislation relating to the duration of the contract or specification of a minimum term is in place in Belarus, Romania, People's Republic of China, Malaysia, Italy and Indonesia. The legislation specifies a minimum term of three years in China and Italy (except in cases of early termination resulting from breach) and five years in Malaysia and Indonesia. A contract must not provide for a term of less than three years in the US state of Connecticut. In Romania the contract duration must be long enough for the franchisee to recover investments. In Belarus the legislation states that the term may be fixed or indefinite which may include territorial restrictions and that the duration of sub-franchise agreements may not extend beyond that of the master agreement.

The extent to which the legislation prescribes how the terms must be addressed in the contract is important. Mandatory terms legislation can be employed at a low level of prescription, to merely suggest that parties include certain terms without prescribing the content of the term. This approach ensures that the parties have addressed a matter but does not dictate how they do so; an example is the Vietnam franchise legislation which merely provides that certain terms 'may' be included. It is less prescriptive, more procedural. Alternatively, the law may be moderately prescriptive, where legislation requires a term and may go further by dictating what the term should state. This requirement can be exact or within certain parameters, for example, setting a minimum or a maximum boundary.

*Table 8.3 Examples of mandatory contract terms in franchise-specific legislation*

| Jurisdiction | Mandatory terms must provide: |
|---|---|
| Mexico | • geographic zone, location, minimum size, investment characteristics must be stated in relation to infrastructure and premises<br>• requirements for inventory, marketing, advertising, and if applicable provisions dealing with merchandise supply and engagement of suppliers<br>• policies and procedures for reimbursement of money by franchisee, financing and other economic terms of relationship<br>• include applicable criteria and methods for determining franchisee's profit and commission margins<br>• include description of criteria, methods, and procedures employed to supervise and evaluate quality of services provided by both franchisee and franchisor<br>• grounds for termination |
| Albania | • specific obligations of the parties<br>• duration<br>• full description of franchise system and obligations |
| Belarus | • franchise fee (either fixed payments, once only payment or periodic payment calculated as a percentage of proceeds)<br>• rights and duties that cannot be modified<br>• cannot grant similar franchises in assigned territory |
| Italy | • exact fees for entry<br>• method of payment of royalties and determination of minimum turnover guaranteed by franchisee<br>• identification of exclusive territory<br>• details of services provided by franchisor<br>• conditions relevant to renewal, termination and transfer |
| Indonesia | The franchise agreement must be governed by Indonesian law and shall minimally contain the following clauses:<br>• names and addresses of parties;<br>• kind of intellectual property right;<br>• business activity;<br>• rights and obligations of parties;<br>• assistance, facilities, operational counseling, training and marketing provided by the franchisor for franchisee;<br>• business area;<br>• validity period of agreement;<br>• procedures for the payment of compensation;<br>ownership, change in ownership and rights of heirs;<br>• settlement of dispute; and<br>• procedures for extending, discontinuing and terminating agreement |

*Table 8.3* (continued)

| Jurisdiction | Mandatory terms must provide: |
|---|---|
| Moldova | • full description of procedure for transfer of franchise and obligations of parties<br>• term of contract<br>• provisions regarding termination and extension |
| Romania | • object of agreement<br>• parties' rights and obligations<br>• financial requirements<br>• duration<br>• conditions of amendment, extension and termination |
| Russia | • object of the contract<br>• rights and obligations of each party<br>• financial conditions of the contract<br>• duration of the contract<br>• amendment, renewal and termination conditions |
| People's Republic of China | • basic information of both parties<br>• content and term of franchise<br>• types, amounts and payment methods of the franchise fee<br>• contents and methods of operational, technical support and business training<br>• quality and standards requirements<br>• promotion and advertising for the products or service<br>• arrangements for protection of consumer interests and compensation<br>• amendment and termination of the franchise agreement<br>• liability for breach of the agreement and<br>• dispute resolution |

Finally, where it requires that parties address certain terms, the legislation may be used to accomplish a highly prescriptive and often specific regulatory purpose, as in Mexico's provisions XI and XII that prohibit a contract from requiring franchisees to sell their interests to the franchisor.

The difficulty with mandatory terms is that, without a high level of specificity, the regulation is less likely to be effective. On the other hand, if it is highly specific, it risks interfering with freedom of contract and the ability of contractors to make arrangements that best serve their particular circumstances. For example, if regulation requires a contract to provide that a franchisor will provide training, but fails to specify what standards must be met, then it is likely to contribute little to the welfare of the intended protected party. But if it does specify standards, such as length, frequency and other aspects of the training, it runs the risk of being ill-suited for some particular applications, and so can be counter-productive. The potential effectiveness of mandatory terms for certain contractual issues that commonly arise in franchising is not at all clear.

- The use of mandatory terms legislation is unlikely to prevent encroachment given the difficulty in making rules that prescribe when a franchisor is or is not encroaching, different standards for different kinds of business, different strategies for each (e.g. a saturation strategy is more likely to run into problems of encroachment, even though it is a legitimate strategy).
- For brand maintenance issues a mandatory term is also unlikely to provide a durable solution. Even if regulation provides a mandatory term requiring a franchisor to maintain the brand, it must be determined to what standard, and what is appropriate to accomplish this for a given size of enterprise, in any given industry, under what market conditions, etc.; it is another example of subjective judgments.
- Mandatory terms legislation offers little recourse as applied to issues related to training. Again, even if legislation requires a mandatory term that a franchisor must train franchisees at its cost, the question arises as to the standard required, what is appropriate to accomplish this for a given size of enterprise in any given industry, under what market conditions, and so on. In employment law, we do not force people to do a job. Similarly, it is difficult to force franchisors to provide training, not only because of the principle against involuntary servitude, but again because of the question of standards, how to ensure that a franchisor delivers this service adequately.
- Minimum performance might be another potential application for mandatory terms legislation. While a franchisor has a legitimate need to monitor franchisees' performance, minimum performance should not be used as a pretext to prematurely and/or unfairly terminate a franchisee. Here again, if there were standards, the question is how and by whom they would be determined. At a minimum it seems they would need to require the reasonableness or good faith of a franchisor.
- With respect to issues of supply, here again a franchisor's legitimate interest in protecting the brand leaves franchisees vulnerable to the exercise of franchisor discretion with respect to conditions of supply. A franchisor needs this discretion. Mandatory terms legislation could only limit it in the most general terms. With respect to duration mandatory minimum terms may help in some cases, but again the minimum term for an investment is not the same across every type of franchise.

- Mandatory terms legislation for right of renewal is problematic as well. A franchisor needs discretion; unfair terms legislation is about making specific requirements and this is not practical. The best approach may be to require reasonableness in franchisor conditions and procedures for renewal; this may equate to a duty of good faith or similar.
- With respect to issues of termination, in the interests of a franchisor's control over the brand, a franchisee should not have a property right in the franchise, but should have certain protections in its own interests and investments. Here again it seems only a franchisor's good faith can help. With respect to restraints of trade mandatory terms legislation could provide some guidance, but there is more here for the courts to contribute in the interpretation of such clauses.

The application of mandatory terms legislation appears to be impractical for many franchise contract terms. This may be one reason why, troublesome as good faith may be, it does provide a standard that is comprehensive, but also broad and flexible. For a sector as diverse as franchising, it may provide the most simple, effective, and comprehensive solution to some of the problems in regulating. In aspects of the relationship where franchisor discretion is particularly prone to abuse, there may be prescriptive legislation that targets particular issues, for example, encroachment, the validity of restrictive covenants, freedom to associate, and supply, in addition to a general duty of good faith.

### Prescriptive Legislation Aimed at Conduct/performance with Respect to Specific Terms or Aspects of the Relationship

In addition to legislation that prescribes form and content of the contract prescriptive legislation can prescribe or proscribe certain conduct directly. This legislation can be similar in form and effect to specific unfair contract terms provisions, in particular where unfair contract terms are highly prescriptive. Applications of this type of legislation are outlined here with respect to, for example, confidentiality, indemnity, the validity of restrictive covenants, freedom to associate, and encroachment. Table 8.4 below catalogues the nature of this legislation in more detail.

More research is needed to determine the effectiveness of these various provisions, and such research could help to clarify whether the specificity of these prescriptive provisions is the most effective means of regulating. It could also explore how these provisions interact with other regulatory requirements such as a general requirement of good faith. There is an argument that mandatory terms destroy whatever market may exist for

*Table 8.4 Legislation prescribing aspects of performance*

| Nature of the provision | Application in particular jurisdictions |
|---|---|
| Confidentiality | Sixteen countries including Mexico, Albania, Belgium, Belarus, Italy, Lithuania, Moldova, Romania, Russia, Spain, People's Republic of China, Georgia, Kazakhstan, Kyrgyzstan, Macau and Malaysia, have some regulation with respect to obligations of confidentiality.<br>• In Albania parties are obliged to maintain confidentiality of information even if the contract is not concluded.<br>• In Belgium Article 6 requires that parties keep confidential all information that they obtain upon the conclusion of the agreement of commercial partnership.<br>• In Mexico franchisee must maintain all information about the franchise confidential.<br>• In Italy Article 5 provides that a franchisee undertakes to respect confidentiality. Lithuania's Article 6.771 provides that a franchisee must not divulge commercial secrets or any other confidential information.<br>• Moldova's Chapter XXI Article 1175 provides that both parties have an obligation to keep commercial secrets confidential.<br>• In Romania and Russia the regulation permits a franchisor to impose a confidentiality clause, and in Russia the law also requires a franchisee to maintain confidentiality.<br>• Georgia's Article 610 places a duty of confidentiality upon both parties. Macau imposes an obligation of confidentiality on both parties. |
| Territorial allocation and encroachment | Some jurisdictions have provisions regarding parties' allocations of competition/territory.<br>• In Belarus, the Ukraine and the Kyrgyz Republic legislation expressly allows territorial exclusivity and noncompetition clauses, but these may be deemed invalid under anti-monopoly or competition law.<br>• Lithuania includes restrictions on a franchisor in encroachment both by a franchisor and in granting rights to other persons for territory allocated to the franchisee. It also imposes restrictions against a franchisee competing with the franchisor. Contracts violating competition law may be deemed null and void.<br>• Similarly, the Civil Code of Russia expressly permits the parties to restrict rights under the contract including |

*Table 8.4* (continued)

| Nature of the provision | Application in particular jurisdictions |
|---|---|
| | obligations regarding exclusive right on the territory and non-compete provisions. Indonesian legislation places limitations on geographic areas where franchising is permitted.<br>• Korea's Fair Franchise Act prohibits a franchisor from opening a shop engaging in a similar line of business to that of the franchisee within the business area of the franchisee during the period of the Franchise Agreement.<br>• The Macau Commercial Code prohibits a franchisee from providing goods or services in competition with a franchisor, and prohibits a franchisor from competing directly or indirectly, except if there is a written agreement to the contrary.<br>• Legislation in five states in the US plus the Virgin Islands prohibit a franchisor from establishing a similar business or granting a franchise for the establishment of a similar business within the franchisee's exclusive territory, if any. |
| Supply and pricing requirements | • The Macau Commercial Code prohibits franchisor restrictions on supply except to the extent necessary to protect intellectual property rights or maintain the common identity and reputation of the franchise network.<br>• Korea's Fair Franchise Act prohibits restrictive supply, pricing restrictions, and other unfair practices.<br>• Four states in the US prohibit requiring a franchisee to supply from designated sources unless reasonably necessary for a lawful purpose justified on business grounds.<br>• Three states in the US prohibit a franchisor receiving kickbacks, except under certain conditions, including disclosure. |
| Restrictive covenants<br><br>(Legislation with respect to competition law often lies outside the scope of franchise-specific regulation, and | • Malaysia legislates against the use of restrictive covenants.<br>• There are prohibitions on vertical restraints in many jurisdictions. Representative of these are Australia, Japan, a number of jurisdictions in the European Community and the US.[a]<br>• Two US states prohibit enforcing any unreasonable covenant not to compete after termination of the franchise relationship. |

*Table 8.4* (continued)

| Nature of the provision | Application in particular jurisdictions |
|---|---|
| may not be included in this survey.) | • In Georgia non-competition within specific territory can be imposed for one year unless it endangers the business where then appropriate monetary compensation is given. |
| Franchisor obligations with respect to training and technical assistance | • A franchisor must provide training and technical assistance under the laws in eight jurisdictions, Estonia, Italy, Moldova, Romania, People's Republic of China, Georgia, Indonesia and Vietnam.<br>• In another seven, Albania, Belarus, Estonia, People's Republic of China, Italy, Moldova and Kyrgyzstan a franchisor must provide instructions, information and updates. |
| Franchisor protection of intellectual property | • Under the law in Belarus, Moldova, People's Republic of China, Georgia and Vietnam a franchisor must provide licences/intellectual property.<br>• Laws in Albania and Moldova require a franchisor to protect rights from third parties. In Romania a franchisor has a right to ensure use of trademarks. |
| Franchisor right to monitor/ quality assurance/ participate in management | • Four states in the US prohibit franchisors requiring or prohibiting a change in management of the franchisee except for reasonable cause.<br>• Under the law in Belarus, Estonia and Romania, a franchisor has a right to review and a right to supervise. In Belarus it can be modified. In Estonia a franchisor has a right to check quality. |
| Changing conditions of the agreement/ Unilateral amendment | The US state of Indiana outlaws substantial modification of the franchise agreement by franchisor without consent in writing of the franchisee. The US state of Wisconsin does not permit a franchisor to substantially change competitive circumstances of a dealership agreement without good cause. |
| Changes in Management | Three US states do not permit a franchisor 'to require or prohibit any change in management of any franchise unless the requirement or prohibition shall be for reasonable cause, which cause shall be stated in writing by the franchisor'. |
| Non-discrimination | • Vietnam requires a franchisor to treat all franchisees equally.<br>• Five states in the US prohibit discriminating that is unreasonable or arbitrary among franchisees in business dealings. |

*Table 8.4* (continued)

| Nature of the provision | Application in particular jurisdictions |
|---|---|
| Performance requirements of a franchisee | • Performance obligations are typically provided for in detail by the contract as a private means of governance by the parties themselves. Some jurisdictions limit performance requirements that can be imposed on a franchisee by a franchisor. With respect to the issue of minimum performance standards imposed upon a franchisee, about four states in the US prohibit the imposition of unreasonable standards of performance upon a franchisee.<br>• In contrast to those jurisdictions where the aim is to limit unreasonable requirements of a franchisee, a number of jurisdictions legislate some of their own requirements for franchisees. For example legislation provides that a franchisee must<br>  • use the trade name in Belarus, Estonia, Romania, and Ukraine;<br>  • ensure quality standards in Belarus, Estonia and Romania;<br>  • follow instructions in Belarus, Estonia, and Moldova;<br>  • provide customers with additional services in Belarus and Estonia;<br>  • conclude the number of sub-franchises in Belarus;<br>  • pay royalties in Moldova; and<br>  • inform customers it is a franchise in Belarus.<br>• Legislation in Macau is interesting from the point of view that it provides for extensive obligations of a franchisee, most of which are included in a typical franchise agreement, for example to undergo training, pay royalties, etc. |
| Marketing and promotions requirements | The US state of Indiana outlaws requiring franchisee to participate in marketing at an indeterminate expense or an expense determined by a third party or by a formula unless the franchise agreement specifies a maximum amount that the franchisee may be required to pay. |
| Indemnity of a franchisor by a franchisee | In Australia a franchisor may not contractually require general indemnity from a franchisee, though there is no restriction or limit on specific indemnities. |
| Franchisees' freedom to associate | • Freedom to associate cannot be denied to franchisees according to legislation in Australia; the Canadian provinces of Alberta, Ontario, and Prince Edward Island; and in eleven US states.[b] |

*Table 8.4* (continued)

| Nature of the provision | Application in particular jurisdictions |
|---|---|
| | • An unusual provision in the Moldovan law assures franchisors' right to associate in national or international associations, but the legislation makes no mention of a right of association for franchisees.[c] |
| Bankruptcy/ Insolvency | The Russian Civil Code provides that the contract of commercial concession shall cease when the user is declared insolvent. |
| General | Some jurisdictions, such as Romania, Korea and Macau require that the contract shall observe certain principles, or a comprehensive list of obligations of a franchisor and/or of franchisees. |

*Notes:*

[a] Many jurisdictions impose these requirements through competition law rather than franchise-specific legislation. Secretariat, International Institute for the Unification of Private Law (UNIDROIT) in collaboration with Philip F. Zeidman, 'Legislation and Regulations Relevant to Franchising (Annex 3 to the UNIDROIT Guide to International Franchise Arrangements)' (2007) UNIDROIT <http://www.unidroit.org/english/guides/2007franchising/annex.htm> at 27 December 2009.

[b] Erik B. Wulff, 'Actions by Franchisee Associations: Antitrust and Other Legal Complications for Franchisors and Franchisees' (1993), 13 *Franchise Law Journal* 37, 58 lists the following states: Arkansas, California, Hawaii, Illinois, Iowa, Michigan, Minnesota, Nebraska, New Jersey, and Washington). See also Barkoff and Selden, *Fundamentals of Franchising* (2nd ed, 2004), Appendix F.

[c] Republic of Moldova, Law Nr 1335 1997, art 17 with respect to franchising.

contract terms,[10] but this is not a strong concern in applications such as franchising because there is virtually no such market to start with.

It is also not clear to what extent the high level of prescription detracts from self-regulatory approaches. It may be preferable to regulate market sectors such as franchising through a process that brings together the two sides of the trade collectively to negotiate some acceptable standard terms, particularly in areas where there is a high incidence of opportunistic behaviour.

## PROCEDURAL LEGISLATION

Franchise-specific legislation may also include procedural measures to influence conduct and performance such as dispute resolution, as well as

[10] Hugh Collins, *Regulating Contracts* (1999) 234.

procedures for transfer, termination and exercise of a right of renewal. Again, there is overlap in the means used. For example, prescriptive and procedural methods can be combined in the form of a requirement that the contract provide for a procedure with respect to a certain event such as conflict resolution or termination.

**Procedural Regulatory Measures for Conflict Resolution**

Most jurisdictions with franchise-specific legislation make no provision for dispute resolution in that legislation. These jurisdictions include the US, Brazil, Mexico, Albania, Belarus, Belgium, Estonia, France, Lithuania, Romania, Russia, Spain, Ukraine, Republic of China (Taiwan), Georgia, Japan, Kazakhstan, Kyrgyzstan, Macau and Malaysia. Table 8.5 summarizes the nature of dispute resolution provisions in franchise-specific regulation.

Provision in franchise-specific regulation with respect to conflict resolution is not as common as one might expect given its importance in the management of contractual relations. The relatively low incidence of the use of dispute resolution in franchise-specific legislation may be due to the fact that provision is made in other legislation. Further research would be useful to determine to what extent this is the case.

Of the countries that do make some provision for dispute resolution, five require that the contract address the issue. Two require disclosure of dispute resolution procedures. Seven jurisdictions make some prescription with respect to process, but most of these are minimal, low-intervention measures. Australia, Alberta, Canada, and Korea, for example, mandate that a mediation process be available to resolve disputes if parties want to use it.

In Australia mediation is a Code-mandated dispute resolution procedure thought to engender greater participation by franchisees in conflict resolution, greater transparency of conflict processes, and assistance to parties in understanding and utilizing conflict management procedures.

In Korea the Fair Franchise Act requires a franchisor to make efforts to resolve disputes through dialogue and negotiations with a franchisee. Parties may apply for mediation; the Mediation Council provides mediation services to the sector free of charge.

In the US two states outlaw contractual provisions requiring that arbitration or litigation be conducted outside the state. One state outlaws limiting litigation brought for breach of the agreement in any manner.

Measures for handling conflict are critical to the health of the franchise relationship. Though it may be 'counter-intuitive as well as counter-cultural', some research suggests that '[r]esisting a breakdown does

*Table 8.5 Dispute resolution requirements*

| Jurisdiction | Mandatory contract term | In disclosure | Prescribed process | Other |
|---|---|---|---|---|
| THE AMERICAS | | | | |
| Canada | | | Prescribed by the Uniform Franchises Act – Mediation Regulation. See also Ontario Franchising Regulation; s 8 of the New Brunswick Act – mediation; Prince Edward Island Franchises Act Regulation – s 16 arbitration, mediation, ADR imposed by franchise agreement | |
| EUROPE | | | | |
| Italy | | | Parties **may** agree that before they resort to courts/ arbitration, they will attempt conciliation through Chamber of Commerce | Rules on Regulation of Franchising |
| Moldova | √ | | Contract **must** specify method of settling disputes; does not say which method | |
| Sweden | | √ | Does not prescribe specific process | Must disclose how the dispute will be settled and who will pay for it |
| EURASIA | | | | |
| People's Republic of China | √ | | | |
| Indonesia | √ | | | |

*Table 8.5* (continued)

| Jurisdiction | Mandatory contract term | In disclosure | Prescribed process | Other |
|---|---|---|---|---|
| Republic of Korea | | | Parties in dispute **may** apply for mediation with the Mediation Council | Franchisor must make efforts to resolve disputes through dialogue and negotiations with franchisee. Franchise Dispute Mediation Council shall be established |
| Vietnam | √ | | Agreement **may** specify settlement of disputes; does not prescribe a method | |
| OCEANIA | | | | |
| Australia | √ | √ | Franchise agreement **must** provide for complaint handling procedure; if procedure not agreed upon, then party **may** opt for mediation | |

nothing to resolve the inevitable failure associated with it. Indeed it is highly likely to cause it to persist'.[11] It follows then that leadership should involve 'shifting organizational culture from breakdowns being seen as problems to culture that regards them as opportunities.'[12] Dispute resolution procedures can play a useful role in the regulation of the sector as they

[11] Allan L. Scherr and Michael C. Jensen, 'A New Model of Leadership', (2007) Harvard NOM Research Paper No. 06-10; and Barbados Group Working Paper No. 06-02.

[12] Werner Erhard, Michael C. Jensen and Steve Zaeeron, 'Integrity: A Positive Model that Incorporates the Normative Phenomena of Morality, Ethics and Legality' (2007) Harvard Negotiations, Organizations and Markets (NOM) Working Paper No. 06-11; and Barbados Group Working Paper No. 03-06.

## BOX 8.1 MEDIATION IN AUSTRALIA

Australia provides an interesting case study in the use of mediation in franchise-specific regulation. Mediation is a consensual process by which the parties meet to resolve their dispute with the assistance of a third party facilitator. Like disclosure, mediation is essentially self-regulatory in nature and has some similar advantages, for example, it requires little or no government involvement for administration or enforcement.

Mediation also has disadvantages. The starting point for mediation is the condition of imbalance in the relationship and it does not usually alter that condition. The flexibility of the process makes it easy for franchisors to control, while the confidentiality of the process means franchisors know the outcomes of disputes while individual franchisees suffer the disadvantage that they do not know these outcomes. Perhaps most importantly, the franchise contract as drafted by a franchisor imposes few enforceable obligations on a franchisor, so that a franchisor has little incentive to reach a negotiated settlement. In these ways mediation can actually reinforce the very imbalance of power that creates problems throughout the franchise relationship.

One Australian practitioner pointed out that trying to remedy a relational problem through mediation often fails to resolve the fundamental problem of a breach of trust; he felt that a reconciliation of the relationship for purely commercial reasons would be unlikely to overcome the suspicion that further attacks against the franchisee, real or perceived, can be expected.

The burden on the parties in the regulation of this sector in this way must overcome significant market inefficiencies with respect to information asymmetry, power imbalance and moral hazard. For franchisees in particular there is a need for more education and training to ensure that franchisees are fairly represented in any dispute resolution process.

offer significant potential to improve parties' abilities to manage relationships and to promote trust and self-sufficiency.

This aspect of the regulatory program for franchising is likely to warrant further development in many jurisdictions. As every jurisdiction will have its own legal framework for handling disputes formally and its own culture and mechanisms for handling them informally as well, however, franchise-specific legislation may not always (or even often) be the appropriate place for such measures.

Other possible procedures for conflict resolution include arbitration, conciliation, the use of an ombudsman, [13] and or expert determination. Tribunals may also be useful to ensure that specialized knowledge and experience can be applied in the adjudication of franchise disputes.

## Other Procedural Standards for Performance of the Contract

In most franchise contracts franchisee obligations are subject to strict standards, schedules, and targets, often to be set and/or changed at the sole discretion of a franchisor. Franchisor obligations are usually minimal and stated in permissive terms such as, 'a franchisor may . . . at its discretion'. Procedural standards in franchise-specific legislation are rarely connected with the terms granting discretion to a franchisor, for example in franchisor training, support or promotional activities, to reduce the potential for franchisor abuse of its discretion in the performance of the franchise contract. This is an important area for further study.

In the case of minimum performance abuses, for example, it may be possible and useful to involve franchisees in the process of the monitoring and enforcement of standards by making available to them the possibility to challenge franchisor's determinations with a committee consisting of both franchisee and franchisor representatives to ensure fairness. In the case of supply, procedures could require involvement of franchisees. Unilateral amendment, if it is not excluded outright as an allowable contract term, could be subject to procedural requirements in order to curb the potential for abuse. Franchise-specific regulation may similarly include procedural provisions for franchisor's changes to territory allocations, selection of franchisees, and matching franchisees to units and territories.

## Substantive and Procedural Requirements for Renewal or Exiting the Relationship Through Transfer or Termination

Among the various types of conduct legislation, the most common procedural provisions are those that apply to end-of-term arrangements such as

---

13 From the Swedish meaning 'go-between'. Christina M. Kuta, 'Universities, Corporations, and States Use Them Now It's Time To Protect Them: An Analysis of the Public and Private Sector Ombudsman and the Continued Need for a Privileged Relationship' (2003) 27 *Southern Illinois University Law Journal* 389.

procedures for termination, transfer, as well as renewal, e.g. notice, time to remedy a breach, and so on. There are also substantive requirements with regard to renewal and exit from the relationship. Transfer, termination, and renewal are subject to disclosure and procedural requirements in about half the jurisdictions with franchise-specific regulation. Some require only disclosure of termination provisions, while others mandate procedures that safeguard rights in the processes and procedures of termination, transfer and renewal.

### Assignment and Transfer by a Franchisee

Transfer of a franchisee's interest in a franchise unit is not extensively regulated. A few prior disclosure regimes, such as France, Romania and Italy, require disclosure of the conditions for the franchisee's entitlement to assign the agreement. In Indonesia all matters between franchisee and franchisor must be settled before a franchisee can transfer. Macau lists conditions where a franchisor can oppose transfer, such as where the transferee does not correspond to standards and/or does not offer sufficient guarantees. In Vietnam a franchisee may transfer as long as the intended transferee satisfies conditions in article 6, and the transfer is consented to by the franchisor. The franchisee must send a written request to which the franchisor must reply within 15 days; otherwise he will be deemed to have consented. There is also a list of conditions under which a franchisor can reasonably reject the transfer of commercial rights. In Australia a franchisor must not unreasonably withhold consent for franchisee to transfer.

Seven states in the US legislate with respect to transfer of a franchise by a franchisee. This legislation typically provides guidelines for the grounds upon which a franchisor may disapprove transfer and some procedures, for example the period of time a franchisor has to disapprove, or it will have been deemed to have approved the transfer. Acceptable reasons for franchisor to disapprove transfer are generally related to qualifications of the transferee. Hawaii allows a franchisor to disapprove only for good cause. The notice period can be as short as 30 days but is most commonly 60 days. Washington State prohibits requiring a transfer fee in excess of the amount necessary to compensate franchisor for expenses incurred in the transfer.

Though transfer is currently regulated only through disclosure and procedural requirements, other measures to improve a franchisee's position in transfer could include collective negotiation, and further specification of procedures to protect franchisee's assets. The courts have a role to play in ensuring that franchisees are compensated for losses, however an enhanced role for the courts would not help the many franchisees who do not litigate.

## Termination by a franchisor

Twenty-one countries' franchise-specific regulation addresses termination in some way. Five countries merely require that termination be adverted to in disclosure, while others require certain procedures such as notice and time to cure.

- In Spain the 2007 Draft allows termination of franchise agreements against payment of liquidated damages equal to two years' earnings; the Draft makes it clear that franchisees will be entitled to the same indemnity payment as commercial agents in certain specific circumstances.
- Moldova provides conditions where parties may request amendment or termination of the contract such as when both parties agree; when one party is in breach; when one party is in liquidation, or is bankrupt; a court finds the company of a party to be void; death; and other circumstances provided by legislation or the contract.
- In Romania when a franchisee breaches the contract a franchisor must notify of its intent to act and give time to remedy the breach. Parties must include precise conditions stipulating termination without notice.
- In Estonia termination is not regulated under franchise-specific legislation but general rules in law of obligations apply.
- In Russia each party has the right to abandon the contract with notification six months in advance unless otherwise provided by the contract. Similarly, in the Kyrgyz Republic, a complex business licence contract can be terminated according to chapter 22 of the code. Either party may waive a term business licence at any time with six months' notification unless the contract provides otherwise. In Lithuania and the Kyrgyz Republic each party to a contract for an indeterminate term has the right to repudiate with six months' notice unless otherwise provided in the contract.
- In Lithuania other conditions may lead to termination of a contract, such as a franchisor's loss of right to the trademark, bankruptcy of a franchisor or franchisee.
- In Albania where the contract is of indefinite duration or term of more than ten years early termination by either party requires one year's prior notice.
- In Georgia if the contract exceeds ten years parties can terminate with one year's notice.
- In Korea just cause must be shown for termination. Restrictions on termination under the South Korea Fair Franchise Act require notification to be sent to a franchisee at least three times with a grace

period of at least two months. Failure to comply with the procedure results in the termination being invalid.

- In Indonesia a 'clean break letter' must be obtained before a new franchisee can be established, and all matters between franchisee and franchisor must be settled.
- In Malaysia parties cannot terminate before the expiration date except for good cause, which shall include but is not limited to the failure of a franchisee to comply with terms of the agreement or any other relevant agreement and the failure of the franchisee to remedy a breach within a stated notice period not less than 14 days. Malaysia also allows early termination of the minimum term of five years in certain circumstances such as where both parties agree or where a court finds conditions which require earlier termination.
- Vietnam provides for right to unilaterally terminate the contract. Vietnam allows a franchisee to unilaterally terminate the contract where a franchisor breaches its obligations specified in article 287 of the commercial law. A franchisor has the right to unilaterally terminate where a franchisee no longer holds the business licence, is dissolved or goes bankrupt, commits serious legal violations which harm the reputation of the system, or fails to remedy immaterial breaches in the contract within a reasonable time limit, despite written notice from franchisor.
- In Australia procedural provisions include termination safeguards.
- There is no provision regarding termination in the federal legislation in the United States. However, 18 states, as well as Puerto Rico and the US Virgin Islands legislate some aspect of the parties' termination of the agreement. The laws typically contain a substantive requirement regarding causes for termination, as well as procedural requirements with respect to notice and cure periods. Of the 20 jurisdictions that legislate with respect to termination, all but two require good cause to terminate. Good cause does not have a uniform definition, if it is defined at all in the legislation. Where good cause is defined it is most often breached where there is failure to substantially comply with franchisor's requirements. Failure by a franchisee to substantially comply with a franchisor's requirements is equated with good cause in five jurisdictions, New Jersey, Nebraska, Rhode Island, Wisconsin and the US Virgin Islands. Some states equate terminating with good cause with the absence of bad faith, and some expressly include a bar on termination in bad faith. Under US state laws notice to terminate can be required as far ahead as 120 days, but a 90 day or 60 day notice requirement is more common. Some states provide for a notice period as short as 30 days, while a few

> do not specify a number of days that require the franchisor to give a reasonable opportunity to cure. There may or may not be both a notice period and a cure period, for example, a notice period of 90 days with a cure period of 30 to 60 days. Note, of course, that some events can lead to immediate termination. California lists 11 such events, while Arkansas lists six, Iowa eight, Minnesota three, Mississippi and Missouri five, Nebraska six and Washington five and Wisconsin three.

Barkoff notes that relationship statutes in the US were devised to provide protections for franchisees against wrongful termination and that unwarranted termination without adequate notice is a less significant problem than in years past. Because most franchise agreements contain such provisions, he questions whether the statutes add much to the current customs in the trade.[14] An argument can be made that the reason such provisions are now almost ubiquitous in franchise agreements is because of the legislation. Certainly, this appears to be the case in Australia, where termination provisions in contracts very often mirror Code requirements.

Termination provisions should be fair for both parties. A franchisor can compensate a franchisee for losses that are not the fault of a franchisee. This should not create an undue burden for a franchisor that terminates only with good cause. Indemnification for franchisee losses can be incorporated into a franchisor's cost of doing business to be spread among all franchisees. Such provisions would increase trust between the parties, by reducing concerns of anticipated franchisor opportunism.

Because of their specific investment, franchisees are more vulnerable than employees, not less so, and they are as vulnerable to franchisors' control as employees are to employers' control. A franchisee, therefore, needs at least as much protection as that afforded to employees. At a minimum they should have the assurance of fair, efficient procedures and terms for ending the business relationship. Table 8.6 below summarizes the nature of franchise-specific legislation with respect to termination and right of renewal.

---

14 Barkoff, 'Franchise Regulation: The American Experience' (Paper presented at Bond University and UNSW School of Business and Taxation Franchise Law Colloquium, Gold Coast, Australia, 20 November 2008).

*Table 8.6 Legislation with respect to termination and right of renewal*

| Jurisdiction | Termination laws including disclosure | Termination only with good cause or similar | Notice requirement | Disclosure must address conditions for termination | Contract must contain term re termination | Right of renewal | Other |
|---|---|---|---|---|---|---|---|
| THE AMERICAS | | | | | | | |
| Barbados | | | | | | | |
| Brazil | | | | | | | |
| Canada | √ | | | √ | | | |
| Mexico | √ | √ | | | √ | | |
| United States | √ | Some US states | Some US states | √ | | 17 US states | |
| EUROPE | | | | | | | |
| Albania | √ | √ | √ | | | √ | |
| Belarus | √ | √ | | | | | |
| Belgium | √ | | | √ | | | |
| Estonia | | | | | | | |
| France | √ | Only for breach | | √ | | | |
| Italy | √ | Only for substantial breach | | | √ | | |
| Lithuania | √ | | | | | | |
| Moldova | √ | | | | √ | | |
| Romania | √ | √ (contract and disclosure must address termination without notice) | | √ | √ | √ | |
| Russia | √ | | | | | | |
| Spain | √ | | | | | | |
| Sweden | | | | | | | |
| EURASIA | | | | | | | |
| Ukraine | | | | | | √ | |
| People's Republic of China | √ | | Only for cause | | √ | | |
| Republic of China | √* | | | | ? | | |
| Georgia | √ | | √ | | | | |

*Table 8.6* (continued)

| Jurisdiction | Termination laws including disclosure | Termination only with good cause or similar | Notice requirement | Disclosure must address conditions for termination | Contract must contain term re termination | Right of renewal | Other |
|---|---|---|---|---|---|---|---|
| Indonesia | √ | | | √ | | | Clean break letter, matters settled |
| Japan | √ | | | √ | | | |
| Kazakhstan | | | | | | | |
| Republic of Korea | √ | | | | | √ | |
| Kyrgyzstan | √ | | | | | | |
| Malaysia | √ | √ | | | | √ | |
| Vietnam | √ | | | | √ (contract may address) | | |
| OCEANIA | | | | | | | |
| Australia | √ | | √ | | | | Procedural requirements |

*Note:* * Not in franchise-specific law – the Civil Code and fair trading laws generally require advance notice of termination and a reasonable period to cure the breach

## Requirements for Renewal and/or Non-renewal of the Agreement

Non-renewal involves a franchisor's failure to renew. There is some confusion with respect to this issue, because there are two points in time when renewal can occur. The first is at the end of a specified first term when there is a contractual 'right to renew'. Franchise contracts typically contain a term entitled 'Right of renewal', 'Right to renew' or similar. If an initial term of the grant is five years, for example, a contract may well provide that a franchisee may renew for a second five-year term provided that she complies with a franchisor's conditions for renewal. As long as a franchisee complies with the conditions for renewal, it should be granted. The issue here is that the conditions are often drafted so that a franchisor will have no difficulty, if it wants to, in finding a justification not to renew.

The second point in time when renewal becomes an issue is at the end of the final term, when there is no further 'right of renewal' provided for in the contract. At this time, a franchisee has no contractual right whatsoever to renewal of the contract. Nevertheless, this has become an issue in the US and particularly in Australia, where franchisees argue that they have a reasonable right to expect the agreement to continue. They suggest that this situation is an important instance in which the power and information advantage enjoyed by franchisors can create undue hardship for franchisees.[15]

Few countries provide a mandatory right for a franchisee to renew. In some jurisdictions this may be due to a concern over creating a property right in a franchisee. A requirement of advance notice of non-renewal is more common.

- In Albania parties are required make an effort to agree on renewal of contract.
- In Estonia renewal is not regulated but is subject to the franchisee agreement.
- Romania requires a franchisor to notify a franchisee of its intention not to renew.
- In Ukraine the legislation provides for the right of the franchisee to conclude an agreement for a new term upon the same conditions and states that the law may determine the conditions under which a title-holder may refuse concluding a concession agreement for a new term.
- In Korea a renewal request must be placed 90–180 days prior to expiration of agreement, and a franchisor cannot decline unless just cause can be shown for non-renewal.
- A franchisor commits an offence in Malaysia if it refuses to renew a franchise agreement or if it does not give written notice of intent not to renew six months prior to expiration date.
- Seventeen states in the United States have legislated with respect to refusal to renew a franchise agreement. This legislation typically declares permitted grounds for refusal, and/or provides for notice periods and procedures. Notice requirements vary from a year to, more commonly, six months but are only required in a handful of states.

The most recent federal inquiry into the regulation of franchising in Australia, 'Opportunity not opportunism: improving conduct in Australian franchising', noted,

---

15 See Economic and Finance Committee, South Australia, 'Franchises (following inquiry into Franchises)' (2008) 65–9. See also <http://www.innovation.gov.au/Section/SmallBusiness/Documents/Accompanying%20RIS%20to%20Government%20response_Franchising.pdf> 28 December 2009 at 63.

> Franchisee expectations about renewal need to be better managed, and the financial implications of non-renewal better understood, before fixed term franchise agreements are initially signed. Franchise agreements should clearly stipulate what the end-of-term arrangements and processes are, and these arrangements should be fully and transparently disclosed to prospective franchisees. In particular, the committee is of the view that pre-agreement disclosure documentation should explicitly discuss the transfer process that will apply to equity in the value of the business as a going concern at the time the agreement ends.[16]

Non-renewal is an issue that raises the possibility of the option of a statutory requirement of good faith. A statutory requirement of good faith for termination and non-renewal has been enacted in approximately half of the US states that have relationship laws for the franchise sector. The following section examines in greater detail the application of a duty of good faith in franchising.

## Requirements of Good Faith in the Conduct of the Relationship

A duty of good faith is common as a part of code-based legislation, particularly in civil law jurisdictions, to ensure fair negotiation at the formation of contract. Some franchise-specific legislation requires parties to act in good faith more broadly. This section begins to examine the complexities of the duty of good faith, but its scope within this survey cannot purport to provide a complete analysis of good faith requirements in common law and civil law jurisdictions.

Most countries that have franchising-specific regulation do not specify a good faith obligation as part of that legislation, but a few do.

- A statutory requirement of good faith is part of franchise-specific legislation in Canada (the Federal Model law and/or legislation at the provincial level in all four provinces).
- A statutory requirement of good faith is part of franchise-specific legislation in the United States in four states. A statutory requirement of good faith is not included in franchise-specific legislation

---

16 Parliamentary Joint Committee on Corporations and Financial Services, Commonwealth of Australia, 'Opportunity not opportunism: improving conduct in Australian franchising' (December 2008), [6.52]. The report is available at <http://www.aph.gov.au/SENATE/committee/corporations_ctte/franchising/report/report.pdf.> at 28 December 2009. See also, A. Terry, 'Issues with Prior Disclosure as a Regulatory Strategy for Franchisee Protection' (Paper presented at 23rd Annual International Society of Franchising Conference, San Diego, CA, USA, 21–22 February 2009).

(the FTC Rule), but is part of a general commercial code (the Uniform Commercial Code) at the federal level in the US.

- Albania includes a statutory implied term of good faith in franchise-specific legislation, as does Italy where the law requires loyalty, fairness, good faith.
- Korea requires a general duty of good faith in the performance of the duties of the parties.
- China requires fairness and reasonableness.
- Malaysia requires performance in an honest and lawful manner.

That so few jurisdictions impose a statutory duty of good faith in franchise-specific legislation does not provide an accurate account of the true requirements of good faith in commercial dealings. Several jurisdictions that have enacted franchise-specific legislation omit to include it in that legislation, as the duty is required of contracting parties under other legislation. Good faith is often an integral part of the fabric of the civil law traditions as many civil law states take an expansive approach to the duty of good faith, applying it both to contract formation and performance.[17] For example,

- The Civil Code of Brazil requires contracting parties to observe principles of good faith in the performance of the contractual agreement.[18]
- In Belgium, although the franchise-specific legislation makes no mention of 'good faith', there is a requirement of 'good faith' in the performance of contracts as prescribed by the Civil Code and contractual interpretations are informed by custom and usage that may include an obligation of good faith.[19]
- In Estonia, while there is no such requirement in the franchise-specific legislation, the statutory duty of good faith requires a franchisor to disclose certain information to franchisees. If a person enters into a transaction due to a mistake or fraud, the injured party may cancel the transaction if the mistake or fraud were caused by

---

[17] See Paul J. Powers, 'Defining the Undefinable: Good Faith and the United Nations Convention on Contracts for the International Sale of Goods' (1999) 18 *Journal of Law and Commerce* 333–53, <http://www.cisg.law.pace.edu/cisg/biblio/powers.html> at 27 December 2009.

[18] Andrew P. Loewinger and Michael K. Lindsey (eds), *International Franchise Sales Laws* (2006).

[19] See Paul J. Powers, 'Defining the Undefinable: Good Faith and the United Nations Convention on Contracts for the International Sale of Goods' (1999) 18 *Journal of Law and Commerce* 333–53, <http://www.cisg.law.pace.edu/cisg/biblio/powers.html> at 27 December 2009.

circumstances where disclosure was required by the principles of good faith.[20]

- In France a pre-contractual duty of good faith is based in tort and after contract formation it is based in contract.[21] The French Civil Code requires good faith and fair dealing under Article 1134.
- In Lithuania a statutory duty of good faith requires franchisors to disclose certain information to franchisees.[22] The Civil Code (2000) of Lithuania also provides that in the course of fulfilling their obligations, parties must act in a manner required by good faith and fairness, and according to the principles of justice, reasonableness and good faith.
- In Moldova the Civil Code imposes an obligation of fair competition for both parties.
- In Spain the Commercial Code contains general provisions applicable to all commercial contracts. The duty to disclose information is an inherent obligation in all business relations, required by the contractual principle of *bona fide*.
- In Finland the Contracts Act[23] states that a transaction that would otherwise be binding upon the parties, will not be so if it was entered into due to circumstances incompatible with 'honour and good faith'.[24] Finland also invokes the principle of good faith in the Consumer Protection Act[25] and Sale of Goods Act,[26] both of which state that if goods purchased are defective, the purchaser must inform the seller of the defect within a reasonable time following the purchase.[27] However, the purchaser may still invoke defects in the goods purchased if the seller's conduct was 'incompatible with honour and good faith'.[28]

---

20 Estonian Civil Code.

21 See Paul J. Powers, 'Defining the Undefinable: Good Faith and the United Nations Convention on Contracts for the International Sale of Goods' (1999) 18 *Journal of Law and Commerce* 333–53, <http://www.cisg.law.pace.edu/cisg/biblio/powers.html> at 27 December 2009.

22 Field Fisher Waterhouse, 'International Franchising: Franchise Disclosure and Registration Requirements' (2008) Field Fisher Waterhouse <http://www.europeanfranchising.com/how-we-can-help-you/disclosure-and-registration.aspx> at 27 December 2009.

23 Contracts Act 228/1929 (Finland).

24 Contracts Act 228/1929 (Finland) s 33.

25 Consumer Protection Act 38/1978 (Finland).

26 Sale of Goods Act 355/1987 (Finland).

27 Consumer Protection Act 38/1978 (Finland) s 16; Sale of Goods Act 355/1987 (Finland) s 20.

28 Consumer Protection Act 38/1978 (Finland) s 16(2)(1); Sale of Goods Act 355/1987 (Finland) s 20(2).

- German legislation requires contracting parties to observe good faith not only in contract negotiation, but also in contract performance. Good faith incorporates the customs practised by the contracting parties as well as a general requirement to act reasonably. The German duty of good faith goes beyond a requirement to act reasonably; it requires a relationship of trust based on the commercial dealing of the parties in a particular transaction. German Bürgerliches Gesetzbuch states that an obligor has a duty to perform in accordance with the principles of good faith, taking into account customary practice.[29] Although the wording of the section is narrow in its meaning, its development by the German courts gave rise to various other duties, such as supply of information and disclosure.[30]
- Though Greece does not have franchising-specific legislation, the sector being regulated by the Civil Code and the laws on competition and commercial agents, Articles 174, 178, 179, 371 and 372 of the Civil Code protect the franchisee from franchisor's abusive practices, and if the agreement is against moral values, good faith or unduly restricts the freedom of the franchisee it may be declared void and not binding on the parties.[31]
- The Civil Code (1999) of Hungary states that in the course of fulfilling their obligations, parties must act in a manner required by good faith and fairness, and according to the principles of justice, reasonableness and good faith.
- In Luxembourg the duty of good faith is a general principle of contract law as well as a statutory duty under article 1135(3) of the Civil Code.[32]
- The Dutch Civil Code states that all parties to an obligation must act in accordance to what is reasonable and equitable. The Supreme Court of the Netherlands has determined that in the course of negotiations, parties must act in accordance to reasonableness and equity,

---

[29] Civil Code 1896 (Germany).

[30] Emily M. Weitzenböck, 'Good Faith and Fair Dealing in the Context of Contract Formation by Electronic Agents' (Proceedings of the AISB Symposium on Intelligent Agents in Virtual Markets, London, United Kingdom, 2–5 April 2002).

[31] Athanassia Papantoniou and Ioanna Lazaridou, 'Greek Franchising Law' (2007) Kelemenis and Co, Attorneys at Law <http://www.kelemenis.com/pdf/pub15.pdf> at 27 December 2009.

[32] Daniel Boone and Michel Schwartz, 'Getting the Deal Through – insurance and reinsurance 2008 Luxembourg' (2008) Kleyr Collarini Grasso, Attorneys at Law <http://www.kckg.lu/download/news/insurance_&_reinsurance_luxembourg_chapter_execution_20080310.pdf> at 27 December 2009.

which imposes upon the parties a duty to take into account the other party's reasonable interests.[33]

- Under Portuguese law, there is a general duty to act in good faith at all stages of a transaction, and the principle of good faith requires that the seller in any type of contractual transaction disclose all relevant information to the purchaser.[34]
- Article 2 of the Swiss Civil Code is applicable to all civil law transactions, including contract law. Impliedly this means that Article 2 is applicable to franchise relationships, even prior to the franchise agreement being executed by the parties.
- The Civil Code of Quebec, Canada at article 1375 states that parties must conduct themselves in accordance to the principles of good faith both at the time the obligation is created, and at the time it is performed.[35]
- Unlike most laws enacted regarding civil court jurisdiction in Thailand, the Unfair Contract Terms Act gives the courts great discretionary power in determining whether contract terms are generally unfair and unreasonable. However, the Act does provide general guidelines under which the court is to consider whether certain terms are unfair or unreasonable.

Common law approaches to good faith are more restrained, typically imposing a narrower duty.[36]A duty of good faith has become an issue with respect to performance in some common law jurisdictions including the UK and Australia, though in most common law jurisdictions any concept of good faith has traditionally resided in the negotiation of agreements. The idea that parties to an agreement should enter into it with full disclosure is the essence of the duty.[37]

In the UK lawyers rely on the common law to find the duty, but UK

---

[33] Arthur S. Hartkamp, 'Judicial Discretion Under the New Civil Code of the Netherlands' (1992) 40(3) *The American Journal of Comparative Law* 551–71.

[34] Avv. Aldo Frignani, 'Disclosure in Franchise Agreements' (Paper prepared for a conference in Brussels on 31 October 1995); Pedro Sáragga Leal, 'Portugal' in Global Legal Group Limited (ed), *The International Comparative Legal Guide to Real Estate 2006* (2006), Chapter 30.

[35] Civil Code of Quebec, S.Q. 1991, c. 64. a. 1375.

[36] Paul J. Powers, 'Defining the Undefinable: Good Faith and the United Nations Convention on Contracts for the International Sale of Goods' (1999) 18 *Journal of Law and Commerce* 333–53 <http://www.cisg.law.pace.edu/cisg/biblio/powers.html> at 27 December 2009.

[37] For a discussion of recent court cases on the issue of good faith in franchising see Andrew Loewinger and John Pratt, 'Recent Changes and Trends in

common law does not require that franchise agreements be subject to duties of good faith.[38] Professor Terry notes that the application of 'derogation from a grant', property law principles in a franchising context suggest that 'good faith' 'may have emerged under another guise'.[39]

There is no statutory requirement of good faith in the regulation of franchising in Australia. A good faith requirement for the franchising sector was recommended by the 2006 Review of the Disclosure Provisions of the Franchising Code of Conduct, 'recognition in the Code of a concept of good faith and fair dealing would provide positive reinforcement to the development of improved relationships and dealings between franchisors, franchisees and prospective franchisees.[40] This recommendation was rejected by the government. Good faith is, however, a factor in the unconscionable conduct statute at the federal level in Australia and in some state fair trading legislation. A requirement of good faith may also be incorporated into unfair contracts legislation.

Good faith may be implied in court interpretation of the contract. Though it has been observed that, 'The sheer volume of cases where courts are asked to rule on good faith indicates that contractual parties have embraced the concept of good faith',[41] the fact is that Australian courts have been inconsistent in their application of the concept of an implied term of good faith and the High Court has not determined that there is a general obligation of good faith in franchise contracts.

In Canada Section 7 of the Alberta Act provides, 'Every franchise agreement imposes on each party a duty of fair dealing in its performance and enforcement.'[42] Ontario has a similar provision.[43] Some observers of franchising in Canada argue in favour of a good faith standard for performance

---

International Franchise Laws' (Paper presented at the American Bar Association 31st Annual Forum on Franchising, Austin, Texas, USA, 15–17 October 2008).

[38] *Jani-King (GB) Limited v. Pula Enterprises and Ors* [2007] EWHC 2433 (QB).

[39] A. Terry, 'Franchising and the Quest for the Holy Grail: Good Faith or Good Intentions?' (Paper presented at 23rd Annual International Society of Franchising Conference, San Diego, CA, USA, 2–3 February 2009). Terry cites *Stone and Anor (t/a Tyre 20) v. Fleet Mobile Tyres Ltd* [2006] EWCA Civ 1209.

[40] See Recommendation 25, Secretariat, Office of Small Business, Commonwealth of Australia, 'Review of the disclosure provisions of the franchising code of conduct' (October 2006) <http://www.innovation.gov.au/Section/SmallBusiness/Documents/Franchising_Code_Review_Report_2006_FINAL_061207200702051342 50.pdf> at 27 December 2009.

[41] Bruno Zeller, 'Good Faith – Is it a Contractual Obligation?' (2003) 13 *Bond Law Review* 214, 239.

[42] Franchises Act, S.A. 1995, (Alberta Act), s. 7.

[43] Arthur Wishart Act (Franchise Disclosure), 2000 (the Ontario Act) , ss. 3(1).

in contracts of sale, recommending the adoption of a standard of good faith similar to that set forth in the Restatement (Second) of Contracts.

In the US a duty of good faith plays an expanded role, implied in every contract governed by the Uniform Commercial Code (UCC).[44] While this is not a franchise-specific law, franchising has generally been held to be subject to this standard.[45] The Restatement (Second) of Contracts also imposes a duty of good faith in the performance and enforcement of contracts.

At the state level a few US states have passed franchise statutes that expressly require the parties to deal in good faith.[46] Approximately 20 US states and territories have 'relationship statutes' that govern various aspects of the franchise relationship;[47] a few have passed franchise statutes that expressly require the parties to deal in good faith.[48]

In the US as in all common law jurisdictions there is a tension between the principle that parties to a contract (including a franchise agreement) are under an implied obligation to deal with one another on the basis of good faith and fair dealing, and the principle that the doctrine of 'good faith and fair dealing' cannot be used to vary the express terms of a contract.

Discrepancies in the application of good faith among various legal traditions notwithstanding, the observance of a principle of good faith has become an element of international law. Good faith is included as

---

[44] Section 1-203 of the UCC provides that 'Every contract of duty within this Act imposes an obligation of good faith in its performance or enforcement.'

[45] A. Terry, 'Franchising and the Quest for the Holy Grail: Good Faith or Good Intentions?' (Paper presented at the 23rd Annual International Society of Franchising Conference, San Diego, CA, USA, 2-3 February 2009).

[46] Jane Cohen and Larry Weinberg, 'Good Faith and Fair Dealing: A primer on the differences between the United States and Canada' (Summer 2002) *Franchise Law Journal* 37–46.

[47] The states with relationship laws are: Arkansas, California, Connecticut, Delaware, Hawaii, Illinois, Indiana, Iowa, Michigan, Minnesota, Mississippi, Missouri, Nebraska, New Jersey, Rhode Island, Washington and Wisconsin. The District of Columbia, Puerto Rico and the Virgin Islands also have statutes that govern the termination of franchises. South Dakota and Virginia's statutes do not directly address termination but they arguably restrict a franchisor's discretion in refusing to renew a franchise. The remaining states do not have franchise relationship statutes, but may have industry-specific (i.e., petroleum or auto dealer) statutes. See Michael J. Lockerby, 'A World Wide Web of Potential Franchise Law Violations' (1999) 6(1) *Richmond Journal of Law & Technology* <http://law.richmond.edu/jolt/v6i1/lockerby.txt> at 28 December 2009; Fisher and Zucker, 'Compliance with state relationship laws' (2004) Fisher and Zucker <http://www.franchise-law-firm.com/franchise_sales_reference/state_relationship_laws.htm> at 28 December 2009.

[48] Jane Cohen and Larry Weinberg, 'Good Faith and Fair Dealing: A primer on the differences between the United States and Canada' (Summer 2002) 'Franchise Law Journal' 37–46.

part of some international conventions. In the first ten years of the UN Convention on Contracts for the International Sale of Goods (CISG), courts have recognized a good faith obligation in contract performance as a requirement for contracting parties. The International Institute for the Unification of Private Law (UNIDROIT) Principles of International Commercial Contracts impose a duty of good faith on contracting parties. An obligation of good faith is also imposed by other international agreements such as the Principles of European Contract Law that include provisions requiring good faith generally and in negotiating a contract.

## The Content of a Duty of Good Faith

Just as the application of the doctrine can vary among legal traditions and jurisdictions, so, too, does the meaning of the duty. Despite (or perhaps because of) extensive case law Germany has not established a definition but does require a contracting party, before and after a contract is formed, to respect the relationship of trust between the parties and to act reasonably in not breaching that relationship. Italy has a pre-contract duty of good faith in negotiating as well as a contract performance duty; good faith becomes an ethical obligation which is an integral part of public policy.[49]

In common law jurisdictions good faith requires parties to perform their obligations under the contract fairly, honestly, and in a manner acceptable in their trade or business. *Black's Law Dictionary* defines good faith as 'an intangible and abstract quality with no technical meaning or statutory definition, and it encompasses, among other things, an honest belief, the absence of malice and the absence of design to defraud or to seek an unconscionable advantage. . . .' The Uniform Commercial Code (UCC) defines good faith as 'honesty in fact in the conduct or transaction concerned'. Good faith is defined in the Restatement as a 'faithfulness to an agreed common purpose and consistency with the justified expectations of the other party'.

The problems that may arise due to this lack of a unified and precise definition of good faith can be circumvented to some extent by inclusion in the statute of what meaning is intended. Relationship statutes in the US provide that franchisors may not terminate franchisees without meeting various standards such as good cause, good cause and notice, just cause, and good faith.[50]

---

49 Paul J. Powers, 'Defining the Undefinable: Good Faith and the United Nations Convention on Contracts for the International Sale of Goods' (1999) 18 *Journal of Law and Commerce* 333–53, <http://www.cisg.law.pace.edu/cisg/biblio/powers.html> at 27 December 2009.

50 Robert Calihan, Steven Emmons, Rochelle B. Spandorf, Craig Tractenberg,

Though it has been observed that, 'Good cause' differs substantially from 'good faith,'[51] the two concepts do overlap where in some instances good faith informs the meaning of good cause. Under most statutes 'good cause' is determined solely by whether or not the franchisee violated the terms of the franchise. In general, the determination as to whether or not there is 'good cause' ignores the business interests of the licensor, especially if the licensed services or products continue to be offered in the territory of the terminated licensee. Termination of a franchise requires prior written notice identifying the 'good cause' for termination by setting forth the reasons in advance. The applicable statute often spells out certain acts, omissions, or circumstances that constitute good cause. If the statutory 'shopping list' is not applicable to a particular situation, there are some commonly applied instances where the good cause requirement will be met.[52]

## Specific Applications of Good Faith

A statutory duty of good faith may be appropriate for broader application in franchise regulation, for example in some of the other instances where franchisor opportunism is an issue. As a starting point, however, it could be particularly useful with respect to non-renewal. Non-renewal is an example of a situation in which franchisor opportunism is a greater risk because there is no contractual or regulatory protection available to franchisees facing non-renewal. It is therefore typical of situations where a franchisee may require protection in the form of a statutory duty of good faith against the damaging consequences of franchisor opportunism.

There are many such situations, which is why good faith holds promise for greater application in the franchise context. It is the strategy that has been examined most closely in recent inquiries into the effectiveness of regulation in Australia. The most promising approach with respect to encroachment seems to be to require a duty of good faith or similar. The most promising approaches for regulating issues related to brand maintenance also seem to involve requiring a duty of good faith or similar and to involve franchisees in formulating promotions programs, in allocating

---

'Franchise transfer, succession and renewal issues' (Paper presented at the International Franchise Association 34th Annual Legal Symposium, Washington, DC, USA, 6–8 May 2001) <http://www.franchise.org/files/franchisee%20transfer%20succession.PDF> at 28 December 2009.

[51] Byron Fox and Bruce Schaeffer, *Franchise Regulation and Damages*, Chapter 17.01 Wrongful Termination.

[52] Byron Fox and Bruce Schaeffer, *Franchise Regulation and Damages*, Chapter 17.01 Wrongful Termination.

funds and in review of same. Training issues again are an appropriate application of a duty of good faith or similar in conjunction with the involvement of current franchisees in the screening of prospective franchisees and the training of new franchisees. A duty of good faith or similar could be part of the answer for minimum performance and supply issues as well as duration and transfer issues. Finally, the tool best suited to address such broad discretion for one contracting party as 'agree to agree' and unilateral amendment clauses is a duty to exercise that discretion responsibly, reasonably and/or in good faith.

Good faith is a useful tool of broad application that makes excellent sense in the governance of the franchising relationship. In her seminal article on the relational nature of franchise contracts Gillian Hadfield concluded that, 'The doctrinal tool necessary to bring the resolution of franchise contract disputes into line with the realities of the franchise relation is the covenant of good faith and fair dealing.'[53] A duty of good faith helps to address many of the conflicts and inconsistencies that are caused not only by the contract's relational nature, but also by the interaction of the relational with the standard form qualities of the contract.

Good faith is particularly appropriate, even essential, to effective relational contracting because it accommodates the incompleteness of contracts and the limits in the forecasting capacity. Professor Terry quotes Thomas J. in *Bobux*, 'Good faith is required to ensure that the requisite communication, co-operation and predictable performance occurs for the advantage of both parties. In short, the obligation seeks to hold the parties to the promise implicit in a continuing, relational commercial transaction.'[54] Good faith accomplishes these ends by emphasizing the participatory nature of contracts, and by encompassing social rules and practices, as well as non-promissory elements. Good faith stresses the moral element of contract relations, counteracts threats to solidarity and helps to overcome barriers for communication. Overall, good faith highlights values and legally protects the trust element, without which no contract is effective.[55]

Good faith addresses the dangers that arise due to the power imbalance, the discretion to a franchisor and the shifting of risk to a franchisee. A franchisor will not relinquish this power and indeed, power in itself is not

---

[53] Gillian Hadfield, 'Problematic Relations: Franchising and the Law of Incomplete Contracts' (1990) 42 *Stanford Law Review* 927, 984.

[54] *Bobux Marketing Ltd v. Raynor Marketing Ltd* [2002] 1 NZLR 506 *per* Thomas J.

[55] Ronaldo Porto Macedo Júnior, 'Relational Contracts in Brazilian Law' (1997) Latin American Studies Association <http://bibliotecavirtual.clacso.org.ar/ar/libros/lasa97/portomacedopor.pdf> at 16 December 2009.

a bad thing. The problem arises when power is abused; and a good faith requirement can deter abuse.

Good faith is also appropriate to meet the conditions created by the commodification of contract (namely the application of traditional contractual doctrine to standard form contracts as discussed above) and the role of a franchisee as a consumer. Good faith is widely used in consumer-protection, including the UCC, where, 'Good faith is specifically mentioned in fifty different UCC provisions.'[56]

Good faith is a principles-based rather than a rules-based regulatory strategy. Principles rather than rules allow regulation to respond effectively to evolving conditions without the need for frequent amendment to rules, amendment that can undermine the effectiveness of such rules.[57] Finally, this principles-based approach offers an aspirational quality that rules cannot offer, which is potentially more conductive to relationships of trust rather than suspicion, for 'If we trust someone simply because legal sanctions apply for breaking rules, we do not, in fact, trust them at all.'[58]

It has taken a place in the governance of commercial relationships in international law, a place it has held for centuries in civil law traditions. Good faith is not a universal solvent for every problem in franchising; it is not the Holy Grail for franchising regulation. The fact that it fails to bring magical properties, however, is no reason to reject a tool that can function effectively to help contain the damage that can be caused due to power imbalance and opportunistic behaviour.

## FRANCHISE TRADE ASSOCIATIONS

No study of the regulation of the franchise sector can be complete without including at least a mention of trade associations and their codes

---

56 Paul J. Powers, 'Defining the Undefinable: Good Faith and the United Nations Convention on Contracts for the International Sale of Goods' (1999) 18 *Journal of Law and Commerce* 333–53, <http://www.cisg.law.pace.edu/cisg/biblio/powers.html> at 27 December 2009.

57 Paul J. Powers, 'Defining the Undefinable: Good Faith and the United Nations Convention on Contracts for the International Sale of Goods' (1999) 18 *Journal of Law and Commerce* 333–53, <http://www.cisg.law.pace.edu/cisg/biblio/powers.html> at 27 December 2009.

58 Stavros B. Thomadakis, 'What Makes Good Regulation?'(Paper presented at the IFAC Council Seminar, Mexico City, Mexico, 14 November 2007) <http://web.ifac.org/download/30th_anniversary_Thomadakis_Pres_Nov_07.pdf> at 28 December 2009.

of conduct or ethics. Today national trade associations for franchising operate in about 45 countries, or about a third of the countries where franchises operate.[59] Virtually all of the countries with a solid history of franchising, such as the US, Canada, France and Australia have franchise trade associations, and many of the countries that regulate franchising also have trade associations, most with Codes of Conduct or Ethics that are binding on members:

- The Brazilian Franchise Association was created in 1987 to promote and defend the development of franchising as a business model. The Association offers support services to allow franchisees to investigate franchises and advises franchisors about steps involved in expanding business. The Association has adopted a Code of Ethics.[60]
- The Canadian Franchise Association has adopted a Code of Ethics which is binding on members.[61]
- The Mexican Association of Franchises was founded in 1989. The association has adopted a Code of Ethics.[62]
- The oldest franchise association in the world, established in 1960, the US[63] trade association was originally called the International Franchise Association (the IFA), and it retains the name today. Members must subscribe to and uphold IFA's Code of Ethics as a condition of membership.[64]

---

[59] These countries are Argentina, Brazil, Mexico, United States, Canada, Austria, Belgium, United Kingdom, Denmark, Finland, France, Germany, Greece, Ireland, Italy, the Netherlands, Norway, Portugal, Spain, Sweden, Switzerland, Croatia, Czech Republic, Hungary, Kazakhstan, Romania, Russia, Slovenia, Ukraine, China, Hong Kong, India, Indonesia, Japan, South Korea, Malaysia, Philippines, Singapore, Taiwan, Vietnam, Australia, New Zealand, Egypt, Morocco, and South Africa, Venezuela and Iceland have franchise regulation but no trade association.

[60] The Association's website is <http://www.portaldofranchising.com.br> at 29 December 2009 and its Code is available (in Portuguese) at <http://www.portaldofranchising.com.br/site/content/interna/index.asp?codA=12&codAf=31&codC=1&origem=sobreaabf> at 29 December 2009.

[61] The Association's website is <http://www.cfa.ca>; the Code is available at <http://www.cfa.ca/About_Us/Code_of_Ethics> at 29 December 2009.

[62] The Association's website is <http://www.franquiciasdemexico.org> at 29 December 2009. The Code of Ethics is available at <http://www.franquiciasde-mexico.org/web-english/index-htm.htm>.

[63] Interview with Matt Shay (Washington, DC, USA, 25 June 2008, 10:30 am).

[64] The Association's website is <http://www.franchise.org> at 29 December 2009. The Code of Ethics is available at <http://www.franchise.org/industrysecondary.aspx?id=3554> at 29 December 2009.

- The Belgian Franchise Federation is a Member of the European Franchise Federation.[65]
- Founded in 1971, the Fédération Française de la Franchise (the FFF) is the oldest franchising association in Europe. Franchisors believed that self-regulation through a Code of Ethics was the only way to avoid externally imposed regulation, thus the first Code of Ethics was established in 1972 with an intention to balance rights and duties within a framework of loyalty and transparency. The FFF now sees the Code of Ethics as the key to self-regulation, advocacy and representation of all stakeholders. The French Franchise Federation also supports the European Franchise Federation's (EFF) Code of Practice that stipulates good conduct of members.
- The Baltic Franchising Association, founded in 2004 with the aim of protecting, enhancing, and promoting franchising in the territory of the Baltic States and bordering regions, is the only franchise association active in Lithuania. The association adheres to the EFF's Code of Ethics.[66]
- Romania has a franchise trade association with a Code of Ethics that is binding on its members.[67]
- The Russian Franchise Association was formed in 1997 for support and protection of the interests of its members and to create a more favourable legal and business environment for the expansion of franchising in Russia. The Association has incorporated a Code of Ethics that applies to the relationship between franchisor and franchisees as well as between master franchisee and franchisees. However, it does not apply to the relationship between a franchisor and its master franchisee.[68]
- The Spanish Franchise Association conforms to the European Code

---

65 The Association's website is <http://www.fbf-bff.be> at 29 December 2009.

66 Schwartz and Zylberman,'Franchise Symposium Materials: International Franchise Regulation' (2008) 8 *Asper Review of International Business and Trade Law* 317, 338.

67 The Association's website is <http://www.francifranchisor.ro> at 29 December 2009. Schwartz and Zylberman, 'Franchise Symposium Materials: International Franchise Regulation' (2008) 8 *Asper Review of International Business and Trade Law* 317, 340.

68 The Association's website is <http://rarf.ru/eng> at 29 December 2009. For more information see Schwartz and Zylberman, 'Franchise Symposium Materials: International Franchise Regulation' (2008). See also 8 *Asper Review of International Business and Trade Law* 317, 342.

of Ethics for Franchising. In addition, it has adopted its own supplementary ethical provisions.[69]
- The Ukrainian Franchise Association was established in 2001.[70]
- The China Chain Store and Franchise Association, founded in 1997, is the leading advocate, representative and resource for entrepreneurs with regular chain, franchise chain, and licensing formats in China. The Association is responsible for mandating rules and codes of conduct for franchise operations and promoting franchise development.[71]
- The Taiwan Chain Store and Franchise Association operates in the Republic of China.[72]
- Indonesia has a franchise trade association.[73]
- The Japan Franchise Association was established in 1972. Members must abide by its Code of Ethics.[74]
- The Korean Franchise Association has adopted a Code of Ethics.[75]
- The Malaysian Franchise Association, established in 1994, enforces a Code of Ethics of Professional Conduct of Franchise Practitioners.
- The Franchise Council of Australia was established in 1983. Information about the Australian Code of Conduct is provided on the association website.[76]

There are three categories of activities typically engaged in by franchise trade associations, branding and promotion of franchising, services to members, and external relations. As part of these activities, many have adopted Codes of Conduct or Ethics.

---

[69] The Association's website is <http://www.franquiciadores.com> at 29 December 2009.

[70] The Association's website is <http://www.franchising.org.ua> at 29 December 2009.

[71] Schwartz and Zylberman, 'Franchise Symposium Materials: International Franchise Regulation' (2008). 8 *Asper Review of International Business and Trade Law* 317, 351.

[72] The Association's website is <http://www.tcfa.org.tw> at 29 December 2009.

[73] The Association's website is <http://www.franchiseindonesia.org> at 29 December 2009.

[74] Schwartz and Zylberman, 'Franchise Symposium Materials: International Franchise Regulation' (2008) 8 *Asper Review of International Business and Trade Law* 317, 355.

[75] The Association's website is <http://www.ikfa.or.kr> at 29 December 2009; the Code is available at <http://www.ikfa.or.kr/manual.htm> at 29 December 2009.

[76] The Council's website is <www.franchise.org.au> at 29 December 2009; see <http://www.franchise.org.au/scripts/cgiip.exe/WService=FCAWWW/ccms.r? PageId=10068>.

Codes of conduct or ethics in 20 countries as well as the EFF Code were evaluated for the provision of 21 categories of requirements contained in the Codes. Of the 21 requirements surveyed Hong Kong and Malaysia each required 15 items; India and Israel each 13 items; Republic of Korea, 14 items; and Japan, 12 items. Canada, the US, the EFF, Belgium, Croatia, Czech Republic, Finland, Greece, Italy, Slovenia, United Kingdom each require about nine items. Ireland requires ten items; Egypt, eight; Mexico, four; and New Zealand, five. Each 'item', however, can comprise a significant amount of information, including subsets of information. This survey therefore offers just a general idea of how the codes are configured; the results are shown in Table 8.7.

The codes, like franchise-specific legislation, appear to rely heavily on disclosure. The main difference seems to be that codes are more likely to include other substantive requirements such as good faith, ensuring the quality of franchisees, and providing support to franchisees.

The literature on inter-firm cooperation and associations within business and industry includes little research into the roles played by franchising associations, and more is needed because of the important role played by associations.[77] According to current conceptions of regulation and governance, the role of trade associations becomes more pervasive.[78]

Trade associations play a role in the governance of the franchise

---

[77] For research on the roles of trade associations generally, see, eg, Robert Bennett, 'Business Associations and their potential contribution to the competitiveness of SME's' (1998) 10 *Entrepreneurship and Regional Development* 243; Khalid Nadvi, *Facing the New Competition: Business Associations in Developing Country Industrial Clusters* (1999); Carmen D. Caruso, 'How Independent Franchisee Associations Can Effectively Influence Franchisor Behavior' (2004) Carmen D. Caruso <http://www.cdcaruso.com/2B4123/assets/files/Documents/cdcaruso%20no11tenlegalissues.pdf> at 29 December 2009; Rochelle Spandorf and Rupert Barkoff, 'Close Encounters: Franchisee Associations and Councils' (Paper presented at the American Bar Association 26th Annual Forum on Franchising, Hollywood, Florida, USA, 22–24 October 2003); Diez-DeCastro, Navarro-Garcia, Rodriguez-Raz, Rondan-Cataluna, 'Membership in the Franchising System: A Worldwide Analysis' (Paper Presented at the 22nd Annual International Society of Franchising Conference, Saint Malo, France, 20–21 June 2008); J.F. Preble, 'Franchising Systems around the Globe: A Status Report' (1995) 33(2) *Journal of Small Business Management* 80–88; Preble and Hoffman, 'The nature of ethics codes in franchise associations around the globe' (1999) 18(3) *Journal of Business Ethics* 239–53; J.C. Real and B. Sanz, 'Study of determinant factors in the associationism of the franchisors in Spain' in Constantin Zopounidis, Panos M. Pardalos, *Managing In Uncertainty: Theory and Practice* (1998), 295–306.

[78] Edward L. Rubin, 'Commentary: The New Legal Process, the Synthesis of Discourse and the Microanalysis of Institutions' (1996) 109 *Harvard Law Review* 1393.

*Table 8.7 Common requirements of trade association codes of conduct or ethics*

| Code Requirement | Number of Codes Surveyed that Contain the Requirement |
|---|---|
| Disclose to prospective franchisees | 19 |
| Resolve disputes fairly and or in good faith | 18 |
| Ensure qualified franchisees | 17 |
| Provide notice to franchisees re termination and time to remedy | 17 |
| Provide full management support to franchisees | 17 |
| Compete fairly | 16 |
| Share information with franchisor | 14 |
| Devote best efforts to the franchise | 12 |
| Own IP | 15 |
| Protect brand/IP | 10 |
| Engage in no misleading or deceptive conduct | 9 |
| Uphold the reputation of the franchise sector | 8 |
| Provide agreement in writing | 8 |
| Clearly state responsibilities and obligations | 7 |
| Obey all laws and regulations | 6 |
| Not discriminate | 5 |
| Communicate with franchisees | 4 |
| Make payments as per agreement | 4 |
| Provide a proven/successful business format | 3 |
| Not engage in pyramid schemes | 2 |
| Not prohibit franchisee association | 0 |

relationship, not just in the most commonly thought-of sense of regulation with respect to lobbying activities in influencing government intervention, but at every layer of governance. Franchising offers a rich context for studying the inter-dependency of private and public ordering, for exploring the role of franchise associations in governance and the extent to which governments should defer to privately-developed standards.[79] The activities of trade associations impact the market interactions between franchisor and franchisee, as well as their contractual expectations and arrangements. Trade associations can also influence judicial decision-

[79] Annette Burkeen, 'Private Ordering and Institutional Choice: Defining the Role of Multinational Corporations in Promoting Global Labour Standards' (2007) 6 *Washington University Global Studies Law Review* 205, 208.

making, government policy and legislative intervention. Further, the internationalization of public decision-making increases the potential for trade associations to be 'important intermediaries for corporate public affairs'. They become a key strand in the web of regulation, not just domestically, but on a global scale.[80]

The role of the association in informing regulatory process by providing information to government and political influence; by advising lawmakers and regulators; and in the promulgation and enforcement of standards is an evolving one.[81] There is an opportunity for associations to become more integrally involved in this process with a benefit to lawmakers of greater expertise, direct experience, legitimacy and political support and benefit to the association of better access in policy formation.[82]

Over the coming years it will be interesting to observe the role of trade associations in the regulation of the sector globally. It may be that the presence of trade associations may act to limit the growth of sector-specific regulation, but alternatively their presence and activities could encourage and shape its continued development. Chapter 9 discusses in greater detail the roles played by the various participants in franchising and its regulation.

## A LARGER ROLE FOR CONDUCT LEGISLATION

Over half of the thirty or so jurisdictions that have implemented franchise-specific regulation have promulgated some laws aimed toward balancing power in the relationship. These relationship laws are comprised primarily of prescriptive and procedural legislation.

Prescriptive legislation includes contract form and language requirements, unfair and mandatory contract terms legislation. Only two countries have proposed unfair contract terms legislation that applies to franchising, and one of these has since abandoned the idea. More common are laws that impose mandatory contract terms. Contract terms of some

---

80 For an excellent overview of regulation of business generally see John Braithwaite and Peter Drahos, *Global Business Regulation* (2000).

81 On the FCA's role see SmartCompany.com.au, 'Franchise Council hits back at critics' (15 September 2008) SmartCompany.com.au <http://www.smartcompany.com.au/Free-Articles/The-Briefing/20080915-Franchise-Council-hits-back-at-critics.html> at 29 December 2009; Stephen Giles (Deacons), Australia: 'FCA Responds To WA & SA Inquiries' (18 September 2008) Mondaq <http://www.mondaq.com/article.asp?articleid=66140> at 29 December 2009.

82 Cornelia Woll and Alvaro Artigas, 'When trade liberalization turns into regulatory reform: The impact on business–government relations in international trade politics' (2007) 1 *Regulation and Governance* 121–38, 121.

kind are required in twelve of the approximately thirty countries that have implemented franchise-specific legislation. Though content requirements are quite common, the particular content specified varies widely. Mandatory contract terms require, variously, specification of fees and payments, training, and listing of obligations of franchisor and franchisee. Such requirements must be carefully calibrated for maximum efficiency and effectiveness. Without a high level of specificity, the regulation is less likely to be effective, but highly specific rules run a greater risk of interference with freedom of contract.

Mandatory contract terms in some jurisdictions involve prescribing a procedure, such as a dispute resolution procedure, as in Moldova, China, Indonesia, Australia, and Vietnam. Other procedural standards for performance of the contract in some countries include substantive and procedural requirements for assignment and transfer, termination, and/or renewal. In most jurisdictions, however, relatively few procedural provisions have been trialled outside of dispute resolution.

Other than content control there is prescriptive legislation aimed at conduct/performance with respect to specific terms or aspects of the relationship. Such legislation addresses variously confidentiality, encroachment, supply and pricing requirements, restrictive covenants, training and technical assistance, protection of intellectual property, unilateral amendment, and others. This legislation can be similar in form and effect to specific unfair contract terms provisions, in particular where unfair contract terms are highly prescriptive.

Good faith is a measure that, though it is not common in franchise-specific legislation, is widely applicable to and potentially effective for the regulation of franchising. Currently, however, approaches to the application of good faith in franchising vary widely among jurisdictions. They are not well understood, and less well harmonized.

Compared with disclosure regulations, 'conduct laws to redress the power imbalance remain more controversial, generate heated debate and have much less support.'[83] This, despite the fact that disclosure is not intended, and has never been proven, to be effective in redressing imbalance of power in the performance of the agreement.

Where disclosure is effective, it is as a tool to balance the positions of contracting parties during the formation of the contract. Disclosure does

---

[83] A. Terry, 'A Census of International Franchise Regulation' (Paper presented at 21st Annual International Society of Franchising Conference, Las Vegas, Nevada, USA, 24–25 February 2007). See also L.G. Rudnick, 'Trends: where do Franchisors and Franchisees stand on Regulation?' (1999) November/December, *Franchising World*, 24–7.

little to address problems of opportunism described in relation to contract terms (discussed in Chapter 3). For example, with respect to scope of grant, disclosure informs a franchisee what the territory is and what rights a franchisor has. Such information may assist franchisees to understand and protect themselves against their risk exposure, but franchisees are still taken by surprise. With respect to franchisor brand maintenance what can be disclosed is that it is a franchisor's role to carry out this function, and that the contract provides that a franchisor will do so at its discretion. Disclosure offers little protection for issues that arise with respect to training, minimum performance, supply, unilateral amendment, contract duration and renewal. Nor do other pre-sales measures such as registration and warnings provide such protection.

The traditional regulatory focus on contract formation that prevails in many jurisdictions is underpinned by the philosophy that while it may be the province of the state to protect parties in entering contracts to ensure the agreement they reach is fair, courts should not re-write agreements once they are made. This approach, however, has been eroded in other areas of contract law, such as employment law and consumer protection. A similar shift in the franchise context is warranted for several reasons. The first is that the terms of the contract deal primarily with performance obligations that are not addressed through regulation of formation and termination of the contract, a fact often overlooked by external regulators.[84] Second, the terms of the contract favour the franchisor in the performance of the contract, explicitly and/or by according to the franchisor a high level of discretion, thus exposing franchisees to uncertainty and risk. Third, the employment and consumer-like attributes of the relationship mitigate in favour of regulation that reflects these multi-faceted roles in franchise relationships.

Performance-oriented intervention offers a range of possibilities, procedural and prescriptive, to supplement pre-sales legislation. Each of these possibilities offers its own particular challenges, which must be considered in the context of interaction with other regulatory measures. International Institute for the Unification of Private Law (UNIDROIT) guidance for relationship/conduct legislation, similar to that provided for disclosure,

---

[84] '[W]hile the [Federal Trade Commission] continues to concentrate its enforcement efforts on pre-sale franchise issues, most of the problems faced by franchisees are post-sale, after the contract is signed, i.e. encroachment, sourcing of supplies, etc.' American Franchisee Association, 'FTC's Franchise Rule requires private right of action to be effective' (2002) American Franchisee Association <http://www.franchisee.org/Blast%20Fax/0207%20Blast%20Fax%20Special%20 Edition.pdf> at 27 December 2009.

would be useful not only on a practical level but also as a general acknowledgement that relationship legislation has the potential to fill gaps where legislation directed toward formation of the contract fails to address power imbalance in the franchise relationship. Relationship legislation for franchising is at present a patchwork. It can be hoped that the next few years of franchising regulation will bring greater unification to these disparate approaches.

# 9. Future directions for the regulation of franchising

This book began by describing the nature of franchising, the franchise relationship and the governance of that relationship in the context of current theoretical approaches to governance. The second half of the book has been devoted to legislative approaches and tools with a survey and analysis of franchise-specific legislation.

While the information presented here offers many interesting points of departure for regulators, practitioners and researchers, there are two key gaps which need to be addressed here by way of conclusion.

One important gap is in the assessment of the effectiveness of regulation. No one has fully tested its costs and benefits. Assessment of the regulation of franchising in any jurisdiction should be part of a program of monitoring and revising the regulatory program to ensure its optimum function, rather than arising on an ad hoc basis often in response to political exigencies that then skew the process. Among the eight countries that have revised franchising legislation since 1990, there seems to be no common standard regarding ongoing monitoring and review of legislation. Regulatory review should be fully participative and transparent and should be scheduled at regular intervals and at various levels of detail in order to mitigate the impact of political pressure on regulatory process.

The second gap, perhaps more important, is that this survey of the *results* of processes of regulating does not peel back this information in order to comment on the processes of regulating themselves. Looking at outcomes is one way to evaluate process, but it is limited in what it can tell us. Process is itself an outcome, an end in itself, and we are not looking at this here. It does appear that many countries' legislative regimes have adopted legislation without first engaging in a regulatory process that would comport with concepts of best practice, not only in the development and implementation phases, but in monitoring and revision. The remainder of this concluding chapter is devoted to process, closing the circle with the discussion of new theories of regulatory process in Chapter 1.

With the understanding that much more work remains to be done with regard to the measuring effectiveness, and that a survey of this kind can comment on regulation, but can never substitute for best practice in regulatory process, this chapter can raise the possibility of revisions to regulation. It can suggest measures that at the municipal level may help to address some of the more pressing issues in the current regulatory program for franchising.

- First, in order to assure the best possible results from regulatory programs currently in place in many jurisdictions, the effectiveness of self-regulatory tools and approaches such as disclosure and dispute resolution should be assured. In conjunction with this, as regulation is revised, alternative approaches can be explored, including ensuring the parties' effectiveness in self-regulatory mechanisms in their market and contractual interactions, and/or through appropriate judicial interpretation and, finally, where necessary, statutory intervention.

Ensuring the effectiveness of self-regulatory tools and approaches means providing the necessary support for the self-regulatory capacities of the parties. Effective self-regulation allows for the parties' and other stakeholders' involvement not only in procedural but also in prescriptive and performance-based measures by including them in regulatory process. Better regulation of franchising is regulation that supports self-regulatory approaches at every layer of interaction in the contractual relationship.

In particular, better support is needed for disclosure and dispute resolution. Disclosure is already a central part of regulatory programs in the majority of countries that regulate the sector. These countries are unlikely to abandon their current regulatory programs, and it is not necessary for them to do so. However, there are many measures that could be taken to improve the capacity of parties to effectively play their role and so enhance the function of disclosure. Education, for example, has been shown to work well with disclosure measures.

Support for the self-regulatory capacities of the parties is needed not only where legislation involves self-regulatory tools such as disclosure, but also in private layers of governance. There is evidence that attitudes toward the regulation of the franchise sector may in some cases involve an internal contradiction with respect to self-regulation. On one hand there seems a firmly-held assumption that self-regulation can be relied upon in private layers, as legal approaches to the arrangement strive to protect the freedom of the parties to make their own bargain at the private layers of governance. Yet the *raison d'être* for legislative intervention is that these dealings are by their nature often inefficient and/or unfair.

A structure of governance for franchising that favours self-regulatory approaches as part of a 'hands-off' approach for government with respect to the parties' private interaction therefore seems at best naïve, as there is in fact an important role for policy-makers to influence the dynamics of private interactions. (Such a structure of governance is also misleading because such influence is actually exercised, but in inchoate ways.)

Possible measures to address this issue at the market layer could include risk statements and greater emphasis on education, which also serves as a form of qualification of participants. Possible measures that might be implemented at the layer of contract are help with negotiation, collective understanding of terms, and the 'contracting community'. Legislation aimed at the conduct of the relationship can include more substantive, prescriptive measures such as mandatory contract terms as well as broader instruments such as an implied duty of good faith.

- Second, where legislation is required, it should employ a full range of tools, not only procedural, but also, where appropriate, prescriptive and performance-based tools. It should also employ tools directed toward performance of the agreement as well as its formation.

Current heavy reliance on self-regulatory and procedural tools means regulators fail to avail themselves of a full range of prescriptive and performance-based tools. The legal convention of regulating formation and refraining from intervention in performance of contracts is outdated. The focus on contract formation should be balanced with measures aimed towards ensuring fairness and efficiency during the performance of the contract. Performance-based and prescriptive measures for specific applications can be used to supplement and provide balance to the current weighting toward procedural measures.

Perhaps the lack of stakeholder input in regulatory process explains the seeming reluctance to employ a wide range of tools. Lack of stakeholder input may also explain why regulatory tools used in statutory intervention in franchising are focused on contract formation. Proper regulatory process, which is the third and most important recommended revision, could help to address these issues.

A regulatory process that involves all stakeholders and all the necessary information in identifying the problems and in selecting the means to address them is the ideal way to ensure that tools are the right tools and that they are effective in implementation. Once thought of as solely the province of governments, the 'new learning' on regulation seeks to reframe regulatory activity in a much broader scope than traditional conceptions. According to this 'new learning' regulation happens at many layers of interaction between stakeholders and participants in a regulated activity. Whatever action is taken at one layer will have impacts on the others. Therefore, exchange of information and participative process is critical to ensure the effective interaction of activities and interventions at all these layers and by various actors.

- Therefore, lastly, but most importantly, it is recommended that those seeking to regulate must recognize the importance of proper process.

The revision to any regulatory program that is most important overall is process. Proper regulatory process will support the self-regulatory capacities of the parties by enhancing their role in public layers of governance. At the same time as the parties' interaction is protected at private layers of governance, the command-and-control role of government appears to persist in legislating, administering and enforcing the regime of legislated intervention. The parties' involvement, so protected in their private interaction, is less evident in processes of government intervention.

This is understandable when one considers that legislative intervention is often a response to failures/inefficiencies of private governance. What makes less sense is that stakeholder participation often appears to be minimal in aspects of regulatory process such as gathering information, in generating alternative measures, and in monitoring and reviewing the effectiveness of regulation. The fact that there is inefficiency at the private layer is not a valid reason to cut out the parties from participating at layers of public governance.

Proper regulatory process will result in increased permeability among layers of governance, and so enhance their effectiveness. Rigid distinctions between private and public governance that seem to prevail in regulatory practice impair the effectiveness of governance at every layer. Permeability among the layers of governance can result in more reflexive and responsive regulation, increased cooperation and a better balancing of the roles of the parties, the regulator and the courts. By improving their interaction, all these layers of governance can interact more effectively together, and complement each other, rather than creating conflicts and dissonances where one layer prevents the effective function or compounds the inefficiencies of another.

Returning to the three fundamental elements of regulatory process outlined in Chapter 1, it is possible to establish a framework upon which to structure process. Such a process starts with orientation toward outcomes based upon better measurements. It continues with selection of the appropriate mix of regulatory tools to meet agreed objectives, and it incorporates collaborative principles throughout the process.

The first of these elements is reliable information. In the interests of a regulatory process that is outcome-oriented and informed by the best information attainable, measures must be put in place to ensure reliable information about the sector and individual franchise systems. Information about what is happening in the sector must be sourced in a balanced way from all participants. Better measurements and information will result in regulatory practice that fits more closely the needs of the sector and has greater legitimacy, accountability and responsiveness. Any deficiency of reliable information seriously compromises any attempt to gauge the risks in informing the design of regulatory process and also compromises the selection of appropriate regulatory tools.

Many avenues are available to obtain meaningful measurements to inform regulatory process generally. These include cooperation with legitimate, independent research initiatives; information from franchisees and franchisors, through, for example, the use of an intranet; studies and surveys that accurately reflect all stakeholders' interests; representation of stakeholders on consultative panels; and as complete information as practicable from dispute processes.

Stakeholders/participants who are equipped with reliable information are best situated to identify problems in the sector. These participants in each jurisdiction must determine the issues to be addressed, for most problems within the sector stem from the opportunism that leads to lack of trust and inefficiencies in terms of costs and risks. While consistency is desirable, there is no universal, ideal formulation. Instead, each jurisdiction must arrive at a regulatory regime best suited to its culture and political, legal and economic conditions, hopefully with an eye toward harmonizing as much as possible with regulatory requirements in other jurisdictions generally, and particularly those that may overlap with its own.

The need to tailor regulatory approaches to particular needs makes even more compelling the need for stakeholders themselves to participate in determining the best regulatory regime through proper regulatory process. Through a democratic, participative, transparent process, the information must be collected, and the important issues identified. Only then can the most appropriate mix of tools be selected to fix the problems, maximizing synergies to improve the efficacy of regulation. Finally, a collaborative mechanism can be put in place to monitor their progress.

Professor Andrew Terry warns that, 'Regulation cannot remove all commercial risk and it cannot guarantee business success. Education, conscientious due diligence and informed advice – legal, financial, commercial – are also integral elements of the protectionary matrix.'[1] And so they are, and so is the full range of solutions that proper process seeks to ensure.

Making the right choices in the process of legislating requires regulatory

---

1 See <http://www.crowtherblayne.com.au/excellence_in_franchising_awards_06_26.pdf> at 26 December 2009.

process that is consultative, identifies the harm, identifies potential solutions, implements an appropriate mix of tools, monitors the outcomes, and adjusts accordingly. This book is not about whether or not there should be franchise-specific legislation (though the imbalance of power at layers of market and contract suggest that it is needed unless and until other strategies can be devised), but rather it is about what the need is and how that need is met.

Collaborative process is critical. Parker writes that the question of how law should react or respond to plural social orderings raises fundamental questions of the role of law in multicultural and trans-national contexts. Pluralized law must incorporate reflexive and responsive catalysing processes that enable consensus on values. Pluralized law must also simultaneously adopt and apply the agreed values to those processes in order to make participation in them possible and to evaluate their outcomes. Reflexive and responsive law do not derive their substantive goals from the law itself, but from political discussion outside the law. That discussion must happen freely, fairly, and continuously to ensure the appropriateness of the substantive goals and outcomes that result. Such a process implies not a dictate of the state but rather the product of plural social orderings within and outside states.[2]

The process of the regulation of the franchise sector is an international concern as well as a municipal one, and it encompasses a range of diverse interests including those of franchisees, franchisors, suppliers, consultants, trade associations, administrators, courts, and legislators. Regulation can be delegated and derived from many sources, via a network of stakeholders, policy makers, consumer groups and international organisations.[3] The state is no longer thought to be the only one doing the regulating, 'The fact of regulation has nothing to do with who does the regulation. A regulator is any person with the power to regulate. Private parties may be regulators just as effectively as many government entities.'[4]

Collaborative principles are incorporated throughout regulatory process that reflects current concepts of best practice.[5] To ensure a commitment

---

[2] And overall Parker suggests there must be an aspiration to universal applicability in order that the concept of law can remain normatively meaningful. Christine Parker, 'The Pluralization of Regulation' (2008) 9(2) *Theoretical Inquiries in Law* Article 2.

[3] Vijaya Nagarajan, 'Reconceiving Regulation: Finding a Place for the Consumer' (2007) 15 *Competition and Consumer Law Journal* 7, 20.

[4] Warren Pengilley, 'Competition Regulation in Australia: A Discussion of a Spider Web and its Weaving' (2001) 8 *Competition and Consumer Law Journal* 2, 51.

[5] One of the most effective techniques for achieving almost any desired change in NLP is the 'six step re-frame'. Institute of Semantic Restructuring,

to collaborative process the role of the regulator makes a transition away from command-and-control in administration and enforcement. The regulator's new role is not to impose rules, but to promote best regulatory process that is democratic, participative and responsive.

This is not an easy transition, but it is a significant one. For, if it imposes rules without the benefit of full participation, the regulator forfeits the opportunity to ensure appropriate regulation, and may hamper the healthy development of the sector. If, on the other hand, the regulator oversees and coordinates regulation at every level, through the operation of the market, the parties' agreements, court interpretations, and, if necessary, through legislation, then it is possible, 'to develop procedures and institutional structures that will enhance deliberation and enable participation'.[6]

In a reflexive regulatory system, the role of the regulator in assisting all stakeholders in the development, enforcement and monitoring of regulation becomes one of facilitator and promoter of the integrity of process. For the regulator a shift in emphasis from command to inducement to facilitation, from ruler to supervisor to servant/enabler of process does not necessarily mean a reduced role, but rather a more multi-faceted one. The inclusion of a wider range of stakeholders creates multiple roles for the regulatory agency such as that of catalyst, facilitator, mediator, broker, and provider of framework rules and regulatory support.[7]

There is in many jurisdictions an unwarranted level of reliance on self-regulatory mechanisms and tools, despite overwhelming evidence that the parties lack the capacity to fulfil their roles as such measures require. At a time when virtually all human endeavour is judged on the basis of its market value, administrative branches of government are not exempt from this calculus. The role of regulators is often no different from that of functionaries in other sectors, where the object of the game is to be (or to be seen to be) as productive and/or effective as possible while actually expending the minimum of effort and/or energy and/or resources. In the regulation of commercial enterprise the administrative branches of many governments have recognized self-regulation's strategic value in this game.

If self-regulation is hampered by a lack of capacity or necessary expertise, a regulator can help to ensure or supply this. Though it may be ill-equipped

---

'Anthropomorphized: Utilization of Ideo-Sensory Responses' (2009) <http://www.semanticrestructuring.com/anthro_ideo.php> at 30 December 2009.

6 Julia Black, 'Proceduralising Regulation: Part I' (2000) 20 Oxford *Journal of Legal Studies* 597.

7 Taskforce on Self Regulation, 'Appendix D: International Policy on Self Regulation' (2007) Australian Government: The Treasury <http://www.treasury.gov.au/documents/1123/HTML/docshell.asp?URL=appd.asp > at 30 December 2009.

to evaluate when to intervene in some forms of self-regulation, such evaluation can be made cooperatively, taking into account the interests of all stakeholders at all stages through the various layers. The regulator can play a coordinating role in ensuring the appropriate forms and levels of regulation for the particular industry context. Regulators can assist participation by designing and facilitating procedures whereby efficient and effective regulation of the franchise sector comprehends and involves the interests of all stakeholders at all stages.

To the extent that collaborative process exists in the regulation of the franchise sector at the present time, it appears to often exclude key stakeholders, notably franchisees. The under-representation of franchisee interests at all 'layers' of regulation is a concern. The focus of regulators is often on the supply side. To improve the ability of franchisees to act on the disclosed information, the regulatory focus needs to shift to a more balanced consideration of both the supply and the demand side.[8]

The intention of a franchisee is not clear in the market interaction; generally, a franchisee enters the relationship with misconceptions about the nature of the relationship. A franchisee is then foreclosed from participating in the contracting process in which it acts as a consumer and as the weaker party to a standard-form contract. With respect to statutory regulation, even though it is the protected interest, a franchisee has a negligible voice at the table with government officials in formulating regulatory intervention.

A franchisee can be marginalized in every aspect of the regulatory process, in contrast to franchisor interests that tend to dominate most aspects of governance of the relationship. Imbalance of power and uncertainty for a franchisee will persist as long as a franchisee is left out of governance processes. Franchisees can play a greater role at the market level, by greater involvement in information dissemination and collective action; at the level of contract through collective understanding of terms; in court proceedings by providing information; and in statutory intervention by taking their proper place in informing legislation as stakeholders.

The harmonious integration of franchisees into the operation of franchise systems may even be the keystone in the future success of this business form. As J.S. Mill observed over 160 years ago, 'The form of association . . . which if mankind continue to improve, must be expected in the end to

---

[8] Organisation for Economic Cooperation and Development, 'Roundtable on economics for consumer policy: summary report' (June 2007) Directorate for Science, Technology and Industry, Committee on Consumer Policy, OECD <http://www.oecd.org/dataoecd/5/38/39015963.pdf> at 22 December 2009.

predominate, is . . . the association of the labourers themselves on terms of equality, collectively owning the capital with which they carry on their operations. . . .'[9] Franchisees already own the capital. What is left to claim are terms of equality, if franchising is to realize its potential as a predominant form of commercial association. Franchisees and franchisors are part of the same system. Because strong franchisees make for more profitable franchise systems for all participants and for a healthier industry sector, empowering franchisees and increasing their participation at all layers of governance ultimately will help to prevent schisms from within and ensure its future success and profitability.

It is also important to revise the roles of franchisors and trade associations in regulatory process. Among the various stakeholder groups, franchisors have the greatest opportunity to enhance the operation and image of the sector. Some researchers in management argue that now more than ever our society needs a massive injection of cooperative culture and cooperative practice.[10] Through better integration of good management and leadership and through commitment to the success of the brand and the system, including the success of each franchise unit, franchisors can ensure better governance at all layers of the interaction.

Regulating the franchise sector is not a task that should be left to a handful of experts and administrators. Best practice in regulation calls for participative, responsive and reflexive process to ensure the provision of accurate and reliable information; to inform baseline measurements; to enable collaborative consultation for identifying the principal problems and goals of regulation; and to draw from a full menu of regulatory measures to meet them.

Quality franchisors sell a right to franchisees that is worth the price; franchisees in well-run systems can themselves enjoy handsome profits. Because opportunistic behaviours are not the norm, well-run franchise systems will benefit from reframed regulatory process and renewed measures to prevent abusive practices where they do occur. This will not only prevent harm to individual franchisees, but will also ensure a favourable image of the sector as a whole.

---

9 John Stuart Mill, *Principles of Political Economy* (ed, 2001) 606.

10 Stefano Zamagni, 'Comparing capitalistic and cooperative firms on the ground of humanistic management' (Paper presented at the 1st IESE Conference: 'Humanizing the Firm and Management Profession', Barcelona, IESE Business School, 30 July 2008) <http://papers.ssrn.com/sol3/papers.cfm?abstract_id=1295314> at 5 December 2009.

# Appendix 1 Franchise legislation worldwide

## THE AMERICAS

### Barbados

Franchises (Registration and Control) Act 1974 as amended, Cap 179A (Barbados)

### Brazil

Law 8.955 2004 (Brazil)

### Canada

**Alberta**
Franchises Act F-23 2000 (Alberta)
Franchises Regulation 240 1995 (Alberta)
Franchises Act Exemption Regulation 312 2000 (Alberta)

**New Brunswick**
Franchises Act F-23.5 2007 (New Brunswick)

**Ontario**
Arthur Wishart Act (Franchise Disclosure) 2000 (Ontario)
Ontario Regulation 581/00 2000 (Ontario)

**Prince Edward Island**
Franchises Act F-14.1 1988 (PEI)
Franchises Act Regulations Reg EC232/06 2006 (PEI)

### Mexico

Industrial Property Law 1991 (Mexico)
Industrial Property Regulations 1994 (Mexico)

### The United States

Title 16 – Commercial Practices; Revised as of January 1, 1986, Chapter I – Federal Trade Commission, Subchapter D – Trade Regulation Rules, Part 436 – Disclosure Requirements and Prohibitions Concerning Franchising and Business Opportunity Ventures (the FTC Rule).

## EUROPE

### Republic of Albania

Civil Code of the Republic of Albania, Chapter XX, Articles 1056 to 1064

### Republic of Belarus

Civil Code No 218-Z 1998 (Republic of Belarus)

### Belgium

Law relative to pre-contractual information in the framework of agreements of commercial partnership 2006 (Belgium)

### Estonia

Law of Obligations Act 2002 (Estonia)

### France

The *Loi Doubin* on Pre-contractual Disclosure 1986 (France)
Decree N° 91-337 1991 (France)
Order 1991 (France)

### Italy

Rules on the Regulation of Franchising 2004 (Italy)

### Lithuania

Civil Code 2000 (Republic of Lithuania)

**Republic of Moldova**

The Civil Code of the Republic of Moldova, Law Nr. 1335 of 01.10.1997

**Romania**

ORDINANCE Nr 52 of 28 August 1997 regarding the franchise legal framework

**Russia**

The Civil Code of the Russian Federation, Chapter 54. The Commercial Concession

**Spain**

Law 7/1996, of 15 of January, Arrangement of Retail Comercio. TITLE I. CHAPTER VI. OF THE COMMERCIAL ACTIVITY IN FRANCHISE. Article 62.

Real Decree 2485/1998 regarding the regulation of franchise and the registry of franchisors. INDUSTRY MINISTRY, TOURISM AND COMMERCE 7458 REAL DECREE 419/2006 of 7 of April, by that Real Decree 2485/1998 modifies, of 13 of November, regarding the regulation of franchise and the registry of franchisors.

**Sweden**

Law on the Duty of a Franchisor to Provide Information (24 May 2006, Law No. 2006:484)

**Ukraine**

Ukraine Civil Code Chapter 36, Business Use Rights – Other Businesses (Commercial Concessions) Articles 366 to 375

## ASIA

**People's Republic of China**

Administrative Measures for Archiving Commercial Franchises 2007 (People's Republic of China)

Measures for the Administration of Information Disclosure of Commercial Franchises 2007 (People's Republic of China)
Regulations for the Administration of Commercial Franchising Operations – China Franchise Regulations (I) 2007 (People's Republic of China)
Commercial Franchise Registration Management Measures – Chinese Franchise Regulations (II) 2007 (People's Republic of China)

**China – Taiwan**

Fair Trade Commission Guidelines on the Disclosure of Information by Franchisors 1999 (Taiwan) 18

**Georgia**

Civil Code of Georgia, (1997) Book Three, Title One, Chapter Seven

**Indonesia**

Regulation on Franchise No 42 2007 (Indonesia)

**Japan**

Medium-Small Retail Business Promotion Act No 101 1973 (Japan)
Ministerial Order No 100 Implementing the Medium-Small Retail Business Act 1973 (Japan)
Unfair Competition Prevention Act 1993 (Japan)
Small and Medium Sized Enterprises Basic Act No. 154 1963 (Japan)
Fair Trade Commission Public Notice No 15 1982 (Japan)
Fair Trade Commission Notification 11 Designation of Specific Unfair Trade Practices by Large-Scale Retailers Relating to Trade with Suppliers 2005 (Japan)

**Kazakhstan**

Law No. 330 of 24 June 2002 concerning the Integrated Business Licence (Franchise)

**Republic of Korea**

Fair Franchise Transaction Act 2002 (Republic of Korea)
Presidential Decree No 17777 Enforcement Decree of the Fair Franchise Transactions Act 2002 (Republic of Korea)

Fair Franchises Transaction Act 2007 (Republic of Korea)
Enforcement Decree of the Fair Franchise Transactions Act 2008 (Republic of Korea)

**Kyrgyz Republic**

Civil Code 1997 (Kyrgyz Republic)

**Macau**

Commercial Code 1999 (Macau)
Law No 6 2000 (Macau)
Decree-Law no. 40/99/M 1999 (Macau)

**Malaysia**

Franchise Act No 590 1998 (Malaysia)

**Socialist Republic of Vietnam**

Decree No 35/2006/ND-CP 2006 (Socialist Republic of Vietnam)

**Australia**

Trade Practices (Industry Codes – Franchising) Amendment Regulations 2007 (No. 1) 2007 (Cth)

# Appendix 2 Content of disclosure

| Country | Content of disclosure |
| --- | --- |
| Canada | None of the Provinces' franchise statutes specifically prescribe the format of a disclosure document, but they all prescribe the list of minimum information that must be provided.<br>Regardless, all disclosure documents must contain all 'material facts', which is any information about the business, operations, capital or control of the franchisor, or its associates, or about the franchise system that would reasonably be expected to have a significant effect on the value or price of the franchise to be offered or the decision to acquire the franchise. The definition of 'material fact' is slightly different, but materially similar, among the Provinces.<br>All four Provinces require the disclosure document to contain the franchisor's prescribed financial statements which must relate to the franchisor and not its parent or associated companies. |
| Alberta | Such disclosure document must contain all material facts, including those facts relating to the matters specifically set out in the Franchises Regulation. 'Material fact' is defined as any information about the business, operations, capital or control of the franchisor or its associate, or about the franchise system, that would reasonably be expected to have a significant effect on the value or price of the franchise to be sold or the decision to purchase the franchise.<br>In addition to copies of all proposed franchise agreements and financial statements, the disclosure document must contain reports and other documents in accordance with the Franchises Regulation.<br>Under Schedule 1 of the Franchises Act, the disclosure document must specifically contain information on the franchisor, previous convictions and pending charges, civil litigation and liabilities, administrative proceedings and existing orders, bankruptcy, nature of the business, initial franchise fee and other fees, initial investment required, financing, working capital, restrictions on sources of products and services and on what franchisees may sell, rebates or other benefits to the franchisor, obligations to participate in the actual operation of the franchise business, existing franchisee and franchisor outlets, franchise closure, earnings claims, termination, renewal and transfer of the franchise, territory, notice of rescission |

| Country | Content of disclosure |
|---|---|
| | and effect of cancellation, right of action for damages, and financial statements.<br>(source: Kendal Tyre, 'Canada: Summary of Franchise Laws of Ontario' 23 December 2007, http://www.lexnoir.org/index_php?option=com_content&task=view&id=98&Itemid=63 at 16 December 2008 |
| Ontario | A disclosure document must contain all material facts, including material facts relating to the matters specified in the Regulations. A 'material fact' is defined as any information about the business, operations, capital or control of the franchisor or its associate, or about the franchise system, that would reasonably be expected to have a significant effect on the value or price of the franchise to be sold or the decision to purchase the franchise.<br>The Ontario Franchise Regulation prescribes that the following shall be disclosed to the prospective franchisee 14 days before either the signing of the document or the payment of fees:<br><br>1. The business background of the franchisor, including,<br>i. the name and address of the franchisor,<br>ii. the name under which the franchisor engages in or intends to engage in business,<br>iii. the principal business address of the franchisor and, if the franchisor's principal address is outside Ontario, the name and address of a person authorized to accept service in Ontario on the franchisor's behalf,<br>iv. the business form of the franchisor, including whether the franchisor is a sole proprietorship, partnership or corporation and, if incorporated, the jurisdiction where the franchisor is incorporated,<br>v. if the franchisor is a subsidiary, the name and principal address of the parent,<br>vi. the length of time the franchisor has engaged in the line of business associated with the franchise,<br>vii. the length of time the franchisor has offered franchises in the line of business associated with the franchise, and<br>viii. if the franchisor has offered a franchise in another line of business, a description of every franchise in each line of business, including for each franchise,<br>A. the length of time the franchisor has offered the franchise to prospective franchisees, and<br>B. the number of franchises sold in the five years immediately preceding the date of the disclosure document. |

| Country | Content of disclosure |
|---|---|
| | 2. The business background of the directors, the general partners and the officers of the franchisor, including<br>3. A statement, including a description of details, indicating whether, during the ten years immediately preceding the date of the disclosure document, the franchisor, the franchisor's associate or a director, general partner or officer of the franchisor has been convicted of fraud, unfair or deceptive business practices, or a violation of a law that regulates franchises or business or if there is a charge pending against the person involving such a matter.<br>4. A statement, including a description of details, indicating whether the franchisor, the franchisor's associate or a director, general partner or officer of the franchisor has been subject to an administrative order or penalty imposed under a law of any jurisdiction regulating franchises or business or if the person is the subject of any pending administrative actions to be heard under such a law.<br>5. A statement, including a description of details, indicating whether the franchisor, the franchisor's associate or a director, general partner or officer of the franchisor has been found liable in a civil action of misrepresentation, unfair or deceptive business practices or violating a law that regulates franchises or businesses, including a failure to provide proper disclosure to a franchisee, or if a civil action involving such allegations is pending against the person.<br>6. Details of any bankruptcy or insolvency proceedings, voluntary or otherwise, any part of which took place during the six years immediately preceding the date of the disclosure document, against any of the following persons as debtors:<br>i. The franchisor or the franchisor's associate.<br>ii. A corporation whose directors or officers include a current director, officer or general partner of the franchisor, or included such a person at a time when the bankruptcy or insolvency proceeding was taking place.<br>iii. A partnership whose general partners include a current director, officer or general partner of the franchisor, or included such a person at a time when the bankruptcy or insolvency proceeding was taking place.<br>iv. A director, an officer or a general partner of the franchisor in their personal capacity.<br>7. An audited financial statement for the most recently completed fiscal year of the franchisor's operations<br>8. Description of mediation or other dispute resolution process<br>9. A list of all of the franchisee's costs associated with the establishment of the franchise, including, |

| Country | Content of disclosure |
|---|---|
| | i. the amount of any deposits or franchise fees, whether the deposits or fees are refundable, and if so, under what conditions,<br>ii. an estimate of the costs for inventory, leasehold improvements, equipment, leases, rentals and all other tangible and intangible property necessary to establish the franchise and an explanation of any assumptions underlying the estimate, and<br>iii. any other costs associated with the establishment of the franchise not listed in subparagraph i or ii, including any payment to the franchisor, whether direct or indirect, required by the franchise agreement, the nature and amount of the payment, and when the payment is due.<br>10. An estimate of annual operating costs for the franchise is provided<br>11. An earnings projection for the franchise is provided<br>12. The terms and conditions of the financing arrangements that the franchisor or the franchisor's associate offers directly or indirectly to franchisees.<br>13. Description of any training or other assistance offered to franchisees by the franchisor or the franchisor's associate, including whether the training is mandatory or optional, and if the training is mandatory, a statement specifying who bears the costs of the training.<br>14. If the franchisee, as a condition of the franchise agreement, is required to contribute to an advertising fund, the projected amount of the contribution<br>15. A description of any restrictions or requirements imposed by the franchise agreement with respect to,<br>i. obligations to purchase or lease from the franchisor, the franchisor's associate or suppliers approved by the franchisor or the franchisor's associate,<br>ii. the goods and services the franchisee may sell, and<br>iii. whom the franchisee may sell goods or services.<br>16. A description of the franchisor's policy, if any, regarding volume rebates, and whether or not the franchisor or the franchisor's associate receives a rebate, commission, payment or other benefit as a result of purchases of goods and services by a franchisee and, if so, whether rebates, commissions, payments or other benefits are shared with franchisees, either directly or indirectly.<br>17. A description of the rights the franchisor or the franchisor's associate has to the trade-mark, service mark, trade name, logo or advertising or other commercial symbol associated with the franchise. |

| Country | Content of disclosure |
|---|---|
| | 18. A description of every licence, registration, authorization or other permission the franchisee is required to obtain, under any applicable federal or provincial law or municipal by-law, to operate the franchise.<br>19. A statement indicating whether the franchisee is required to participate personally and directly in the operation of the franchise or, if the franchisee is a corporation, whether the principals of the corporation are so required.<br>20. A description of any exclusive territory granted to the franchisee.<br>21. The name, last known address and telephone number of each franchisee in Ontario who operated a franchise of the type being offered that has been terminated, cancelled, not renewed or reacquired by the franchisor or otherwise left the system within the last fiscal year immediately preceding the date of the disclosure document.<br>22. For each closure of a franchise of the type being offered within the three fiscal years immediately preceding the date of the disclosure document, the reasons for the closure.<br>23. A list of the locations of all franchises in Ontario of the type being offered, including the business address, telephone number and name of the franchisee who operates the franchise and, if there are less than 20 franchises in Ontario, the list shall include those franchises which are geographically closest to Ontario, until information on 20 franchises is provided.<br>24. A description of all restrictions or conditions in the franchise agreement related to, termination or renewal of the agreement and transfer of franchise. |
| New Brunswick | The Franchises Act requires that the franchisor provide the franchisee with the following information at s 5(4):<br><br>(a) financial statements as prescribed,<br>(b) copies of all proposed franchise agreements and other agreements relating to the franchise to be signed by the prospective franchisee,<br>(c) statements, as prescribed, that are for the purpose of assisting the prospective franchisee in making informed investment decisions,<br><br>S 5(5) states that in addition to the statements, documents and information required by subsection (4), the disclosure document shall contain all material facts. |

| Country | Content of disclosure |
|---|---|
| | 'material fact' means any information, about the business, operations, capital or control of the franchisor or franchisor's associate or about the franchise or the franchise system, that would reasonably be expected to have a significant effect on the value or price of the franchise to be granted or the decision to acquire the franchise. |
| Prince Edward Island | Schedule I of the Franchises Act Regulations prescribes that the following information shall be disclosed to the franchisee 14 days prior to the signing of the document of the payment of any consideration:<br><br>1. business background of the franchisor, including name, business experience, principal business address, other types of franchises offered by the franchisor<br>2. business background of its directors<br>3. whether during the last 10 years, the franchisor or any of its directors or associates have been convicted of fraud, unfair or deceptive pending charges, administrative orders or proceedings, civil actions and liability, bankruptcy<br>4. costs of establishing the franchise, including initial fees, an estimate of the costs for inventory, supplies, leasehold improvements, fixtures, furrnishings, equipment, signs, vehicles, leases, rentals, prepaid expenses and all other tangible or intangible property<br>5. recurring or isolated fees<br>6. guarantees and security interests required of the franchisees<br>7. estimate of operating costs and the basis for the estimate<br>8. earnings projections<br>9. terms and conditions of any financing arrangements<br>10. training and other assistance provided by franchisor<br>11. restrictions and requirements to purchase/lease products and what/to whom the franchisee may sell<br>12. franchisor's policies and practices re rebates, commissions, payments or other benefits<br>13. territory and proximity between franchisees<br>14. trademarks and other proprietary rights related to the franchise<br>15. extent to which the franchisee is required to personally participate in the operation of the franchise<br>16. renewal, termination and transfer of franchise<br>17. dispute resolution<br>18. list of current franchisees<br>19. list of former franchisees |

| Country | Content of disclosure |
|---|---|
| | The Franchises Act under s 5 states that the franchisor disclose to the franchisee all material facts. A material fact means any information, about the business, operations, capital or control of the franchisor or franchisor's associate or about the franchise or the franchise system, that would reasonably be expected to have a significant effect on the value or price of the franchise to be granted or the decision to acquire the franchise. |
| United States | The FTC Rule (2007 version), which, as indicated above, is a disclosure law, requires franchisors to provide prospective franchisees with a document with detailed information regarding:<br>the franchisor and any parents, predecessors and affiliates<br>business experience<br>litigation<br>bankruptcy<br>initial fees<br>other fees<br>estimated initial investment<br>restrictions on sources of products and services<br>franchisee's obligations re financing<br>franchisor's assistance, advertising, computer systems and training<br>territory<br>trademarks<br>patents, copyrights and proprietary information<br>obligation to participate in the actual operation of the franchise business<br>restrictions on what the franchisee may sell<br>renewal, termination, transfer and dispute resolution<br>public figures<br>financial performance representations<br>outlets and franchisee information financial statements. |
| Brazil | Article 3 specifies the information that the franchisor should provide the franchisee:<br><br>(1) Resumed abstract, business structure and full name or commercial style of franchisor and all enterprises to which it is directly linked, as well as the respective trade names and addresses<br>(2) balance sheets and financial statements of the franchise for the last two years<br>(3) all litigations in which the franchisor, controlling enterprises and all title holders of trademarks, copyrights and patents relative to the operation and their sub-franchisors may be involved, challenging the |

| Country | Content of disclosure |
|---|---|
| | franchise system or those that would render the functioning of the franchise system an impossibility<br>(4) detailed franchising description, detailed description of the business and activities to be performed by the franchisee<br>(5) profile of the 'ideal franchisee' re previous experience, education, compulsory or preferable characteristics<br>(6) requirements re direct involvement of franchisee in the operation and administration of franchise<br>(7) estimated initial investment, initial fees, estimated value of the installations, equipment and initial stock and their payment conditions<br>(8) periodical remuneration, rent of equipment or place of business, publicity fee, insurance, other fees due to franchisor or third parties<br>(9) complete list of franchisee, sub-franchisee (including those that left the system in the last 12 months – stating name, address and phone number)<br>(10) territory – whether exclusive or preference for a certain territory is guaranteed to franchisee and the conditions thereof; possibility that franchisee realises sales/services outside the territory<br>(11) obligation that franchisee acquire real estate, services or manufacturing components only from specific suppliers and a list thereof<br>(12) what is offered by the franchisor ie – supervision of chain, training of franchisee or its employees, manuals, assistance in analysis and choice of place of business, layout of franchisee plants<br>(13) situation of trademarks or patents<br>(14) situation of franchisee after expiry of contract re know-how or industrial secrets<br>(15) whether the franchisee may engage in concurrent activities similar to those of the franchisor after the expiry of the contract<br>(16) model of standard agreement |
| Mexico | At Part 65 of the Regulation under Law on Industrial Property the franchisor is required to provide the prospective franchisee with Disclosure documents AFTER the entering into the appropriate agreement.<br>The pre-sale information required to be provided to prospective franchisees includes: I. Name, designation or business, address and nationality of the franchisor; II. Description of the franchise; III. Age of the original franchising company and, where appropriate, main franchisor in the franchise transaction; IV. Intellectual property rights involved in the franchise; V. Amounts and purposes of the payments to be made by the franchisee to the franchisor; VI. Types of technical assistance and services that the franchisor has |

| Country | Content of disclosure |
|---|---|
| | to afford the franchisee; VII. Definition of the territorial area of operation of the business that uses the franchise; VIII. Right of the franchisee to grant or not to grant sub-franchises to third parties, and where appropriate the requirements to be met in order to do so; IX. Obligations of the franchisee regarding information of a privileged character supplied to him by the franchisor; X. In general, the obligations and rights of the franchisee that derive from the conclusion of the franchise contract. |
| Belarus | The Civil Code of the Republic of Belarus does not require the franchisor to provide the franchisee with Disclosure documents.<br>At article 910(3) it states that the franchisor is obliged to:<br>transfer to the user technical and commercial documentation and other information necessary to the user in order to exercise the exclusive rights granted to him under the contract of franchise, and also instruct the user and his employees with regard to questions connected with the exercise of these rights:<br>issue to the user the licences, provided for by the contract of franchise, for the right of using the objects of the intellectual property, specified in Article 910(1) of this Code, ensuring the formalization thereof in the established procedure. |
| Belgium | The disclosure document must contain the following information:<br><br>The main terms of the agreement<br>– whether the agreement is specific to the proposed contracting party and therefore cannot be transferred;<br>– the obligations accepted by the parties;<br>– the consequences of failure to comply with the contractual obligations;<br>– how fees are calculated and details of fee review provisions during the course of the agreement and on its renewal;<br>– non-compete provisions;<br>– the duration of the agreement and the conditions for renewal;<br>– notice provisions, provisions for termination and the consequences of termination; and<br><br>The information on the franchisor and its system<br>– the name of the franchisor, together with details of its address, contact numbers, etc.;<br>– if the franchisor is a corporate entity, the identity and capacity of the person acting as its authorized representative;<br>– the nature of the franchisor's commercial activities; |

| Country | Content of disclosure |
|---|---|
| | – the intellectual property rights to be licensed;<br>– the annual financial statements of the franchisor for the three previous financial years;<br>– details of the franchisor's experience both in franchising and in the use of the 'system' generally;<br>– the background, status and prospects of the market and market shares at the national and local franchisee level;<br>– for each of the three previous years, the number of franchisees in Belgium and internationally, and the prospects for expansion of the network;<br>– for each of the three previous years, the number of agreements entered into, the number of agreements terminated by the franchisor or by franchisees, and the number of agreements that were not renewed upon the expiration of their term; and<br>– the amount and purpose of the charges and investment required from the franchisee, at the start and in the course of the contractual term, together with the depreciation period and the consequences upon termination of the agreement. |
| Estonia | Chapter 19 of the Law of Obligations does not require the franchisor to provide the franchisee with any detailed disclosure, it does require the franchisor to provide the franchisee with instructions for the exercise of the rights thereof and to provide permanent assistance related thereto to the franchisee.<br>It further states that a franchisor has the right to check the quality of the goods manufactured or services provided on the basis of a franchise contract by the franchisee. |
| France | The Decree contains three articles, the first of which specifies the information that must be disclosed.<br>In the event that the conditions are met, certain disclosures must be made 30 days prior to the execution of the franchisor licence agreement. The disclosures include the following items:<br><br>the address of the franchisor and the nature of its activities and the identity of its CEO; the corporate registration details and details about the trade marks; bankers' details; details of the franchisor's history over the preceding five years and a presentation of the general state of the market in respect of the products or services which are subject to the contract as well as the prospects of development of this market. The annual accounts in respect of the last two financial years must be annexed to this part of the document and public companies must exhibit the report established during the |

| Country | Content of disclosure |
|---|---|
| | last two financial years; and details of the franchise network, which must include information about franchisees, the agreement and so on.<br><br>The document must also give full details as to the size of the required investment. The market report and analysis can be an onerous and time consuming requirement, particularly for foreign franchisors. As a rule it is the French master licensee who knows the French market much better than the foreign franchisor. Accordingly, the franchisor has to spend resources and money to retain a third party to prepare the market analysis for it. Another factor which can cause problems is the 30 day waiting period. On many occasions the parties are not willing to wait one month before they commence doing business and in some cases, customers or sub-franchisees which have already been lined up may lose interest if there is significant delay. |
| Italy | At least 30 days before the date of execution of the franchise contract, the franchisor must deliver to the franchisee a definitive draft of the contract, together with:<br><br>corporate information relating to the franchisor;<br>when requested by the franchisee, the franchisor's balance sheets for the three previous financial years;<br>documentation relevant to the franchisor's trade marks;<br>description of the characteristic elements of the franchisor's commercial system;<br>a list of all the franchisees belonging to franchisor's network, together with a list of the franchisor's direct points of sale;<br>an indication of any fluctuations in the number of franchisees during the previous three years;<br>a concise description of any judicial lawsuits or arbitral procedures filed against the franchisor in the previous three years. |
| Lithuania | Does not deal with disclosure in any detailed manner, but does provide in Article 6.770 for duties of the franchisor that include transfer to the franchisee of technical and commercial documentation and other information necessary to the franchisee in order to implement the rights granted to him under the contract of franchise, likewise train the franchisee and his employees with regard to the questions related with the implementation of the transferred rights. |
| Macau | Under the Commercial Code of Macau at art 680 the franchisor is obliged to disclose the following information: |

| Country | Content of disclosure |
|---|---|
| | a) the identification of the franchiser;<br>b) the franchiser's annual accounts of the last two accounting periods;<br>c) any judicial proceedings in which the franchiser, the holders of trademarks, patents and other industrial or intellectual property rights related to the franchise are or have been involved, as well as their sub-franchisers, which may directly or indirectly come to affect or render impossible the functioning of the franchise;<br>d) a detailed description of the franchise;<br>e) the profile of the ideal franchisee regarding previous experience, level of education and other characteristics that compulsorily or preferably he must have;<br>f) the necessity and extent of the franchisee's personal and direct participation in the exercise of the franchise;<br>g) the specifications as to the estimated sum of the initial investment needed for acquisition, installation and entry into functioning of the franchise;<br>h) the value of the periodic payments and other amounts to be paid by the franchisee to the franchiser or to third parties indicated by him, specifying the respective bases of calculation and what these remunerate, or the purpose for which they are destined;<br>i) the composition of the franchise network, lists of franchisees, sub-franchisees and sub-franchisers of the network, as well as of those who have left the network in the last 12 months;<br>j) the profitability of the franchisees' enterprises and the incidence of bankruptcies;<br>l) the professional experience gained, his know-how and entrepreneurial methods;<br>m) any services that the franchiser obliges himself to render to the franchisee for the duration of the contract.[a] |
| Moldova | Article 8 of Law 1335 of 1997 states that the franchisor must provide the franchisee the following disclosure information:<br><br>(1) the business plan specifying the production and/or sale of products (goods),<br>(2) the provision of services, parameters of the production process,<br>(3) the remuneration of employees,<br>(4) anticipated income,<br>(5) the amount and purpose of additional investments,<br>(6) any other clauses, at the request of the franchisor or franchisee. |

| Country | Content of disclosure |
|---|---|
| Romania | Disclosure requirements:<br>In the pre-contractual phase the franchisor is required to provide the prospective franchisee certain information by the way of a Disclosure Document. In order to enable the franchisee to make an informed and conscious decision as to entering into the franchise relationship, the disclosure document must be submitted before he undertakes any legal obligations with respect to the proposed business. The disclosure document shall include, among others, the following items:<br>name of the franchisor;<br>experience gained by the franchisor in the proposed business;<br>information concerning financial conditions of participating in the franchise network;<br>exclusivity;<br>further information enabling the prospective franchisee to join the franchise network in full awareness of the relevant facts. |
| Russia | It may be observed that although the Chapter does not deal with disclosure in any detailed manner, Article 1031 does provide that the right-holder has the obligation to transfer technical and commercial documentation to the user, and provide other information necessary for the user to exercise the rights granted to him under the agreement.[b] |
| Spain | The law requires a franchisor to disclose certain information to a prospective franchisee before signing the contract or before payment. Article 62 of the Spanish Law of Retail Commerce Planning together with Royal Decree 2485/1998 lists a number of items which need to be disclosed to potential franchisees. It is applicable to all franchises and not limited to retail franchises as the name might suggest.<br>Spanish legislation also requires the franchisor to disclose in writing to the franchisee – within 21 days before closing a deal with a franchisee (i.e. within 21 days prior to the signing of a franchising contract, or pre-contract, or prior to any payment to the franchisor) – all information necessary to enable the franchisee to freely and knowingly decide on whether to join the franchise network.[c] |
| Sweden | The third article describes what information must be provided and when it should be provided to franchisees. The law requires the information to be provided in 'ample time', which is likely to be 14 days, but if the franchise agreement is complex then more than 14 |

| Country | Content of disclosure |
|---|---|
| | days would be appropriate. There is no definition of 'complex' in the legislation. Only in exceptional cases would less than 14 days be acceptable.<br>The information must be 'clear and understandable'. The information must be in writing and must contain at least the following information:<br><br>– a description of the franchised business;<br>– information on other franchisees and the scope of their businesses;<br>– information on direct or indirect payments from franchisees to the franchisor and any other financial terms for the business;<br>– information on intellectual property rights that are licensed to the franchisee;<br>– information on the products or services that franchisees are obliged to purchase or rent;<br>– information on all limitations on competition during and after the term of the franchise agreement;<br>– information on the duration of the franchise agreement, how the agreement may be amended, renewal of the franchise agreement, termination and the financial consequences for franchisees of termination; and<br>– information on how disputes are to be resolved and how costs arising from disputes will be borne by the parties. |
| Ukraine | Legislation not in English.<br>Although the legislation does not impose any disclosure requirements, the law follows the Russian model generally. |
| United Arab Emirates | UAE's franchise sector is governed by the Company Law, Federal Law 8 of 1984, Law 19 of 1988 Commercial Agency Agreement, Law 18 of 1981 Commercial Agency Agreements and Law 13 of 2006 Commercial Agency Agreement.<br>There is no requirement for disclosure from franchisor to franchisee. Franchising is regarded as a commercial agency agreement. |
| China, People's Republic of | The following materials must be provided to the prospective franchisee a minimum of 30 days prior to the signing of the Franchise Agreement:<br><br>1. Basic information on the franchisor and franchise activities:<br>a. Franchisor's name, address, contacts, legal representative, general manager, registered capital, scope of business, and the number of regular chains including their addresses and phone numbers; |

| Country | Content of disclosure |
|---|---|
| | b. A brief introduction to the commercial franchise activities of the franchisor;<br>c. Basic information on the archival filing of the franchisor;<br>d. If the franchisor's associated company provides products and services to the franchisee, the associated company's basic information must also be disclosed; and,<br>e. Information on any bankruptcy and/or application for bankruptcy of the franchisor or of its associated company in the preceding five years.<br><br>2. Basic information on the business resources of the franchisor:<br>a. Information available on registered trademarks, company logos, patents, proprietary technologies, and business methods, etc;<br>b. If the owner of any of the above-mentioned business resources is the associated company of the franchisor, then the basic information of the associated company must also be disclosed (the franchisor is also required to explain how to manage the franchise system upon termination of the licence contract); and,<br>c. Information on the business resources of the franchisor (or its associated company) in relation to litigation or arbitration.<br><br>3. Basic information on franchise expenses:<br>a. If the type, amount, criteria and payment method of fees collected by the franchisor or on behalf of a third party cannot be disclosed, then the franchisor must explain the reason for the non-disclosure; if the fee collection standards are inconsistent, then the franchisor is required to disclose both the maximum and minimum standards, and explain the reason thereto;<br>b. The collection thereof, return conditions, return time, and return on investment; and,<br>c. If the franchisee is required to pay a fee before the franchise.<br><br>Agreement is concluded, then the franchisor must explain in writing the use of the fee and the conditions and method of return.<br><br>4. Information on the prices and conditions of the products, services and equipment provided to the franchisee:<br>a. Whether the franchisee must purchase products, services or equipment from the franchisor (or its associated company), including the prices and conditions thereof; |

| Country | Content of disclosure |
|---|---|
| | b. Whether the franchisee must purchase products, services or equipment from the suppliers appointed or approved by the franchisor; and,<br>c. Whether the franchisee has the discretion to choose its own suppliers and the standards for the selection of its suppliers.<br><br>5. Information on the continuous provision of services to the franchisee:<br>a. Detailed content, manner of provision and implementation plans for professional training, including the training location, approach and duration; and,<br>b. Details regarding technical support and a catalogue of the operation manual of the franchise including the number of pages therein.<br><br>6. Methods and content of guidance and supervision over the franchise activities of the franchisee:<br>a. The franchisor's methods and content of guidance and supervision over the franchise activities of the franchisee, the franchisee's obligations and consequences for failing to fulfil them.<br>b. Whether the franchisor is jointly liable with the franchisee for complaints by and compensation to consumers, and how to share such liability.<br><br>7. Information on the investment budget of the franchise:<br>a. The expenditure for the investment budget may include the following: initial fee; training fee; real estate and decoration fee, procurement fee for equipment, office supplies, furniture, etc; initial inventory; water, electricity and gas fees; fees needed to obtain licences and other governmental approvals; and working capital; and,<br>b. The statistical source and estimation basis for the above-mentioned fees.<br><br>8. Information on franchisees within China:<br>a. Information on the present and estimated number of franchisees, geographical distribution, scope of licence, and as to whether or not they are subject to an exclusive regional licence (if so, details of the scope thereof must also be explained);<br>b. Information on the evaluation of the performance of the franchisee, the actual or estimated average sales volume, |

| Country | Content of disclosure |
|---|---|
| | costs, gross and net profits of the franchisee, the source of the above-mentioned information, duration of and franchise networks involved (if the information is speculative, then the franchisor shall explain the basis for its speculation, and specify that the actual performance of the franchisee may differ from its speculation).<br><br>9. Abstracts of the franchisor's financial and accounting reports and of the audit reports in the last two years audited by the accounting or auditing firms.<br><br>10. Information on any major litigation or arbitration involving any franchises of the franchisor in the last five years:<br>a. Major litigation or arbitration refers to litigation and arbitration involving litigation fees of more than RMB 500 000; and,<br>b. Basic information as to the location of the litigation or arbitration and the judgment or award must also be disclosed.<br><br>11. Information on any record of major illegal operations of the franchisor and its legal representative:<br>a. Where either the franchisor or its legal representative has been imposed with a fine, by the competent administrative law enforcement authorities, exceeding not less than RMB 300 000 but not more than RMB 500 000; and,<br>b. Where the franchisor and its legal representative have been subject to criminal penalization.<br><br>12. Franchise Contract:<br>a. Sample franchise contract; and<br>b. If the franchisor requires its franchisee to sign with the franchisor (or its associated company), other franchise contracts (sample contract shall be provided at the time of contracting).<br><br>Note that where the franchisor is found to have concealed or provided false information, the franchisee may rescind the Franchise Agreement. |
| Taiwan | The Fair Trade Commission Guidelines on the Disclosure of Information by Franchisors requires the franchisor to provide the franchisee with the following information 10 days prior to the signing of the franchise agreement: |

| Country | Content of disclosure |
|---|---|
| | (1) The name of the franchiser's enterprise, its operating capital, place of business, business items, date of establishment and date on which it began franchising operations.<br>(2) The names of the responsible person and the chief management personnel of the franchiser, and information on their relevant business experience.<br>(3) The franchise fees and other charges collected by the franchiser before the entry into the franchising contracts and duration of the franchising contracts, including their types of fees, amounts, methods of collection, and conditions for refunds.<br>(4) The intellectual property rights including trademarks, patents, copyrights and so on that the franchiser authorizes the usage to the franchisee, in regard to the time that the intellectual property rights are filed or granted, the content and duration of the rights, plus the scope and any restriction of the authorization to the franchisee.<br>(5) The content and methods of management assistance, training guidance and so forth to be provided by the franchiser to the franchisee.<br>(6) The franchiser's management program concerning the franchisee's areas of operation with those of other franchisees or directly operated stores.<br>(7) All the other franchisees' names and business addresses of the franchiser in the city, county (city) where the franchisee will be located, as well as, within the last accounting year, the statistic data number of other franchisees and terminated numbers of the franchising contracts with the franchiser in the whole country and also the city, county (city) where the franchisee will be located.<br>(8) Within duration of the franchise contract, the restrictions over the business relationship between the franchiser and franchisee in their operations of business.<br>(9) Conditions and resolved means to modify, terminate and/or rescind the franchise contract. |
| Georgia | Although the legislation does not impose any disclosure requirements, the law follows the Russian model generally. |
| Indonesia | GR 42 also has introduced certain new – and in some cases, potentially burdensome – disclosure requirements and retained certain significant other ones. In the disclosure document the franchisor must now include: |

| Country | Content of disclosure |
|---|---|
| | the business licences of the franchisor;<br>the identity cards of the owners or members of the management of the franchisor;<br>the history of the franchisor's business activity;<br>the financial statements for the past two years; and<br>the number of outlets and the list of franchisees.<br><br>The financial statement requirement has been increased from one to two years. In addition, inclusion of both the number of outlets and the list of franchisees is new. It is not clear whether these latter requirements relate just to Indonesian franchisees or those worldwide.<br>Article 11 states that the franchisor shall register franchise agreement. Article 12 provides that the application for the registration of the franchise-offering prospectus shall be submitted by enclosing a copy of the franchise-offering prospectus and a copy of business legality and that application for the registration of the franchise agreement as meant in article 11 shall be submitted by enclosing the following documents: copy of business legality; copy of franchise agreement; copy of franchise-offering prospectus; and copy of citizenship identity card of the owner/executive of company. The application for the registration of franchise shall be submitted to the Minister which shall issue Certificate of Registration of Franchise if the application for the registration of franchise has met the requirements. The certificate of registration of franchise shall be valid for five years. In the case of the franchise agreement not yet expiring, the Certificate of Registration of Franchise can be extended for five years. The application and issuance of certificate of registration of franchise shall not be subject to cost. Article 13 states that further provisions on procedures for the registration of franchise shall be regulated by the Minister. |
| Japan | The guidelines list the following as examples of the items to be disclosed:<br><br>1. the conditions regarding the supply of goods to the franchisee (e.g. recommendation of the supplier);<br>2. the details of the assistance to be offered the franchisee, such as a description of the assistance to be offered, its manner, frequency and costs;<br>3. the nature, amount and conditions of repayment, if any, of the fee to be paid at the time of entering into a franchise agreement;<br>4. the amount, method of calculation, as well as the timing and manner of payment of royalties; |

| Country | Content of disclosure |
|---|---|
| | 5. the description of any settlement arrangement between the franchisor and the franchisee, as well as the interest rate of any loan to a franchisee offered by the franchisor;<br>6. whether or not the franchisor is prepared to indemnify the franchisee for its deficit or to render assistance to the operation of a franchised unit that is not doing well;<br>7. the terms of the franchise agreement and the conditions of its renewal, resolution as well as termination; and<br>8. whether or not the franchisor in the franchise agreement reserves a right to operate a unit on its own or to grant another franchise close to the franchisee and whether or not the franchisor plans to do so.<br><br>The guidelines also require that if the franchisor provides the franchisee with the projected sales or profits, such projection shall be made in a reasonable manner, on the basis of reliable data. The underlying data as well as the way in which the projected sales or profits are worked out must be disclosed to the franchisee. |
| Kazakhstan | Although the legislation does not impose any disclosure requirements, the law follows the Russian model generally. |
| Korea, Republic of | The South Korean Act on Fairness in Franchise Transactions (the Act) was created on 7 November 2001. Under the Act a franchisor must provide a disclosure document upon a written request by a prospective franchisee.<br>The Act required that the franchisor provide the following information in its disclosure document:<br><br>description of general status of the franchisor;<br>any legal violation by an executive of the franchisor;<br>obligations of the franchisee;<br>conditions and restrictions on franchised business operations;<br>current status of the franchisor's franchise;<br>description of instruction and training programs; and<br>description of procedure and period for commencement of the franchised business.<br><br>The Act as initially enacted did not require that franchisors or franchisees make any filing or register the franchise offering, the franchise disclosure document, or any executed franchise agreement. |
| Kyrgyzstan | The Civil Code of the Kyrgyz Republic does not require the franchisor to provide the franchisee with disclosure documents. |

| Country | Content of disclosure |
|---|---|
| | It does, however, require under article 870 that the licensor transfer to the licensee technical and commercial documents and provide him with other information necessary for the licensee to exercise his rights, conferred on him under the contract, as well as to give instructions to the licensee and his employees on issues which relate to these rights. The contract may provide for other licensor's obligations. |
| Malaysia | The disclosure documents must be submitted to the prospective franchisee at least ten days before the agreement is signed. The disclosure documents given to the prospective franchisee are the same as those handed in to the Registrar as required by Article 7.(1), 'A franchisor shall make an application to register his franchise by submitting to the Registrar the application in the prescribed form together with:<br><br>(a) the complete disclosure documents with all the necessary particulars;<br>(b) a sample of the franchise agreement;<br>(c) the operations manual;<br>(d) the training manual;<br>(e) a copy of the latest audited accounts, financial statements, and the reports, if any, of the auditors and directors of the applicant; and<br>(f) such other additional information or documents as may be required by the registrar for the purpose of determining the application.'<br><br>A person who fails to comply commits an offence.<br>At s 21 the Act states that the franchisor must disclose to the franchisee the amount of franchise fees or royalties. Section 23 states that the amount of promotional fees must be as disclosed in the disclosure document. |
| Vietnam | The information that must be disclosed in the disclosure document is set forth in the standard form of the Introduction of the Franchise Business which is attached to Circular 9. The disclosure document must include the following categories of information:<br><br>(1) general information about the franchisor;<br>(2) initial fees payable by the franchisee;<br>(3) other financial obligations of the franchisee;<br>(4) initial investment of the franchisee;<br>(5) franchisee's obligations to buy or lease equipment under the franchise agreement; |

| Country | Content of disclosure |
|---|---|
| | (6) obligations of the franchisor;<br>(7) description of the market for the goods and services to be franchised;<br>(8) a summary of the franchise contract;<br>(9) information about the franchise system;<br>(10) the franchisor's financial statements;<br>(11) rewards, acknowledgements the franchisor has received and organizations in which it participates.<br><br>Circular 9 requires that the information be presented in the order described above.<br>Section IX of the Decree requires a franchisor to provide the number of outlets under its franchise system (worldwide) which includes all outlets that are operating or cease operation.[d] |
| Australia | A franchisor that intends to enter into, extend or renew a franchise contract covered by the Code must provide to the prospective franchisee at least 14 days prior to signing the contract a copy of the Code, a copy of the franchise contract and a disclosure document that provides information about contract terms. Annexure One prescribes a 21-item disclosure document provided to a franchisee 14 days before signing a contract. The following items of information must be included: 1) A seven-day cooling-off period; 2) Details of the franchisor; 3) Franchisor business experience; 4) Litigation proceedings and judgments; 5) Payments made by a franchisor to recruiting agents; 6) Numbers of existing franchises and numbers of franchisees terminated by a franchisor in the last three years; 7) Description of a franchisee's right to use, and judgments pertaining to trademark, patent, design, copyright; 8) Site or territory, exclusivity and franchisor right to change; 9) Supply of goods or services to franchisee; 10) Supply of goods or services by franchisee; 11) Sites or territories; 12) Marketing and other cooperative funds; 13) Payments; 14) Financing arrangements; 15) Franchisor obligations; 16) Franchisee obligations; 17) Summary of other conditions of the franchise agreement; 18) Obligation to sign related agreements; 19) Earnings information; 20) Financial details; 21) Updates; 22) Other relevant disclosure information; 23) Acknowledgment of receipt.[e]<br>With disclosure a franchisor must also provide a copy of the Code and a copy of the franchise contract. The disclosure process also requires a prospective franchisee to attest that it has consulted with legal and accounting professionals prior to signing the franchise contract or that it has been advised to but has declined to seek such assistance.[f] |

| Country | Content of disclosure |
|---|---|
| | In addition to the requirements of Annexure One for disclosure at the time of contract formation, a franchisor must on an ongoing basis also provide financial statements for marketing or other cooperative funds to which franchisees have made financial contributions.[g]<br><br>DISCLOSURE REQUIREMENTS: PART TWO OF THE CODE<br>Where an agreement is covered by the Code, a franchisor is required to prepare a disclosure document which is to be updated annually within three months after the end of the franchisor's financial year. The franchisor must give a copy of the Code and the disclosure document to the prospective franchisee at least 14 days before the prospective franchisee enters into the franchise agreement or pays a non-refundable amount in connection with the proposed franchise agreement (at least 14 days before the renewal or extension of the franchise agreement). |

*Notes:*

[a] See: http//bo.io.gov.mo/bo/i/99/31/coclcomo601. asp#a680.

[b] Taken from: www.unidroit.org/english/guides/2007franchising/country/russia.htm.

[c] http://www.europeanfranchising.com/how-we-can-help-you/disclosure-and-registration.aspx.

[d] See 36 Circular No,09/2006/TT-BTM, of May 25, 2006, 'Guiding The Commercial Franchising Registration' (last accessed on 25 July 2008) http://www.itpc.hochiminhcity.gov.vn/en/business_news/ vietnam_legend_update/Full%20Text/folder.2006-06-14.7979682921/2006_05_25a/view (Vietnam).

[e] The Code is available at <http://www.comlaw.gov.au/ComLawithLegislation/LegislativeInstrumentCompilation1.nsf/0/4FA9F21A9489DC27CA256F71004E4CCB?OpenDocument at 30 July 2006.

[f] Trade Practices (Industry Codes – Franchising) Regulations 1998 (No 162) (Cth), Clause 13.

[g] Ibid. Clause 17. Note that the Code applies concurrently with the Petroleum Retail Marketing Franchise Act 1980 (Cth) (PRMF Act); see Stephen Giles and Fiona Wallwork, 'Franchising and Co-operatives – The Franchising Code of Conduct' (2002) Australian Centre for Co-Operative Research and Development <http://www.accord.org.au/social/infobriefs/franchising_code_of_conduct.html at 1 August 2005.

# Index

adhesion contracts 78, 142, 150
advertising 185, 198, 224, 238, 239
  funds 62, 72, 97–9, 169, 210
advice, risk statements and warnings 257–9, 311
Africa 214
agent/principal perspective
  transaction cost theory 51–4
Albania 152–4, 214, 215, 249, 265, 272, 276, 278
Americas 212–14
  *see also individual countries*
annulment of contracts 161, 224
antitrust/competition law 64, 66, 130, 253, 276
  Belarus 155
  Japan 191
  Kyrgyzstan 196, 276
  Lithuania 164, 271, 276
  Romania 171
  Russia 173
  Vietnam 208
arbitration 149, 150–52, 168, 281, 285
Asia 214, 223–5, 244
  *see also individual countries*
assignment *see* transfer of franchise
association
  franchisees 63–4, 66, 130, 140, 148, 167, 210, 279
  franchisors *see* trade associations
asymmetry
  information *see under* information
  power *see separate entry*
Australia 9, 22, 49, 55, 64–5, 208
  code of conduct 306
  contracts 71, 99, 108, 111, 113
    unfair terms 82, 267–70
  Franchise Council of (FCA) 28, 60–64, 306
  franchise-specific legislation 126, 208–11, 215, 216, 249, 257–8
    conduct/performance 209–10, 221, 265, 267–70, 277, 279, 281, 283, 284, 310
    disclosure 127, 209, 210, 221, 227, 228, 229, 240, 241, 242, 247–8, 256, 348–9
    dispute resolution 66, 210, 221, 281, 283, 284, 310
    exemptions 127–8
    good faith 210–11
    objectives 117, 119
  good faith 210–11, 297, 298, 301
  mediation 66, 210, 281, 284
Austria 227

Baltic Franchise Association 227, 305
Barbados 133–4, 212, 215, 216, 249
Belarus 125, 126, 154–6, 215, 223, 227, 333
  conduct/performance 154–5, 276, 278, 279
    mandatory terms 265, 271, 272
  registration 154, 249
Belgium 8, 125, 156–8, 215, 241, 249, 265, 305, 307
  confidentiality 158, 276
  disclosure 157–8, 222, 227, 229, 335–6
  good faith 294
Bernstein's life-cycle theory 17
best-practice model for regulatory process 38–9
  core elements 39–44
  scope and effectiveness 44–5
*bluemaumau.org* 28
Bolivia 212
bounded rationality 52
boycotts 66
Braithwaite, J. 25, 41–2, 45

brand 61, 92, 93, 95, 112, 176
  awareness 9, 58, 96, 110, 112
  free-riding 69–70
  maintenance of 100, 267, 268, 274, 301
    franchisor's obligations 97–9
    transfer by franchisee 109
    uniformity and 66–8, 79, 90, 91
  mandatory terms 274, 275
  nature of franchise contract 76
Brazil 126, 134–7, 214, 215, 304
  disclosure 135–6, 221, 227, 228, 229, 247–8, 334
  good faith 294
  registration 136, 221, 249, 253
brokers 202, 228, 260
burden of proof 142
Burger King 107
business-format franchises, features of 48, 49

Canada 8, 22, 28, 126, 137–42, 212, 215, 216, 221
  code of ethics 227, 304, 307
  conduct/performance 139–40, 141, 221, 279, 281, 282
  disclosure 138–9, 140–41, 142, 221, 227, 228, 229, 240, 247–8, 327–33
  dispute resolution 141, 221, 281, 282
  exemptions 127
  exit stage 140–41
  good faith 141–2, 293, 297, 298–9
  registration not required 139, 218, 249
capital 50–51, 61
capture theory 17
Caribbean islands 212, 214
  Barbados 133–4, 212, 215, 216, 249
categories of franchise systems 47–9
centralized law 20
certification 194–5, 229, 259
China 126, 180–85, 215, 224, 278, 310
  contract duration 184, 224, 271
  cooling-off period 257
  disclosure 182, 224, 227, 228, 229, 231, 240, 242, 340–43
  franchisee qualifications 185
  Hong Kong 28, 181, 224, 227, 307
  Macau *see separate entry*
  mandatory terms 265, 271, 273
  objectives 117, 118, 119
  registration 182–3, 224, 249, 253
  trade association 306
  'two plus one' rule 183–4, 224, 259
civil law 216, 217
  civil code-based model 223
  communist legal conventions and 204
  cultural and 187–8
  good faith 36, 142, 161, 186, 198, 200, 293, 294–7
  socialist and 180–81
co-branding 95
co-regulation 25, 36
codes of ethics and conduct 27, 28–9, 214, 224, 227, 241, 259–60, 303–9
collaborative process 318–20
collective agreement clause 79–80, 105–6
common law 200, 208, 216, 217
  good faith 36, 297–9
communities, interpretive 27
compensation *see* damages
competition 26, 27–8, 36–7, 51, 103
  defined territories: protection from 58, 63, 94–7, 149, 155, 173, 180, 197, 276–7
  fair 153, 171, 295
  law *see* antitrust
conciliation 162, 285
conditions conducive to franchising 49–50
  *see also* motivations
conduct/performance: franchise-specific legislation 129, 130, 218–20, 225, 263, 302, 315
  Albania 153, 265, 272, 276, 278
  Australia 66, 209–10, 221, 265, 267–70, 277, 279, 281, 283, 284, 310
  Belarus 154–5, 265, 271, 272, 276, 278, 279
  Belgium 265, 276
  Canada 139–40, 141, 221, 279, 281, 282
  China 184–5, 265, 271, 273, 278
  dispute resolution *see separate entry*
  Estonia 158, 270, 278, 279
  exit stage *see separate entry*

Georgia 187, 276, 278
good faith *see separate entry*
Indonesia 189, 265, 271, 272, 277, 278
Italy 161–2, 265, 271, 272, 276, 278, 282
Japan 191–2, 277
Kazakhstan 192–3, 276
Kyrgyzstan 265, 276, 278
larger role 309–12
Lithuania 163–4, 265, 271, 276
Macau 198–9, 224, 265, 276, 277, 279, 280
Malaysia 203, 271, 277
Mexico 145, 265, 272, 273, 276
Moldova 166, 167, 168, 265, 273, 276, 278, 279, 280, 282
prescriptive legislation 263–5, 309–10
conduct directly proscribed 275–80
contract form 265
language 265
mandatory contract terms 271–5, 309–10, 315
unfair competition 271
unfair contract terms 265–70
procedural legislation 280–81, 285
conflict resolution 281–5
Romania 170–71, 265, 271, 273, 276, 278, 279, 280
Russia 172–3, 273, 276–7, 280
South Korea 195, 265
Spain 265, 276
Ukraine 180, 265, 276, 279
United States 148–52, 222, 271, 277, 278, 279
Vietnam 207, 265, 271, 278, 283
confidentiality 81
franchise-specific legislation 130, 276
Albania 153, 276
Belarus 155
Belgium 158, 276
China 184–5
Georgia 187, 276
Italy 161, 276
Kazakhstan 192
Macau 198, 199, 276
Malaysia 203
Mexico 145, 276
Moldova 167, 276
Romania 170, 171, 276
Russia 173, 276
mediation 66, 284
operations manuals 92–3, 241
conflict of interests 62, 63, 65–6, 72, 80, 93, 111
consent
changes to contracts 149
standard-form contracts and 82–3, 88, 90
transfer by franchisee 109, 185
*contra proferentum* principle 224
contract formation: franchise-specific legislation 89–90, 129, 130, 131, 218, 220, 225, 226, 260–62, 311
cooling-off period 129, 193, 194, 202, 209, 218, 221, 225, 257
disclosure 227, 260–61, 262
analysis of 243–8
content requirements 229–42
effective disclosure 244–8
individual countries *see* by country *under* disclosure
procedural requirements 228–9
performance requirements
prescriptive requirements 260
standards and qualifications 131, 183–4, 185, 224, 259–60
registration 248–53, 311
costs and benefits 253–7
individual countries *see under* registration
review period 129, 257
revising and ongoing disclosure 147, 202, 210, 242
risk statements, advice and warnings 257–9, 311
contract terms 72, 93–4, 104–5
collective agreement 79–80, 105–6
exiting relationship 106
duration 33, 38, 95, 106–7, 108
release form 110
renewal 107–9
restraint of trade 29, 110, 111–13
termination by franchisor 101, 110–11
transfer by franchisee 109–10, 112
express 29, 299
franchisor's obligations 97–100

implied 29–30, 34, 111, 299
management of business 53, 101
mandatory 130, 153, 166, 169–70, 184, 189, 271–5, 309–10, 315
minimum performance and reporting requirements 55–6, 100–102, 274
scope of grant/encroachment 94–7
sole control and discretion 105
supply requirements 103–4
underperforming franchisees 55–6, 101, 107, 110, 112
unfair 82–3
legislation 265–70, 275, 297, 298, 309
contracts 29–34, 76–8
court interpretation 29, 30, 34–6, 83, 87, 90, 115, 275, 286
default rules analysis 30, 34–5
drafted by franchisor 30, 70–72, 261, 284, 291
duration 33, 38, 95, 106–7, 108, 271, 274
express terms 29, 299
freedom of contract 34, 84, 90, 114, 273
imbalance: market and contract interaction 113–15
implied terms 29–30, 34, 111, 299
reasonableness 30, 34, 35, 36, 91, 96, 98, 105, 113, 296–7, 300
relational 29, 33, 35, 77–8, 84–7, 114, 115, 246, 247
discretion, uncertainty and risk 90–93
erosion of bargained-for-exchange 89, 90
good faith 302
inconsistent with standard-form 86, 88, 89–90, 113
specificity and flexibility 30, 33, 115
standard-form 29, 33, 77–9, 114, 115, 224, 246–7
discretion, uncertainty and risk 90–93
erosion of bargained-for-exchange 82–4, 88, 89, 90
good faith 302
imbalance of power 79–81
impact on relationship 82–4
inconsistent with relational 86, 88, 89–90, 113
no negotiation 81
unfair terms 266–7, 268, 270
uniformity 70–72, 79
terms *see* contract terms
cooling-off period 129, 193, 194, 202, 209, 218, 221, 225, 257
coordination costs 52–3, 55
copyrights 238, 239
corporate social reporting 27
cost effectiveness/costs and benefits 29, 33, 225, 253–7, 261
disclosure 240–41, 243, 244–8
courts
good faith 115, 298
layer of governance 29, 30, 34–6
relational contracts 87, 90, 115
restraint of trade clauses 275
standard-form contracts 83, 90, 115
transfer by franchisee 286
unfair contract terms 297
Croatia 307
Czech Republic 307

damages/compensation 289
Albania 153
Australia 211
Belarus 156
Brazil 136
Canada 142
China 184
France 161
Georgia 187
Indonesia 189
Lithuania 164, 165
Macau 200, 224
Malaysia 203
Mexico 144
Romania 171
Russia 174
Spain 177, 287
United States 152
Vietnam 207
death 155–6, 165, 167–8, 173–4, 200, 287
decentralization 20
defamation 63, 66
definitions
co-branding 95

discretion 90
franchise 47, 120–26, 128–9, 223
Australia 209
Belarus 154
Belgium 157
Brazil 135
Canada 138, 142
China 181
Estonia 158
Georgia 186
Indonesia 188
Italy 160
Lithuania 162
Macau 197
Mexico 143
Moldova 166
Romania 168
Russia 171–2
Spain 174–5
Taiwan 185–6
United States 146–7
Vietnam 204
globalization 6
good faith 300
operating risk 69
private regulation 25
regulation 15–16
relational contract 84–5
self-regulation 19
standard-form contract 78
transaction costs 51
democratic process 15, 22, 37, 41, 317, 319
Denmark 227
direct intervention *see* statutory intervention
disclosure 25, 92, 115, 119–20, 129, 218, 225, 227, 260–61, 262, 314
analysis of 243–4
effective disclosure 244–8
by country 89–90
Albania 153
Australia 127, 209, 210, 221, 227, 228, 229, 240, 241, 242, 247–8, 256, 348–9
Belgium 157–8, 222, 227, 229, 335–6
Brazil 135–6, 221, 227, 228, 229, 247–8, 334
Canada 138–9, 140–41, 142, 221, 227, 228, 229, 240, 247–8, 327–33
China 182, 224, 227, 228, 229, 231, 240, 242, 340–43
exemptions 127
France 159–60, 222, 227, 229, 247–8, 286, 336–7
Georgia 186
Germany 296
Indonesia 188, 222, 227, 228, 229, 231, 344–5
Italy 161, 222, 227, 229, 241, 286, 337
Japan 191, 222, 227, 228, 231, 345–6
Macau 197, 198, 224, 228, 231, 337–8
Malaysia 201, 202, 222, 227, 228, 229, 231, 240, 347
Mexico 143–4, 222, 227, 229, 231, 335
models of 221–3
Moldova 227, 231, 240, 338
Portugal 297
Romania 168–9, 171, 222, 227, 228, 229, 231, 240, 241, 286, 339
South Korea 193, 194, 222, 227, 228, 229, 231, 242, 346
Spain 175, 177, 227, 228, 229, 240, 295, 339
Sweden 178, 222, 227, 228, 229, 240, 339–40
Taiwan 186, 225, 227, 229, 231, 343–4
United States 127, 147, 149, 150, 221, 222, 227, 228, 229, 240, 242, 243, 246, 247–8, 333
Vietnam 205, 222, 227, 228, 229, 231, 241, 242, 347–8
closed and open 240–41
codes of conduct or ethics 227, 307
content requirements 229–42, 327–49
due diligence by franchisees 55
electronic delivery 228
European Union 126, 214, 241–2
exit stage 140–41, 242
from franchisee to franchisor 241

good faith 227, 297
power asymmetry and 247, 310–11
procedural requirements 228–9
registration and 256
revising and ongoing 147, 202, 210, 228, 242
transfer of documents to franchisee 223, 227
Belarus 154, 227, 333
Estonia 223, 227, 336
Kazakhstan 192, 227, 228, 346
Kyrgyzstan 196, 227, 346–7
Lithuania 162, 163, 227, 240, 337
Russia 172, 227, 339
Ukraine 179, 227, 340
unfair contract terms legislation and 266
UNIDROIT Model Law 127, 131, 228, 238, 248
uniformity 70
discretion, franchisor 90–93
discrimination 149, 278
dispute resolution 29, 31, 32, 33, 111, 314
arbitration 149, 150–52, 168, 281, 285
conciliation 162, 285
confidentiality 66, 284
EU proposed disclosure law 242
franchise-specific legislation 129, 220, 221, 223, 225, 239, 281–5
Australia 66, 210, 221, 281, 283, 284, 310
Canada 141, 221, 281, 282
China 184, 310
Indonesia 189, 310
Italy 162, 282
Kazakhstan 193
Moldova 168, 282, 310
no provision 281
South Korea 195, 281, 283
United States 150–52, 222
Vietnam 207, 283, 310
mediation *see separate entry*
distributorships 128
due diligence: franchisee 55, 59, 247
duty of care 34

e-commerce 95
economies of scale 9, 52, 58, 70, 73
education 189, 259, 260, 261, 262, 284, 314, 315
*see also* training
Egypt 8, 214, 227, 260, 307
England 2, 48, 216
Estonia 158–9, 215, 227, 249, 270, 278, 279
good faith 294–5
estoppel, promissory 35
Europe 108, 214, 216–18, 227
Eastern 243–4
*see also individual countries*
European Franchise Federation (EFF)
code of ethics 29, 227, 241, 260, 305, 307
European Union 214, 277
Principles of European Contract Law 300
proposed disclosure law 126, 214, 241–2
evolution of regulatory theory 15–24
exemptions from franchise-specific legislation 127–9
exit stage 101, 107–11, 112, 285–93
contracts: exiting relationship 106
duration 33, 38, 95, 106–7, 108
release form 110
renewal 107–9
restraint of trade 29, 110, 111–13
termination by franchisor 101, 110–11
transfer by franchisee 109–10, 112
Estonia 158–9, 287, 292
franchise-specific legislation 127, 129, 130, 220–21, 225, 239, 285–93
Albania 153–4, 287, 292
Australia 111, 210, 288, 289, 292–3
Belarus 155–6
Canada 140–41
China 184, 185
France 286
Georgia 187, 287
Indonesia 189, 286, 288
Italy 286
Kyrgyzstan 196, 287
Lithuania 164–5, 287
Macau 199–200, 286
Malaysia 202, 203, 288, 292

mandatory terms 275
Mexico 145
Moldova 167–8, 287
Romania 169–70, 171, 286, 287, 292
Russia 173–4, 287
South Korea 193, 287–8, 292
Spain 177, 287
Ukraine 180, 292
United States 150, 286, 288–9, 292, 300–301
Vietnam 206–7, 286, 288
good faith 111, 293
Taiwan 186
expert determination 285
externalities 28, 36, 67, 69–70, 79, 93

fairness 71, 107, 129, 153, 161, 171, 195, 294, 295
fair dealing 34, 35, 114, 141–2, 185, 224, 295, 299
fair trading 186, 190–92, 298
unfair contract terms 82–3, 265–70, 275, 297, 298, 309
*see also* good faith
federated model 9, 52, 53
fees 60, 61, 238, 239, 242
Albania 153
Belarus 155, 156
China 184
Georgia 187
joining 56, 61, 96, 184, 202, 239
Lithuania 163
Macau 198
Malaysia 202, 203
Moldova 166
Romania 170
Russia 172, 174
transfer 109, 149, 286
United States 149, 286
fiduciary duties/obligation 34, 36
field staff 62
financial performance 239, 242
fines 160, 177, 178, 190
Finland 8, 295, 307
Fletcher, G. 120–21
force-of-ideas theory 18
fractional franchises 127
France 125, 126, 159–60, 215, 227, 249
code of ethics 227, 305
disclosure 159–60, 222, 227, 229, 247–8, 286, 336–7
exemptions 127
good faith 295
objectives 118
franchise-specific legislation 133
conduct/performance *see separate entry*
contract formation *see separate entry*
exemptions 127–9
exit stage *see separate entry*
objectives 116–20
scope of: defining a franchise 120–26, 128–9
tools to achieve objectives 129–32
trends in 212–15
adoption and implementation 215–18
models 221–5
tools used 218–21
fraud 294–5
free-riding 69–70, 72, 91, 93, 97, 100, 107, 108
future directions for regulation 313–21

Georgia 186–7, 215, 223, 227, 249, 278
confidentiality 187, 276
Germany 2, 8, 48, 216, 227, 296, 300
good cause 288, 300–301
good faith 34, 35, 36, 38, 114, 115, 293–300, 310, 315
civil law 36, 142, 161, 186, 198, 200, 293, 294–7
codes of conduct or ethics 307
commercial and consumer law 227
common law 36, 297–9
content of duty of 300–301
encroachment by franchisor 97
franchise-specific legislation 220, 221, 275, 293–4
Albania 294
Australia 210–11
Canada 141–2, 293, 297, 298–9
China 185, 294
Italy 294
Malaysia 203, 294
South Korea 195, 294
United States 222, 293–4, 299, 300
franchisee association 66

international law 299–300
marketing funds 99
renewal 107, 275, 293, 301
specific applications of 301–3
termination process 111, 293
goodwill 67, 109–10, 112
governance *see* layers of governance
Greece 227, 253, 296, 307

hard and soft law 15
Hong Kong 28, 181, 224, 227, 307
hostages 26, 28, 29
Hungary 227, 296

imbalance of power *see* power asymmetry
imperfect competition 28
independent small business ownership vs franchising
trade association claims 58–64
India 8, 227, 307
Indonesia 126, 187–90, 215, 259, 265, 277, 278, 310
contract duration 189, 271
disclosure 188, 222, 227, 228, 229, 231, 344–5
exit stage 189, 286, 288
mandatory terms 271, 272
objectives 118
registration 188, 222, 229, 249, 256
trade association 306
information 262, 316–17
access to, franchisor 102
asymmetry 28, 36, 52–3, 63, 64–6, 74, 260
contract terms 102
disclosure 243
mediation 66, 284
renewal 292
restrictive covenants 112
disclosure *see separate entry*
market regulation 26, 27, 72
asymmetry 28, 36, 52–3, 63, 64–6, 74
exchange at recruitment stage 59, 65
monopolies 19
privacy 62, 102
registration 254–5, 256–7, 261
relational contracts 85, 87
standard-form contracts 82
transaction cost theory 52–3
UNIDROIT Model Law 117
injunctions 152, 192, 211
insolvency 280, 287
institutional theories 17–18
intellectual property 7, 9, 47, 93, 223, 227
franchise-specific legislation 128, 130, 238, 239, 248, 253, 278
Belarus 154, 278
Georgia 187, 278
Indonesia 189
Italy 160
Kazakhstan 192
Kyrgyzstan 196
Macau 198, 199, 200
Mexico 144
Moldova 167, 278
Romania 169, 253
Spain 175, 176
Ukraine 180
restrictive covenants 112
scope of grant/encroachment 94–7, 109–10
uniformity to protect 66–8, 72
Vietnam 208, 278
*see also* trademarks
international law: good faith 299–300
Internet 95, 228, 261
interpretive communities 27
investment, transaction-specific 26
Ireland 227, 307
Israel 227, 307
Italy 125, 126, 160–62, 215, 222, 227, 249, 259, 278, 307
confidentiality 161, 276
contract duration 161, 271
contract in writing 265
disclosure 161, 222, 227, 229, 241, 286, 337
dispute resolution 162, 282
Franchise Association 28
good faith 161, 300
mandatory terms 271, 272
objectives 118

Japan 8, 126, 190–92, 215, 249, 277
code of ethics 227, 306, 307

disclosure 191, 222, 227, 228, 231, 345–6
objectives 118
joint liability 174
joint and several liability 156, 180, 197

Kazakhstan 125, 192–3, 215, 227, 276
objectives 117, 119
kickbacks 62, 103–4, 149, 277
Kyrgyzstan 125, 195–7, 215, 223, 227, 265, 276, 278

language 261, 265
large investors 127
layers of governance 16, 24–5, 314–16, 320
best-practice model for regulatory process 38–9
core elements 39–44
scope and effectiveness 44–5
contract as regulation 29–34, 315
court interpretation 29, 30, 34–6
market regulation 26–9
statutory intervention 30, 36–8, 315
legal representation 80, 81, 114
legislation *see* statutory intervention
licenses 128
life-cycle theory 17
Lithuania 125, 126, 162–5, 215, 223, 227
conduct/performance 163–4, 265, 271, 276
good faith 295
registration 162–3, 256
trade association 305
Luxembourg 296

Macau 181, 197–200, 215, 224, 277, 279, 280
confidentiality 198, 199, 276
contract in writing 265
definitions 197, 198, 224, 228, 231
disclosure 197, 198, 224, 228, 231, 337–8
registration not required 249
McDonald's 7, 49, 52, 107, 212, 214, 215
Malaysia 6–7, 8, 126, 200–204, 215, 271, 277, 307
code of ethics 227, 259–60, 306
contract duration 203, 271
disclosure 201, 202, 222, 227, 228, 229, 231, 240, 347
registration 201–2, 222, 229, 249, 253, 256, 260
manufacturing/processing franchise 48–9
market regulation 26–9, 46, 73–5
conditions conducive to franchising 49–50
motivations *see separate entry*
contract and 29
early stages of franchise system development 54–5
information asymmetry 28, 36, 52–3, 63, 64–6, 74
power asymmetry 67–8, 71, 72, 74, 113–15
recruitment and screening of franchisees 55–6, 59, 65–6
uniformity 66–7, 74, 79, 81
brand maintenance 66–8, 79, 90, 91
fairness 71
franchisee perspective 72–3, 246
legal advice and franchisees 80
price of 71–2
risk reduction 68–70, 72, 73, 74
transaction costs 70–71, 79
marketing 146, 147, 149, 190, 210, 279
brand maintenance 97–9
franchisor to prospective franchisees 56, 57–64, 65, 73–4, 79
materiality 240
mediation 25, 115, 246
Australia 66, 210, 281, 284
Canada 141, 281
South Korea 195, 281
United States 150–52
Mexico 143–5, 212, 215, 222, 276
code of ethics 304, 307
disclosure 143–4, 222, 227, 229, 231, 335
language 265
mandatory terms 272, 273
objectives 117, 118
registration 144, 222, 249, 256
misrepresentation 142
mistake 294–5

models of franchise-specific legislation 221–3
Moldova 126, 165–8, 215, 265, 278, 279
  associate, right to 167, 280
  confidentiality 167, 276
  disclosure 227, 231, 240, 338
  dispute resolution 168, 282, 310
  fair competition 295
  mandatory terms 273
  registration 166, 223, 249
moral hazard 36, 67, 69, 71–2, 284
Morocco 214
motivation costs 52, 53, 55
motivations
  franchisee 56–7, 73
    franchisor marketing 56, 57–64, 65, 73–4, 79
    psycho-social 57
  to franchise 50–54, 59, 73

negotiation *see* contract formation
Netherlands 2, 8, 216, 227, 296–7
New Zealand 8–9, 28, 212, 215, 227, 307
non-discrimination 149, 278
Norway 8

objectives of franchise-specific legislation 116–20
Oceania 215
  *see also individual countries*
OECD: principles for best practice in regulation 39, 40
offences 134, 136, 152, 203, 204
ombudsman 285
operations manuals 92–3, 100, 101, 112, 184, 241
opportunism 53, 55, 72, 74, 91, 92, 98, 280, 317, 321
  good faith 301, 303
  registration 256–7
  termination provisions 289
opportunity costs 248

patents 162, 181, 238, 239
performance *see* conduct
Peru 8
Philippines 28
plain language 261
Portugal 227, 297
power asymmetry 67–8, 71, 72, 74, 318, 320–21
  conduct laws 310, 312
  disclosure and 247, 310–11
  franchise contract 77–81, 82–3
  franchise-specific legislation 129, 150
  good faith 302–3
  market and contract interaction 113–15
  mediation 284
  renewal 292
  termination provisions 289
pre-investment education and advice
  franchisees 80, 92
price fixing 95
principal/agent perspective
  transaction cost theory 51–4
privacy 62, 102
private interest theory 16–17
private regulation, definition of 25
processing/manufacturing franchise 48–9
product franchise 48
product-tying requirements 103–4
promissory estoppel 35
promotions 62, 97–9, 177, 185, 203, 301–2
psycho-social motivations 57
public goods 37
public interest theory 16
Puerto Rico 150, 288
purpose of franchise-specific legislation 116–20

qualifications and standards, pre-sale 131, 183–4, 185, 224, 259–60

Reagan, Ronald 14
recruitment and screening of franchisees 55–6, 59, 65–6, 170
reflexive regulation 18, 21, 22–3, 41, 318, 319
registration 129, 218, 221, 222, 223, 225, 244, 248–53, 261, 310
  Barbados 134, 249
  Belarus 154, 249
  Brazil 136, 221, 249, 253
  China 182–3, 224, 249, 253

costs and benefits 253–7
disclosure documents 229
Estonia 249
exemptions 127
Greece 253
Indonesia 188, 222, 229, 249, 256
Italy 249
Japan 249
Kazakhstan 192
Lithuania 162–3, 256
Malaysia 201–2, 222, 229, 249, 253, 256, 260
Mexico 144, 222, 249, 256
Moldova 166, 223, 249
not required 249
Canada 139, 218, 249
Romania 169, 223, 249, 253
Russia 172, 249, 256
South Korea 193, 194–5, 222, 229, 249
Spain 176, 249, 256
Ukraine 179, 249, 256
United States 147–8, 218, 222, 229, 246, 249, 253–4
Vietnam 205, 222, 249, 253
regulators 38, 43, 64, 244, 248, 256, 262, 311, 318–20
capture theory 17
educational initiatives 261
franchise-specific legislation 220
institutional theories 18
life-cycle theory 17
public interest theory 16
responsiveness and reflexivity 21–2, 23
standard-form contracts 83–4, 267
relational contracts and 89–90
regulatory theory 14, 261
best-practice model for regulatory process 38–9
core elements 39–44
scope and effectiveness 44–5
definitions of regulation 15–16
evolution of 15–24
layers of governance 16, 24–5
contract as regulation 29–34
court interpretation 29, 30, 34–6
market regulation 26–9
statutory intervention 30, 36–8
relational contracts 29, 33, 35, 77–8, 84–7, 114, 115, 246, 247
discretion, uncertainty and risk 90–93
erosion of bargained-for-exchange 89, 90
good faith 302
inconsistent with standard-form 86, 88, 89–90, 113
renewal of franchise 107–9, 291–3
Australia 292–3
Estonia 159, 292
EU proposed disclosure law 242
franchise-specific legislation 127, 130, 221, 239, 291–3
Albania 292
Canada 140–41
Georgia 187
Indonesia 189
Lithuania 164–5
Malaysia 203, 292
mandatory terms 275
Romania 169, 292
South Korea 193, 292
Ukraine 180, 292
United States 292
good faith 107, 275, 293, 301
repeat deals 26–7, 28
reporting requirements
minimum performance and 100–102
reputation 27, 28, 102, 170–71
risk to 56, 69
rescission
Canada 142
China 184
Mexico 145
United States 152
resource acquisition theory 50–51
responsive regulation 21–3, 318
restitution 35
restraint of trade clauses 29, 110, 111–13, 130, 149, 187, 275
review periods 129, 257
risk 74–5
business 51, 54, 62, 73
contract 101, 103, 311
duration 107
exit 106
standard-form and relational qualities 77–8, 89, 90–93

franchisee: perceived levels of 57, 58, 59, 74, 93
good faith 302
legal representation 80
marketing claims by franchisors 58–9, 62
operating 53, 68–9
pre-investment discovery of 93, 261
recruitment and screening of franchisees 56
reputational 56, 69
statements 315
strategic 67, 69
systems theory 19
uniformity and 68–70, 72, 73, 74
risk statements, advice and warnings 257–9, 311
Romania 8, 126, 168–71, 215, 259, 278, 279, 280
code of ethics 305
confidentiality 170, 171, 276
contract duration 271
disclosure 168–9, 171, 222, 227, 228, 229, 231, 240, 241, 286, 339
mandatory terms 265, 271, 273
registration 169, 223, 249, 253
Russia 125, 171–4, 215, 223, 227, 276–7
code of ethics 305
confidentiality 173, 276
insolvency 280
mandatory terms 273
registration 172, 249, 256

scarce goods 37
screening of franchisees 55–6, 59, 65–6, 109
self-regulation 6, 14, 18, 19–20, 23–4, 37, 116, 280
contracts *see separate entry*
definition of 19
disclosure plus registration model 222–3
education 262
future directions 313–21
market regulation *see separate entry*
prescribed disclosure model 221
public regulation in conjunction with 25
reflexivity and responsiveness 21–3, 318
Sharia law 200
Singapore 8, 28
Slovenia 227, 307
small businesses 4, 9
independent small business ownership vs franchising 58–64
and medium-sized businesses 189, 191
social reporting 27
soft and hard law 15
solicitors 80
South Africa 28, 214, 267
South America 216
*see also individual countries*
South Korea 126, 193–5, 215, 260, 277, 280
code of ethics 227, 306, 307
cooling-off period 193, 194, 257
disclosure 193, 194, 222, 227, 228, 229, 231, 242, 346
dispute resolution 195, 281, 283
language 265
objectives 117, 119
registration 193, 194–5, 222, 229, 249
Spain 126, 174–7, 215, 265, 276
*bona fide* principle 295
code of ethics 305–6
disclosure 175, 177, 227, 228, 229, 240, 295, 339
objectives 118
registration 176, 249, 256
standard-form contracts 29, 33, 77–9, 114, 115, 224, 246–7
discretion, uncertainty and risk 90–93
erosion of bargained-for-exchange 82–4, 88, 89, 90
good faith 302
imbalance of power 79–81
impact on relationship 82–4
inconsistent with relational 86, 88, 89–90, 113
no negotiation 81
unfair terms 266–7, 268, 270
uniformity 70–72, 79
standards and qualifications, pre-sale 131, 183–4, 185, 224, 259–60

statutory intervention 38, 114–15
pre-contractual measures 92
purposes 30, 36–7
*see also* franchise-specific legislation
subsidiary liability 165
sunk investment 26, 28
supply and product-tying requirements 103–4
Sweden 2, 126, 178, 215, 282
disclosure 178, 222, 227, 228, 229, 240, 339–40
registration not required 249
Switzerland 297
systems theory 18–19, 39

Taiwan 118, 126, 185–6, 215, 257, 306
disclosure 186, 225, 227, 229, 231, 343–4
taxonomy of franchising 47–9
termination 101, 110–11, 242
Estonia 158–9, 287
franchise-specific legislation 129, 130, 220–21, 225, 239, 287–91
Albania 153–4, 287
Australia 111, 210, 288, 289
Belarus 155–6
Canada 140–41
China 184
Georgia 187, 287
Indonesia 189, 288
Kyrgyzstan 196, 287
Lithuania 165, 287
Macau 200
Malaysia 202, 203, 288
mandatory terms 275
Mexico 145
Moldova 167–8, 287
Romania 169, 171, 287
Russia 173–4, 287
South Korea 193, 287–8
Spain 177, 287
Ukraine 180
United States 150, 288–9, 300–301
Vietnam 206–7, 288
good faith 111, 293
Taiwan 186
Thailand 297
time limits
commercial rights, grant of: Vietnam 205
company-owned stores: China 183–4
contract duration 107, 108
Barbados 134
China 184, 224, 271
Indonesia 189, 271
Italy 161, 271
Macau 197
Malaysia 203, 271
United States 149, 271
cooling-off period
Australia 209, 257
Malaysia 202, 257
South Korea 194, 257
disclosure 228–9
Australia 209, 210, 229
Belgium 157–8, 229
Brazil 135–6, 229
Canada 229
China 182, 224, 229
France 160, 229
Indonesia 188
Italy 161, 229
Malaysia 201, 229
Mexico 229
South Korea 194, 229
Spain 175, 229
Taiwan 186, 225, 229
UNIDROIT Model Law 131, 228
United States 229
Vietnam 205, 229
dispute resolution: Canada 141
exemptions 127
registration
China 182
Greece 253
Malaysia 202
Spain 176
renewal 292
rescission
Canada 142
China 184
restraint of trade clauses: Georgia 187
review period: Taiwan 257
termination
Albania 153–4, 287
Australia 111
Belarus 155, 156
Georgia 187, 287
Kyrgyzstan 287

Lithuania 164, 165, 287
Malaysia 203, 288
Moldova 168
Russia 287
South Korea 287–8
Spain 177
United States 288–9
transfer: Vietnam 206, 286
trade associations, franchise 167, 215, 280, 303–4, 307–9, 321
codes of ethics and conduct 28–9, 214, 224, 227, 259–60, 303–9
marketing 59–64, 65
recognition and awards programs 28
trade practices law 95
trademarks 58, 61, 67, 76, 99, 112
franchise-specific legislation 126, 128, 136, 138, 238, 239, 241
Australia 209
China 181
Estonia 158
France 159
Lithuania 162, 163, 164, 165, 287
Mexico 143, 144
Moldova 166, 167
Romania 168, 169, 170, 278
Russia 172
Taiwan 185
Ukraine 180
United States 146, 147
training 60, 61, 99–100, 101, 302
franchise-specific legislation 130, 238, 239, 278, 284
China 183, 184, 224, 278
Indonesia 189, 278
Lithuania 163
Macau 199, 224, 279
mandatory terms 273–4
Romania 170, 278
Russia 172
transaction costs
contracts 29, 31, 33
relational 85
standard-form 82
definition 51
disclosure 243, 245, 248
inefficiencies 36
motivation to franchise 51–4
recruitment 55
uniformity contains 70–71, 79
transaction-specific investment 26
transfer of franchise 109–10, 112, 242, 286
franchise-specific legislation 127, 129, 221, 239, 286
Australia 210
Canada 140–41
China 185
Indonesia 286
Macau 199–200, 286
Romania 169–70, 286
Russia 173
United States 286
Vietnam 206, 286
trust, principles of 153
'two plus one' rule 131, 183–4, 224, 259–60

Ukraine 125, 126, 179–80, 215, 223, 227, 306
conduct/performance 180, 265, 276, 279
registration 179, 249, 256
uncertainty 90–93, 101, 104, 108, 113, 129, 311
*see also* relational contracts
unconscionability 35, 36, 83, 298
unfair contract terms 82–3
legislation 265–70, 275, 297, 298, 309
unfairness *see* fairness
UNIDROIT 300, 311–12
Model Law 2, 116–17, 129, 131–2, 227, 249
definition of franchising 121, 126
disclosure 127, 131, 228, 238, 248
exemptions 127
uniformity 66–7, 74, 79, 81
brand maintenance 66–8, 79, 90, 91
fairness 71
franchisee perspective 72–3, 246
legal advice and franchisees 80
price of 71–2
risk reduction 68–70, 72, 73, 74
transaction costs 70–71, 79
United Arab Emirates 340
United Kingdom 22, 28, 99, 120, 227, 297–8, 307
England 2, 48, 216

United States 3, 8, 83, 99, 112, 145–6
- *bluemaumau.org* 28
- code of ethics 28, 304, 307
- conditions conducive to franchising 49–50
- franchise-specific legislation 118, 119, 145–52, 212, 215, 216, 222
  - conduct/performance 148–52, 222, 271, 277, 278, 279
  - contract duration 149, 271
  - disclosure 127, 147, 149, 150, 221, 222, 227, 228, 229, 240, 242, 243, 246, 247–8, 333
  - exemptions 127
  - registration 147–8, 218, 222, 229, 246, 249, 253–4
  - solvency 259
  - warnings 257–8
- good faith 222, 293–4, 299, 300–301, 303
- goodwill 112
- International Franchise Association 28, 304
- survey 95

Venezuela 2, 214, 216, 227
vertical integration 70
Vietnam 126, 204–8, 215, 259, 271, 278, 283, 310
- disclosure 205, 222, 227, 228, 229, 231, 241, 242
- language 265
- registration 205, 222, 249, 253

Virgin Islands 150, 277, 288
voluntarism 130

waivers 140, 160, 203
warnings 257–9, 311
wasting asset 109

Yum! Brands 7